LAY INTELLECTUALS
CAROLINGIAN WC

Did the laity have a part in the Carolingian Renaissance? If so, how were lay elites, and through them the laity at large, affected? This wide-ranging volume examines these questions through a study of lay involvement in literary and artistic activity in early medieval Europe. Leading historians explore a diverse range of Latin and vernacular texts written by secular authors and use richly drawn case studies to illuminate such key issues as the extent of lay literacy, the contexts in which learned laity could flourish, the transformative impact of the Carolingian Renaissance, and the interaction of 'lay' and 'clerical' values on both sides of the English Channel. This volume demonstrates that the learned laity, both women and men, contributed much more as writers and patrons to early medieval culture than was previously thought, and it will be essential reading for scholars of Carolingian and Anglo-Saxon history.

PATRICK WORMALD was a College Tutor and University Lecturer at Christ Church, Oxford.

JANET L. NELSON is Professor of Medieval History at King's College London.

LAY INTELLECTUALS IN THE CAROLINGIAN WORLD

EDITED BY
PATRICK WORMALD AND JANET L. NELSON

CAMBRIDGE UNIVERSITY PRESS
Cambridge, New York, Melbourne, Madrid, Cape Town,
Singapore, São Paulo, Delhi, Tokyo, Mexico City

Cambridge University Press
The Edinburgh Building, Cambridge CB2 8RU, UK

Published in the United States of America by Cambridge University Press, New York

www.cambridge.org
Information on this title: www.cambridge.org/9780521174091

© Cambridge University Press 2007

This publication is in copyright. Subject to statutory exception
and to the provisions of relevant collective licensing agreements,
no reproduction of any part may take place without the written
permission of Cambridge University Press.

First published 2007
First paperback edition 2011

A catalogue record for this publication is available from the British Library

ISBN 978-0-521-83453-7 Hardback
ISBN 978-0-521-17409-1 Paperback

Cambridge University Press has no responsibility for the persistence or
accuracy of URLs for external or third-party internet websites referred to in
this publication, and does not guarantee that any content on such websites is,
or will remain, accurate or appropriate.

Contents

List of illustrations	page	vii
List of contributors		viii
Preface		ix
List of abbreviations		x

1 In place of an introduction
   Janet L. Nelson 1

2 Secular sanctity: forging an ethos for the Carolingian nobility
   Thomas F. X. Noble 8

3 Einhardus peccator
   David Ganz 37

4 The world, the text and the Carolingian: royal, aristocratic and masculine identities in Nithard's *Histories*
   Stuart Airlie 51

5 Eberhard of Friuli, a Carolingian lay intellectual
   Paul J. E. Kershaw 77

6 Dhuoda
   Janet L. Nelson 106

7 Learned women? Liutberga and the instruction of Carolingian women
   Valerie L. Garver 121

8 Charles the Bald, Hincmar of Rheims and the ivory of the Pericopes of Henry II
   Celia Chazelle 139

9	Problems of authorship and audience in the writings of King Alfred the Great *David Pratt*	162
10	'Stand strong against the monsters': kingship and learning in the empire of King Æthelstan *Michael Wood*	192
11	The lay intellectual in Anglo-Saxon England: Ealdorman Æthelweard and the politics of history *Scott Ashley*	218
12	Concluding *Richard Abels*	246

Index 255

Illustrations

8.1 Pericopes of Henry II, cover   *page* 141
8.2 Utrecht Psalter, illustration of Psalm 18   155

Contributors

RICHARD ABELS is Associate Professor of Military History at the United States Military Academy, Annapolis, MD, USA

STUART AIRLIE is Senior Lecturer in History at the University of Glasgow, UK

SCOTT ASHLEY is Lecturer in Medieval History at the University of Newcastle, UK

CELIA CHAZELLE is Professor of History at The College of New Jersey, USA

DAVID GANZ is Professor of Palaeography at King's College London, UK

VALERIE L. GARVER is Assistant Professor of Medieval History at Northern Illinois University, USA

PAUL KERSHAW is Assistant Professor of History at the University of Virginia, USA

JANET L. NELSON is Professor of Medieval History at King's College London, UK

THOMAS F. X. NOBLE is Professor of History and Conway Director of the Medieval Institute at the University of Notre Dame, USA

DAVID PRATT is Senior Tutor in History at Downing College, Cambridge, UK

MICHAEL WOOD is a British writer and film-maker specialising in historical subjects

PATRICK WORMALD was Tutor in Medieval History at Christ Church, University of Oxford, UK. He died on 24 September 2004.

Preface

Patrick Wormald invited nearly all the papers in this book for delivery at sessions he conceived and organised at the annual International Conference on Medieval Studies at Kalamazoo, Michigan, in 1999 and 2000; the concluding paper was commissioned shortly afterwards. He wanted the book to be published as soon as possible after the contributions were written, read and revised, and he worked very hard to achieve that end. He died in September 2004. Despite the inevitable delay in getting this collection into print, it is the hope of all the contributors that their efforts have not dated. In fact it is their fervent belief that this book is every bit as timely as Patrick's original project. Their collective wish is to assure readers that this book is as Patrick intended it to be – with one exception: it lacks the introduction he planned to write. The one I have written can be no substitute for what is lost. It attempts merely to situate this project in Patrick's career and within the intellectual preoccupations of what proved, alas, to be his final years. In making final preparations for the book's publication, I have incurred debts of gratitude: to Cambridge University Press, and, above all, to the contributors, for their help and patience, to Rachel Stone for preparing the Index, and most of all, to Jenny, Tom and Luke Wormald for their moral support throughout.

La Marteille, JINTY NELSON
August 2006

Abbreviations

AB	*Annales Bertiniani*, ed. F. Grat, J. Vielliard, S. Clémencet and L. Levillain; *Les Annales de Saint-Bertin* (Paris, 1964), English translation by J. L. Nelson, *The Annals of St-Bertin* (Manchester, 1991)
AF	*Annales Fuldenses*, ed. F. Kurze, *MGH SRG* 7 (Hanover, 1891), pp. 33, 34, English translation by T. Reuter, *The Annals of Fulda* (Manchester, 1992)
AHR	*American Historical Review*
ARF	*Annales Regni Francorum*, ed. F. Kurze, *MGH SRG* 6 (Hanover, 1895)
ASC	*Anglo-Saxon Chronicle*
ASE	*Anglo-Saxon England*
Astronomer	Astronomer, *Vita Hludowici imperatoris*, ed. E. Tremp, *MGH SRG* 64 (Hanover, 1995)
CCCM	*Corpus Christianorum, Continuatio Medievalis* (Turnhout, 1966–)
CCSL	*Corpus Christianorum, Series Latina* (Turnhout, 1952–)
DA	*Deutsches Archiv für Erforschung des Mittelalters*
Dhuoda	*Liber Manualis*, ed., with French translation by B. de Vregille and C. Mondésert, by P. Riché, *Manuel pour mon fils*, SC 225 (Paris, 1975); also ed., with English translation, by M. Thiébaux, *Dhuoda, Handbook for her Warrior Son: Liber Manualis* (Cambridge, 1998)
EHR	*English Historical Review*
EME	*Early Medieval Europe*

Ermold	Ermoldus Nigellus, *In honorem Hludovici pii*, ed. (with French translation) E. Faral, *Ermold le Noir: Poème sur Louis le Pieux*, 2nd edn (Paris, 1964)
FMS	*Frühmittelalterliche Studien*
HJ	*Historisches Jahrbuch*
HZ	*Historische Zeitschrift*
JEH	*Journal of Ecclesiastical History*
JMH	*Journal of Medieval History*
KL	S. Keynes and M. Lapidge, eds., *Alfred the Great. Asser's Life of King Alfred and other Contemporary Sources*, translated with introduction and notes (London, 1983)
LM	*Lexikon des Mittelalters*
MGH	*Monumenta Germaniae Historica*
AA	*Auctores antiquissimi*
Capit. episc.	*Capitularia episcoporum*
Capit.	*Capitularia regum Francorum*
MGH Conc.	
Const.	*Constitutiones et acta publica imperatorum et regum*
DD	*Diplomata regum et imperatorum; Die Urkunden der deutschen Könige und Kaiser*
Epp.	*Epistulae* III–VII (= *Epistulae merovingici et karolini aevi*, Hanover, 1892–1939)
Epp. DK	*Epistulae der deutschen Kaiserzeit*
Epp. sel.	*Epistulae selectae in usum scholarum*
Fontes	*Fontes iuris germanici antiqui in usum scholarum*
Form.	*Formulae Merowingici et Karolini Aevi*
Poet.	*Poetae latini aevi carolini*
Quellen	*Quellen der deutschen Kaiserzeit*
MGH Schriften	
SRG	*Scriptores rerum Germanicarum in usum scholarum separatim editi*
SRL	*Scriptores rerum Langobardorum*
SRM	*Scriptores rerum Merovingicarum*
SS	*Scriptores* in folio
SSDM	*Scriptores des deutsches Mittelalters*
MIÖG	*Mitteilungen des Instituts für Österreichische Geschichtsforschung*

NCMH	*The New Cambridge Medieval History*, vol. II, ed. R. McKitterick (Cambridge, 1995); vol. III, ed. T. Reuter (Cambridge, 1999)
Nithard	Nithard, *Historiarum Libri IV*, ed. with French translation by P. Lauer, *Nithard: Histoire des fils de Louis le Pieux* (Paris, 1964)
Notker	Notker, *Gesta Karoli magni imperatoris*, ed. H. F. Haefele, *MGH SRG* n.s. 12 (Berlin, 1959)
P&P	*Past and Present*
PBA	*Proceedings of the British Academy*
PL	J.-P. Migne ed., *Patrologia Latina*, 217 plus 4 index vols. (Paris, 1841–64)
QFIAB	*Quellen und Forschungen aus italienischen Archiven und Bibliotheken*
S. (with number)	P. H. Sawyer, *A Hand-List of Anglo-Saxon Charters*, Royal Historical Society Guides and Handbooks 8 (London, 1968); a revised edition by S. E. Kelly is ongoing and available online at www.trin.cam.ac.uk/chartwww/
SC	*Sources Chrétiennes*
SCH	*Studies in Church History*
Settimane Spoleto	Settimane di Studio del Centro italiano di studi sull'alto medioevo
Thegan	Thegan, *Gesta Hludovici imperatoris*, ed. E. Tremp, *MGH SRG* 54 (Hanover, 1995)
TRHS	*Transactions of the Royal Historical Society*
VA	Asser, *Life of King Alfred (Asserius, De Gestis regis Ælfredi)*, ed. W. A. Stevenson (Oxford, 1904), repr. with Introduction by D. Whitelock (Oxford, 1959)
VK	Einhard, *Vita Karoli Magni*, ed. O. Holder-Egger, *MGH SRG* 25, 6th edn (Hanover and Leipzig, 1911)
WMGR	William of Malmesbury, *Gesta regum Anglorum*, vol. I, ed. R. A. B. Mynors, R. M. Thomson and M. Winterbottom (Oxford, 1998)
Whitelock, *EHD*	D. Whitelock, ed., *English Historical Documents*, vol. I: *c. 500–1042*, 2nd edn (London, 1979)
Wormald, *Making*	P. Wormald, *The Making of English Law: King Alfred to the Twelfth Century*, vol. I, *Legislation and its Limits* (Oxford, 1999)

ZRG, GA	*Zeitschrift der Savigny-Stiftung für Rechtsgeschichte, germanistische Abteilung*
ZRG, RA	*Zeitschrift der Savigny-Stiftung für Rechtsgeschichte, römanistische Abteilung*

CHAPTER I

In place of an introduction

Janet L. Nelson

Patrick Wormald will ever be remembered as, above all, a bravura solo performer of originality and power: an academic Barenboim. His many writings, particularly in the genre of learned papers, were each and all sole-authored productions of distinctive and enduring value;[1] and in *The Making of English Law*, he produced a scholarly master-work. But there was more to Patrick's distinction than that. He was a wonderfully inspiring teacher, whose influence and intellectual generosity extended far beyond his own students. He was engaged in literally hundreds of scholarly exchanges, in speech and in writing and latterly email, to the huge benefit of his partners in dialogue. He enjoyed the collaborative work of symposia, nowhere more so than with colleagues in the Bucknell Group.[2] International contacts, in North America and, increasingly, in Continental Europe, evoked new applications of his extraordinary mental energy.[3] He thrived on the buzz of conferences, and always gave as much as (sometimes as good as) he got. All this, well known as it is to students

---

[1] The exceptional value and coherence of this corpus of work has lately become apparent in Patrick's two collections of papers: *Legal Culture in the Early Medieval West: Law as Text, Image and Experience* (London, 1999); and now *The Age of Bede*, ed. S. Baxter (Oxford, 2006). I am especially grateful to Stuart Airlie, Wendy Davies and Simon Keynes for bibliographical and other help during the final stages of getting the present book into press.

[2] Patrick himself gave currency to this label, which derived from the home-place in the 1980s of Wendy Davies, the group's convenor from the outset to the present. Though she moved house to Woolstone in Oxfordshire (Patrick's housewarming gift was an account of the Anglo-Saxon history of Woolstone), the name Bucknell Group stuck. Patrick's contributions to the group's published volumes were major ones: see 'Charters, law and the settlement of disputes in Anglo-Saxon England', in W. Davies and P. Fouracre, eds., *The Settlement of Disputes in Early Medieval Europe* (Cambridge, 1986), pp. 149–68, and 'Lordship and justice in the early English kingdom: Oswaldslow revisited', in Davies and Fouracre, eds., *Property and Power in the Early Middle Ages* (Cambridge, 1995), pp. 114–36.

[3] See, for instance, Patrick's contributions to conferences at Spoleto in the mid-1990s (publications cited below, nn. 9 and 10) and at Vienna in 2000 ('Pre-modern "state" and "nation": definite or indefinite?', in S. Airlie, W. Pohl and H. Reimitz, eds., *Staat im frühen Mittelalter* (Vienna, 2006), pp. 179–89).

I

and practitioners of early medieval history, is worth repeating, and celebrating.

Less well known, but worth adding here, is Patrick's less-often practised quality as a skilled conductor working from the keyboard: another Barenboim. Patrick could bring colleagues together, and help their combined product to be more than the sum of its parts. He did this, for instance, in his editorial work on the *Festschrift* for Michael Wallace-Hadrill.[4] He did something akin in seminars, whereof he was so often the life and soul. He did it again in organising a series of sessions at two successive meetings of the annual International Conference on Medieval Studies at Kalamazoo, Michigan, USA in 1999 and 2000. Here he deployed all the gifts just mentioned: he invited apt contributors from among former students and present colleagues on both sides of the Atlantic; he chaired and commented sessions *con brio*, so that then, and later, he enhanced every speaker's contribution; above all, he chose a theme dear to his own heart which, like so many of Patrick's enthusiasms, once applied to early medieval scholarship worked like yeast in dough – or, to use a more contemporary metaphor, proved to be absolutely at the cutting edge. It was, more or less, the theme of the present book: the Lay Intellectual in the Carolingian World.

Behind that formulation – which caused (and may still cause)[5] some jibbing at its deliberately provocative anachronism – was an agenda that had been bubbling away in Patrick's mind for well over twenty years. In the mid-1970s, he began to grapple with three problems fundamental to any understanding of the early medieval West: first and foremost, the nature of its law, new or old, Roman or German, authoritative or customary, royal or consensual; second, the impact of Christianity on aristocratic values and conduct, contradictory or complementary, destructive or adaptive; third, the significance of literacy, instrument of power or collective medium, clerical monopoly or tool of secular elites, learned or popular.[6] Not only was Patrick prescient and exemplary in insisting on British as distinct from merely English history, inspired by Michael Wallace-Hadrill, his

---

[4] P. Wormald, D. Bullough and R. Collins, eds., *Ideal and Reality in Frankish and Anglo-Saxon Society: Studies Presented to J.M. Wallace-Hadrill* (Oxford, 1983). As the order of the co-editors' names indicates, Patrick did the lion's share of editorial work on this volume.

[5] See Richard Abels, below, p. 247.

[6] Key papers were: '*Lex scripta* and *verbum regis*: legislation and Germanic kingship from Euric to Cnut', in P. Sawyer and I. N. Wood, eds., *Early Medieval Kingship* (Leeds, 1977), pp. 105–38; 'The uses of literacy in Anglo-Saxon England and its neighbours', *TRHS*, 5th ser. 27 (1977), pp. 95–114; and 'Bede, Beowulf and the conversion of the Anglo-Saxon Aristocracy', in R. T. Farrell, ed., *Bede and Anglo-Saxon England*, BAR 46 (Oxford, 1978), pp. 32–95.

vision always extended beyond these Isles[7]. His early published work showed him deeply well informed on Continental law and politics, and he had important new insights to offer on the Lombards as well as the Franks.[8] He was always interested in contact, and comparison. In the 1990s, as he toiled on the big synthesis, Patrick pondered ever more deeply on the Carolingian Renaissance. Here he saw Christianity impacting in new and lasting ways on politics and polities, communities and social structures. Equally interested in ideals and realities, he saw that impact both in normative texts and in the charters that embodied legal practice.[9] The Carolingian period was the transformative moment when law, no longer thought of as secular, a thing (only) of this world, came to be understood and used as the means to secure the collective good of the Christian people. That good was expressed by the one word 'justice' – the watchword of Carolingian government, a word loaded with religious and this-wordly values.[10] Law-making was an activity engaged in co-operatively by clergy and secular men. In the Carolingian regime, the delivery of law, through the holding of courts, and the imposing, and recording, of legal judgments, necessarily entailed such collective action. Normative decrees and case records needed to be brought together in a single field of vision. Having once grasped these essentials, Patrick could read in and from records of dispute settlement the implementation of Carolingian justice; and having grasped the inspirational significance of Carolingian justice for Anglo-Saxon rulers and elites from the ninth century onwards, Patrick could set early medieval legal ideals and realities on both sides of the Channel within a single frame.[11]

For Patrick, as for the scholar whose work most inspired and challenged him, F. W. Maitland,[12] to think about medieval law was always to engage with medieval men making and using law. In this scholarly exercise, history, not law, had priority. A thorough knowledge of legal texts and

---

[7] See, for instance, his yeasty comparative paper, 'Celtic and Anglo-Saxon kingship: some further thoughts', in P. E. Szarmach with V. Oggins, eds., *Sources of Anglo-Saxon Culture* (Kalamazoo, 1986), pp. 151–83.
[8] '*Lex scripta*'.
[9] See especially '"*Inter Cetera Bona … Genti Suae*": law-making and peace-keeping in the earliest English kingdoms', *La Giustizia*, Settimane Spoleto, 2 vols. (1995, 1997), I, pp. 963–96; 'Bede and the conversion of England: the charter evidence', The Jarrow Lecture, 1984.
[10] 'Giving God and king their due: conflict and its regulation in the early English state', *La Giustizia* (1997), II, pp. 549–92; Wormald, *Making*, pp. 122–5.
[11] Wormald, *Making*, pp. 29–108.
[12] It was a characteristic achievement (much more than a gesture) of Patrick's, after much effective networking and lobbying, to get a memorial plaque to Maitland put up in Westminster Abbey in December 2000.

legal practice was crucial. The object, though, was not historic law but legal history – which in turn was part of social history, or as historians tend to say nowadays, emphasising the importance of representations and meanings for the people we study, cultural history. Finding what is the law, enunciating that, and giving it social force, can be, and in many parts of Western Europe in the early Middle Ages, before professional lawyers, was, a field of collective action involving a wide swathe of people.[13] Learning in the academic sense is necessarily something confined to a caste or very restricted elite – both because, historically, it has been a scarce resource and source of social power and because, especially in our own democratic age of mass values and mass media, it is not everyone's cup of tea. But learning can take applied forms: as with the law. Thus, though in the early Middle Ages, law was instrumentalised by the powerful, often aided and abetted by the learnèd themselves, it could at the same time empower the less powerful, even the powerless and the unlearnèd, by embodying and protecting the rights of individuals and groups.[14]

In a similar way, religious knowledge, while it most certainly empowered the clergy, and in the early Middle Ages legitimised that new elite, was power qualified in several important ways. The clergy themselves were divided by yawning chasms of wealth and rank: poor rural priests were among the powerless. As for bishops and abbots, powerful as well as learned they might be, but their churches' institutional wealth depended for security and protection on rulers and the secular elite. Further, before the growth of papal government run by professional canon lawyers, religious knowledge and status could be claimed by more non-specialists – whether *soi-disant* holy men and women or do-it-yourself practitioners of beneficent magic. The early medieval world, deeply unequal as it was, offered access to Faith – a universal empowerer. The Carolingian Church preached the duties as well as the claims of that accessibility, in imposing such religious obligations as tithe payment and Sunday observance at the same time as it affirmed the entitlement of all the faithful to the clergy's services (in both senses).[15] Secular men were now to think of themselves as faithful men; and non-clerical persons of either gender were encouraged to think of themselves as lay.

---

[13] Wormald, *Making*, pp. 53–92, 468–9; cf. pp. 11–12 and n. 44 for succinct observation of the significance of learned lawyers in Celtic societies, in contrast to their absence among 'the Germans'.

[14] S. Reynolds, *Kingdoms and Communities in Western Europe, 900–1300*, 2nd edn (Oxford, 1996); cf. several of the contributions to P. Stafford, J. L. Nelson and J. Martindale, eds., *Law, Laity and Solidarities: Essays in Honour of Susan Reynolds* (Manchester, 2001).

[15] Wormald, *Making*, pp. 316, 302–3, 306.

Patrick saw that Christianity confronted barbarian elites with new demands and new tensions; but what struck him most forcefully in the end was the way potential clash yielded to mutual accommodation.[16] The Carolingian age saw a transformation of lay values, and, on the ecclesiastical side, a re-evaluation of lay action in the world. Alcuin in *Virtues and Vices* affirmed that lay status did not exclude any person, man or woman, from heaven: on the contrary, the lay person could work toward their own salvation through good works.[17] Even at court, Alcuin thought, the busy lay aristocrat could engage in daily prayer, and understand its religious significance. By implication, away from court, and in a less busy life, prayer was easier to accommodate. The Carolingian Church is very clearly on record as legitimising the powers that were. It also made demands on them. The responses of a few kings, above all, as well as a tiny number of high aristocrats, have survived, directly or indirectly, in the evidence.[18] Intellectuals, in the early Middle Ages as in later ages, necessarily constituted a small elite, just as they by definition sought an audience. The *scientia* cultivated by prayer and righteous action was amongst the things that that elite aimed to diffuse. In practice it may have been limited to those with enough Latin to recite psalms; but if so, the constituency of the knowledgeable was probably already wider than the high aristocracy. This was learning of a kind: learning sufficient to permit active participation in Christian observance, and acknowledgement of Christian duties, and – crucially in the present context – to respond to the moral messages emanating from social superiors. For if Charlemagne asked all household heads to share responsibility for pushing forward the project of Christian education, he asked *a fortiori* those heads of magnate households who were fully enrolled at court as exemplars of the project.[19] Aristocrats, and they included women, whom the patriarchal Carolingian world had ways of accommodating and deploying,[20] pushed out the project's frontiers in the provinces, in ecclesiastical and secular houses, halls and meeting-places. They, along with the rulers who enlisted them, were

---

[16] Three of Patrick's Oxford teachers and colleagues, Maurice Keen, Henry Mayr-Harting and Peter Brown, encouraged him to wrestle life-long with these problems.
[17] See Noble, below, p. 10.
[18] For the kings, see below, especially the chapters of Chazelle, Pratt and Wood; for great, royally connected aristocrats, see especially the chapters of Ganz, Airlie, Kershaw, Nelson and Ashley.
[19] Among recent work on these lines, see the papers of Airlie, Nelson and Innes, referred to in Airlie, pp. 51, 55, 60 nn. 2, 16, 37, below. I am especially grateful to Stuart Airlie, Wendy Davies and Simon Keynes for bibliographical and other help during the final stages of getting the present book into press.
[20] See below, especially the chapters of Nelson and Garver.

among the lay intellectuals with whom Patrick wished *his* enlisted team to be concerned. Few such people left much individual trace in the written record, as authors, patrons or educators. Those few who did, all of them of the highest social rank, must stand for however many others wrote works that have perished, or taught by the spoken word. Those few are the subjects of the various chapters that follow.

Given that cluster of Patrick's concerns, and the consistency of the textual raw material, the theme of his Kalamazoo conference sessions, and of this book, has brought its own benefits of focus and coherence. What Patrick wanted to suggest in making Lay Intellectuals the subject, and in presenting them thus in this book's title, was that they were imbued with Christian learning, worked with their minds as well as their spears or distaffs, were self-consciously committed to a moral project of social transformation, and sought and addressed a public.[21] If we make all due allowance for the specifics of early medieval conditions, the label 'intellectuals' fits well enough.[22] They saw themselves, too, as *lay* intellectuals: needing ecclesiastical guidance and reassurance, yet active indispensable members and leaders of God's people. This was, as Alcuin put it in a letter to Charlemagne, the age of the laity.[23]

Richard Abels ends our book with some cautionary words: 'How widespread the appeal of learning, of pursuing holy wisdom, actually was among the lay elites of Carolingian Francia and Anglo-Saxon England must remain an open question.'[24] This contributor respects his caution. Nevertheless, she ends these reflections, in what she hopes is the spirit of Patrick's original project, with a surmise not wild but warranted: warranted, that is, by much evidence presented in the chapters below. To return to one of Patrick's original questions, the surmise is this, that the Carolingian Renaissance, far from inhibiting the laity, gave them a new

---

[21] Cf. Nelson, below, pp. 106–7.

[22] The label was one Patrick very much wanted to keep in the title of this book: cf. *Making*, p. 429: 'That [King] Alfred had an unrivalled grasp of the material necessities of government brooks no denial. The fact remains that he was also a ninth-century intellectual.' See below, Pratt, pp. 162–91.

[23] Alcuin Ep. 136, ed. E. Dümmler, *MGH Epp.* IV (Berlin, 1895), p. 205: 'I am absolutely delighted whenever laymen blossom to the extent of asking questions about the Gospels. True, I have heard a certain wise man say somewhere that it is for clerics, not laymen, to study the Gospels. What is my response? All things have their time [citing Ecclesiastes 3: 1; and Alcuin now interprets]: often a later hour provides what an earlier hour could not. Whoever the layman is who asked this question, then, he is a wise man in his heart even if he is a warrior in his hands; and your most wise authority needs many men like that' (my translation). Cf. Nelson below, p. 106. I confess I have exploited whatever licence is due to a provider of editorial finishing touches to add a couple of fairly recent references to my chapter.

[24] Abels, below, p. 254.

agenda, a new 'ministry'.[25] In the courts and court-connected places of the early medieval world where wisdom was taught, and 'bought',[26] not only did kings, counsellors, churchmen, patrons and parents intend that lay persons commit themselves to wisdom's pursuit, but unnumbered individual quests fulfilled, however imperfectly, that high intent. Recovering the traces of those quests and that intent was what, I will dare to say, drew Patrick to the subject of this book.

[25] Cf. Noble, below, pp. 16, 19.   [26] Nelson, below, pp. 118–20.

CHAPTER 2

Secular sanctity: forging an ethos for the Carolingian nobility

Thomas F. X. Noble

Towards the end of the eighth century a Bavarian count expressed the hope that one of his sons would succeed him 'if any should be found worthy to do so'.[1] This chapter seeks to explore what that count might have had in mind when musing about his son's worthiness. Put a little differently, the following pages constitute an attempt to discern some aspects of the ethos of the Carolingian nobility. For reasons that will be explained in due course, I call this ethos 'Secular sanctity', and I will show that this label comes close to actual Carolingian usage.[2] But it must be acknowledged at the outset that it is easier to find sources in which certain ideals were urged upon the Carolingian lay elite than to find such laymen speaking in their own voices. It might be objected that the 'Secular Sanctity' sketched here is only normative, prescriptive, aspirational. I must admit that such an objection cannot be destroyed. But, I insist, it can be met, worried and weakened. Accordingly, after a brief recitation of the relevant sources and a presentation of secular sanctity's key components, I turn to the persons to whom this ethos was addressed and ask a series of questions: Who were the members of the Carolingian elite? Where was the ethos formulated and might laymen have had a hand in its elaboration? In so far as the ethos is now found in Latin texts, how might laymen have gained access to those texts or to the ideas contained in them? In what ways might the ethos have been attractive to Carolingian laymen? What place did this ethos hold within the broader spectrum of Carolingian culture?

A wide array of sources provide insights into the noble ethos of the Carolingian age. Einhard's *Life of Charlemagne* and the *Lives* of Louis the

---

[1] T. Bitterauf, ed., *Die Traditionen des Hochstifts Freising* (Munich, 1905), no. 319.
[2] This chapter had gone through several versions when I discovered that D. Baker had once used the term 'secular sanctity': '*Vir Dei*: secular sanctity in the early tenth century', *Sanctity and Secularity: The Church and the World*, SCH 10 (1973), pp. 41–53. Baker and I treat the 'Life of Gerald of Aurillac' very differently.

Secular sanctity

Pious are full of examples and exhortations.[3] Capitularies often spell out parts of an ethos. Those capitularies also explicitly extended to nobles a royal *ministerium* which is itself delineated in a group of *specula principum* (mirrors for princes) addressed to Charlemagne, Louis the Pious, Pippin of Aquitaine and Charles the Bald.[4] Numerous hortatory epistles were written to noblemen by, among others, Agobard of Lyons, Alcuin, Hrabanus Maurus, Lupus of Ferrières, Ermoldus Nigellus and Jonas of Orléans.[5] Hrabanus Maurus preached at least six sermons on the virtues and vices.[6] Most important of all, however, are the ethical treatises written by Ambrosius Autpertus, Paulinus of Aquileia, Alcuin, Jonas of Orléans, Hincmar of Rheims and Rather of Verona.[7] Nor should we overlook the

---

[3] *VK*, Thegan, the Astronomer, and, to a lesser degree, Ermold, pp. 2–201. The themes of example and imitation in these texts are discussed by H. Siemes, *Beiträge zum literarischen Bild Kaiser Ludwigs des Frommen in der Karolingerzeit* (Freiburg, 1966).

[4] These texts are cited and analysed in Anton; the background to Carolingian ideas about rulership is discussed by: E. Ewig, 'Zum christlichen Königsgedanken im Frühmittelalter', in *Das Königtum: Seine geistigen und rechtlichen Grundlagen*, Vorträge und Forschungen 3 (Sigmaringen, 1956), pp. 7–73; M. Reydellet, *La royauté dans la littérature latine de Sidoine Apollinaire à Isidore de Seville*, Bibliothèque des écoles françaises d'Athènes et de Rome 243 (Rome, 1981); N. Staubach, 'Germanisches Königtum und lateinische Literatur vom fünften bis zum siebenten Jahrhundert', *FMS* 17 (1983), 1–54; J. L. Nelson, 'Kingship and Empire in the Carolingian World', in R. McKitterick, ed., *Carolingian Culture: Emulation and Innovation* (Cambridge, 1994), pp. 52–87. Smaragdus of St Mihiel and Jonas of Orléans are the subject of books since Anton: O. Eberhardt, *Via Regia: Der Fürstenspiegel Smaragds von St. Mihiel und seine literarische Gattung*, Münstersche Mittelalterschriften 28 (Münster, 1977); R. Savigni, *Giona d'Orléans: Una ecclesiologia carolingia* (Bologna, 1989).

[5] Agobard of Lyons, *Epistolae*, ed. E. Dümmler, *MGH Epp.* III (Berlin, 1899), 10, pp. 201–3; Alcuin, *Epistolae*, ed. Dümmler, *MGH Epp.* II (Berlin, 1895), nos. 16, 18, 30, 61, 67, 108, 119, 122–3, 174, 188, 217, 224, 249, 251, pp. 42–5, 49–52, 71–2, 104–5, 110–11, 155, 174, 178–81, 287–9, 315–16, 360–1, 367–8, 401–4, listed and discussed by L. Wallach, *Alcuin and Charlemagne*, Cornell Studies in Classical Philology 32 (Ithaca, NY, 1959), pp. 61–3, cf. S. Mahl, *Quadriga Virtutum: Die Kardinaltugenden in der Geschichte der Karolingerzeit* (Cologne, 1969), pp. 83–96; Hrabanus Maurus, *Epistolae*, ed. Dümmler, *MGH Epp.* III (Berlin, 1899), nos. 15, 16, 17a, 17b, pp. 403–15, 416–20, 420–2, cf. Mahl, *Quadriga Virtutum*, pp. 128–47; Lupus of Ferrières, *Epistolae*, ed. Dümmler, *MGH Epp.* IV (Berlin, 1902–25), nos. 64, 93, pp. 63–4, 82–3; Ermold, *Epp.* 1–2, pp. 202–33; Jonas, *Epistolae Variorum*, ed. Dümmler, *MGH Epp.* V, nos. 29, 31, pp. 346–7, 349–53.

[6] C. Woods, 'Six New Sermons by Hrabanus Maurus on Virtues and Vices', *Revue Bénédictine* 107 (1997), pp. 280–306.

[7] 'De conflictu vitiorum atque virtutum', ed. R. Weber, *Ambrosii Autperti Opera*, CCCM XXVIIb (1979), pp. 909–31, cf. J. Winandy, 'L'oeuvre littéraire d'Ambroise Autpert', *Revue Bénédictine* 60 (1950), pp. 93–119, F. Brunhölzl, *Histoire de la littérature latine du moyen âge: L'époque carolingienne*, trans. H. Rochais (Louvain, 1991), pp. 69–70; Paulinus, *Liber exhortationis*, *PL* 99, cols. 197–232, cf. M. Manitius, *Geschichte der lateinischen Literatur des Mittelalters*, 3 vols. (Munich, 1911–31), II, pp. 368–70, R. McKitterick, *The Frankish Church and the Carolingian Reforms* (London, 1977), pp. 166–8, Brunhölzl, *Histoire*, pp. 14–20, esp. 16–17; Alcuin, *De virtutibus et vitiis liber*, *PL* 101, cols. 613–38, cf. Manitius, *Geschichte*, pp. 273–88, Brunhölzl, *Histoire*, pp. 29–46, esp. 40–1, Anton, pp. 83–7, McKitterick, *Frankish Church*, pp. 168–70, R. Newhauser, *The Treatise on Vices and Virtues in Latin and the Vernacular*, Typologie des sources du moyen âge occidentale 68 (Turnhout, 1993), pp. 116–18; Jonas, *De institutione laicali*, *PL* 106, cols. 121–78, cf. Manitius, *Geschichte*, pp. 374–80, Brunhölzl, *Histoire*, pp. 155–9; Hincmar, *De cavendis vitiis et virtutibus exercendis*, *PL* 125, cols. 857–930,

remarkable *Liber Manualis* of the noblewoman Dhuoda.[8] The *Life of Gerald of Aurillac* is especially revealing too.[9]

What, then, do these sources say? Virtually all of the sources with which I am dealing here stress both a private and a public dimension of the life that nobles will lead. Both Alcuin and Jonas say that they were asked to explain how busy, powerful laymen could discharge their duties in the world and meet the requirements of the Christian faith. The authors stress that the goal of life is salvation and go on to admit that the life of a public man, or of a soldier, might not be conducive to heavenly rewards. Thus our texts encourage men to do the corporal works of mercy, to pray constantly, to read the Bible, to listen to the clergy, to attend mass and the sacraments.[10]

In addition to these exhortations, the texts provide guidance in the form of lists of vices, usually versions of the capital sins, to which are opposed the beatitudes, the seven gifts of the Holy Spirit (wisdom, understanding, justice, fortitude, knowledge, piety and fear of the Lord), the Christian virtues (Faith, Hope, Love), the cardinal virtues (Prudence, Justice, Temperance, and Fortitude), or the Ten Commandments.[11] These remedies for vice are

---

cf. Manitius, *Geschichte*, pp. 339–54; Brunhölzl, *Histoire*, pp. 199–205; Rather, *Praeloquiarum libri sex*, *PL* 136, cols. 145–344; best on Rather is the introduction to P. L. D. Reid, trans., *The Complete Works of Rather of Verona*, Medieval and Renaissance Studies and Texts 16 (Binghamton, NY, 1991), pp. 3–16 and if it seems unusual to find Rather here, he was born to a noble family in Liège *c.* 880 and had a typical Carolingian education and outlook; his writings are too seldom set next to those of the Carolingian period with which they are most similar. Newhauser, *Treatise* (as above) serves as a good introduction but neglects Paulinus, Jonas, Hincmar and Rather, and says little about Ambrosius Autpertus.

[8] *Liber Manualis*; for an excellent translation, with introduction and notes, see C. Neel, *Handbook for William: A Carolingian Woman's Counsel for her Son* (Lincoln, NE, 1991); cf. Brunhölzl, *Histoire*, pp. 159–61; P. Dronke, *Women Writers of the Middle Ages: A Critical Study of Texts from Perpetua (+203) to Marguerite Porete (+1310)* (Cambridge, 1984), pp. 31–54; C. W. Atkinson, *The Oldest Vocation: Christian Motherhood in the Middle Ages* (Ithaca, NY, 1989), pp. 96–100. A study which has some interesting things to say but which also makes mistakes and covers too little of the sources and literature is Y. Bessmertny, 'Le monde vu par une femme au IXe siècle: La perception du monde dans l'aristocratie carolingienne', *Le Moyen Age* 93 (1987), pp. 161–84. See now Nelson, 'Dhuoda', below chapter 6.

[9] Odo, *Gerald*. Like Rather, Odo was Carolingian in education and outlook and his subject Gerald was Carolingian *tout court*.

[10] Paulinus, *Liber*, I, cols. 3, 5, 28, 51, 57, 63, 197C–198C, 199A–200A, 200C–201A, 223A–225B, 254B–255A, 265B–D, 272C–274C; Alcuin, *De virtutibus* c. 5, col. 616D; *Liber Manualis* II, 3, III, II, VIII, I, pp. 124–8, 184–96, 306; Jonas, *De institutione laicali* I, cc. 6, 11–12, 14, 19–20, II, cc. 20–1, 23, III, cc. 13–14, cols. 132B–C, 143A–144D, 145A–147A, 149D–151A, 158B–161A, 161A–166A, 208D–213A, 216A, 257D–258D, 258D–261B; Hincmar, *De cavendis vitiis*, preface and *c.* 9, cols. 857B–C, 915A–920A.

[11] These are based on Is. II: 2. Alcuin Ep. III, p. 160, stresses the gift of wisdom and adds the gift of speech for the laity while reserving to the clergy 'charismata' (based on Rom. 12: 6–8 or I Cor. 12) such as healing, miracles, prophecy, tongues. Here is another of the functional distinctions noted already. See J. Chélini, *L'aube du moyen âge: Naissance de la chrétienté occidentale. La vie religieuse des*

usually mixed up in varying combinations. The military theme, *conflictus*, the battle between good and evil, is almost certainly deliberate, even if it is derivative. That is, our authors draw directly or indirectly upon Prudentius, Julianus Pomerius, John Cassian, Gregory I, Isidore and Aldhelm, all of whom wrote accounts of the battle of virtue with vice.[12] In the middle of the eighth century Ambrosius Autpertus wrote a *Conflictus* that enjoyed a fairly wide dissemination. He says that in ancient times there was persecution and martyrdom to test those who wished to follow Christ. In these later times, however, there is only the battle to oppose evil by doing good. He says, 'We see how the camps of heaven and hell fight, how the arms of Christ and the devil crash into one another.'[13] Paulinus introduces his battle of vices and virtues in the following terms: 'You', he is addressing Duke Eric of Friuli, 'as a *miles terrenus*, go forth to battle against the visible enemy but the invisible enemy does not cease to struggle. You struggle to fight the enemies of your body using carnal arms ... but God fights with spiritual arms. You fight with weapons but God fights by opposing virtues to vices. You vest yourself with armour; God will vest you with his gifts.'[14] In a treatise on faith, hope and charity, Paschasius Radbertus called the cardinal virtues 'the armour and tools of faith' and he says that 'armed with this kind of weapon, faith can repel the spears of the enemy'.[15] These are fine examples of messages couched in terms that were immediate, relevant and understandable to those to whom they were directed. The quest for salvation was described to warriors in themes of battle. Dhuoda, too, stresses the struggle of good against evil and tells her son William that while 'carnal man fears the loss of the things of this world, spiritual man fears the loss of heaven'.[16] A noble could save his soul by keeping God's commands and obeying the rules of the Church. This message was suited to the nobility in so far as it was encouraging to men whose routine duties might place their souls in jeopardy.

More relevant to the nobility itself are further counsels offered by each of our authors. Not a single one of these texts ever, in any circumstances,

---

laïcs dans l'Europe carolingienne, 750–900 (Paris, 1991), p. 38; Giles Brown, 'The Carolingian Renaissance', in McKitterick, ed., *Carolingian Culture*, pp. 1–51, at 25.

[12] Wallach, *Alcuin and Charlemagne*, pp. 236–47; Mähl, *Quadriga Virtutum*, pp. 19–34, 163. Some sources are discussed by Newhauser, *Treatise*, pp. 26–8, 99–115.

[13] *De conflictu*, 1, ed. Weber, p. 910. Ambrosius, who wrote for monks, departs from the conventions of his genre in having virtue and vice fight for the soul of a man rather than, as in (say) Prudentius, fighting one another directly.

[14] Paulinus, *Liber c.* 20, col. 213A.

[15] Paschasius, *De fide, spe et caritate c.* 12, ed. B. Paulus, *CCCM* 97 (1990), pp. 48–52. His source is Ephesians 6: 14–17.

[16] *Liber Manualis*, v, 1, p. 260.

recommends that a nobleman save his soul by entering the clergy. Ascetic practices are not usually recommended. Odo of Cluny reports of Gerald of Aurillac that when he considered entering a monastery those people did well who talked him out of it.[17] Gerald's place was in the world where he might be a good example to others. But, then, Odo tells us that Gerald was moderate in food, drink and clothing, and that he eschewed marriage, and that he fought with blunt weapons. Indeed, it was precisely as a public man that Gerald could best be *vir sanctus*.[18] All the texts, though with varying degrees of emphasis on particular points, stress public actions such as: attendance at mass in the basilica; open, sincere confession of sins; visible, but not ostentatious, generosity in almsgiving; true hospitality to pilgrims and strangers.[19]

Paulinus reminds Eric of the story of the widow's mite by way of telling him that while for the salvation of his own soul interior disposition is more important than exterior performance, public actions are nevertheless crucial to the salvation of those who will take a good example from so exalted a man as the duke of Friuli.[20] Paulinus tells Eric to preach to those in his household since he will answer for them at the last judgement and he tells him to set a good example for them.[21] Paulinus reminds him that Christ taught by both word and deed and he suggests imitating Christ's renunciations, such as having only one garment and fasting in the desert. Paulinus also calls the public performance of the beatitudes the *opus Dei*, an interesting choice of terms, and then goes on in what is almost a motto to say that 'Holiness is found in the works of righteousness' (*Sanctitas vero in justitiae operibus constat*).[22]

Jonas held up to Matfrid as an example to be shunned houses where one would find 'huge, handsome dogs and pallid, staggering men'.[23] Mayke de Jong has recently stressed the preoccupation of numerous writers in the time of Louis with the idea of scandal and of the danger posed for the Church and for Christian society by scandalous behaviour on the part of

---

[17] Odo, *Vita Geraldi* II, 2, cols. 670C–671A; cf. II, 16, cols. 679B–680B, where Gerald himself decides that instead of becoming a monk he could be of more use in his lay state.
[18] *Ibid.*, II, 22, col. 682D.
[19] Jonas, *De inst.* I, 6, II, 14–16, II, 29, III, II, cols. 132C–133A, 143A–144D, 149D–150A, 151B–154B, 231A–234A, 253D–255C; Alcuin, *De virtutibus* cc. 12, 17, cols. 621B–622B, 625B–626B; *Liber Manualis* V, 2, pp. 272–4; Paulinus, *Liber c.* 5, col. 201A.
[20] Paulinus, *Liber c.* 5, col. 201A.
[21] Paulinus, *Liber* cc. 6, 29, cols. 201A–202A, 225B–226A; cf. Jonas, *De inst.*, I, 6, cols. 132C–133A.
[22] Paulinus, *Liber c.* 54, cols. 260B–262A, cf. cc. 5, 9, cols. 200C, 205B.
[23] Jonas, *De inst.* II, 23, col. 216C–D.

leaders.²⁴ This concern with public scandal is an important part of the impetus behind the attempt in these years to restore public penance for at least the most notorious of offences.²⁵ In other words, one crucial component of the noble ethos was personal moral conduct of the highest and most exemplary sort. The nobility was not to usurp or to mix in the clergy's responsibilities, but in their own lay state they had a share in the great task of saving the souls of the *populus Dei* who lived in the *imperium Francorum*. This sense of shared responsibility is just what Charles and Louis meant when they talked of extending their *ministerium* to the nobility. Smaragdus and Jonas stressed in their mirrors that kings had to set a good example, and Louis the Pious repeatedly sounded this theme in his capitularies, never more meaningfully than when he stated that the bishops at Attigny in 822 performed public penance following his own 'most salubrious example'.²⁶ This *ministerium* was not a privilege, not something to be grasped at. It was a burden, an awesome responsibility.²⁷ Carolingian nobles were expected to be 'saintly' in public, partly to save their own souls and partly to save others. The Carolingian reform of society was to be carried out by men who taught by deed the lessons codified by other men who taught by word. Indeed, Louis II asked the bishops of his realm to inquire into the religious practices of the laity for fear that laxity on the part of *potentes* and *nobiles* might set a bad example for others.²⁸

The ethical treatises also contain a good many examples drawn from the daily life of public figures. I take this to be further evidence for the

---

[24] M. de Jong, 'Power and Humility in Carolingian Society: The Public Penance of Louis the Pious', *EME* 1 (1992), 29–52.
[25] On Carolingian penance: S. Hamilton, *The Practice of Penance, 900–1050* (Woodbridge, 2001), pp. 1–24; M. Driscoll, *Alcuin et la pénitence à l'époque carolingienne*, Liturgiewissenschaftliche Quellen und Forschungen 81 (Münster, 1999), pp. 88–98 and *passim*; R. Meens, 'The Frequency and Nature of Early Medieval Penance', in P. Biller and A. J. Minnis, eds., *Handling Sin: Confession in the Middle Ages* (Woodbridge, 1998), pp. 35–61; de Jong, 'What Was Public About Public Penance?', *La giustizia nel medioevo*, 2 vols., Settimane Spoleto XLIII (1996), II, pp. 863–902; wide-ranging but less acute is Chélini, *L'aube du moyen age*, pp. 362–441.
[26] *MGH Capit.* I, no. 174, p. 357; Smaragdus, *Via regia* c. 18, *PL* 102, col. 958A–B, 'debent etenim caput sequi membra'. Jonas, *De institutione regia* c. 3, ed. J. Reviron, *Jonas d'Orléans et son 'De Institutione Regia'* (Paris, 1930), pp. 138–9, 'bonis exemplis exuberare faciat, ut ab ea ceteri subiecti bonum exemplum semper capiant. Ipse etiam salutiferis Christi preceptis fideliter atque obedienter obsecundet, et recte agendo eos, quibus temporaliter imperat, in pace et concordia atque caritate, ceterorumque bonorum operum exhibitione, quantum sibi divinitus datur, consistere faciat et dictis atque exemplis ad opus pietatis et iustitiae et misericordie sollerter excitet, adtendens, quod pro his Deo rationem redditurus sit…'.
[27] A. Vauchez, *La spiritualité du moyen âge occidental: VIIIe–XIIe siècle* (Paris, 1975), pp. 18–19 says that this ministerial conception of the lay role in society was a natural consequence of an anointed royalty in the sense that anointed kings were seen to share in the ministry of the priesthood; I agree.
[28] *MGH Capit.* II, no. 210, p. 210.

practical and almost pastoral side of these tracts. They tend to treat sensitively real-life situations. Counts are told that they will be constantly tempted by gifts or by outright bribes.[29] They are told they will be asked to make unjust judgements in courts. They are warned to watch out for friends and family members who will expect preferential treatment.[30] They are counselled to be alert for persons of rank and eminence who will abuse their station to gain unjust ends. Finally, they are even cautioned against members of the clergy who may ask for things to which they are not entitled.[31] In a letter to Count Matfrid, Agobard of Lyons stated many of the same themes that appear in the treatises. He told Matfrid that before all time God had chosen him to be count and that God had honoured and endowed him before all other men with not only his office but also the gifts needed to exercise it well: prudence, justice, fortitude and temperance. Armed with these gifts, Agobard said, Matfrid should restrain iniquity, destroy fraud and evil, make depravity vanish, eliminate cruelty and erect justice. He concluded by saying that Matfrid ought to emend his own behaviour and that of his subordinates so that they would be the keenest possible ministers of God and the most fitting helpers (*adiutores*) of the emperor. Good conduct would make them worthy of reward in the eyes of both their lords, that is, the emperor and God.[32] Secular sanctity was again required but this time in specific reference to the public duties of great men. Such people were told to conduct their affairs in open and exemplary fashion and then they were told to be just as honest and irreproachable in the conduct of their public duties. André Vauchez notes that a deliberate consequence of the increasing ritualisation of society was that ordinary people became accustomed to watching the elite do things for them.[33] Once again, the great danger is scandal. Agobard and Jonas and the others fall neatly into line with the admonitions of the capitularies. There are some not so subtle warnings in these writings. Good behaviour will result in earthly and heavenly reward while bad behaviour will just as certainly result in condemnation here and hereafter.

---

[29] Paulinus, *Liber c.* 62, cols. 271A–272B; Rather, *Praeloquia* I, 7.17, cols. 162B–163B. A powerful warning against official temptation and misconduct is Theodulf, *Carmen* 28, ed. E. Dümmler, *MGH Poet.* 1 (Berlin, 1881), pp. 493–517.
[30] Alcuin, *De virtutibus* cc. 19–21, cols. 627C–629D; Jonas, *De inst.* II, 24, cols. 218C–221C; Paulinus, *Liber c.* 6, cols. 201A–202A.
[31] Jonas, *De inst.* II, 20, 22, 24, cols. 208D–211C, 213A–215B, 218C–221C; Rather, *Praeloquia*, I, 10.23, cols. 166C–168A.
[32] Agobard Ep. 10, pp. 201–3.   [33] Vauchez, *La spiritualité*, pp. 14–15.

Our texts also sketch out a hierarchy of loyalties that Carolingian nobles were expected to observe. First is loyalty to God. Paulinus, for example, opens his treatise by reminding Eric that he was created by divine plan and in God's image; that he can do nothing without God's help; that he owes all he has to God; and that he will answer to God alone in the end. Dhuoda tells her son to place his love of God above all earthly attachments.[34] It is not surprising, and calls for no further comment, that Carolingian writers would have placed loyalty to God in the first place.

Second came loyalty to one's lord, especially to one's highest lord, namely the king or emperor.[35] Dhuoda actually has the most to say on this subject but her comments may be supplemented by those of many ninth-century writers, notably Hincmar and Hrabanus Maurus.[36] Authors draw clear analogies between loyalty to God and loyalty to one's lord. We already noted Agobard's comments to Matfrid to the effect that proper conduct vis-à-vis God and Louis would bring rewards from each. Loyalty was so important to Agobard that when he found himself in the anti-imperial camp in the 830s, he had to explain to Louis' sons, who had rebelled against their father, that their cause was just because of the evils perpetrated by Louis' wife Judith.[37] Disloyalty to the ruler was seen as sinful, and thus as dangerous to the soul of the disloyal party, but also as a bad example to others, and thus potentially damaging to their souls too.

Finally, the texts stress loyalty to family. Dhuoda is positively eloquent in telling her son to remember his family in prayer. She tells him all that she can about his family and says that in time he will have to pass that information on to the next generation.[38] Peter Dronke says of Dhuoda that her 'world-picture' was one 'in which the bonds of loyalty to the human father, to the emperor, and to a father God are seen concentrically'.[39] Alcuin and Paulinus have almost nothing to say about marriage and the

---

[34] Paulinus, *Liber* cc. 1–4, cols. 197C–200B; *Liber Manualis* I, 1–7, pp. 96–116.
[35] For very interesting comments on the encounter between Germanic ideas of loyalty and Christian ideas see D. H. Green, *The Carolingian Lord: Semantic Studies on Four Old High German Words* (Cambridge, 1965), pp. 216–32.
[36] *Liber Manualis* III, 4, VIII, 6, pp. 148–52, 308. C. Bouchard, 'Family Structure and Family Consciousness among the Aristocracy in the Ninth to Eleventh Centuries', *Francia* 14 (1987), pp. 642–3 says the tenuous position of Dhuoda's family made her urge young William not to place loyalty to Charles the Bald over loyalty to his own father, something Bouchard thinks such men were likely to do. For some very perceptive comments on this issue see J. L. Nelson, 'Ninth-Century Knighthood: The Evidence of Nithard', in Christopher Harper-Bill *et al.*, eds., *Studies in Medieval History Presented to R. Allen Brown* (Woodbridge, Suffolk, 1989), pp. 255–66, esp. 257–62.
[37] Agobard, *Libri duo pro filiis et contra Iudith uxorem Ludovici Pii*, *MGH SS* XV, pp. 275–9.
[38] *Liber Manualis* VIII, 7, 14–15, 17, X, 5, pp. 310, 318–20, 320–2, 324, 354–6.
[39] Dronke, *Women Writers*, p. 38.

family, concentrating instead on the virtue of chastity in an almost monastic understanding – a position not unlike that taken later by Odo of Cluny with respect to Gerald of Aurillac.[40] We may suppose this advice to have been neither welcome nor useful. But Jonas, Hrabanus, and Rather stress the importance of the honour and reverence that must be shown among husband, wife and children, and they have a great deal to say about the dignity and value of the married life.[41] These writers, and Jonas especially, evince considerable evolution in social thought in the generation between the 790s and the 820s. Pierre Toubert argues persuasively that Jonas's comments about family solidarity and the need to avoid sexual abuses would have been understood to argue for the integrity of the family and the greater certainty of succession.[42] In other words, the writers of these treatises played upon the natural sense of kin solidarity among the Frankish nobles and turned it to higher moral purposes.

Let us sum up this ideal, this noble ethos, which it might not be an exaggeration to call an ideology. It is remarkably simple and is solidly coherent with the central tenets of the Carolingian reform programme as those began to be articulated in the central years of Charlemagne's reign. Basically, it held that nobles must live an active public life, that they must accept the responsibilities that go with that life. The daily life of a nobleman will present temptations and challenges that threaten his soul and the souls of all those people for whom he has responsibility in a great hierarchy of ministerial duty. God will provide aid to the aristocrat in fulfilling his *ministerium* and when that ministry is being fulfilled properly the aristocrat will be a *vir sanctus* who does the *opus Dei*, that is, the *opera iustitiae*, in public. The nobleman's sword, wife and extended family were the chief badges of his rank. Secular sanctity kept each of them brightly polished.

Carolingian society was hierarchical and elitist.[43] The elite constituted a governing class whose rank and status were plain for all to see. It was to this

---

[40] Alcuin, *De virtutibus* c. 18, cols. 626C–627C; Paulinus, *Liber* c. 24, cols. 219B–220A.
[41] Jonas, *De inst.* II, 1–4, cols. 167A–177C; Hrabanus Ep. 15–17, pp. 403–22; Rather, *Praeloquia* II, cols. 189A–218C.
[42] P. Toubert, 'La théorie du marriage chez les moralistes carolingiens', in *Il matrimonio nella società altomedioevale*, 2 vols., Settimane Spoleto XXIV (1977), 1, pp. 246–54.
[43] For general observations on ideas of rank, order, and hierarchy see: K.-F. Werner, *Naissance de la noblesse* 2nd edn (Paris, 1998); L. Kuchenbuch, 'Ordnungsverhalten im grundherrlichen Schriftgut vom 9. bis 12. Jahrhundert', in J. Fried, ed., *Dialektik und Rhetorik im früheren und hohen Mittelalter*, Schriften des historischen Kollegs, Kolloquien 27 (Munich, 1997), pp. 175–268; G. Duby, *The Three Orders: Feudal Society Imagined*, trans. A. Goldhammer (Chicago, 1980), chs. 5, 7, 10, and *passim*; H. Fichtenau (tr. P. J. Geary), *Living in the Tenth Century: Mentalities and Social Orders* (Chicago, 1991), chs. 1–3.

elite that secular sanctity was proposed as a code of values and conduct, and among this elite that the ideal of secular sanctity arose and circulated. We can capture a sense of this group's identity from both impressionistic sources of the Carolingian world and objective criteria formulated in our own times. Recent general studies of the Carolingian nobility are so thorough and comprehensive that we can here dispense with detailed efforts to define the nobility.[44]

One indicator of noble status consciousness that can serve as a bridge to a wider discussion of rank and hierarchy pertains to the Carolingian version of knighthood. The early eleventh-century *Decretum* of Burchard of Worms records the case of a Lombard named Aistulf who murdered his wife and was assigned stiff penances by Paulinus of Aquileia. Aistulf had to forego wine, beer and meat except on Christmas and Easter. He had to eat bread, water and salt and perform vigils and almsgiving. Moreover, he could never bear arms, sit in judgement in a court, or take a wife or concubine. He had to avoid baths and banquets and to give up riding horses.[45] Taking away wine, beer and meat was a real deprivation for a member of the elite but even more serious was the denial of weapons and horses, for these were the marks of the aristocrat *par excellence*.[46] By the middle of the ninth century, aristocrats took great pride in their fine weapons and their noble horses. Investiture with weapons, in particular with the sword-belt, the *cingulum militare*, was a key *rite de passage* for a young nobleman. Stripping a man of his weapons was a way of taking away his rank in the world. Historical sources of many kinds, and even literary works such as *Waltharius*, emphasize many aspects of the noble life well lived: fine clothes, lavish banquets, large entourages and joyful entertainment.[47] But horses and weapons were absolutely central to the

---

[44] In addition to its own distinguished contribution Werner's *Naissance*, pp. 20–67 and 125–42 provides a superb account of the history of research into the nobility. See also R. Le Jan, *Famille et pouvoir dans le monde franc (VIIe–Xe siècle): Essai d'anthropologie sociale* (Paris, 1995); Le Jan, ed., *La royauté et les élite dans l'Europe carolingienne* (Lille, 1998); S. Airlie, 'The Aristocracy', in R. McKitterick, ed., *NCMH* II (Cambridge, 1995), pp. 431–50.

[45] *Decretum*, 6.40, *PL* 140, cols. 774A–775B; also Paulinus, *Epistolae*, ed. Dümmler, *MGH Epp.* IV (Berlin, 1899), no. 4, pp. 520–2.

[46] The case is discussed by Leyser, 'Early Medieval Canon Law and the Beginnings of Knighthood', in L. Fenske *et al.*, eds., *Institutionen, Kultur und Gesellschaft im Mittelalter: Festschrift für Josef Fleckenstein zu seinem 65. Geburtstag* (Sigmaringen, 1984), pp. 549–66, repr. in his *Communications and Power in Medieval Europe*, ed. T. Reuter, 2 vols. (London, 1994), I, pp. 51–71, esp. 59–60. See also J. Fleckenstein, 'Adel und Kriegertum und ihre Wandlung im Karolingerzeit', in *Nascita dell'Europa ed Europa Carolingia: Un equazione da verificiare*, Settimane Spoleto XXVII (1981), pp. 67–94; Nelson, 'Ninth-Century Knighthood'.

[47] *Waltharius and Ruodlieb*, ed. and trans. D. M. Kratz, Garland Library of Medieval Literature 13 (New York, 1984), pp. 2–71; Kratz's Introduction, pp. xiii–xxiv, sums up current thinking on this

lives of the aristocracy. Across the course of the ninth century the profession of arms changed from a duty theoretically incumbent on all free men to an exclusive and jealously guarded preserve of the nobility. In other words, if you spot a person in the sources with expensive weapons and many horses, that person is noble.[48]

Other examples are ubiquitous in the sources, as a few examples will serve to show. In a letter to Arn of Salzburg, Alcuin urged his friend 'to bring counsel to every person according to his condition and status: justice and mercy to the powerful and officials, obedience, humility and confidence in their elders to the young, to everyone equity, love of God and neighbours, chastity of body, generosity and piety in alms'. In a letter to the priests Calvinus and Stephen, Alcuin reminded his correspondents to 'consider time, place and person; in what time, at what place, and to which person something should be said'.[49] In this same vein, Theodulf of Orléans, in the dedicatory epistle to Magnus of Sens that precedes his treatise *De ordine baptismi*, quoted almost *verbatim* a letter which Paulinus of Aquileia had addressed to Charlemagne: 'It is most suitable for you, venerable prince, that you urge prelates to investigations of sacred scriptures and to healthy and sober learning; every cleric to discipline; the learned to an understanding of divine and human affairs; monks to religion; everyone in general to holiness; nobles to good counsel; officials to justice; soldiers to experience in arms; prelates to humility; subjects to obedience; and all in general to prudence, justice, fortitude and temperance, peace and concord.'[50] The poet known as 'Hibernicus Exul' called down blessings on king, clergy, counts and warriors in a neatly hierarchical series of ranks.[51]

---

poem that has been authoritatively dated from the early ninth to the early tenth century. The most recent discussion, profoundly learned and destined to be controversial is Werner, '*Hludovicus Augustus*: Gouverner l'empire Chrétien – Idées et réalités', in P. Godman and R. Collins, eds., *Charlemagne's Heir: New Perspectives on the Reign of Louis the Pious* (Oxford, 1990), pp. 3–123, at 101–23. Walter and his associates share bountifully in everything the unfortunate Aistulf was denied.

[48] J. France, 'The Military History of the Carolingian Period', *Revue belge d'histoire militaire* 26 (1985), pp. 81–99, usefully distinguishes between the possession and importance of horses and that hearty bloom in the Carolingianist's garden of debate, cavalry and mounted shock combat.

[49] Alcuin *Epp*. 184, 209, pp. 310, 348.

[50] Paulinus Ep. 18c, ed. E. Dümmler, *MGH Epp*. IV, p. 527; Theodulf, letter to Magnus of Sens, in S. Keefe, *Water and the Word: Baptism and the Education of the Clergy in the Carolingian Empire*, 2 vols., II, *Editions of the Texts* (Notre Dame, IN, 2002), no. 15, pp. 280–1. This text has been called *De ordine baptismi* from Sirmond's edition reprinted in *PL* 105, where the letter to Magnus occupies cols. 223C–224B.

[51] Hibernicus Exul, *Versus Karoli Imperatoris*, ed. Dümmler, *MGH Poet*. I, pp. 399–400.

These private records accord well with public ones on the theme of specific duties for particular people, especially the nobility. In the preface to the *Admonitio generalis* of 789, a text which Alcuin probably drafted, Charlemagne explicitly extended his royal ministry, his royal duty and burden, to the nobility whom he asked to be his *adiutores*. Charlemagne asked 'the most brilliant lights of the world' to be especially vigilant 'to lead the people of God to the pastures of eternal life'. A series of specific responsibilities was spelled out: the promotion of peace and concord; the correction of abuses (presumably judicial ones); honest judgements; avoidance of bribes; refusal to consider rank and privilege.[52] In a capitulary of 802 Charles insisted that only the wisest and most religious of the nobles were fit to share in his ministry and he asked that men show their fitness by concern for the unfortunate, for widows, orphans, paupers, pilgrims and children. In that same capitulary, Charlemagne urged every person to keep to his own purpose and profession.[53] Jonas and Rather later echoed this sentiment.[54] Louis the Pious repeated and even intensified these themes in his capitularies. In 818 he emphasised his own responsibility for the souls of all of those whom God had entrusted to his care and then in the early 820s he said 'although the totality of this ministry is seen to be in our person, nevertheless by divine authority and human arrangement it is recognised to be so divided into parts that each one of you is known to have a share in our ministry in his own place and rank. Hence it is clear that I ought to be admonishing all of you and you ought to be my helpers.'[55] These texts, then, recognise that people in society have different roles and responsibilities and that some people have an obligation to lead by word and example.

Who are those leaders? The most memorable passage in Thegan's *Life of Louis the Pious* is surely the one where he castigates Ebo of Rheims for turning on the emperor. He tells the Saxon goatherd's son that 'he [Charles] made you free but he did not make you noble, for that is impossible'. This passage may be about status, or it may be about raw power, but it reveals a

---

[52] MGH *Capit.* 1, no. 22, p. 53. D. Bullough, *Alcuin: Achievement and Reputation* (Leiden, 2004), pp. 379–84; Wallach, *Alcuin and Charlemagne*, p. 62; F.-K. Scheibe, 'Alcuin und die *Admonitio Generalis*', *DA* 14 (1958), pp. 221–9.

[53] MGH *Capit.*, no. 33, p. 93. In a well-known study F.-L. Ganshof stressed the heightened sense of social and spiritual fitness called for by this capitulary: 'Charlemagne's Programme of Imperial Government', in his *The Carolingians and the Frankish Monarchy*, tr. J. Sondheimer (Ithaca, NY, 1971), pp. 55–85.

[54] Jonas, *Admonitio et opusculum de munere regio* (=*De institutione regia*), c. 4, ed. A. Dubreucq, *Le métier du roi*, SC 407 (Paris, 1995), p. 198; Rather, *Praeloquia* 1, 1.1, cols. 147C–149A.

[55] MGH *Capit.* 1, no. 137, pp. 273–4, no. 150, c. 3, p. 303.

genuine awareness of social difference.[56] Thegan is upset that a person of low birth had risen to an archbishopric, a station for which high birth was a virtual *sine qua non*. Another revealing story is the one told by Notker about Charles's visit to Clement's school. There he found *nobiles, mediocres et infimi* studying together but to his displeasure the aristocratic youth were malingerers while the others were eager and successful at their studies. Charles thus told the noble boys that he was disappointed in them and that they might not get the preferments that they had every right to expect, and he told the other boys that he would reward them with bishoprics and abbacies.[57] There is no question that nobly born boys were powerful, but low-born boys could become powerful too, could enter the elite. This is exactly what upset Thegan so much. Finally, it is interesting to see how both of the prose biographers of Louis the Pious emphasised the nobility – the paternal and the maternal nobility – of Louis' mother Hildegard and also of his second wife, Judith of Bavaria.[58] One might have supposed that marriage to the king or emperor was enough. Perhaps, too, Thegan and the Astronomer were seeking to remind the high-born aristocrats who had so violently opposed Louis and Judith that they were attacking not, as it were, the Ebos of the world but that world's grandees, people just like themselves, people they ought to be supporting.

The same conclusion can be drawn from the addresses of papal letters to Francia. For instance, in 800 Leo III wrote to Bavaria and addressed himself to 'bishops, abbots, priests, deacons, monks and clerics, abbesses, nuns, officials, all nobles (*primates*) and the whole people' and he reminded them all to work in their own order (*ordo*) and to fulfil their own duty (*officium*) for the good of all.[59] Here we see two hierarchies, one clerical and one lay. I do not think one needs to see the entire clerical order as superior to the entire lay order. It is simply listed first. Lay officials are assumed to be *primates* and they are further assumed to be different from everyone else. A few years later Paschal I used different words to sound the same themes. He addressed: 'All our most holy brothers, our fellow bishops, all priests or other ecclesiastical orders, the glorious princes, dukes, and magnificent

---

[56] Thegan *c*. 44, pp. 599–600; S. Airlie, 'Bonds of Power and Bonds of Association in the Court Circle of Louis the Pious', in Godman and Collins, eds., *Charlemagne's Heir*, pp. 191–204.
[57] Notker, *Gesta Karoli* 1, cc. 1–3, pp. 2–5.
[58] Thegan *c*. 2, p. 590: 'desponsavit sibi nobilissimi generis Suavorum puellam, nomine Hildegardum'; *c*. 26, p. 596: 'accepit filiam Hwelfi ducis sui, qui erat de nobilissima progenie Bawariorum'; Astronomer *c*. 2, p. 607: 'Hildegardum nobilissimam'; *c*. 32, p. 624: 'Iudith, filiam Welponis nobilissimi comitis'.
[59] Leo III *Ep*. 5, ed. K. Hampe, *MGH Epp*. v (Berlin, 1899), p. 62.

counts, and all Christians faithful to God.'⁶⁰ Decades earlier Pope Zachary, in a letter to Pippin, had said that 'to the princes, to the men of the world, and to the warriors falls the task of guarding against the enemy's cunning and of defending the country; to bishops, priests, and servants of God it is given to act by offering salutary counsel and prayer so that, thanks to God, with our praying and their fighting, the country may remain safe'.⁶¹ Here the laymen are mentioned before the clergy and each group is assigned a discrete task. Readers of these words will almost certainly think of the well-known letter of Charlemagne to Pope Leo III in which the king urged the pope to lift his hands to God in prayer for the success of Carolingian arms.⁶² Memorial book entries are also arrayed hierarchically. That of St Peter in Salzburg lists both the dead and the living in carefully ranked hierarchies, and the Reichenau book starts with the royal family and follows with the clerical orders of bishops, abbots and priests and then goes on to counts and ordinary laymen.⁶³ While it is true that descriptions of Carolingian society are frustratingly inconsistent, it is also true that every one of them is hierarchical, and that every one of those hierarchical schemes assigns tasks according to position in the hierarchy. The people at the top of that hierarchy are the nobility, designated in texts as *primores, primates, proceres, principes, optimates, nobiles* and the like.⁶⁴ These are the people discussed above whom we can identify by the marks of birth, office, power, landed wealth, access to the royal court, status and, sometimes, education. It was an extremely fluid group. Because an understanding of the nobility's very shapelessness and changeability will help to show why the Carolingian noble ethos took the form it did, we need to pursue the nobility's structure just a bit further.

Let us go back to Thegan. He clearly hated *arrivistes* like Ebo and I suspect that he represented a broad current of opinion. But can we say that the archbishop of Rheims was not noble? Yes and no. Thegan after all was at pains to refute the idea so it must have enjoyed some currency. Thegan may have been concerned about Ebo's status as an archbishop or

---

⁶⁰ Paschal I *Ep.* 11, ed. Hampe, *MGH Epp.* v, p. 69.
⁶¹ *Codex Carolinus* 3, ed. W. Gundlach, *MGH Epp.* III (Berlin, 1892), p. 480.
⁶² Alcuini Ep. 93, p. 138.
⁶³ K. Schmid, 'Über das Verhältnis von Person und Gemeinschaft im früheren Mittelalter', *FMS* 1 (1967), pp. 243–4; Schmid, 'Einleitung', in Schmid *et al.*, eds., *Verbrüderungsbuch der Abtei Reichenau (Einleitung, Register, Faksimile)* (Hanover, 1979), p. lxii.
⁶⁴ For discussion of this terminology see: J. Martindale, 'The French Aristocracy in the Early Middle Ages: A Reappraisal', *P&P* 75 (1977), pp. 3–17; H.-W. Goetz, 'Der Adel im Selbstverständnis der Karolingerzeit', *Vierteljahrschrift für Sozial- und Wirtschaftsgeschichte* 70 (1983), pp. 161–3, and esp. 188–91 on nobility as a 'relative concept'.

he may have been worried about the archbishop's lack of moral fitness. In either case, a decisive mark of 'nobility' was absent. To the point is a letter of Lupus of Ferrières to Charles the Bald. He told the king not to worry too much about some of the *potentes* who were giving him so much trouble because just as he had made them, so he could unmake them, when he wished.[65] Rather of Verona was also conscious that men could rise and fall rapidly and unexpectedly.[66] This sense of changeability and fragility is the corollary to Notker's story about Clement's school. The noble boys there had a natural expectation of high office but the king could, on the spot, grant to low-born boys the positions and privileges that themselves could confer power, status, and, eventually, nobility. Relevant too is Joachim Wollasch's sensitive reading of Dhuoda's *Manual*.[67] His argument is that the family of William of Gellone, although noble and well known, was neither wealthy nor powerful and, as a result, was nearly destroyed in a quest for the kind of *honores* that would have solidified its social and political position and that, as noted, the boys in Clement's school got as a reward for their industry. The Fulda annalist tells a revealing story about Bishop Liutward of Vercelli. He was, as Charles the Fat's arch-chancellor from 878 and his arch-chaplain from 883, one of the most powerful men in the East Frankish kingdom. Nevertheless, 'Liutward was honoured and feared by all more than the emperor. For he carried off the daughters of the most noble men in Alemannia and Italy … and gave them to his relatives in marriage. He went so far in his stupidity … that he invaded the nunnery in Brescia [San Salvatore] and had certain of his friends carry off by force the daughter of Count Unruoch, a relative of the emperor, and gave her to his relative in marriage.'[68] Shortly after this Liutward was deposed. Obviously he had been trying to gain for his family some guarantee of a noble rank that his own exalted status could not assure. What these observations mean is that while an Ebo was not yet noble, he was in a position to ennoble his family, and that while William of Gellone's family was noble it was perilously close to losing that status. Liutward can be reckoned as noble on the basis of his high offices but his personal status could not automatically be transferred to his relatives.

---

[65] Lupus Ep. 64, p. 64: 'Ne metuatis potentes, quos ipsi fecistis et quos, cum vultis, extenuare potestis.'
[66] *Praeloquia* 1, 10.23, cols. 166C–168A.
[67] 'Eine adlige Familie des frühen Mittelalters: ihr Selbstverständnis und ihre Wirklichkeit', *Archiv für Kulturgeschichte* 39 (1957), pp. 150–88.
[68] *AF* s.a. 886, p. 105, tr. Reuter, pp. 101–2.

To various Carolingian attempts to come to grips with the nobility we may add the reflections of recent scholars. Wilhelm Störmer identifies as noble those who practised distinctive traditions of name-giving, who usually married within their own class, who held landed possessions, who led a military-aristocratic life-style, who possessed high offices in the Church and empire, and who controlled their own churches and others too through advocacy. Hans K. Schulze invites us to imagine as noble all of those who appeared as donors, witnesses or judges in counts' courts; who were recipients of fiefs or other royal gifts; who possessed public offices; or who held monasteries and canonries. Reinhard Wenskus, in a huge study of the relationships between the Saxon nobility and the 'imperial nobility', found that local families of some significance often joined in what he calls 'donation-communities' with some of the great families that had interests all over the kingdom and, later, empire. Régine Hennebicque (Le Jan), in a study of some families from the Middle Rhine–Mosel region, reaches the same conclusions. She points out that many of the greatest imperial families had imbricated themselves in local societies in ways that strengthened their own position while elevating the status of the locals among whom they had settled and, not infrequently, intermarried. Hans-Werner Goetz agrees that there was a large group of *potentes* but he sees within that group a smaller set of genuinely noble people who were seen by contemporaries as noble, who transmitted their status through blood, who intermarried with one another, who had close relations with the royal/imperial court, who routinely held, indeed who expected to hold, high offices in both Church and state, and whose habits and customs marked them off as different.[69]

The criteria offered by these scholars are useful in general but vague in some respects. Land-holding, for instance, was not the preserve of the nobility. It is not clear how many of these proposed characteristics must be present simultaneously for a person to be labelled noble. Wealth in land and the possession of public offices appear to be the two criteria on which everyone agrees. Moreover, there is a broad consensus that offices were acquired and that lands were gained or expanded through *Königsnähe*

---

[69] Störmer, *Früher Adel: Studien zur politischen Führungsschicht im fränkisch-deutschen Reich vom 8. bis 11. Jahrhundert*, 2 vols., Monographien zur Geschichte des Mittelalters (Stuttgart 1973), 1; Schulze, 'Reichsaristokratie, Stammesadel und fränkische Freiheit', *HZ* 227 (1978), pp. 353–73, at p. 369; Wenskus, *Sächsischer Stammesadel und fränkischer Reichsadel*, Abhandlungen der Akademie der Wissenschaften in Göttingen, Phil.-Hist. Kl. 93 (Göttingen, 1976); Hennebique, 'Structures familiales et politiques au IXe siècle: Un groupe familial de l'aristocratie franque', *RH* 265 (1981), pp. 289–333; Airlie, 'The Aristocracy', p. 431; Goetz, 'Selbstverständnis', pp. 153–91.

(proximity to the king) and marriage.⁷⁰ Various spiritual bonds, such as godparenthood, could also affect relationships within the nobility.⁷¹

To make things more concrete, we can say that there were at any given time somewhat more than 600 counts.⁷² They were unquestionably noble. To them may plausibly be added subordinate officials such as *vicecomites, centenarii* and *vicarii*, high officers such as *duces, marchiones* and the like, as well as the major ecclesiastical officials. Bishops and abbots were typically noble and they came from the same families as their lay relatives. The Carolingian elite, the people with whom this chapter is concerned, probably numbered a few tens of thousands of persons across the whole of the eighth and ninth centuries. They were the visible, recognised leaders of the social and political order.

Having identified the people to whom secular sanctity was proposed, we may ask about the settings in which the ideal was formulated to see if laymen can be identified as having been present at the creation, so to speak, or if they might have had some role in the creative process. As a start, we may return to the sources enumerated above and note the contexts in which they were produced. Alcuin probably drafted the preface to the *Admonitio Generalis*, and he wrote a major ethical treatise on the request of Count Wido of the Breton March. Alcuin also wrote no fewer than thirteen other hortatory documents, addressing them to kings, clerics and laymen. Alcuin also taught Hilduin and Hrabanus. Hrabanus wrote many hortatory and ethical letters and treatises and taught Lupus of

---

⁷⁰ K. Schmid, 'Zur Problematik von Familie, Sippe und Geschlecht, Haus und Dynastie beim mittelalterlichen Adel: Vorfragen zum Thema "Adel und Herrschaft im Mittelalter"', *Zeitschrift für die Geschichte des Oberrheins* 105 (1957) p. 26; Schmid, 'Heirat, Familienfolge, Geschlechterbewußtsein', *Il matrimonio nella società altomedioevale*, Settimane Spoleto XXIV (1977), pp. 103–37; Leyser, 'Maternal Kin in Early Medieval Germany', *P&P* 49 (1970), pp. 126–34, repr. in his *Communications and Power*, I, pp. 181–8: an article that was in part a riposte to D. Bullough, 'Early Medieval Social Groupings: The Terminology of Kinship', *P&P* 45 (1969), pp. 3–18; Fleckenstein, 'Adel und Kriegertum', pp. 74–5; G. Althoff, *Verwandte, Freunde, Getreue: Zum politischen Stellenwert der Gruppenbildung im früheren Mittelalter* (Darmstadt, 1990), pp. 34–6.

⁷¹ A. Angenendt, *Kaiserherrschaft und Königstaufe: Kaiser, Könige und Päpste als geistliche Patrone in der abendländischen Missionsgeschichte* (Berlin, 1984); J. Lynch, *Godparents and Kinship in Early Medieval Europe* (Princeton, NJ, 1986).

⁷² Synthesising older work, E. Perroy, *Le monde carolingien*, 2nd edn (Paris, 1974), pp. 203–4, estimated a fluctuating number of counts between 200 and 250. F.-L. Ganshof, *Frankish Institutions Under Charlemagne*, trans. B. Lyon and M. Lyon (New York, 1968), p. 28, suggests 'about four hundred' in the time of Charlemagne. On the basis of careful mapping of the empire's 600–700 *pagi* Werner raises the estimate above 600: '*Missus-Marchio-Comes*: Entre l'administration centrale et l'administration locale de l'empire carolingien', in W. Paravicini and K.-F. Werner, eds., *Histoire comparée de l'administration (IVe–XVIIIe siècles)*, Beihefte der Francia 9 (Munich, 1980), p. 191, n. 2.

Ferrières who himself dispensed moral guidance freely.[73] Hilduin is not known to have circulated social advice but his greatest pupil, Hincmar of Rheims, was never reluctant to provide advice, whether asked or not. Theodulf, too, mostly in his poems, sounded themes that appear frequently in the ethical treatises and Theodulf, along with Alcuin and Paulinus of Aquileia, point us to the court of Charlemagne, a place of lively discussion and intellectual exchange revealed to us by a good number of poetic and epistolary sources.[74] Ebo of Reims asked Halitgar of Cambrai for a penitential book and got a strange compilation whose first two books discuss virtues and vices. Moreover, these two books are very much like books I and II of a three-book ethical work that has long been attributed to Hrabanus Maurus but is probably not his.[75] Agobard of Lyons wrote to Count Matfrid of Orléans to tell him how to exercise his comital responsibilities in the best way and Matfrid requested and received from Jonas of Orléans a long ethical treatise.[76] Jonas was arguably the most important cleric in the Frankish world in the 820s and he had links to the court of Louis the Pious. Matfrid was one of the most influential laymen in the empire and the close associate of Count Hugh of Tours whose daughters married Louis the Pious' son Lothar and brother-in-law Conrad. Finally, Hincmar tells us in *De ordine palatii* that at the annual assemblies of the Franks the king spent his time meeting individually and in groups with the nobles who had assembled to conduct the business of the realm. He also tells us that the greatest of the people there assembled recommended to the rest what actions should be taken.[77] Those actions usually came in the form

---

[73] *De virtutibus* preface, col. 613C: 'Memor sum petitionis tuae et promissionis meae … Aliqua tuae occupationi, quam te in bellicis rebus habere novimus, exhortamenta brevi sermone conscribere…' See also above n. 5; and on Hrabanus see Manitius, *Geschichte*, pp. 288–302; Brunhölzl, *Histoire*, pp. 84–98.

[74] Theodulf, *Carmina* 1, 2, 4, 5, 6, 7, 8, 10, 12, 17, 28, pp. 445–51, 452–8, 459, 459–60, 460, 460–2, 462–3, 464–5, 466–7, 472–4, 493–517; see P. Godman, *Poets and Emperors: Frankish Politics and Carolingian Poetry* (Oxford, 1987), pp. 38–92; M. Garrison, 'The Emergence of Carolingian Latin Literature and the Court of Charlemagne (780–814)', in McKitterick, ed., *Carolingian Culture*, pp. 111–40.

[75] For the texts see R. Kottje, *Die Bussbücher Halitgars von Cambrai und des Hrabanus Maurus: Ihre Überlieferung und ihre Quellen*, Beiträge zur Geschichte und Quellenkunde des Mittelalters 8 (Berlin, 1980); and for discussion see Mahl, *Quadriga Virtutum*, pp. 128–47, esp. 146–7; McKitterick, *Frankish Church*, pp. 170–2; Brunhölzl, *Histoire*, p. 95 and n. 24.

[76] Agobard Ep. 10, pp. 201–3; Jonas, *De inst., praefatio*, cols. 121D–123A: 'tuae nuper strenuitatis litteras suscepi, quibus meam extremitatem commone fecisti, ut tibi citissime et quam brevissime [!] scriberemus qualiter te caeterosque qui uxorio vinculo ligantur, vitam Deo placitam ducere oporteret'.

[77] Hinkmar, *De ordine palatii* cc. 6–7, ed. T. Gross and R. Schieffer, *MGH Fontes Iuris* 10 (Hanover, 1980), pp. 82–6, 92–6 (cf. Nelson, below, p. 118). Fascinating new material has come to light on the preliminaries behind the preparation of capitularies: H. Mordek, 'Recently Discovered Capitulary Texts Belonging to the Legislation of Louis the Pious', in Godman and Collins, eds., *Charlemagne's Heir*, pp. 437–53.

of capitularies and now we have closed the circle: capitularies were among the first sources I cited as revealing the aristocratic ethos.

My point in setting forth this selection of evidence is that in the ethical treatises to which we shall now turn I think we can hear the authentic voice of a wide swathe of the Carolingian elite and not simply the voices of those clerics who took it upon themselves to counsel the nobility in proper behaviour. Richard Newhauser may exaggerate slightly when he says that 'literary compositions of all kinds remained bound to a communicative situation, and the more practical the subject matter was, the more decisive and direct was the relationship between the expression of (implied) authorial intention and the audience'; but he is surely on the right track.[78] The evidence reveals a discourse that resounded for well over a century and that was almost always carried out in the same terms. That discourse was centred on the Carolingian court but extended far outside that court too. If laypeople, apart from Dhuoda, do not appear as authors of ethical advice, we cannot say that they were uninformed about its basic formulations. Capitularies speak the same language as the ethical treatises and they were the result of deliberations among lay magnates.

Can the Carolingian nobility actually have received the message that was being broadcast? One might approach this question indirectly and say that nobles were, after all, present at the public assemblies and Church Councils where we know many of these ideas to have been discussed and later incorporated into various written formulations, especially capitularies. Several historians have begun speaking of 'consensus politics' in the Carolingian world.[79] It is not far-fetched to see the secular ethos we have been discussing as one element in that consensus. Or we might note that many Carolingian sermons raise exactly the same themes as do the written materials examined above.[80] Given that both secular and ecclesiastical

---

[78] Newhauser, *Treatise*, p. 60.
[79] J. Hannig, *Consensus Fidelium: Frühfeudale Interpretationen des Verhältnisses von Königtum und Adel am Beispiel des Frankenreiches*, Monographien zur Geschichte des Mittelalters 27 (Stuttgart, 1982); J. L. Nelson, 'Legislation and Consensus in the Reign of Charles the Bald', in P. Wormald *et al.*, eds., *Ideal and Reality in Frankish and Anglo-Saxon Society* (Oxford, 1983), pp. 222–7; G. Schmitz, 'The Capitulary Legislation of Louis the Pious', in Godman and Collins, eds., *Charlemagne's Heir*, pp. 425–36 (longer version *DA* 42 (1986), 471–516); T. F. X. Noble, 'From Brigandage to Justice: Charlemagne 785–794', in C. Chazelle, ed., *Literacy, Politics, and Artistic Innovation in the Early Medieval West* (Lanham, MD, 1992), pp. 49–76, at 56–7.
[80] Fundamental is the unpublished work of T. L. Amos, 'The Origin and Nature of the Carolingian Sermon' (Ph.D. dissertation, Michigan State University, 1983). See, more briefly, his 'Preaching and the Sermon in the Carolingian World', in T. L. Amos *et al.*, eds., *De ore Domini: Preacher and Word in the Middle Ages*, Studies in Medieval Culture 27 (Kalamazoo, 1989), pp. 41–60. See also Woods as in n. 6. More than 900 sermons survive, and there is considerable evidence for the preaching of

legislation from the last years of Charlemagne's reign demanded preaching on the virtues and vices, we have some reason to be confident that the ideas we have been tracking did at least circulate.[81]

Or else one can take an approach that leads into the quicksand surrounding all questions having to do with Carolingian literacy. As we have seen, Paulinus, Alcuin, Jonas and Hincmar say clearly, and with neither qualification nor emphasis, that the persons to whom they addressed their ethical treatises asked for them. Alcuin and Dhuoda recommend that Count Wido and young William read their handbooks frequently, the better to commit their contents to memory. Dhuoda says she hopes that as her son acquires other books, which he will surely do, he does not forget to read hers.[82] Even so, she urges him to read the Bible and the church fathers. This is precisely the advice that Eric got from Paulinus: read the Bible and the church fathers. Alcuin too pronounced himself pleased at Eric's 'sacred reading'.[83] Jonas assumed that Matfrid could read and he is one of the considerable number of laymen from the Carolingian period who were the recipients of surviving letters.

But Jonas also provides a hint that pushes us in a slightly different direction. He says to Matfrid 'that you might frequently read this [book], or have it read to you',[84] and Hincmar says much the same thing: 'There are many who willingly read the words of God, or who hear them ... and there are those who so read or hear the words of God ... and there are not a few who, having heard or read the word of God.'[85] The 'hearing' in these instances may refer not only to treatises like *De institutione laicali* but also to the lessons in church or to sermons. None of these possibilities should be discounted as a source for the circulation of ideas. But hearing could have a different meaning. Einhard relates that Charlemagne had books read during dinner.[86] Fair enough, one might say, but that is the royal/imperial

---

sermons, sometimes in the vernacular, immediately after the Creed. See W. Haubrichs, *Von den Anfängen zum hohen Mittelalter*, Teil 1, *Die Anfänge: Versuche volkssprächiger Schriftlichkeit*, 1 (Frankfurt, 1988), pp. 305–11; thus the comments of R. E. McLaughlin, 'The Word Eclipsed? Preaching in the Early Middle Ages', *Traditio* 46 (1991), pp. 77–122 (preaching was 'a useful and exciting accessory', p. 122) seem needlessly pessimistic.

[81] *MGH Capit.* 1, no. 81 (810/13) *c.* 15, p. 179; Conc. Rheims (813) 13, ed. A. Werminghoff, *MGH Conc.* 11.1 (Hanover, 1906), p. 255.
[82] Alcuin, *De virtutibus*, Ep. nunc., cols. 613C–614C; Liber Manualis Pref., 1, 7, X, 2, XI, 2, pp. 114–16, 340, 368.
[83] Alcuin *Ep.* 98, p. 142.   [84] Jonas, *De inst.*, Praef., col. 124C.
[85] Hincmar, *De cavendis vitiis c.* x, *PL* 125, col. 857B.
[86] Einhard, *VK c.* 24, p. 29: 'Inter caenandum aut aliquod acroama aut lectorem audiebat. Legebantur ei historiae et antiquorum res gestae. Delectabantur et libris sancti Augustini praecipueque his qui De civitate Dei praetitulati sunt.'

court. Revealing, then, is Odo's remark that Gerald of Aurillac had the scriptures read as he dined.[87] Can other elite laymen have done likewise? Is it possible that such practices were a desirable mark of status?

Rosamond McKitterick argues for very widespread lay literacy in the Carolingian world.[88] The great contribution of her study is to gather together, and to force reflection upon, the huge number and the wide array of written materials produced by the Carolingians. One might suggest that McKitterick jumped too quickly from readable materials to readers when more case-by-case demonstrations would have been helpful. McKitterick's discussion of potential audiences is also too diffuse to be completely conclusive. Religious materials – liturgy, exegesis, etc. – were obviously read, but read by clergy, a class one of whose distinguishing characteristics was reading. Charters may well have been read by counts, judges and lay magnates, but can hardly be taken to point to widespread lay literacy. Yet what does widespread mean? I think that what McKitterick has actually demonstrated is that the existence of a basic, functional literacy among the Carolingian elite must be taken very seriously.

Janet Nelson has laid out clearly the centrality of written words to Carolingian government.[89] Wilfried Hartmann argues that a knowledge of the law was fairly common among the Carolingian elite.[90] Pierrre Riché identifies the wide reading, implying a substantial library, of Dhuoda, and comments on the numerous books bequeathed by Eberhard of Friuli and Eccard of Mâcon. Among Eberhard's books, significantly, was Alcuin's treatise on virtues and vices.[91] A dozen counts received letters from Hincmar, and two got letters from Lupus of Ferrières.[92] André Wilmart published in 1940 four prayerbooks prepared for Carolingian laymen, and one of them exists in a manuscript with Alcuin's *De virtutibus et vitiis*.[93] Both Eberhard and Eccard had prayerbooks and Dhuoda probably did

---

[87] Odo, *Gerald*, 11, 14, col. 678B.
[88] R. McKitterick, *The Carolingians and the Written Word* (Cambridge, 1989).
[89] J. L. Nelson, 'Literacy in Carolingian Government', in McKitterick, ed., *The Uses of Literacy in Early Mediaeval Europe* (Cambridge, 1990), pp. 258–96.
[90] W. Hartmann, 'Rechtskenntnis und Rechtsverständnis bei den Laien des früheren Mittelalters', in Hubert Mordek, ed., *Aus Archiven und Bibliotheken: Festschrift für Raymund Kottje zum 65. Geburtstag*, Freiburger Beiträge zur mittelalterlichen Geschichte 3 (Freiburg, 1992), pp. 1–20; but see Wormald, *Making*, pp. 91–2, n. 316, who points out that Hartmann's evidence is limited in quantity and in geographical distribution.
[91] P. Riché, 'Les bibliothèques de trois aristocrates carolingiens', *Le Moyen Age* 69 (1963), pp. 87–104.
[92] Nelson, 'Literacy', p. 283.
[93] *Precum libelli quattuor aevi karolini*, ed. A. Wilmart (Rome, 1940). Alcuin's was in fact a widely disseminated text: P. Szarmach, 'The Latin Tradition of Alcuin's *Liber de Virtutibus et Vitiis*, cap. xxvii–xxxv, with Special Reference to Vercelli Homily xx', *Medievalia* 12 (1989), pp. 13–41.

too. Vauchez thinks these permitted laymen to imitate to some extent the spiritual routines of the clergy. Dhuoda tells her son how to divide up the psalms for recitation.[94] Not all laymen had prayerbooks, but many probably had psalters; both Eberhard and Eccard did.[95] Odo says that Gerald of Aurillac recited the psalter daily.[96] Let us look at one of the prayers from Wilmart's collection:

> Prayer on the Holy Trinity: You are my help, Holy Trinity. Hear me, O hear me, my Lord. For you are my God, living and true. You are my holy father. You are my pious Lord. You are my great king. You are my just judge. You are my one master. You are my fitting support. You are my most powerful healer. You are my loveliest delight. You are my living and true bread. You are a priest forever. You lead me away from this world. You are my true light. You are my holy sweetness. You are my shining wisdom. You are my pure simplicity. You are my Catholic unity. You are my peaceful harmony. You are my entire protection. You are my good portion. You are my eternal salvation. You are my great mercy. You are my sturdiest wisdom, O Saviour of the world, you who live and reign for ever and ever, amen.[97]

I suspect that this text brings us close to the level of religious culture of most Carolingian nobles. The ethical treatises are not this simple, but neither are they very complex. In fact, I am struck by a quality that marks all of them, except perhaps Hincmar's, which was addressed to Charles the Bald. The portions that actually carry the discussion are quite simple in terms of syntax, vocabulary and content. What is more, the authors' central points almost always come right at the start of each section or chapter. The texts get a bit more difficult when they cite lengthy patristic passages. In most cases, though, a reader in the ninth century (or the twenty-first) can skip over these reference sections – one might almost call them notes or appendices – and not miss anything really important. Ethical treatises, psalters and prayerbooks share much with lawbooks, capitularies and charters. They are direct, unadorned and formulaic. They could be read and understood reasonably well without great native intelligence or intensive education. For persons in the

---

[94] *Liber Manualis* XI, 1, pp. 360–8.   [95] Riché, 'Bibliothèques', pp. 97, 101–2.
[96] Odo, *Gerald*, 1, 11, col. 650B–C.
[97] Wilmart, *Libelli precum*, p. 13: 'Oratio de sancta Trinitate: Auxiliatrix es tu mihi trinitas sancta. Exaudi me, exaudi me deus meus. Tu es deus meus vivus et verus. Tu es pater meus sanctus. Tu es dominus meus pius. Tu es rex meus magnus. Tu es iudex meus iustus. Tu es magister meus unus. Tu es adiutor meus oportunus. Tu es medicus meus potentissimus. Tu es dilectus meus pulcherrimus. Tu es panis meus vivus. Tu es sacerdos in aeternum. Tu es dux meus a patria. Tu es lux mea vera. Tu es dulcedo mea sancta. Tu es sapientia mea clara. Tu es simplicitas mea pura. Tu es unitas mea catholica. Tu es concordantia mea pacifica. Tu es custodia mea tota. Tu es portio mea bona. Tu es salus mea sempiterna. Tu es misericordia mea magna. Tu es sapientia mea robustissima salvator mundi qui sine fine vivis et regnis in saecula saeculorum amen.'

lands where Romance was evolving, moreover, it is possible that relatively simple Latin texts were not far from the vernacular of the elite.[98] The eastern lands, where Old High German was emerging, may have presented linguistic difficulties more serious than those encountered in Romance lands. Before arguing that ideas circulated more slowly in incipient Germany, however, it would be necessary to take more accurate stock of the large and sophisticated corpus of materials in Old High German.[99]

To speak of literacy, therefore, is not to make dramatic claims for the Carolingian elite. In so far as my remarks focus on the governing class I am not claiming literacy for a large group of people across the whole of Carolingian history. I am referring to dukes and counts, their principal subordinates, and, probably, the members of their families: a few thousand people at any given time. And, finally, this discussion does not depend solely or even primarily on literacy. The elite could either read or hear accounts of the ethos that was appropriate to their station. But they also discussed that ethos in councils, synods and courts. The critical point is that this information was widely disseminated by various means over more than a century.[100]

Let us now ask whether secular sanctity might have been attractive to the nobility. First of all, the major ethical treatises say that the men to whom they were addressed asked for them so that they might be able to save their souls. Dhuoda was deeply concerned about the soul of her son William. We would be ill advised to discount the significance of salvation

---

[98] McKitterick, *Carolingians*, pp. 7–22. There has been a good deal of recent work on transfers between oral and written cultures in the early Middle Ages and between Latin and the vernaculars. McKitterick reflects on this scholarship in 'The Written Word and Oral Communication: Rome's legacy to the Franks', in R. North and T. Hofstra, eds., *Latin Culture and Medieval Germanic Europe*, Germania Latina 1 (Groningen, 1992), pp. 89–112. Her chief inspiration is R. Wright, *Late Latin and Early Romance in Spain and Carolingian France* (Liverpool, 1982).

[99] An excellent introduction to the Germanic vernacular and its richness is C. Edwards, 'German Vernacular Literature: A Survey', in McKitterick, ed., *Carolingian Culture*, pp. 141–70; for more detail see Haubrichs, *Die Anfänge*, pp. 313–89.

[100] In developing my argument this way I disagree with A. Guerreau-Jalabert, 'La renaissance carolingienne: Modèles culturels, usages linguistiques et structures sociales', *Bibliothèque de l'École des Chartes* 139 (1981), pp. 5–35. Her central point is that an exclusively Latin and ecclesiastical culture was cultivated on the Continent thanks to the work of Anglo-Saxon scholars. I take the 'cultural models' and the 'social structures' in a broader sense than she does. Moreover, I think there is room to question the exclusively Latin element – the 'linguistic usages' – in light of Edwards, 'German Vernacular Literature'. Continental scholars are beginning to assess the degree to which ideas were transferable between Latin and vernaculars; for a start see Banniard, 'Rhabanus Maurus and the vernacular Languages', in Roger Wright, ed., *Latin and the Romance Languages in the Early Middle Ages* (London, 1991), pp. 164–74 and M. Richter, *The Formation of the Medieval West: Studies in the Oral Culture of the Barbarians* (Dublin, 1994), a book that sparks agreement and argument by quick turns.

as a motivation for the articulation and the adoption of a particular way of life. Or, to put it a little differently, the fear of hell can be a potent pedagogical device.[101] Second, this ethos was rigorously elitist. It was addressed to men in positions of leadership and it was expressed in terms that confirmed that leadership as divinely ordained and fundamentally good. I know of no other body of evidence from the Carolingian period that so powerfully confirms the status of a particular group of people. Given that Carolingian society was fluid and changing, nobles will have found most welcome this divinely and publicly sanctioned approval of their status and rank. Not only did this ethos confirm the status and rank of nobles, it also dignified that rank in solemn ways. Nobles were given a share in the royal ministry and they were said to hold offices that were divinely assigned and important for the salvation of others in their society. In other words, this ethos dignified nobles as individuals and also dignified their roles in society. The ethos also stressed the importance of holding these roles or offices. To men who wanted offices, *honores*, as well as the power and wealth that went with them, it must have been most agreeable to be told that seeking office was actually a duty and that holding office was pleasing to God. This point about the dignification of roles can be extended. I have emphasised that the ethos was secular as well as public. Although many clerics were noble, and although high ecclesiastical office was seen as a way to gain or to enhance noble status, none of our sources tells a noblemen to enter the clerical life as a way to save their souls or as a way to fulfil their *ministerium*. Still, an important dimension of the Carolingian noble ethos was religious. Secular sanctity was an instrument of broader social sanctification.

Carolingian spirituality was marked by certain characteristics. Conformity is one of these, and our treatises urge common standards of behaviour. Another characteristic was the movement to the private and away from the ecclesial spirituality that was the hallmark of the patristic age. In practice this meant that religion was more and more a matter of individual acts rather than of community celebrations or of intellectual assent to theological doctrines. As the Carolingian period unfolded, more and more of the visible acts of which Christianity was comprised were restricted to the clergy. The liturgy became a more priestly enterprise as the priest stood with his back to the people and offered prayers on their behalf, and as choirs alone possessed the competence to sing the complex melodies that accompanied

---

[101] As Mähl points out, *Quadriga Virtutum*, p. 167.

the celebration.[102] Even as formal religion became more remote from people of all stations, our treatises found new roles for aristocrats to play. For example, they were constantly urged to frequent the sacraments for in this way they could share in the celebration that was in other respects excluding them. The virtual sacramentalising of matrimony in Book II of Jonas's *De institutione laicali* may be seen as a concession to aristocratic sensitivity. Janet Nelson stresses that the late ninth-century *Oratio super militantes* is the 'earliest known piece of the liturgy of knighthood' and that, from at least the time of Charles the Bald, soldiers were considered to be '*ministri Dei*'. Karl Leyser comments that bearing arms was a dignity that was increasingly seen as incompatible with sinful behaviour.[103] This may explain, at least in part, why Gerald was only willing to fight God's enemies.[104] It is interesting to think of Walter, the hero of *Waltharius*, praying over the corpses of the men he has killed.[105] If religion was becoming more private, and if in the private realm crucial duties were being largely reserved for a functionally distinct *ordo*, the clergy, then it cannot be mere coincidence that the public realm was increasingly reserved for the nobility and in that realm they were allocated visible, important, quasi-religious roles.

Here is the fate of the 'noble sanctity' identified by Karl Bosl and Friedrich Prinz in the Merovingian period.[106] As Bosl once noted, some Merovingian saints' lives draw a virtual equivalence between nobility and sanctity. Yet as Frantisek Graus replied, this ideal of noble sanctity might have been good in the long run for certain families, but it required that its saints actually withdraw from the world.[107] Joseph-Claude Poulin observes

---

[102] For some perceptive remarks on these issues see Vauchez, *Spiritualité*, pp. 5–32; M. McLauglin, *Consorting with Saints: Prayer for the Dead in Early Medieval France* (Ithaca, NY, 1994), pp. 29–35, 103–6, 212–34; F. S. Paxton, *Christianizing Death: The Creation of a Ritual Process in Early Medieval Europe* (Ithaca, NY, 1990), pp. 92–200.

[103] Nelson, 'Ninth-Century Knighthood', pp. 259, 262–3; Leyser, 'Canon Law and the Beginnings of Knighthood', p. 70.

[104] Odo, *Gerald*, I, 33, 36, 37, 38, 40, cols. 661C–662A, 664A–C, 664D–665A, 665A–C, 666B–667A; F. Lotter, 'Das Idealbild adliger Laienfrömmigkeit in den Anfängen Clunys: Odos *Vita* des Grafen Gerald von Aurillac', in W. Lourdaux and D. Verhelst, eds., *Benedictine Culture, 750–1050*, Medievalia Louvanensia II (Leuven, 1983), pp. 89–90, 94–5; Airlie, 'The Anxiety of Sanctity: St Gerald of Aurillac and his Maker', *JEH* 43 (1992), pp. 372–95, at 375–6, 384–95.

[105] *Waltharius*, ed. Kratz, ll. 116–67.

[106] Bosl, 'Der "Adelsheilige": Idealtypus und Wirklichkeit, Gesellschaft und Kultur im merowingischen Bayern des 7. und 8. Jahrhunderts', in C. Bauer *et al.*, eds., *Speculum Historiale: Geschichte im Spiegel von Geschichtsforschung und Geschichtsdeutung. Festschrift für Johannes Spörl* (Munich, 1965), pp. 167–87; F. Prinz, 'Heiligenkult und Adelsherrschaft im Spiegel merowingischer Hagiographie', *HZ* 204 (1967), pp. 529–44.

[107] F. Graus, 'Sozialgeschichtliche Aspekte der Hagiographie der Merowinger- und Karolingerzeit: Die Viten der Heiligen des südalemannischen Raumes und die sogennanten Adelsheilige', in A. Borst ed.,

that in the middle of the eighth century there was simply no ideal of lay sanctity. Down to the time when Odo wrote about Gerald, a lay ethos of sanctity was created in treatises and sermons, but not in saints' lives. Then Odo did something quite new in holding up Gerald, a layman, as an example to other laymen.[108] Saints' lives could always evoke admiration for their subjects, encourage people to seek the saint's intercession, display the action of God in the world, promote cult-centres, show off the literary skills of the hagiographer, contribute to contemporary polemics, or promote imitation of the saint.[109] But in so far as the saints whose lives were written were members of the clergy, their *vitae* had only limited value as models for laymen. Saints were different from everyone else, and it was precisely their differences that were to be emulated. Typically, key aspects of that difference involved retreat from the world and the cultivation of a life that made one a friend of God rather than a friend of man. In the Carolingian period, noble behaviour, ennobling behaviour, in this world came to be equated with sanctity of a new kind. The new Carolingian secular sanctity was no less exemplary, but it was wholly a matter of life lived in the hurly-burly realm of daily realities. This kind of sanctity had deep repercussions in the age of the Peace of God and in the Crusades, but finally, could not find a permanent place between clerical ideas of sanctity and the aristocratic values of later times. Stuart Airlie astutely observes that Gerald was 'something of a misfit'.[110]

Pierre Riché says that the Carolingian age did not see the creation of many new saints, except in missionary regions on the frontiers.[111] Considered in

---

Mönchtum, Episkopat und Adel zur Gründungszeit des Klosters Reichenau, Vorträge und Forschungen 20 (Sigmaringen, 1974), pp. 131–76, at 160.

[108] J.-C. Poulin, *L'idéal de sainteté dans l'Aquitaine carolingienne d'après les sources hagiographiques (750–950)*, Travaux du laboratoire d'histoire religieuse de l'Université de Laval 1 (Québec, 1975), pp. 33–7, 48–9, 81–2, 140. See also Airlie, 'Anxiety', p. 378: 'including sanctity in secularity was a new and difficult task'; Lotter, 'Laienfrömmigkeit', pp. 80–2. M. Heinzelmann, 'Sanctitas und "Tugendadel": Zu Konzeptionen von Heiligkeit im 5. and 10. Jahrhundert', *Francia* 5 (1977), pp. 741–52, agrees with Poulin's basic thesis but asserts that the ideal of exemplary lay sanctity was not new because it had appeared in certain late antique writings. That does not change the validity of Poulin's point that on the eve of the Carolingian era no such ideal was in evidence. For another extended reaction to Poulin's work see W. Pohlkamp, 'Hagiographische Texte als Zeugnisse einer "histoire de la sainteté": Bericht über ein Buch zum Heiligkeitsideal im karolingischen Aquitaine', *FMS* 11 (1977), pp. 229–40. J. M. H. Smith goes to the heart of the issues when she notes that the Carolingians preferred dead saints whose charisma could be managed: 'The Problem of Female Sanctity in Carolingian Europe c. 780–920', *P&P* 146 (1995), pp. 3–4.

[109] Poulin, *Sainteté*, pp. 119–25; Smith, 'Problem of Female Sanctity', p. 7.

[110] Airlie, 'Anxiety', p. 393.

[111] P. Riché, 'Les Carolingiens en quête de sainteté', in *Les fonctions des saints dans le monde occidental (IIIe–XIIIe siècle)*, Collection de l'École française de Rome 149 (Rome, 1991), pp. 217–24.

relation to the secular sanctity that has been my theme, Carolingian saints' lives are revealing. Benedict of Aniane, for instance, 'got over' his early attraction for asceticism and then worked as a public man to reform monastic institutions. Willehad of Bremen, an Anglo-Saxon who was outside the Bonifatian circle, is described by his anonymous biographer writing around 840 not as a charismatic wonder-worker, but as a work-a-day administrator. Rimbert constructed his life of Anskar almost like a set of annals, or a chronicle.[112] That is, a dense and detailed account of Anskar's actual deeds in this world is what commanded respect and attention. Secular holiness involved what you did in this world, not your ability to manipulate the potency of the other world. Friedrich Lotter says that 'holiness was based on a way of life',[113] and Julia Smith insists that 'no charismatic ascetics, healers, prophets or visionaries made their mark' on the Carolingian Church. Commenting on some contemporary Byzantine saints, Marie-France Auzépy says, 'It is not the adjective that counts in these texts, but the verb. It is not the state of sanctity that is valorized, but action.' That could be said of Carolingian lives too. Look where one might, the charismatic, miraculous dimension is almost absent from Carolingian history both sacred and secular. In an ironic way, the lay saintly ideal that Poulin and others find missing from Carolingian hagiography before Odo's *Gerald* is present precisely in its absence.

Two qualifications before ending. One: the Carolingian noble ethos was exclusively male. This may have owed something to the fact that males, celibate clerics and public officials, formulated it. It may have been crucial that the ethos was designed for powerful, public men and Carolingian women, even queens, could rarely operate in the public realm. Whether there was an ethos for Carolingian noble women remains to be seen.[114] Two, the ideal sketched here was prescriptive, not descriptive. No matter how saintly a Gerald of Aurillac or Walter might appear, the sources are teeming with men who met few of the most basic dictates of the ideal of secular sanctity. It is paradoxical that Carolingian nobles contributed significantly to formulating an ideal to which many paid only lip service.

---

[112] Ardo, *Vita Benedicti abbatis Anianensis et Indensis*, ed. G. Waitz, *MGH SS* xv (Hanover, 1887), pp. 200–20; *De sancto Willehado primo Bremensis episcopo et inferioris Saxoniae apostolo*, A. Poncelet, ed., *Acta Sanctorum*, Nov. III (Brussels, 1910), pp. 842–6; Rimbert, *Vita Anskarii*, ed. G. Waitz, *MGH SRG* 55 (Hanover, 1884).

[113] Lotter, 'Laienfrömmigkeit', p. 82; Smith, 'Problem of Female Sanctity', p. 4; M.-F. Auzépy, 'L'analyse littéraire et l'historien: l'exemple des vie des saints iconoclastes', *Byzantinoslavica* 53 (1992), pp. 57–67, at 58.

[114] A start has been made by V. I. Garver, 'Carolingian Aristocratic Women and the Transmission of Culture' (Ph.D. dissertation, University of Virginia, 2003); see also below, pp. 121–38.

The student of Carolingian history often confronts lofty aspirations that yielded modest results.

In concluding, we may ask what was the point of this ethos? I think it had three basic objectives. First, it was intended as a stage in the Christianisation of the warrior aristocracy of Carolingian Francia. Numerous scholars – I mention only Jean Chélini, Emmet McLaughlin and John Van Engen – have argued that the Carolingian reform programme did little to alter the basic religious beliefs of the people living in the Carolingian world.[115] That is undoubtedly true, but it is most useful as an observation when it is coupled with an appreciation of the persistent attempt that the Carolingians made to alter the *behaviour* of their contemporaries.[116]

The first stage in Carolingian Christianisation was inclusion: Saxons, Slavs and others were forced to accept baptism and, by that act alone, to become members of the *populus christianus*.[117] The second stage was an attempt to reach the already baptised. In part, this was to be achieved by post-baptismal instruction by godparents and parents.[118] The outcome of such instruction was supposed to be the ability to recite the *Pater Noster* and the Creed. From the elite, however, more was expected. Their knowledge, in terms of theology and the mysteries of the faith, was not very high. Look again at the prayer text quoted above. It represents a set of simple, but rather elegant, reflections on Christian basics. More important were the ethical treatises we have been considering, and all the sources that are in some way related to them. The purpose of these materials was not to teach people the essentials of theology. Instead, these texts aimed to change the behaviour of Christians. In a hierarchical society with limited means of communication, the public behaviour of the elite could be a powerful example for others. It is surely no coincidence that aristocrats were so regularly urged to set a good example or that Paulinus reminded Eric that Christ himself had taught by word and by example.[119]

---

[115] Chélini, *Aube du moyen âge*, passim; McLaughlin, as in n. 80 above; J. Van Engen, 'Faith as a Concept of Order in Medieval Christendom', in T. Kselman, ed., *Belief in History: Innovative Approaches to European and American Religion* (Notre Dame, IN: 1991), pp. 19–67. See also A. Mirgeler (trans. E. Quinn), *Mutations of Western Christianity* (Notre Dame, IN, 1968), pp. 44–65; A. H. Bredero (trans. R. Bruinsma), *Christendom and Christianity in the Middle Ages* (Grand Rapids, MI, 1994), pp. 10–18.

[116] C. S. Jaeger, *The Envy of Angels: Cathedral Schools and Social Ideas in Medieval Europe, 950–1200* (Philadelphia, PA: 1994), pp. 23–5 stresses that the purpose of the Carolingian educational programme was both the inculcation of letters and the enhancement of morals.

[117] P. Cramer, *Baptism and Change in the Early Middle Ages, c. 200–1150* (Cambridge, 1993), pp. 185–8.

[118] *Capitulare generale* (813) c. 29, eds. Hubert Mordek and Gerhard Schmitz in 'Neue Kapitularien und Kapitulariensammlungen', *DA* 43 (1987), pp. 361–489 at 421.

[119] Paulinus, *Liber*, col. 261A–B.

The second point of this ethos, then, was to translate into practical terms the central message of the Carolingian reform programme that had begun taking shape in the 780s. Too often that programme has been analysed by ecclesiastical historians, who are mainly interested in church structures, or by intellectual historians, who discuss the 'Carolingian Renaissance' in terms too narrowly focused on classical texts and Latinity. I would not dispute that these are important topics or that they figured prominently in Carolingian efforts. But I have tried to identify another dimension of, another goal of, the reform programme.

Third, Charlemagne and Louis the Pious attempted to draw the City of God down to earth, and to make the nobility sharers in the burdens of citizenship in that city. A Christian ideal of public service, of ministry, was both a vision and a plan of action. It was meant to provide a common foundation of belief, but especially of conduct, for a nobility that was fluid, mobile, diverse in origin and uncertain of its status.[120]

[120] I would like to thank Patrick Wormald for a careful reading of this chapter and Owen Phelan for help with editing and references.

CHAPTER 3

Einhardus Peccator

David Ganz

In any discussion of the outlook of early medieval lay intellectuals the life and the writings of Einhard can supply crucial evidence.[1] But to label Einhard a layman is over-simple. For his younger contemporary, the biographer of Louis the Pious whom we can only call the Astronomer, Einhard was 'the most prudent man of his time, inspired by holy devotion'.[2] And every Christian layman should have been inspired by such devotion. But for the Carolingian author of the *Lives of the Abbots of Fontanelle* he was 'Abbot Einhard, the most learned of men'.[3] As lay-abbot of St Bavo and St Peter at Ghent, St Servatius at Maastricht, of Fontanelle and of his own foundations at Michelstadt and Seligenstadt, Einhard was apparently not a cleric; even though he had not risen in ecclesiastical orders, he had been granted the estate at Michelstadt on which he built a church soon after the accession of Louis the Pious.[4] In his verses for Seligenstadt, Hrabanus Maurus, abbot of Fulda and archbishop of Mainz, clearly distinguished between the status of 'that excellent man Einhard' and his successor as abbot of Seligenstadt 'Ratleig the priest'.[5] As we shall see, Einhard was an abbot but not a cleric: he blurs those categories which we use to distinguish identities. Not only did he fight, he could also pray.

Einhard is one of the few Carolingian authors who names himself in a wide range of different texts. While it is easy to find instances in which contemporaries characterise one another, personal statements such as those of Einhard or Dhuoda are much less common. Are they more revealing, or

---

[1] They are now conveniently translated in *Charlemagne's Courtier: the Complete Einhard*, ed. and trans. P. E. Dutton (Peterborough, ON, 1998).
[2] Astronomer, *Vita Hludowici* c. 41, p. 442.
[3] *Gesta sanctorum patrum Fontallenensium coenobii*, ed. F. Lohier and J. L. Laporte (Rouen, 1936), p. 94.
[4] On Einhard's career, Dutton's introduction to *Charlemagne's Courtier* gives references to all previous discussions.
[5] Hrabanus, Carmen 83, ed. E. Dümmler, *MGH Poet.* II (Berlin, 1884), p. 237, translated by Dutton, *Charlemagne's Courtier*, p. 10.

37

do they merely satisfy our own search for the emerging individual? Like most important lay figures Einhard attested charters. He witnessed as Abbot Einhard,[6] and even as 'venerable abbot in Christ', a standard epithet for an abbot witness, but not what we might expect from a lay abbot. The frequency of standard formulae in witness lists is but one instance of the nature of early medieval Latinity: words and phrases are borrowed so often that we may doubt how strictly they were being used.[7] Modern readers expect originality and a developed sense of personal identity – most Carolingians thought of themselves as members of groups, unhappy with notions of the individual or the private.[8]

In addition to the charters we have a collection of some of Einhard's letters, assembled at the monastery of St Bavo at Ghent some thirty years after his death, probably to provide a model for the monks to write letters. Here again we see Einhard through the formulae of his chancery. (Some letters may have been written by his notary, the priest Ratleig, others seem to have been written by Einhard on behalf of Louis the Pious.) The letters open with a standard greeting formula such as 'Einhard wishes salvation in the Lord to the holy and justly venerable lord Bishop N.' or 'Einhard in the name of Christ to his deputy N.' (The letter N. is used by the scribe of the collection in place of the name which Einhard had used in his original letter, though in some of the letters the name of a recipient is preserved, or can be deduced.) This letter collection is a remarkable insight into the concerns of a lay magnate, dealing with vassals, runaway serfs and food supplies.[9]

But in letters written to thirteen abbots and bishops Einhard used a very different epithet. He called himself *Peccator* or Sinner. He used the same term at the start of his account of the translation of the relics of Marcellinus and Peter from Rome to Michelstadt and Seligenstadt. 'To the true worshippers and genuine lovers of the true God, of our Lord Jesus Christ

---

[6] Maastricht manumission, 7 March ?821, *Formulae imperiales* no. 35, ed. W. Schmitz, *MGH Form.*, ed. K. Zeumer (Hanover, 1886), p. 313; Mont Blandin charters of 21 January 830 and 7 September 839, ed. M. Gysseling and A. C. F. Koch (Brussels, 1950), pp. 139, 141; 'Einhardus Peccator' in the charter granting the estate of Michelstadt to Lorsch, 12 September 819, *Chronicon Laureshamense*, ed. G.H. Pertz, *MGH SS* XXI (Hanover, 1869), p. 360; 'Einhardus Peccator' in the remarkable letter to Louis the Pious, ed. K. Hampe, *MGH Epp.* V (Berlin, 1899), letter 10, p. 113: 'they deigned to stay with me, a sinner', and in letter 53 to the monks of Seligenstadt, *ibid.*, p. 136 (dated 834–40).

[7] Matthew Innes, *State and Society in the Early Middle Ages: The Middle Rhine Valley 400–1000* (Cambridge, 2000), p. 15, has written of 'the mind-numbingly formulaic tradition of the documents'.

[8] Recent discussion of the public/private debate is best summarised by J. L. Nelson, 'The Problematic in the Private', *Social History* 15 (1990), pp. 355–65.

[9] For a good account in English, see Innes, *State and Society*, esp. pp. 80–147. I am preparing a new study of the manuscript.

and of his saints, Einhard, a sinner.' And on the arch-reliquary, which he gave to St Servatius at Maastricht, he set up a monumental inscription: 'Einhard, a sinner, strove to set up and dedicate to God this arch to support the cross of eternal victory.' This consistent usage is hard to parallel: we do not see Carolingian writers signposting their own sins. No one is called a sinner in the lists of names of those joined in prayer in Carolingian confraternity books. What did it mean, in the first half of the ninth century, to call yourself a sinner?

Of course we cannot answer this question with any certainty. What Einhard may have meant may not have been what those who received his letters understood. The scribe of the only surviving manuscript of those letters abbreviated *Einhardus Peccator* to E. P. It was a formula, an expression of humility used when asking a favour or addressing a spiritual superior. But Einhard used it in the *Translatio* and on the arch, neither settings where such formulae were standard. The Carolingian reader encountered the name of Einhard, on the page or on the shrine, with a clear label emphasizing Einhard's fallen condition.

Einhard might have called himself a sinner because it was a conventional formula, because he felt himself guilty of specific or of general sins, because all men are born in sin or even because as he says in the *Translatio* he wanted, like other Christian writers, 'to inspire the spirits of all people to emend their evil ways and to sing the praises of God's omnipotence'. The arch was to support a relic of the Cross, the emblem of Christ's redemption of human sin.[10] Each of the texts which Einhard composed was a moment of self-definition, in a world in which the terminology of identity depended on the vocabulary of Bible and liturgy, a world defined by clerics as the temporal sphere in which men stray away from God. What is surprising is that Einhard so often echoed the same definition.

Isidore, in his *Etymologiae* x, 228, set out the etymology of *Peccator*. 'Peccator a pelice, id est meretrice vocatus, quasi pelicator; quod nomen apud antiquos tantum flagitiosum significabat, postea transiit hoc vocabulum in appellationem omnium iniquorum.'[11] It had been a legal term, and later became a Christian one, the bond of all the unrighteous. It is used very frequently in the Psalms, where it sometimes becomes an individual

---

[10] For full discussion, see V. Elbern, 'Einhard und die karolingische Goldschmiedekunst', in H. Schefers, ed., *Einhard: Studien zu Leben und Werk* (Darmstadt, 1997), pp. 155–78, and K. Hauck, ed., *Das Einhardskreuz* (Göttingen, 1974).

[11] 'Sinner comes from skin, that is, from a prostitute, like *pelicator* (concubine). The ancients used this name for any kind of criminal and the word later was used to describe all sorts of wicked men.'

statement of sin rather than a condemnation of the unrighteous.[12] The standard Carolingian prayer ascribed to Bede focused on sin and redemption: 'Liberator of the souls of the world, Redeemer Jesus Christ, Eternal God, immortal king, I a sinner beg for your great clemency.'[13] At death, prayers were said asking for God's forgiveness even for those unable to speak so as to do penance.[14] A series of votive masses for those who confessed their sins includes the prayer, 'Omnipotent and merciful God who would rather correct each penitent soul confessing than lose it, look with favour on this your servant N. and by these sacraments of which we have partaken turn from him the anger of your wrath and forgive him all his sins.'[15] 'Omnipotent Lord and Father who art truly holy and protector of all the saints, we offer you pious Lord with devout minds sacrifices of praise, and in commemoration of the faithful saints we humbly pray you for your servant, that you grant him forgiveness for all his sins, and keep him lest he return to a will to sin.'[16] 'Free us Lord from all our sins we beg, that having received the pardon of sinners we may serve you with free minds.' Prayers to the Cross asked for freedom from sin. Christ's persecution and crucifixion were the holy punishments which enabled him to free man from the punishments for sin.

After the Bible and the liturgy the most celebrated literary usage of *'peccator'* is by Patrick in his *Confessio*, which begins 'Ego Patricius peccator, rusticorum et minimus.'[17] This echoes the words of Peter to Christ in Luke's Gospel at the miraculous draught of fishes, 'Depart from me for I am a sinful man O Lord', and the words of the publican in the parable, 'God be merciful to me a sinner' (Luke 18: 13). Patrick's terminology is echoed by Cummian, who calls himself *supplex peccator*. This Hiberno-Latin usage is not to be equated with the stock epithet used in letters: it is rather a measure of the writer's distance from divine grace. Carolingian usage may draw on this tradition: *peccator* was always a word astride categories, for it entailed the possibility of looking at the world through God's eyes, and seeing into men's hearts. Of early medieval authors only Rather of Verona ever used *peccator* to confess to specific sins.

---

[12] Psalms 9, 27, 36, 118, and 139.
[13] *Orationes tres, oratio prima*, PL 94, 529 and used by Smaragdus, *Collectiones in Epistolas et Evangelia*, PL 102, 493.
[14] 'Missa pro Defunctis', *Le Sacramentaire Grégorien. Supplementum Anianense*, ed. J. Deshusses (Fribourg, 1988), I, no. 1424, p. 465.
[15] *Le Sacramentaire Grégorien*, ed. Deshusses, II, no. 2721, p. 184.   [16] *Ibid.*, no. 2378, p. 136.
[17] The *Confessio* has most recently been edited by David Howlett, *Liber Epistolarum Sancti Patricii Episcopi* (Dublin, 1994) with accounts of *peccator* in Patrick at pp. 26 and 52. I am grateful to Dr Howlett for discussions of Patrick's style.

Bede on the Catholic Epistles quotes Augustine on the Epistle of John: 'No one says I am a sinner, but I am not wicked.'[18] The awareness of sin as a defining category of fallen man is explicit in the prayers for forgiveness of sin in the Gregorian Sacramentary.[19] But there it is a general category. For Einhard it has become a personal one. To evaluate how Einhard was using the term we must sketch its history.

It is first used as a characterisation of the writer in Christian letters by Paulinus of Nola, writing to Augustine and to Sulpicius Severus.[20] Paulinus seems to use it only in letters to spiritual superiors, as a way of highlighting his own lesser status. When St Germanus of Paris wrote to Queen Brunhild in 575 he began his letter, 'To the daughter of the church, Queen Brunhild, Germanus the sinner'.[21] In the extensive register of his papal letters Gregory the Great only called himself *peccator* twice, in each case in letters to the Emperor Maurice.[22] Again it defines status: sinner was not used in letters to a subordinate. But in Gaul there seems to be a more widespread use of the term by ecclesiastics. Sixth-century Merovingian bishops sometimes attested the acts of Church councils using the term *peccator*[23] and also witnessed charters using the word *peccator*.[24] The term is frequent in the important early seventh-century Merovingian episcopal letter-collection of Bishop Desiderius of Cahors, with many bishops using *peccator* in their opening salutation formula. But this epistolary practice was much less common in the Carolingian age. The only instance I have found is in the pastoral letter to the clergy of his diocese composed by Archbishop Wulfad of Bourges which opens 'Wulfad though unworthy and a sinner ... bishop'.[25]

In departing from standard Carolingian practice Einhard set himself in a world of redemption, achieved both by the prayers of the living and the intercession of the saints in heaven. Sinners needed prayers. Einhard asked

---

[18] *PL* 93, 100.
[19] *Le Sacramentaire Grégorien*, I, nos. 840–75, pp. 311–17.
[20] *Paulini Nolani Epistolae* III, IV, VI, XXIV, ed. G. de Hartel, *CSEL* XXIX, revised edn (Vienna, 1999), pp. 13, 18, 39, 201.
[21] *Sancti Germani Epistola ad Brunichild-em reginam, PL* 72, col. 77.
[22] *Gregorii Magni Epistolae*, ed. D. Norberg, *CC* 140 (Turnhout, 1982), V, 36 and VII, 70.
[23] Vaison (529), Paris (556x73), ed. J. Gaudemet and B. Basdevant, *SC* nos. 353, 354 (Paris, 1989), I, 192, II, p. 424.
[24] 'Chrodegangus acsi peccator Metensis urbis episcopus', Council of Compiègne (757), ed. A. Werminghoff, *MGH Conc.* II, i (Hanover, 1906), p. 60, and a number of other episcopal subscribers at pp. 62–3.
[25] *MGH Epp.* VI, ed. E. Dümmler (Berlin, 1925), p. 188. On Wulfad, see J. Marenbon, 'Wulfad, Charles the Bald and John Scottus Eriugena', in M. T. Gibson and J. L. Nelson, eds., *Charles the Bald: Court and Kingdom*, 1st edn (Oxford, 1981), pp. 375–83, and the references there cited.

for such prayers in a letter which we can set in a clear context of letters of confraternity. It was common practice in the early Middle Ages for religious houses to maintain records of the names of those whom they wished to remember in their prayers. The lists of names organized in the form of a *Liber memorialis*, an earthly counterpart to the celestial Book of Life, would be brought to the altar during mass, and some of the names might be read out during the celebration.[26] Boniface and Alcuin had been the first to write asking to be included in such lists and to receive special prayers from devout congregations.[27] Einhard's letter to the monks of Seligenstadt is the clearest of the *Einhardus peccator* letters in setting out the spiritual economy of prayer exchange. The text in the St Bavo manuscript is damaged, but the fragmentary text asks the monks 'to undertake to remember me carefully, as you promised, in the presence of the holy martyrs, our patrons, whom you are known to serve daily. In this way the pious Lord may allow me to find you safe through their intercession. I beg you therefore, with a father's concern, my dearest ones, to remain mindful of your promise and that you are daily commending yourselves to the Lord and his saints ... and that you are always anxiously on guard lest the ancient enemy may not be able to deceive and seduce you with any trickery ... Let this letter of mine be devoutly read out in the presence of all the brothers, and let it be obeyed.'[28]

Einhard writes from a position of power: he had founded and endowed the monastery at Seligenstadt. He wants the older monks to set a model of salvation to the younger ones, he sees worship at the altar as the means to gain the eternal kingdom. But that reward cannot be won without the intercession of the saints. Daily commendation to Christ is the only security, and Einhard's monks are asked especially to pray for him. In the exchange of letters with Lupus of Ferrières after the death of Einhard's wife Imma he reveals his own anguish at the apparent breakdown of this spiritual reciprocity. 'For what human being full of reason and sound in mind would not weep over his fate and count himself unhappy and the most pitiful of humans, when, overcome by troubles, he learns that the one he had believed would support him in prayers had turned against him and was unmoved?'[29] Einhard is here confronting the reality of

---

[26] S. D. Keynes, *The Liber Vitae of the New Minster and Hyde Abbey Winchester*, Early English Manuscripts in Facsimile XXVI (Copenhagen, 1996), pp. 49–58.
[27] Boniface, *Die Briefe des heiligen Bonifatius und Lullus*, ed. M. Tangl, *MGH Epp. sel.* I (Berlin, 1916), nos. 33, 81, 38, pp. 57, 181, 63. There are similar passages in the letters of Lull; and cf. Alcuin *Epp.* 67, 301, ed. E. Dümmler, *MGH Epp. Karolini Aevi* II (Berlin, 1895), pp. 110–11, 459–60.
[28] Einhard Ep. 53, ed. Hampe, p. 136.
[29] *Lupi Epistolae* 3, ed. P. K. Marshall (Leipzig 1984), pp. 4–6.

predestination and grace, the issue which was to divide the Carolingian Church in the mid-century. For Carolingian religious practice encouraged a belief in divine intercession, in the presence of 'invisible companions' who could 'bind their fellow men even closer to God than could the angels'.[30] Yet Carolingian religious experience might cause the hope of such intercession to grow dim. The invisible network of prayer, stretching across the Christian world, linking the living and the dead, offered the most certain hope of that release from the bondage of sin and death which Christ had promised to his elect. But the moment of release was not in this world, and the only certainty, as Einhard wrote to Emperor Louis the Pious was that 'by being penitent and calling upon the mercy of God they may work towards avoiding future danger'.[31] As the demon Wiggo told Einhard, 'There are many other, almost an endless number of, sins committed every day both by the people themselves and by their rulers.'[32] It was the shared sense of being a community of sinners deserving of divine punishment which both explained Viking invasions and exposed the fragility of any human hope. Einhard was profoundly concerned with his relations with God. In a telling quotation ascribed to the Jewish writer Philo, Einhard says: 'ask for divine assistance, since human assistance fails'.[33] 'Brevis est ista vita, et incertum est tempus mortis, quid aliut agendum est, nisi ut semper parati simus. Cogitemus quam terribiliter est incidere in manu Dei.'[34] We must hope for God's compassion, that our daily sins be redeemed by confession and penance.[35] 'Humanum est peccare, angelicum est emendare, diabolica est perseverare in peccato.' Priests were to preach with all diligence for what crimes people would be sent with the devil into eternal punishment.[36] Theodulf reminded the sinner that every day we must confess our sins in our prayers to God, once, twice or as often as we can. The confession of sins to God helps us to rid ourselves of the stain of sin, for as often as we remember our sins, so

---

[30] The vocabulary is that of Peter Brown, *The Cult of the Saints* (Chicago, IL, 1981), p. 61.

[31] Einhard Ep. 40, ed. Hampe, pp. 129–30.

[32] *Translatio* III, c. 14, ed. G. Waitz, MGH SS XV(i) (Hanover, 1887), p. 253, trans. Dutton, *Charlemagne's Courtier*, p. 104.

[33] Einhard Ep. 31, ed. Hampe, p. 125.

[34] *Missi cuiusdam admonitio*, MGH *Capit.* I, ed. A. Boretius (Hanover, 1883), no. 121, pp. 238–40, at 240. The source of this admonition was very probably Charlemagne himself. See next note.

[35] MGH *Capit.* I, no. 121, p. 240. The text is discussed by T. M. Buck, *Admonitio und Praedicatio: Zur religiös-pastoralen Dimension von Kapitularien und kapitulariennahen Texten (507–814)*, Freiburger Beiträge zur mittelalterlichen Geschichte 9 (Frankfurt, 1997), pp. 157–238, 376–94, with a new edition of the *Admonitio* at 397–401.

[36] *Admonitio generalis*, MGH *Capit.* I, no. 22, c. 82, p. 61.

often does the Lord forget them, but as often as we forget them, the Lord remembers them.[37]

The vision of a certain pious priest of the land of the English, revealed to him after Christmas while he was transported out of his body was sent to Louis the Pious by King Æthelwulf and the text is preserved in the *Annals of St. Bertin* for 839. It includes the prophecy that for three days and nights a very dense fog will spread over their land and then all of a sudden pagan men will lay waste with fire and sword most of the people and land of the Christians. But instead, if they are willing to do true penance immediately and carefully atone for their sins according to the Lord's command with fasting, prayer and alms-giving, then they may still escape those punishments and disasters through the intercession of the saints.[38]

In the account of the *Translation of the Relics of Marcellinus and Peter*, Einhard recounted miracles which showed how the saints might intervene to help the living. 'I gave praise and thanks for the mercy of the almighty God, because he had deigned to help and console us in our time of need because of the merits of his saints.'[39] The process of intercession was carefully regulated. In a letter to Lupus, written in 836, dealing with the worship of the Cross, Einhard notes: 'When we entreat God, seeking to gain something other than that which is laid out in the Lord's Prayer, then the attainment of that request remains in doubt because we are praying not for what He commanded but for what pleases us.'[40]

The tension between worldly values and sanctity was well expressed in the preface to the Life of the lay saint Gerald of Aurillac: 'Some men, trying to excuse their own sins, cry him up, saying that Gerald was powerful and rich, lived very well and yet is a saint.'[41] The values of the lay aristocracy are seldom presented without this sort of ecclesiastical filter. Their secular culture was characterised by fighting, hunting, feasting, family and office. A remarkable document from Le Mans tells of a young noble named Rigrannus, raised in a monastery after his father's death, who

---

[37] *MGH Capitula Episcoporum*, ed. P. Brommer (Hanover, 1984), 1, *Theodulfi Capitula* 1, c. 30, pp. 127–8.
[38] *AB* s. a. 839, pp. 29–30, trans. Nelson, pp. 42–3. The role of the Vikings as the visible instrument of God's punishment is repeatedly stressed in Carolingian legislation of the second half of the ninth century, cf. S. Coupland, 'The Rod of God's Wrath or the People of God's Wrath? The Carolingians' theology of the Viking Invasions', *JEH* 42 (1991), pp. 535–54.
[39] *Translatio* III, 19, p. 255, trans. Dutton, *Charlemagne's Courtier*, p. 108.
[40] *De adoranda cruce* as translated by Dutton, *ibid.*, pp. 171–4. The text was most recently edited by K. Hauck 'Einhard beantwortet 836 Lupus von Ferrières dessen *Questio de adoranda cruce*', in *Das Einhardskreuz* (Göttingen, 1974), pp. 211–16.
[41] Odo of Cluny, *Vita sancti Geraldi*, preface, *PL* 133, col. 639.

wished to become a monk, as his father had intended. 'The Holy Church strives daily to induce not only those who scorn the world, but also, what is a far greater task, those whom worldly activity makes prosperous, to seek the lot of the elect and the beatitude of eternal life. Rigrannus' uncle wanted him to become a priest and 'other relations took it badly that the boy was lost to the world and acquired for God.' His uncle angrily addressed him:

What have you done, wretch? Why have you chosen one small loaf of bread rather than a hundred, and a little wine rather than goblets to be drained in abundance. Why do you want to be satisfied with a pig-like life of beans and vegetables? Where will be the pleasures of the meats that you have rejected, the sweetness of drinks, the enjoyment of dogs and hawks, the voluptuous touch of women? Why do you want to dishonour us? Our family had no business with poor men and beggars. The world has prospered for us; quantities of gold and silver and precious stones were ours. For us shining arms gleamed, horses preened themselves with gilded bridles and arched necks.[42]

These were the values which most wealthy laymen were assumed to have adopted. But it was not always quite so clear-cut. Rigrannus was assured that he could share in these values as a priest and canon. Einhard knew that laymen had to live in a Christian world.

To use Einhard as a source for the views of lay intellectuals in the early Middle Ages also entails an investigation of the ideology of his own account of a lay intellectual in the *Vita Karoli*. The work has long been regarded as a secular biography, adapting the language of Sulpicius Severus' *Vita Martini* to praise a figure whose acts were not a model, like those of Martin, but were explicitly characterised as 'scarcely able to be imitated'. In describing the characteristics of such figures Carolingian authors approached personality in terms of the attributes of persons. Both Alcuin, and Paschasius Radbertus, abbot of Corbie, in his *Life* of Charlemagne's cousin Adalhard, follow this scheme, though their lists of attributes are slightly different. The eloquence of rhetorical art can tackle personality, for according to that art persons have many attributes, namely:

Si figuram nobilitatis ejus a puero describere voluero, quae Graece Χαρακτηριβμὸς dicitur, ero inefficax, quia, etsi secundum rhetoricae artis facundiam ipsius persona consideretur, possitne laudis idonea comprobari. … Personae quippe iuxta prefatam artis peritiam plurima sunt attributa, ex quibus optime dignoscatur. Consideratur

---

[42] G. Constable, 'Monks and Canons in Carolingian Gaul: The Case of Rigrannus of Le Mans', in *After Rome's Fall: Narrators and Sources of Early Medieval History. Essays presented to Walter Goffart*, ed. A. C. Murray (Toronto, 1998), pp. 320–36 re-editing *PL* 129, cols. 1263–8.

enim perfecti viri qualitas, juxta oratores, nomine, patria, genere, dignitate, fortuna, corpore, institutione, moribus, victu; si rem bene administret; qua consuetudine domestica teneatur; affectione mentis, arte, conditione, habitu, vultu, incessuque, oratione, affectu ...[43]

Alcuin discusses the *attributa personarum* in Chapter 24 of his *Rhetoric*. They are *Nomen, Natura, Victus, Fortuna, Habitus, Affectio, Studia, Consilia, Facta, Casus, Orationes* (name, nature, way of life (*victus*), condition, custom, feelings, tastes, intentions, conduct, fortune, words spoken). This scheme derives from Cicero, *De inventione* I, xxiv, 34, a section on the attributes of persons.[44] Einhard used a Suetonian scheme of rubrics (*species*) to cover many of the same features. This was how secular biography was written.

Einhard's account of the debt which he owed to his friend and patron, set in the preface to the *Vita Karoli*, is an important secularisation of Christian terminology. Einhard praises Charles as his *nutritor*, his patron. Isidore had defined *nutritor* as *quasi nutu eruditor*, someone who teaches with a nod.[45] Augustine had used the term when describing Ambrose, and Bede used it of Coelfrid *nutritor* and tutor of his monks in his *History of the Abbots* of Wearmouth-Jarrow.[46] The only instance I have found before Einhard of *nutritor* used of a secular ruler is in Paul the Deacon's *Historia Langobardorum*, where King Liutprand is called *nutritor gentis*.[47] But Charlemagne was not only commemorated because of Einhard's loyalty to his patron and friend, the ruler at whose court he had been educated. Isidore affirms that the heroic dead had attained their own immortality. *Heroicum enim carmen dictum, quod eo virorum fortium res et facta narrantur. Nam heroes appellantur viri quasi aerii et caelo digni propter sapientiam et fortitudinem ... Quo nomine appellant alicuius meriti animas*

---

[43] 'If I wished to describe the figure of his nobility from boyhood, which is called characterismos in Greek, I would be incapable, for even if the person is considered according to the eloquence of the art of rhetoric it could not furnish fitting praise ... According to the skill of that art there are many attributes of a person from which he may be best discerned. According to orators, the quality of a perfect man should be considered in his name, his nation, his family, his worth, his fortune, his body, his rank, his way of life, his food, if he administered his property well, how he ran his household, his affection, his mind, his skill, his status, his dress, his face, his gait, his speech, his feelings', Paschasius, *Vita Adalhardi* c. 55, *PL* 120, col. 1536, cf. Paschasius, in Ps. 44 XLIV, iii, Prologus, *PL* 120, col. 1039. See A. Cizek, 'Der Charakterismos in der *Vita Adalhardi* des Radbert von Corbie', *Rhetorica* 7 (1989), pp. 185–204.
[44] For an essential discussion of Einhard's debt to Ciceronian forensic oratory, see M. Kempshall, 'Some Ciceronian Models for Einhard's Life of Charlemagne', *Viator* 26 (1995), pp. 11–37.
[45] Isidore, *Etymologiae* x, 189.
[46] Augustine, *Confessiones* VIII, vi, 15, ed. J. J. O'Donnell (Oxford, 1992), p. 94; Bede, *Historia Abbatum* II, 14, ed. C. Plummer, *Venerabilis Baedae Opera Historica* (Oxford, 1896), p. 393.
[47] Paul the Deacon, *Historia Langobardorum* VI, 58, ed. L. Bethmann and G. Waitz, *MGH SRL* (Hanover, 1878), p. 242.

defunctorum, quasi ἀηρωαζ, *id est viros aerios et caelo dignos propter sapientiam et fortitudinem.*[48] If Charlemagne is regarded as such a hero, then his biography has even stronger parallels with the lives of the saints. The commemoration of a layman belongs in a tradition of epics for heroes.

In investigating the picture Einhard presents of a lay subject it is necessary to assess his attitude to Charlemagne's Christianity. Einhard's hero was an explicitly Christian ruler, concerned to protect Christians throughout the world, and to worship God in a fitting way. His victory over the Saxons depended on his condition that the Saxons abandon the cult of demons and their native rites to take up the sacraments of Christian faith and worship. Throughout the biography Christian values are implicit: the pope made Pippin king and Charles and Carlomann succeed him by God's will, Charles is granted symbolic authority over the Holy Places in Palestine and he restored the churches throughout his kingdoms. He had been brought up a Christian from his youth and he went to church morning and evening and for the night office. He was concerned with the splendour of the church at Aachen and with the church of St Peter's. And at the end of his life his decision to make Louis co-emperor seemed divinely inspired. Heinz Löwe suggested that Einhard's account of Charles as protector of the church and of Rome may reveal an awareness of the implications of the Donation of Constantine.[49] But while we may recognise such subtle nuances in Einhard's text, that text is not the exemplary biography of a Christian ruler that Thegan and the Astronomer provided in their lives of Charlemagne's son. It is Thegan, not Einhard, who describes the dying Charlemagne correcting the Gospels.[50] It is the Astronomer who reminds us that Charlemagne died as the most pious emperor.[51]

It is the account of Charlemagne's private life which has attracted readers to Einhard's biography. The thick neck, the bulging belly, the weak voice for so large a man, even the limp can all be found as details in the

---

[48] 'For verse is called "heroic" when the deeds and achievements of courageous men are told of therein. For men who are, as it were, "airy", and worthy of heaven, are called "heroes", because of their wisdom and courage ... People call the souls of dead men who had merit of some kind by the name of "airy", signifying worthy of heaven, because of their wisdom and courage', Isidore, *Etymologiae* I, xxxix, 9; VIII, xi, 98. These passages were discussed by R. E. Kaske, '*Sapientia et Fortitudo* as the Controlling Theme in Beowulf', *Studies in Philology* 55 (1958), pp. 423–56, and by F. Robinson, *The Tomb of Beowulf* (Oxford, 1993), pp. 3–19.
[49] H. Löwe, '"*Religio Christiana*", Rom und das Kaisertum in Einhards *Vita Karoli Magni*', in *Storia e storiografia in onore di E. D. Theseider* (Rome, 1973), pp. 1–20.
[50] Thegan, *Gesta Hludowici* c. 7, p. 186.
[51] Astronomer c. 20, p. 344, and note the frequent scriptural quotations about kingship in both the Astronomer and Thegan.

descriptions of Suetonian Caesars, but they were not the stuff of medieval biography. It is the measure of Charlemagne's greatness that these details do not damage him. And they are enhanced by Einhard's care to make his hero another intellectual; enjoying the *City of God*, educating his children in the liberal arts as well as the Frankish ones, learning grammar and astronomy and even trying to write with his tablets kept under his pillow. The 'leisure and learning' which Einhard found in Cicero and exhorted his readers not to abuse had become the hallmark of the civilised rule of his hero. Tiberius had also most diligently cultivated the liberal arts, and Einhard probably found the word *dicaculus* (talkative), which he uses to praise Charles' eloquence, in the *Scriptores Historiae Augustae*.[52] But he was reporting on the court life in which he had shared, where poets were prized and courtiers discussed comets. This revival of learning was admired by Walahfrid and Lupus: it has become Charlemagne's undisputed legacy.

Earthly society was distinguished from the world of the saints by military achievement and by marriage.[53] Stuart Airlie has characterised the ways in which the *Vita Karoli* 'features most of the items on our checklist of aristocratic qualities. Charlemagne's ancestors, their lands, wealth and office are all celebrated. Much space is devoted to the king's family life and notably, Charlemagne's union with concubines is neither glossed over nor apologised for. War too has a crucial place in Einhard's picture and for Einhard the success of Charlemagne's aggressive campaigning was sufficient justification: Charlemagne doubled the size of his kingdom. Hunting and feasting are also highlighted facets of Einhard's portrait.'[54] The lay ethos of the biography is best conveyed in Einhard's account of how Charlemagne's children were educated: 'He believed that his children, both his daughters and his sons, should be educated, first in the liberal arts which he himself had studied. Then he saw to it that when the boys had reached the right age they were trained to ride in the Frankish fashion, to fight and to hunt. But he ordered his daughters to learn how to work with wool, how to spin and weave it, so that they might not grow dull from inactivity and learn to value work and virtuous activity (*ad omnem honestatem erudiri*).'[55] The pride in Frankish values, including Frankish royal acclamation and Frankish dress, is a constant feature of the *Vita Karoli*.

---

[52] *Scriptores Historiae Augustae, Vita Hadriani* 20.8.1, ed. J. P. Callu (Paris, 1992), pp. 40–1. The word is very rare, as Gottschalk noted, and is not in Cicero or Suetonius.
[53] S. Airlie, 'The Anxiety of Sanctity: St Gerald of Aurillac and his Maker', *JEH* 43 (1992), pp. 372–95.
[54] *Ibid.*, pp. 381–2.   [55] *VK* c. 19, p. 23.

We get closest to Einhard's explanatory scheme in an aside in the account of the Saxon war: 'Charlemagne was able to endure and to bear anything, not yielding in adversity nor assenting to a false smiling fortune in prosperity.' Einhard may have found his false smiling Fortune in Boethius, but not in any Christian source. The suggestion that humans can be deceived by Fortune set a distance between human endeavour and human understanding of God's purposes. It is a part of Einhard's classical vocabulary, and may derive from Suetonius' *Life of Nero*. For Regino of Prüm, at the end of the ninth century, Fortune was the best means of explaining the vicissitudes of history.[56]

Einhard wrote a great biography of a lay intellectual, and in the preface to that biography he presents himself to his readers. And here again we can detect the voice of the layman, expressing a sense of a new kind of writing. 'But to write and account for such a life (*scribendae atque explicandae*) what was required was Ciceronian eloquence, not my feeble talent, which is poor and small (*exile et parvum*) and indeed almost non-existent. There is nothing in it that you should admire but his accomplishments, except perhaps that I, a barbarian with little training in the language of Rome, should have imagined that I could write something correct and even eloquent in Latin.'[57] The language here is also borrowed, the feeble talent comes from Jerome, who frequently used the word *ingeniolum* and who was echoed by Alcuin. Einhard's feeble talent is characterised as *exile et parvum*, a combination found in Pliny, Letters, Book II, 14, 1. It may seem an excessive protestation of modesty, but it is a measure of Einhard's desire to be judged by classical standards. He is a *homo barbarus*, which must imply a German speaker, and his term for training derives ultimately from Cicero. Einhard never names himself in the preface. He has established himself as a friend of Charlemagne, a courtier, a truthful witness, a Frank, but he effaces Einhard: the preface is not about the particularity of who he is. Instead it establishes a cultural identity, that of the untrained barbarian whose every word is redolent of the culture he is adopting. The unabashed Ciceronianism is stunning, everything is staked on the possibility of creating a fitting memorial. But the values of the *Vita Karoli* are heroic values, the only hint of a more overreaching ethos is when Einhard supplies the text of Charlemagne's will and lists the portents which foretell his death. The portents reveal to everyone, even to Charlemagne, that the end

---

[56] H. Löwe, 'Regino von Prüm und das historische Weltbild der Karolingerzeit', reprinted in his *Von Cassiodor zu Dante* (Berlin, 1973), pp. 149–79.
[57] *VK* preface, p. 2.

is near. Glory will fade, just as the letters of Charlemagne's inscription *Karolus Princeps* became so faint that they were almost invisible. In the will there is reference to Christian practice, and the remarkable suggestion that Charlemagne might abandon the world (*aut voluntariam saecularium rerum carentiam*).[58] And that retreat from the world of the court was accomplished by Einhard, it was perhaps a part of his master's legacy to him.

If we look for a statement of Einhard's literary aims, the clearest testimony is at the very beginning of the *Translatio*.

> Those who have set down in writing and recorded the lives and deeds of the just and of people living according to divine commands, seem to me to have wanted to accomplish nothing but to inspire by means of examples of this sort the spirits of all people to emend their evil ways and to sing the praises of God's omnipotence. These writers did this, not only because they lacked envy, but because they were completely full of charity, which seeks the improvement of all. Since their praiseworthy intention was so obviously to accomplish nothing other than those goals I described, I do not see why their plan should not be imitated by many other writers.[59]

By 830 moral reform and divine praise had become Einhard's goals, and in a letter written to Louis the Pious to explain the significance of the comet which had appeared in June 837 he again places them at the centre of his world-view: 'I suspect that this comet supplies us with fitting signs of our just deserts and announces an approaching disaster that we deserve. For what does it matter whether humans are forewarned of impending anger by a human, by an angel, or by a star announcing it? Only this is necessary to understand that the appearance of the star was not without meaning, but warned humans that by being penitent and calling upon the mercy of God they may work towards avoiding future danger.'[60] In a world of impending danger, a world in which the divine opinions were not being followed,[61] the consciousness of sin and the appeal to God's mercy was the last measure of the unity of fallen man.

---

[58] *Ibid. c.* 33, p. 39. [59] *Translatio*, preface, p. 239, trans. Dutton, *Charlemagne's Courtier*, p. 69.
[60] Einhard Ep. 40 (on the comet of 837), ed. Hampe, pp. 129–30, trans. Dutton, *Charlemagne's Courtier*, pp. 160–1.
[61] Einhard Ep. 11 (to Lothar), ed. Hampe, pp. 114–15, trans. Dutton, *Charlemagne's Courtier*, pp. 145–6.

CHAPTER 4

The world, the text and the Carolingian: royal, aristocratic and masculine identities in Nithard's Histories

Stuart Airlie

'I listen and the voice is of a world collapsing endlessly under a frozen sky.' This citation sums up the wintry view that Nithard came to take of the key secular institutions of his own world. The fact that it actually comes from the peculiarly twentieth-century work of Samuel Beckett (his novel, *Molloy*) does not diminish its relevance here. It is appropriate as my subject is Nithard's *Histories*, one of the bleakest prose works of the Carolingian era. The bleakness of Nithard's text may be surprising, not least because it was as a layman that he composed such a withering critique of his political society.[1] A negative view of the institutions and way of life of the secular elite in the Carolingian world is not in itself a surprising thing to encounter. A host of clerical authors from Alcuin in the eighth century to Odo of Cluny in the tenth lambasted this elite for its pride in its earthly nobility, its devotion to war, display, hunting, feasting, etc.[2] The clergy and the laity formed two separate orders (*ordines*) and members of the former were forbidden, for example, to sport the fancy clothes of the

---

[1] 'His *Histories* are the wry, gaunt and ... melancholy story of a Carolingian predicament', according to K. Leyser, 'Nithard and his Rulers', in Leyser, *Communications and Power in Medieval Europe*. 1, *The Carolingian and Ottonian Centuries*, ed. T. Reuter (London, 1994), pp. 19–25, at 19. I owe much to this article as I do to the indispensable studies of Nithard by Janet L. Nelson; see her 'Public *Histories* and Private History in the Work of Nithard', *Speculum* 60 (1985), pp. 251–93, and repr. in Nelson, *Politics and Ritual in Early Medieval Europe* (London, 1986), pp. 195–237, to which reference is made; 'Ninth-Century Knighthood: The Evidence of Nithard', in C. Harper-Bill, C. Holdsworth and J. L. Nelson, eds., *Studies in Medieval History Presented to R. Allen Brown* (Woodbridge, 1989), pp. 255–66, repr. Nelson, *The Frankish World* (London, 1996), pp. 75–87, to which reference is made; 'Nobility in the Ninth Century', in A. J. Duggan, ed., *Nobles and Nobility in Medieval Europe* (Woodbridge, 2000), pp. 43–51. I cite the edition of Nithard's *Histories* by P. Lauer, as listed in Abbreviations at p. xii of this volume, with French translation, hereafter cited simply as 'Nithard'.
[2] S. Airlie, 'The Anxiety of Sanctity: St Gerald of Aurillac and his Maker', *JEH* 43 (1992), pp. 372–95; M. Alberi, '"The Better paths of wisdom": Alcuin's Monastic "True Philosophy" and the Worldly Court', *Speculum* 76 (2001), pp. 896–910.

latter, as well as often being urged to avoid the vernacular, tainted as it was by the 'stench of dung and the sweat of the warrior'.³

Nithard, on the other hand, seems to be, as Michael Wallace-Hadrill put it, 'of firmly secular outlook', writing history 'with a certain degree of detachment'.⁴ But distinctions, and therefore identities, were not that clear. A text contemporary with Nithard, and generated in the court circle of his king, Charles the Bald, the agreement of Coulaines of 843, refers to 'our faithful men, in both the venerable clerical order and the illustrious men of the noble laity'. Nithard himself was a layman but he was also an abbot. The ruling elite formed a community.⁵ Further, Nithard wrote his *Histories* in Latin, not in the vernacular (apart from one famous section). If *fides* (faith in its religious and political sense) was a key term for Nithard, and a key value, it was a term charged with religious as well as secular meaning in Carolingian culture. Thus Hrabanus Maurus, writing in 819, described baptism in terms of escaping from Satan's service to that of Christ: 'after he has commended himself into the lordship of the other by his confession of the true faith (*vera fides*), he separates himself from the power (*servitium*) of the previous owner …'⁶ Not for nothing were the 'faithful men' of the Carolingian world called the 'faithful of God and the king (*fideles Dei et regis*)', and, as we shall see, *fides* as understood by Nithard embraced women too. Nithard reveals the perceptions of the Frankish aristocracy in the ninth century to be firmly Christian, and rooted and expressed within Christian institutions, as Janet Nelson has demonstrated.⁷ It is Nithard who tells us how the bishops were called upon to interpret the meaning of the great conflict at Fontenoy in 841, and it is Nithard who tells us that Charles the Bald and Louis the German turned 'first of all' to their bishops and priests to prepare the way for

---

³ See, for example, the Preface to the Synod of Meaux-Paris (845–6), in W. Hartmann, ed., *Die Konzilien der karolingischen Teilreiche 843–859, MGH Conc.* III (Hanover, 1984), p. 82; on clothing, see, echoing other pronouncements, the 'Canones extravagantes' 8, in *MGH Capit.* II, ed. A. Boretius and V. Krause (Hanover, 1883), no. 252, p. 248; on the low status of the vernacular, C. Edwards, 'German Vernacular Literature: A Survey', in R. McKitterick, ed., *Carolingian Culture: Emulation and Innovation* (Cambridge, 1994), pp. 140–70, at p. 141.
⁴ J. M. Wallace-Hadrill, *The Frankish Church* (Oxford, 1983), p. 238; similar stress on secularity in Leyser, 'Nithard and his Rulers', p. 25.
⁵ 'Fideles nostri, tam in venerabili ordine clericali quam et inlustres viri in nobili laici habitu', *Konzilien 843–859* 3, p. 14, with an older edition in *MGH Capit.* II, no. 254, p. 254; on lay-abbacies, Nelson, 'Public *Histories*', pp. 236–7; and M. de Jong, 'Carolingian Monasticism: The Power of Prayer', in *NCMH* II, pp. 634–6; and see below, nn. 17, 28.
⁶ Hrabanus, *De clericorum institutione* I, 27, *PL* 107, col. 311, cited and discussed in J. M. H. Smith, 'Religion and Lay Society', in *NCMH* II, pp. 654–78, at 659.
⁷ Nelson, 'Public *Histories*', pp. 228–9; Nelson, 'Ninth-Century Knighthood', pp. 83–7.

The world, the text and the Carolingian 53

excluding their brother Lothar from the division of the realm. Nithard does not include in his text Charles the Bald's fierce dressing-down of the archbishop of Ravenna, captured fighting on Lothar's side, even though he may have witnessed Charles' stagey tirade.[8] It is true that Nithard's picture of Lothar's supporter the archbishop of Mainz is not flattering as he yokes him with his own *bête noire*, Count Adalbert, but Nithard concentrates his firepower not on Otgar but on Adalbert, and indeed on members of the secular aristocracy, as we shall see. For a stinging attack on a bishop in the great period of crisis stretching from 830 to 843 we need to turn to a clerical author, Thegan the assistant bishop of Trier, whose savage attack on Archbishop Ebo of Reims is based on Ebo's unsuitability for high office because of his lowly birth, grounds that we might expect to find expressed among the secular aristocracy rather than the clerical.[9] In general, Nithard's respect for bishops recalls another contemporary secular text: Dhuoda's advice to her son to revere priests.[10]

Nithard's medieval readership, such as it was, did not see his text as being purely 'secular'. It may appear in the only early manuscript along with Flodoard's *Annales*, but the interpolations into Nithard's text designed to enhance the saintly aura of the church of Saint-Médard of Soissons do indeed reveal that Nithard's text, like other Carolingian texts, could be very 'fluid ... [and] able to be amended or excerpted as their readers saw fit', as David Ganz has put it.[11] Further, extracts from Nithard's text appear in the collection of material relating to the history of the abbey of St Riquier compiled by or for Hariulf, whose history of that

---

[8] Nithard III, 1, p. 82, IV, 1, p. 116, IV, 3, p. 126; see J. L. Nelson, 'The Lord's Anointed and the People's Choice: Carolingian Royal Ritual', in Nelson, *Frankish World*, p. 116; bishops on Lothar's side took a different view of the battle: R. Kottje, *Die Bussbücher Halitgars von Cambrai und des Hrabanus Maurus* (Berlin, 1980), pp. 6, 241–3; and see also below for other lay reactions to Fontenoy. For Charles' clash with the archbishop of Ravenna, captured at Fontenoy, Agnellus, *Liber Pontificalis Ecclesiae Ravennatis c.* 174, ed. O. Holder-Egger, *MGH SRL* (Hanover,1878), pp. 390–1, with J. L. Nelson, *Charles the Bald* (London, 1992), p. 116.

[9] Nithard II, 6, p. 58, for Otgar and Adalbert; and for depictions of Otgar as cowardly III, 4, p. 100, III, 7, p. 114; on Ebo, see Thegan, *Gesta Hludowici* cc. 44, 56, pp. 232–8, 252; and note the rather sinister Otgar at *c.* 47, p. 240.

[10] Dhuoda, *Liber Manualis* III, 11, ed. Riché, pp. 184–96, and ed. Thiébaux, pp. 117–25; see Nelson in this volume, below, pp. 106–20.

[11] D. Ganz, 'The *Epitaphium Arsenii* and Opposition to Louis the Pious', in P. Godman and R. Collins, eds., *Charlemagne's Heir: New Perspectives on the Reign of Louis the Pious* (Oxford, 1990), pp. 537–50, at 538. Nithard's text survives in only one early manuscript, Paris BNF lat. 9768, and Rosamond McKitterick takes a pessimistic view of its circulation, *The Carolingians and the Written Word* (Cambridge, 1989), p. 237; but see the suggestive comments of J. L. Nelson, 'History-Writing at the Courts of Louis the Pious and Charles the Bald', in A. Scharer and G. Scheibelreiter, eds., *Historiographie im frühen Mittelalter* (Vienna, 1993), pp. 435–42, at 440, repr. Nelson, *Rulers and Ruling Families in Early Medieval Europe* (Aldershot, 1999), ch. 9; see also next note.

abbey was composed in the late eleventh century. It was thus seen as a useful quarry for a church history.[12] Nithard's own high regard for the abbey of St Riquier is a mixture of admiration for its spectacular ecclesiastical architecture, and as a site of sanctity and of family, one might say proprietorial, pride. Categories could become mixed and Nithard's epitaph at St Riquier blends qualities – bravery in battle, knowledge of sacred wisdom, care for monks, pride in descent from Charlemagne – that we might initially think of as separate.[13] Like the tenth-century Anglo-Saxon Æthelweard, Nithard was royal and a member of the aristocracy; occupied with war and government in a Christian kingdom, he was also a writer. And Christian symbols resonated in the war that he described.[14]

It can thus be difficult, in examining Nithard's text, to separate it, or elements within it, into a category that we can label as purely secular. The secularity of secular institutions is therefore not entirely clear-cut. The concerns of the secular and clerical elite overlapped. Like Einhard in his *Life of Charlemagne*, Nithard was a connoisseur of the rhythms of the royal household, of the trappings of patrimonial rule. Nithard tells us that on his accession Louis the Pious made his half-brothers his 'table-companions (*participes mensae*)', and thus demonstrated their political status (in marked contrast to the fate of Louis' sisters, whose expulsion from court he summarily commanded, and which Nithard also records, though he does not mention that one of these sisters was his own mother). He also records Lothar's elaborate surrender to his father's will at Worms in 839, a ceremony that included a feast (*prandium*), and Nithard describes other such ritualised feasts.[15] But such concern with the ceremonies and the political ups and downs of court life is hardly the exclusive preserve of

---

[12] Hariulf, *Chronique de l'abbaye de Saint-Riquier* III, 5; IV, 5; IV, 17, ed. F. Lot (Paris, 1894), pp. 101–2, 219–20, 264; M. Tischler, *Einharts Vita Karoli: Studien zur Entstehung, Überlieferung und Rezeption*, 2 vols., MGH Schriften 48 (Munich, 2001), I, pp. 687–94.
[13] Nithard IV, 5, pp. 138–40; his epitaph is in *MGH Poet.* III, ed. L. Traube (Berlin, 1896), pp. 310–11.
[14] On Æthelweard, see Ashley in this volume, below, pp. 218–45; for Charles the Bald's use of the cross as symbol of the justice of his claims, see Nithard II, 6, p. 56, and Nelson, 'Ninth-Century Knighthood', p. 85; for the cross as battle-standard of Frankish armies under Carolingian rule, *Opus Caroli regis contra synodum (Libri Carolini)*, ed. A. Freeman, *MGH Conc.* Supplementum 1 (Munich, 1998), II, 28, p. 296; see also Widukind, *Res Gestae Saxonicae*, ed. P. Hirsch and H.-E. Lohmann, MGH SRG 60 (Hanover, 1935), I, 33, pp. 45–6; and G. Althoff, *Amicitiae und Pacta: Bündnis, Einung, Politik und Gebetsgedenken im beginnenden 10. Jahrhundert*, MGH Schriften 37 (Munich, 1992), pp. 25–6.
[15] Nithard I, 2, p. 6 (Louis' brothers); I, 7, p. 30 (Lothar at Worms); and see G. Althoff, *Spielregeln der Politik im Mittelalter* (Darmstadt, 1997), pp. 118–19; for Charles extending the hospitality of his table to envoys from his enemy Lothar, Nithard II, 8, p. 62. For Einhard's view of life in the royal household, see *VK* cc. 18, 19, pp. 21–5.

secular authors; few texts imagine the texture of Carolingian court life as vividly as the late ninth-century *Deeds of Charlemagne*, written by Notker, a monk. Even when Nithard gazes upon the royal bedchamber of Louis the Pious, his gaze is matched by that of the bishops who also watched the bedchamber of Louis and of other kings, though their perspective may not be Nithard's one, of public honour.[16]

Nithard was no monk or bishop, but in seeking to categorise him as a lay author we may be in danger of simplifying him and his culture. That culture did, however, seek to draw some key distinctions between the secular and clerical worlds. The synod of Ver at the end of 844 insisted that secular and church properties were not to be mixed up.[17] For its part, the secular aristocracy could find the monastic experience distasteful and destabilising.[18] There remains something distinctive about Nithard's work. Notably, it is concerned with contemporary history. This may not be unusual in itself; much Carolingian historical writing was concerned with contemporary events and sought to influence them. Thegan's *Deeds of Louis the Pious*, written some half-dozen years before Nithard, is a good example of this. What does appear to be unusual is the fact that a work of such immediately contemporary history was written for a king, indeed at royal command. Kings seem to have preferred 'biblical history and its commentary ... [to] historiography of contemporary events'. One reason for this royal preference was, again to cite Mayke de Jong, that 'a teleological perspective was not easily combined with an intelligent approach to contemporary events', and only such a perspective offered a view of the true significance of history.[19] Nithard's text was so close to the events

---

[16] Nithard describes how Judith was not received in the 'royal bed' until she had purged herself of accusations of adultery, 1, 4, pp. 18–20; on the ecclesiastical accusations against Judith, see E. Ward, 'Agobard of Lyons and Paschasius Radbertus as critics of the Empress Judith', in W. J. Sheils and D. Wood, eds., *Women in the Church*, SCH 27 (Oxford, 1990), pp. 15–25; on ninth-century views, lay and ecclesiastical, of the marriage-bed as an actively sexual site, see J. L. Nelson, 'Monks, Secular Men and Masculinity, *c*. 900', in D. M. Hadley, ed., *Masculinity in Medieval Europe* (London, 1999), pp. 121–42, at 127–8. On the court as viewed by Notker and other churchmen, S. Airlie, 'The Palace of Memory: The Carolingian Court as Political Centre', in S. Rees Jones, R. Marks and A. J. Minnis, eds., *Courts and Regions in Medieval Europe* (Woodbridge, 2000), pp. 1–20, at 4–8.

[17] *Konzilien 843–859* 7, *c*. 12, p. 44; with context in F. J. Felten, *Äbte und Laienäbte im Frankenreich* (Stuttgart, 1980), pp. 297–300, and de Jong, above n. 5.

[18] Nelson, 'Monks, Secular Men', pp. 132–3. The clerical aristocracy's activities in secular business were not uniformly approved of by the clerical establishment, as can be seen in the later examples of Franco of Liège and Brun of Cologne: F. Prinz, *Klerus und Krieg im früheren Mittelalter* (Stuttgart, 1971), pp. 115–46, 176–96.

[19] M. de Jong, 'The Empire as *ecclesia*: Hrabanus Maurus and Biblical *Historia* for Rulers', in Y. Hen and M. Innes, eds., *The Uses of the Past in the Early Middle Ages* (Cambridge, 2000), pp. 198, 200; this topic would bear further investigation.

it was describing that a teleological perspective was not available to it. This makes it rather different even from other texts concerned with contemporary events. Even Einhard and the Astronomer, in writing their biographies of Charlemagne and Louis the Pious respectively, had the death of their subjects to provide a 'closure' for their accounts. Thegan wrote while Louis the Pious was still alive but after the storms of the early 830s, and thus was able to end his work with his hero safe in harbour.[20] The annalistic texts of the Carolingian period may seem to tell a simple story in the simple manner of one damn thing after another but were in fact often elaborately composed long narratives. Further, in their very repetition of accounts of royal journeys, assemblies, wars, etc., they revealed and reinforced contemporary perceptions of the deep structures of royal authority.[21] As we shall see, these deep structures offered no comfort to Nithard, whose text artfully portrays their disintegration.

His text is different. When he started to write, there was no prospect of a clear outcome to the war of Louis' sons, so he could not be sure of the direction of the events to which his text was so closely connected. Further, even after the victory of Charles and his brother ally Louis the German at Fontenoy seemed to offer him the opportunity to shape his account as a unified text designed to justify Charles the Bald's actions and claims, his view of his work changed. Books III and IV, which were probably not part of his original plan for the work, came to express ideas that, as Janet Nelson has argued, were simultaneously broader than the justification of Charles' actions and seemingly more narrowly personal to himself.[22] Nithard's text thus did not have the clear trajectory towards closure that is so characteristic of the royal biographies composed by Einhard, Thegan and the Astronomer. It is not so much that Nithard could not find a pattern. After all, in England at the end of the ninth century Asser set out to write a biography of King Alfred while his hero was still alive and menaced by events, but this did not prevent Asser from imposing a clear pattern on

---

[20] Relating Charlemagne's death, the portents heralding it and the contents of his will, Einhard gives his work a long-drawn-out final cadence, *VK* cc. 30–33, pp. 34–41; the Astronomer gives Louis a vivid death-bed scene and highlights the importance of Carolingian family harmony, Astronomer, *Vita Hludowici* cc. 63, 64, pp. 546–54; Thegan ends with a formal prayer, Thegan c. 58, p. 254, though a contemporary was happy to carry on the narrative past this point, see 'Continuatio Anonyma', *ibid.*, pp. 254–8. On Nithard's ending, see below.
[21] R. McKitterick, 'Political Ideology in Carolingian Historiography', in Hen and Innes, eds., *Uses of the Past*, pp. 162–74.
[22] Nelson, 'Public *Histories*', pp. 197–9, 203, 225; but see also Nelson's later thoughts on Nithard's audience in her 'History-Writing at the Courts of Louis the Pious and Charles the Bald', p. 440.

The world, the text and the Carolingian

his material.²³ Nithard's lack of unity was a response to the swift pace of events but he was ultimately to be able to impose a retrospective unity upon his work, as we shall see at the conclusion of this chapter.

It is this immediacy, which should not be taken to mean artlessness, that relates Nithard's *Histories* to a whole series of other texts generated by the crisis of 840–3, texts that also offer lay perspectives. We shall briefly examine them as indications of the concerns of lay aristocrats in this time of turmoil, and then go on to examine Nithard's own text. This will reveal that Nithard was not isolated in his concerns, though his expression of them was distinctive.

Our first witness is a woman. Like Nithard, Dhuoda wrote because of events of the war, she wrote at almost exactly the same time as he did, and she shared his urgent concerns with the importance of faithfulness and loyalty in politically uncertain times, though her treatment of these themes was notably more optimistic than his.²⁴ These concerns were further shared by another lay author, the writer of a letter to the Empress Ermengard, wife of Lothar I. Its editor has dated this text to the time of the war and plausibly suggested that its author was Adalhard 'the seneschal', a powerful magnate at the court of Louis the Pious who went on to support Charles in the war.²⁵ In this letter, Adalhard eloquently defends himself against accusations of dishonourable behaviour, and stoutly denies that he has been unfaithful to Lothar or that he has fomented conflict among the royal brothers. He stresses that he wants 'justice', which we may understand as his rights, and this may be a reference to his properties in areas under Lothar's control; but he is concerned above all to defend his honour and reputation: 'Some think of me as being unfaithful to your lord [Lothar I] because I have not abandoned my own lord [Charles] and submitted myself to the former. But if I were to do that for short-lived

---

[23] A. Scharer, 'The Writing of History at King Alfred's Court', *EME* 5 (1996), pp. 185–206. The attack on the genuineness of Asser by A. Smyth, *King Alfred the Great* (Oxford, 1995) has triggered a powerful defence of Asser's urgency and distinctiveness: see, for example, J. L. Nelson, 'Waiting for Alfred', *EME* 7 (1998), pp. 115–24; and P. Kershaw, 'Illness, Power and Prayer in Asser's *Life of Alfred*', *EME* 10 (2001), 201–24; and see Pratt in this volume, below, pp. 162–91.

[24] Dhuoda, *Liber Manualis* III, 4, ed. Riché, pp. 92–5; see Nelson in this volume, below, pp. 106–20.

[25] The letter is ed. E. Dümmler, *MGH Epp.* III, no. 27, pp. 343–5; see Dümmler, *Geschichte des ostfränkischen Reiches*, 3 vols. (Leipzig, 1887), I, p. 184, n. 2; J. L. Nelson, 'The Intellectual in Politics: Context, Content and Authorship in the Capitulary of Coulaines, November 843', in L. Smith and B. Ward, eds., *Intellectual Life in the Middle Ages: Essays Presented to Margaret Gibson* (London, 1992), pp. 1–14, repr. Nelson, *Frankish World*, esp. p. 157, and Nelson, 'The Search for Peace in a Time of War: The Carolingian *Bruderkrieg*, 840–843', in *Vorträge und Forschungen* 42, Konstanzer Arbeitskreis für mittelalterliche Geschichte (Sigmaringen, 1996), pp. 87–114, esp. 102–4.

rewards (*res transitorias*), I would be despised by him and all right-thinking people.'²⁶ Adalhard is here living up to the general precepts of Dhuoda who urged her son to be unwavering in his loyalty to his lord as an aspect of his family honour. But he also precisely parallels Nithard's account of those magnates who did defect from Charles in the face of Lothar's threats and blandishments. For Nithard, such figures were aristocratic trimmers who 'chose, like slaves, to break their fidelity and renege on their oaths rather than abandon their properties for a brief time'.²⁷ In direct contrast to such men, including his own brother, Adalhard described himself as having rejected 'short-lived rewards', and in fact he was behaving exactly as Nithard had done. Further, Adalhard was, like Nithard, a lay-abbot, and in that capacity subscribed an 843 document confirming the properties and rights of the monastery of Saint-Lomer, a transaction that sought to repair the 'violence of the recent civil war'.²⁸ One would not guess that Adalhard had such interests from a reading of Nithard.

Adalhard was also concerned with his own honour and reputation and did not hesitate to speak frankly to Ermengard: 'you can remember my services, if you choose to do so'; 'I am faithful and wish to remain so, even if you have changed towards me.' Nithard included a hostile portrait of Adalhard in his *Histories*, but it is worth noting here not simply that Nithard's text is tendentious but also that Adalhard claims to act by a code of positive values. He seeks only his rights. He has remained steadfast while the kings have changed their attitudes, their conflict is a tragedy, but he did not foment such conflict as he has never wanted to 'sow discord among the sons of my lord [Louis the Pious] who brought me up'.²⁹ In referring to the bond of *nutritor* and *nutritus*, i.e., to the role of Carolingian royal courts as places where the aristocracy learnt loyalty to the dynasty and formed bonds with it and its followers, Adalhard echoes Einhard, whose gratitude for such a bond was one of the motives for his writing his *Life of Charlemagne*.³⁰ Adalhard's determination to defend his rights and his articulateness in doing so, together with his palpable sense of annoyance at the kings' behaviour and at Lothar's attempt to tarnish his reputation, illustrate contemporary aristocratic responses to the war as vividly as Nithard's text does and should make us more sympathetic to the

---

[26] *MGH Epp.* III, p. 344.
[27] Nithard II, 3, p. 44; Nelson, 'Public *Histories*', p. 215; for Dhuoda, see above, n. 24.
[28] *Konzilien 843–859* I, p. 6; Adalhard is immediately followed in the subscription list by one Ratbaud, identified by the editor as Richbod, Nithard's kinsman and rival for control of St Riquier.
[29] *MGH Epp.* III, pp. 344–5.   [30] *MGH Epp.* III, pp. 344–5.

dilemmas of figures such as Bernard of Septimania, portrayed by Nithard as coolly calculating political operators.[31]

Further, Adalhard's letter was a reply to a letter sent by the Empress Ermengard and thus points to the fact that the crisis of 840–3 generated heavy signals traffic. More messages and texts were composed and written than have survived. Ermengard's letter shows that Dhuoda was not the only woman who was forced into writing by the events of the war; who knows how many other letters were sent by Ermengard in an attempt to win over followers for her husband's cause? Lothar himself sent messengers across Francia to announce his coming after the death of Louis the Pious, and Nithard's text is packed with references to envoys and messengers.[32] The war triggered a whole series of messages, contacts and texts stemming from or involving the secular aristocracy and not all of this has come down to us. Warriors who had fought at Fontenoy, the great set-piece battle of the war, responded to churchmen's calls for penitence with the claim that they had been obeying orders of the rulers, and penitence was thus unnecessary, though we can catch only an echo of this in ecclesiastical sources.[33] The fighting at Fontenoy drove a contemporary supporter of Lothar to describe it in sombre verse and this poem may well be the product of a secular author.[34]

In this highly charged time, a time of competing royal claims to rule, royal charters were not simply 'normal' documents but were instruments to justify such claims. This can be seen in royal charters for churches.[35] But royal charters also came the way of secular followers. Thus Lothar's instruction of February 841 to 'all our counts and officials of the fisc (*exactoribus rei publice*)' to respect the privileges of the abbey of Prüm signalled to a politically significant audience that Lothar was the protector of this quintessentially Carolingian abbey in the line of his ancestors. Lothar's charters also now began to include a 'fidelity clause' that demanded

---

[31] Nithard's hostile account of Bernard's negotiations with Charles after Fontenoy shows that Bernard was concerned to press claims for territories (*honores*) that he thought he had a claim to, Nithard III, 2, p. 84; this is Adalhard's claim for his rights (*justitia*) seen from the outside.
[32] Nithard II, 1, pp. 36–8; see also III, 2, p. 86, for disinformation spread by Lothar and his supporters after Fontenoy.
[33] See the letter from Hrabanus Maurus to Archbishop Otgar of Mainz, *MGH Epp.* III, no. 33, pp. 462–5; Kottje, *Die Bussbücher*, pp. 6, 241–3 and S. Hamilton, *The Practice of Penance 900–1050* (Woodbridge, 2001), pp. 190–6.
[34] *MGH Poet.* II, p. 138, with English translation in P. Godman, *Poetry of the Carolingian Renaissance* (London, 1985), pp. 263–5; McKitterick, *Carolingians and the Written Word*, p. 231.
[35] See, for example, Lothar's charter for St Arnulf's, Metz, *Die Urkunden Lothars I. und Lothars II*, ed. T. Schieffer, *MGH DD Karolinorum* III (Munich, 1966), no. 46; and the parallel from Charles the Bald, *Recueil des Actes de Charles le Chauve*, ed. G. Tessier, 3 vols. (Paris, 1943–55), I, no. 9.

unwavering loyalty.³⁶ Royal charters such as these of Lothar, or the series of charters issued by Charles the Bald to a number of 'faithful men' in the period before the definitive settlement of Verdun in the summer of 843, were, in their grand format, majestic formulaic language and important dating clauses, miniature versions of a text such as Nithard's, active documents that targeted claims to rule at an important audience.³⁷

The flavour of chancery documents is also detectable in the texts of the Oaths of Strasbourg as written up by Nithard, the famous vernacular promises made in 842 by Charles the Bald, Louis the German and their followers to be mutually true to one another. The fact that these texts appear in the vernacular should not seduce us into thinking that Nithard simply recorded what was actually spoken at Strasbourg; as Rosamond McKitterick has said, Nithard here gave his material 'literary and formulaic oral structure' to serve his own rhetorical purposes.³⁸ In fashioning what was spoken at Strasbourg into a text, Nithard here highlights for us the links between oral and written material. But what is undeniable is that Louis and Charles were making great efforts actively to involve their followers, and not simply the great magnates, in the current political situation.³⁹ That active involving of the aristocracy generated further texts, such as the surveys (*descriptiones*) of the resources of the empire; these were the essential sources of information on which the great division of that empire made at Verdun in 843 was to be based. The survey of the empire was made by some 120 members of the aristocracy.⁴⁰ Previous projects to divide the empire in the last years of Louis the Pious had probably resulted in the writing of official documents outlining the division and such

---

[36] *DD Lothars I*, no. 57; see M. Mersiowsky, 'Regierungspraxis und Schriftlichkeit im Karolingerreich: Das Fallbeispiel der Mandate und Briefe', in R. Schieffer, ed., *Schriftkultur und Reichsverwaltung unter den Karolingern* (Opladen, 1996), pp. 109–66, at 141. For the 'fidelity clause' in this period, see *DD Lothars I*, nos. 66, 69–70, with comment in K. Brunner, *Oppositionelle Gruppen im Karolingerreich* (Vienna, 1979), p. 15.

[37] *Recueil*, ed. Tessier, nos. 5, 10–11, 15–17, 19. Such documents could carry messages of what nobles stood to lose; see Louis the German's charter of December 840 granting to Corvey what had been a benefice held by Banzleib, brother of Lothar's supporter Adalbert, *Die Urkunden Ludwigs des Deutschen, Karlmanns und Ludwigs des Jüngeren*, MGH DD regum Germaniae I, ed. P. Kehr (Berlin, 1932–34), no. 29, with comment on Banzleib's family in M. Innes, *State and Society in the Early Middle Ages: The Middle Rhine Valley 400–1000* (Cambridge, 2000), pp. 205–6.

[38] Nithard III, 5, pp. 104–8; R. McKitterick, 'Introduction: sources and interpretation', in *NCMH* II, pp. 11–12.

[39] P. Classen, 'Die Verträge von Verdun und Coulaines 843 als politische Grundlagen des westfränkischen Reiches', *HZ* 196 (1963), pp. 1–35; Nelson, 'Public *Histories*', pp. 210–11; G. Althoff, *Amicitiae und Pacta*, pp. 24–5; Althoff, *Spielregeln*, pp. 140–3.

[40] 'Descriptio' is the term used by the *Annals of St Bertin* s.a. 842 (hereafter *AB*), p. 43, trans. Nelson p. 54; see also *Annales Fuldenses* s.a. 843, pp. 33, 34, trans. Reuter pp. 21, 22.

documents may well lie behind Nithard's account of these divisions, as well as behind the account of the Astronomer, whose biography of Louis the Pious was written in 840–1.[41]

A wave of documents and communications thus poured down upon and out from the secular aristocracy in this period of crisis and tension. Nithard's text was not isolated and there was certainly an audience for textual gestures such as his. But Nithard's contribution was distinctive in its intellectual anatomising of the greatness and, above all, of the limitations of the key (secular) institutions of his world: Carolingian royalty and the secular aristocracy and perhaps masculinity itself.

Nithard was himself a member of the Carolingian house. Through his mother he was a grandson of Charlemagne; he does not, however, describe any of the individual Carolingians mentioned in his text as his relatives. We can thus see his text as a Carolingian house history and place it beside other such texts, notably the continuations of Fredegar produced under the aegis of Count Childebrand and Count Nibelung, kinsmen of Pippin III, in the eighth century and the so-called *Annals of Metz*, probably produced under the supervision of Charlemagne's sister Gisela in the early ninth.[42] What I wish to draw attention to here is not any 'secular' characteristics of such texts but their Carolingian character. This Carolingian aspect of Nithard's text has not yet been sufficiently explored. What is important here is the sheer fact of literary activity by members of the royal house. Nithard's text can be placed, not just beside these other historical works, but beside the copying of the *Life* of St Arnulf of Metz, ancestral holy man of the royal line, by a very junior member of the Carolingian family, the nine-year-old son of Charles Martel.[43]

Such literary activity was part of the Carolingian house's strategy of legitimation, a way of making the Carolingians prominent in the landscape

---

[41] See Tremp's introduction to his edition of the Astronomer, pp. 88–91.
[42] Nithard on his Carolingian descent, IV, 5, pp. 138–40, and see Nelson, 'Public *Histories*', pp. 213–15; see also Nithard's reference to 'our *genus*', III, preface, p. 78, and see below for comment on this. For the work of Childebrand and Nibelung, see the continuations of Fredegar's chronicle, *The Fourth Book of the Chronicle of Fredegar c.* 34, ed. J. M. Wallace-Hadrill (London, 1960), pp. 102–3, with commentary in R. Collins, *Fredegar*, Authors of the Middle Ages IV (Aldershot, 1996), pp. 32–7; the slender basis of evidence for the ascription of this chronicle to Childebrand and his son is stressed in R. McKitterick, 'The Illusion of Royal Power in the Carolingian Annals', *EHR* 115 (2000), pp. 1–20, at 5–6. On Chelles and the *Annales Mettenses Priores*, J. L. Nelson, 'Gender and Genre in Women Historians of the Early Middle Ages', in Nelson, *Frankish World*, pp. 191–4.
[43] B. Kasten, *Königssöhne und Königsherrschaft*, MGH Schriften 44 (Munich, 1997), p. 119; a very prominent Carolingian layman, Charlemagne himself, lay behind an anecdote on St Arnulf, according to Paul the Deacon, *Liber de Episcopis Mettensibus*, MGH SS 11 (Hanover, 1829), p. 264. Cf. Ashley on Æthelweard, below, pp. 218–45.

of the past as well as in that of the present. Such a strategy was necessary in order to make the rule of the Carolingians, whose royalty stemmed not from timeless right, but from the specific historical context of the reign of Pippin III (751–68), appear as inevitable, as part of the natural order. This is certainly the effect of Nithard beginning his narrative proper with a portrait of Charlemagne himself, even if this Charlemagne appears to belittle his successors. In terms of presenting Carolingian legitimacy, Nithard's Charlemagne appears, not as a beginning, but as a given, a tremendous natural phenomenon of the political landscape.

The nature of Nithard's achievement in this opening section is thrown into sharp relief if we heed some remarks of the late Pierre Bourdieu: 'There is no more potent tool for rupture than the reconstruction of genesis: by bringing back into view the conflicts and confrontation of the early beginnings and therefore all the discarded possibles, it retrieves the possibility that things could have been otherwise.'[44] This, rather surprisingly, is the risk that Einhard runs in his famous opening to his *Life of Charlemagne*. There, he highlights the pre-royal past of the Carolingians and actually opens his text with the Merovingian dynasty; but this simply serves to highlight his literary skill in fashioning a vision of the inevitability of Carolingian royalty so convincing as to hold historiographical sway for centuries. Writing a generation or so later, Nithard, who may have read Einhard, avoids any possibility of rupture, that is, of referring to a time when the Carolingians were not the hereditary royal family of the Franks, by presenting Charlemagne as the starting point of his work. None of Charlemagne's predecessors are named; there is no reference to Pippin III or to earlier Carolingian mayors of the palace, let alone to any Merovingian ruler. There was no logical narrative reason for Nithard to begin his history with Charlemagne. As he says himself, the story he had to tell required him to begin with the reign of Louis the Pious, as an account of it would help the reader better understand the subsequent conflicts. But there was no such need to include Charlemagne in the history. Nithard realised this, but he could not resist beginning with him: 'it seems most unwise to omit completely the remembrance, so worthy of respect, of your grandfather, and so my text starts from there'.[45]

In fact, Nithard uses the figure of Charlemagne to give point and contrast to his account of the unhappy reign of Louis and, as it turned out, his

---

[44] P. Bourdieu, *Practical Reason: On the Theory of Action* (London, 1998), p. 40 (trans. R. Johnson from *Raisons Pratiques* (Paris, 1994)).
[45] Nithard 1, 1, p. 4; contrast *VK* cc. 1–2, pp. 2–5.

opening hymn of praise to Charlemagne provided a bitter counterpoint to his final book's gloomy picture of the era of another Charles, Charles the Bald himself, though Nithard can hardly have planned this when he began to write. But the figure of Charlemagne also serves to enhance the aura of Carolingian royalty in Nithard's text. Nithard locates Charles the Bald in a hereditary series of rulers ('in the times of your pious father', 'the remembrance of your grandfather').[46] On one level, this is designed to justify Charles' claim to a throne, such justification being the immediate cause of Nithard's writing. But, on a deeper level, it forms part of a general discourse of the hereditary royal quality of the Carolingian family. On this level the fact that Nithard's text is full of Carolingian fathers, sons and brothers continually quarrelling is less important than the fact that they *are* fathers, sons and brothers. Carolingian authority, status and identity are thus represented as being produced through the natural structure of the family.

Louis the Pious functions in Book I as one of the points from which members of the royal family take identity and status. Nithard describes Louis as the heir of Charlemagne, as the only one of his legitimate sons to survive.[47] Louis' legitimacy, if not his competence, is thus secure as it is grounded in Nithard's fundamental starting point. Other members of the family are then defined in Book I in terms of their relationship to Louis: his sisters, brothers, nephew, his own sons and grandsons.[48] All this is part of a general discourse of Carolingian familial authority. Nithard's account of Louis' death fits into this. His account is terser and much less richly detailed than that given by the Astronomer, which draws on eyewitnesses, but it is awash with the royalty of the Carolingian family: 'while Lothar was in Italy, Louis [the German] was on the other side of the Rhine and Charles [the Bald] was in Aquitaine, the emperor Louis their father died on an island close to Mainz on 20 June. His brother Drogo, bishop and archchaplain, with bishops, abbots and counts, buried him with fitting honour in his city of Metz at St Arnulf's.'[49] All the far-flung parts of the empire were in the hands of legitimate successors, explicitly labelled as sons of

---

[46] Nithard, preface, p. 2; for the closing reference to Charlemagne, see IV, 7, p. 144, and see below.
[47] Nithard I, 2, pp. 4–6.   [48] Nithard I, 2, pp. 6–8; I, 8, p. 32.
[49] Nithard I, 8, pp. 34–6; Astronomer cc. 63–4, pp. 546–54; and see J. L. Nelson, 'Carolingian Royal Funerals', in F. Theuws and J. L. Nelson, eds., *Rituals of Power: From Late Antiquity to the Early Middle Ages*, The Transformation of the Roman World 8 (Leiden, 2000), pp. 131–84, at 159. Nithard does not explicitly refer to Arnulf as an ancestor of Louis but we can safely assume that this family connection was widely known; Thegan certainly thought so, Thegan *c*. 1, pp. 174–6, and see the *Carmen de exordio gentis Francorum*, ed. E. Dümmler, *MGH Poet*. II (Berlin, 1884), p. 143, a text contemporary with Nithard and drawing on genealogical compilations; see also Charlemagne's own testimony, above n. 43.

Louis, while Louis himself was buried by his brother in the shrine of his sacred ancestor, St Arnulf. An aura of glorious Carolingian continuity from the holy ancestor in the past to the new rulers of the future, with their royal names unique to the Carolingian family, surrounds death, which threatens dissolution, but which is here masterfully orchestrated into a hymn to Carolingian splendour by Drogo, brother of Louis. Nithard, himself a descendant of Charlemagne, recapitulates Drogo's action by deploying in his text the figures of the emperor, his sons, his brother and his ancestor as elements in a system to represent Carolingian royalty as present across time and space, to give depth and reality to Carolingian hegemony.

Like the contemporary landscape, Nithard's text was full of members of the Carolingian family and he is usually alert in noting their status or changes to it. It is only Nithard who identifies a Pippin who held lands between the Meuse and the Seine as 'son of Bernard king of the Lombards', just as only he gives details on the death of that ill-fated Bernard.[50] Nithard is the only source to tell us that Louis the Pious made his half-brothers his 'table companions' at the beginning of his reign but while other sources also tell us that Louis, in the uneasy period after the revolt of his nephew Bernard, had them tonsured, it is Nithard who tells us that this ritualised humiliation took place in public, at an assembly.[51] Nithard looks at the royal family from a particular angle. Having a daughter of Charlemagne for a mother did not obliterate Nithard's feeling for his father Angilbert's kin and that kinship came to be more important for him as he wrote the *Histories*. Nonetheless, he simultaneously stressed his descent from Charlemagne: 'by a daughter of that great king [Charlemagne] named Bertha he [Angilbert] had Hartnid my brother and me, Nithard'. He also highlights his Carolingian family identity in his preface to Book III, where he admits that the story he has to tell is hardly flattering to 'our family (*genus nostrum*)'.[52] We shall return to this gloomy reference but for now we

---

[50] Nithard II, 3, p. 44; Regino of Prüm also knew that Pippin was a son of Bernard, see his *Chronicon*, ed. F. Kurze, *MGH SRG* (Hanover, 1890), s.a. 818, p. 73. Nithard I, 2, p. 6, has the unique detail of the name of Bernard's executioner, as noted by K. F. Werner, '*Hludovicus Augustus*: Gouverner l'empire chrétien – idées et réalités', in Godman and Collins, *Charlemagne's Heir*, pp. 3–123, at 48. On Nithard's informed accounts of his Carolingian kin, Nelson, 'Public *Histories*', pp. 213–15.

[51] Nithard I, 2, pp. 6–8; M. Diesenberger, 'Hair, Sacrality and Symbolic Capital in the Frankish Kingdoms', in R. Corradini, M. Diesenberger and H. Reimitz, eds., *The Construction of Communities in the Early Middle Ages*, The Transformation of the Roman World 12 (Leiden, 2002), pp. 173–212, at 206.

[52] Nithard IV, 5, pp. 138–40, with Nelson, 'Public *Histories*', pp. 213–14, 231–3; 'genus', Nithard III, preface, p. 78, and on the associations of this term, R. Le Jan, *Famille et pouvoir dans le monde franc (VIIe–Xe siècle)* (Paris, 1995), p. 34.

will focus on what Nithard tells us of the structure and make-up of the key secular institution of his world, the Carolingian family itself.

Nithard's view of that family is actually quite narrow, deep but not broad. He himself, together with his brother Hartnid, is the only 'peripheral' Carolingian to be explicitly referred to as a Carolingian in his text. He gives unique details on many Carolingians, as we have seen, but his picture of the royal house is tightly focused, linear. Apart from himself and his brother, the only Carolingians that are identified as such in his text are the children, male and female, of kings. This contrasts with Thegan and the Astronomer. Thegan signals that Bernard of Septimania was a member of the royal house (*stirps regalis*), while the Astronomer notes that Wala was the emperor's kinsman (*adfinis*). Nithard mentions both these men but makes no reference to them belonging to the Carolingian house.[53] His text is royal in the quite specific sense that it is king-centred. He does not refer to any of the Carolingian actors in it as being his kinsmen, apart from Charlemagne(!). To that extent he may testify to the success of the kings in imposing shape and rank on a royal family. He thus served the system of making Carolingians special but also ensuring that some Carolingians were more special than others.

Among those special Carolingians were women, the daughters of kings. He gives the name of his own mother, Bertha, and specifies that she was the daughter of Charlemagne. Further, Nithard is the only source to tell us that Charles the Bald faced a military challenge from his half-sister Hildegard in the autumn of 841.[54] But his text makes clear that what Hildegard did was less important than what she was, i.e., her identity as a Carolingian, and how this helped constitute a generally present Carolingian identity. This Hildegard, daughter of Louis the Pious and his first wife, bore the prestigious name of her paternal grandmother, the great Hildegard who had married Charlemagne and who had successfully been 'incorporated' into the royal family. Charles the Bald was a son of Louis' second marriage, but for Nithard Hildegard is simply his 'sister'. At Laon, she was probably abbess of Notre-Dame and St-Jean-de-Laon; here she took her place in a succession of Carolingian women, and the property which she lost to her brother Charles seems to have ended up in the hands of his wife

---

[53] Bernard: Thegan *c.* 36, p. 222, and Nithard I, 3, p. 10, II, 5, p. 50, III, 2, pp. 82–4; Wala: Astronomer *c.* 35, p. 408, and Nithard I, 4, p. 15. The Arnulf referred to by Nithard II, 6, pp. 54–6, is not identified as Carolingian, though he was the illegitimate son of Louis the Pious and we can assume that Nithard knew this.

[54] Bertha: Nithard IV, 5, p. 138; Hildegard: Nithard III, 4, pp. 96–8.

Ermentrude and thus remained in the pool of what was marked out for the women of the royal house.[55] We know very little about her; Nithard is the only source to mention her activity at Laon. For contemporaries, however, her name and her position in a series of royal women at Laon meant that she was part of a structure that replicated the identity, and thus the aura of specialness, of the ruling house. The clash at Laon may not have been remembered, but Hildegard herself was, and as a Carolingian.[56] Nithard's narrative presents Hildegard's surrender to Charles in 841 as a restoration of family harmony: 'she came into his faithfulness' (*fides*: this probably means that she swore an oath to Charles); 'Charles received his sister kindly and forgave her all the wrongs that she had done him and ... promised her the kindness that a brother ought to show to a sister.' Harmony in the royal family betokened harmony in the public sphere. Conversely, the royal family's problems were public problems; according to Nithard, when Charles' men threatened to get out of hand at Laon, Charles restrained them because he was moved by pity for 'the churches of God, *his sister* and the Christian people'.[57] In his account of family conflict, his Hildegard story turns out to carry a message of family harmony. It also sounds some fairly sonorous Carolingian chords: those present at Laon in 841, as well as Nithard's intended audience, would see a picture of concord between a Charles and a Hildegard. The aura of Charlemagne is evoked by his grandchildren, Charles, Hildegard and the narrator Nithard. In this light, family quarrels and Hildegard's individual loss of power matter less than the continuing assertion of the identity and aura of the royal family and, at this level, Hildegard was a success.

Nithard's text may work within the grand system of Carolingian legitimation, but this does not mean that it is uniformly favourable to all members of the royal house, nor that it lacks distinctiveness. The tension of the period went deep. Nithard's verdict on the rule of the Carolingian family is not a simple positive one. The endless references to family relationships are often expressed in a bitter minor key. The very opening of Nithard's preface to Book I, addressed to Charles the Bald, refers to the 'persecution by your brother', and the unstable nature of the patrimonial rule of the Carolingian family is clearly highlighted in the references to

---

[55] E. Ewig, '*Descriptio Franciae*', in H. Beumann, ed., *Karl der Grosse I, Persönlichkeit und Geschichte* (Düsseldorf, 1965), pp. 143–77, at 164; K. F. Werner, 'Die Nachkommen Karls des Grossen bis um das Jahre 1000 (1.-8. Generation)', in W. Braunfels and P. E. Schramm, eds., *Karl der Grosse IV: Das Nachleben* (Düsseldorf, 1967), pp. 402–82, at 447.
[56] Witger, *Genealogia Arnulfi Comitis*, ed. L. Bethmann, *MGH SS* IX (Hanover, 1851), p. 303.
[57] Nithard IV, 3, p. 98 (my emphasis).

voluntas patris, the ever-changing will of the father (Louis the Pious) as the constant motor of change and instability in the 830s.[58] But it is in his portrait of Lothar that Nithard really draws blood. Scornful of the ties of blood reinforced by godparenthood that bind him to this father and brothers, dominated by his own followers, seducing the followers of others by *cupiditas* and *terror* (in contrast to Charlemagne, who used *terror* to create order), forgetful of the plight of the poor, widows and orphans, Lothar is a parody of a proper king. In bitingly sarcastic tones, Nithard describes Lothar as indeed possessing the indisputably kingly qualities of *virtus* and *industria* but as deploying them only to foment civil war.[59] Ultimately, Lothar subverts the empire of Charlemagne. Nithard praises Charlemagne's subjection of the Saxons, but this only acts as a prologue to Lothar's stirring them up into rebellion and chaos.[60] By focusing on the royal virtues that Lothar so signally lacks, Nithard depicts Lothar as a parody of true kingship, a polemic against a living king that, in its satiric stance, anticipates the attack on Henry IV in Bruno of Magdeburg's *On the Saxon War*, written in the eleventh century when kingship itself came under attack.[61] Carolingian blood was not enough. Pippin, son of King Bernard of Italy, bore a royal name and identity but, like Lothar, he failed to live up to royal standards and instead behaved like a slave in his shameful betrayal of his lord.[62]

If the central institution of the empire, the Carolingian family, was found wanting by Nithard, so too was the aristocracy. Historians have seen Nithard's text as enshrining the positive values of the secular aristocracy, its corporate identity, its sense of Christian knighthood. But in scrutinising the behaviour of individual aristocrats in action, Nithard tends to provide a negative picture. A contrast with Einhard brings this

---

[58] Nithard I, 3, p. 12; I, 6, p. 28, and see also IV, 6, p. 142; compare this with Louis' destabilising proposals of 831 to his sons, in the projected division of the realm, *MGH Capit.* II, no. 194, p. 23.

[59] Nithard himself reminded Lothar to his face in 840 that he was brother and godfather to Charles, II, 2, p. 40; for count Adalbert's domination of Lothar, II, 7, p. 58; for a whole catalogue of royal and familial duties neglected by Lothar, III, 3, p. 92; contrast Nithard's account of Lothar and Charlemagne in II, 1, p. 38, I, 1, p. 4, and see next note; for Nithard's bitingly ironic use of *virtus* and *industria*, II, preface, p. 36, with Nelson, 'Public *Histories*', p. 199. For Nithard's criticism of rulers, Leyser, 'Nithard and his Rulers', and E. Screen, 'The Importance of the Emperor: Lothar and the Frankish Civil Wars, 840–843', *EME* 12 (2003), pp. 25–51, esp. 27–31. For Paschasius Radbertus on the wilfulness of rulers, Ganz, '*Epitaphium Arsenii*', pp. 544–50.

[60] Nithard IV, 2, pp. 120–2.

[61] *Brunos Buch vom Sachsenkrieg*, ed. H.-E. Lohmann, *MGH SSDM* (Leipzig, 1937); H.-H. Kortüm, 'Zur Typologie der Herrscheranekdote in der mittelalterlichen Geschichtsschreibung', *MIÖG* 105 (1997), pp. 1–29, at 21–4.

[62] Nithard II, 3, p. 44.

instructive point into focus. In his *Life of Charlemagne*, Einhard mentions only five aristocrats by name, all of whom he describes in two episodes as dying in loyal service to the Carolingians. Nithard's first book alone mentions by name some eighteen aristocrats.[63] He thus peoples his narrative with a far larger supporting cast of aristocratic actors than Einhard does. But they do not play a heroic part. Of these eighteen, three appear as greedy and treacherous, one is mentioned merely to be set up for a later treacherous appearance in the narrative, and six are slaughtered in the civil wars of the royal family; and a noble woman is also cruelly killed on Lothar's orders (in contrast to Charles the Bald's firm but fair disciplining of his sister at Laon in Book III).[64] And all this in Book I, written when Nithard is usually assumed to have been fairly optimistic about the political scene!

It is almost as if Nithard had set out to mock the advice given by Dhuoda to her aristocratic son. Her references to royal dignity, to the virtues of the royal court and to proper aristocratic pride clash discordantly with Nithard's stories of kings and aristocrats destroying themselves. Nithard's magnates use access to court only to advance themselves, to strive for the second place in the empire (and even monks are infected by this self-aggrandisement). Dhuoda urges her son to be 'wise (*prudentius*) ... in affairs that matter to the royal power (*utilitatis regiae potestati*)', but Nithard depicts figures who despise 'public concerns (*utilitas publica*)', and who are imagined to be *prudens* in counsel when they advise kings to join in civil war.[65]

---

[63] *VK* c. 9, p. 12 (Eggihard, Anselm, Roland, though the name of Roland does not appear in every manuscript class), c. 13, p. 16 (Eric and Gerold); Einhard does name several aristocratic women, but they marry into the Carolingian family and thus are presented as royal; the will does of course list the names of many noble witnesses but this does not appear in Einhard's main narrative, *VK* c. 33, p. 41. For Nithard's aristocratic *dramatis personae*, see next note.

[64] Greedy and treacherous (Hugh, Matfrid, Bernard and Lambert): Nithard I, 3, pp. 8–10, I, 4, p. 16; guilty of later treachery (Gerard), I, 6, p. 26, and cf. II, 3, p. 44; victims (Wido, Odo, Vivian, Fulbert, Gozhelm, Sanila): I, 5, pp. 20–2; execution of Gerberga, I, 5, p. 22. Conrad, Rudolf and Herbert are presented as victims of the civil wars: I, 3, p. 10; Warin has to swap sides because of Lothar's force, I, 5, p. 22; Bertmund, count of Lyon, appears as doing his duty, but that duty involves the blinding of Bernard of Italy, I, 1, p. 6; the one 'neutral' reference is to Richard, I, 7, p. 30. Nithard refers to fewer members of the clerical aristocracy, and he does not always bother to identify them as churchmen, but they too are shown to be involved in the power struggles, see I, 4, p. 14, I, 6, p. 26, and see I, 3, p. 12 for the ambitious monk Guntbald, on whom see P. Depreux, *Prosopographie de l'entourage de Louis le Pieux 781–840* (Sigmaringen, 1997), pp. 218–20.

[65] Dhuoda III, 4, p. 94; Nithard sees Charlemagne as concerned for 'publica utilitas', while the individualistic actors of his text subvert it, I, 1, p. 4, IV, 7, pp. 142–4; for 'wise counsel (*prudens consilium*)', from Adalbert of Metz, leading to more war, II, 7, p. 58; on Nithard's terminology of 'publica utilitas' and 'res publica', Leyser, 'Nithard and his Rulers', pp. 20–1.

He sketches the careers of three men as anti-types of fitting aristocratic behaviour. His Adalhard the seneschal is wilful and selfish, scornful of *utilitas publica*; his Bernard of Septimania is a slippery barrack-room lawyer as well as cowardly, preferring to sit out the great battle of Fontenoy. These vivid sketches are caricatures and simplifications, in which Nithard highlights what he sees as the glaring discrepancy between ideal and reality in the behaviour of the secular aristocracy.[66] His most savage portrayal is that of a third figure, Adalbert count of Metz. Adalbert had been a major player on the political scene of the 830s, though his political career probably stretched back further than that. His political influence and interests were not confined to Metz and the middle Rhineland but reached into east Francia and Saxony. These interests have been well analysed by Matthew Innes and Eric Goldberg; the latter clearly demonstrates that Adalbert's unrelenting hostility to Louis the German sprang from his determination to prevent the 'formation of an independent east-Rhenish kingdom'.[67] The creation of such a kingdom, precisely what Louis was trying to create, would break up Adalbert's own power networks. Adalbert's opposition to Louis the German was thus consistent and comprehensible.

But Nithard does not examine Adalbert's career in these terms. He takes Adalbert's hostility to Louis and deploys it as one element in a sombre portrait of a man driven by hatred and blood-lust: he 'felt a deadly hatred for Louis. Adalbert had just recovered from the illness that had laid him low for about a year, so that he could now help with the fratricide. He was so shrewd (*prudens*) in counsel that no-one would challenge his advice.' What Nithard presents here is a picture of a man anxious to arise from his sick-bed, but only in order to take part in 'fratricide', as if the very prospect of that had lent him strength. One might think that Nithard had Dhuoda's *Manual* for her son in front of him as he wrote, since his picture of Adalbert rushing from sick-bed to scenes of slaughter contrasts directly with her urgent reminders to her son that bodily health should lead to salvation of the soul.[68] Nithard was surely relying on his audience's knowledge of such commonplaces for the impact of his negative picture of Adalbert.

---

[66] Adalhard: Nithard IV, 6, p. 142, but it must be admitted that Nithard's hostility to Adalhard is only a feature of this last book, see Nelson, 'Public *Histories*', pp. 218, 222–3; Bernard: Nithard II, 5, p. 50.
[67] E. J. Goldberg, 'Popular Revolt, Dynastic Politics, and Aristocratic Factionalism in the Early Middle Ages: the Saxon *Stellinga* Reconsidered', *Speculum* 70 (1995), pp. 467–501, at 485–7, 493–4; Innes, *State and Society*, pp. 206–8, 213, n. 180; Depreux, *Prosopographie*, pp. 69–72 surveys his career. He counted Einhard among his contacts.
[68] Nithard II, 7, p. 58; Dhuoda III, 8, p. 178.

Nithard's Adalbert was not a wholly invented figure. As we have seen, there really was no love lost between Adalbert and Louis the German. Nor was Nithard the only contemporary to see Adalbert as a troublemaker. The *Annals of Fulda* record his death in a clash with Louis and explicitly label him as 'instigator of these disputes (*incentor discordiarum*)'.[69] Such perceptions are valuable in themselves, not least as evidence for the seething personal resentments among the elite of the period, and there is little point in us trying to whitewash grimly active political figures such as Adalbert. There is, however, every reason for us to understand just how partial are such views as Nithard's and the Fulda annalist's (presumably Rudolf). Even within Fulda, it was possible to take a more detached view of Adalbert, as seen in the fact that his memory was recalled in the abbey's solemn memorialising of the dead. This more positive commemoration of Adalbert was also made elsewhere in the east: in Würzburg, in a calendar dating from the time of bishop Gozbald (843–55), and in the abbey of Reichenau, in an entry in its *Liber Vitae* deriving from Archbishop Liutbert of Mainz (863–89).[70]

The existence of such alternative memories of Adalbert in non-narrative sources has not been evoked here in order simply to provide a form of balance to Nithard's picture of him. They are useful for us here precisely because they highlight just how carefully crafted, in its tendentious way, his portrait of Adalbert is. That is to say, Nithard's text is highly wrought and we have to treat it as such; that is one of its primary qualities. Nithard gives us no 'back-story' on Adalbert; his Adalbert appears on the scene abruptly, motivated by hatred and with an appetite for slaughter. Nithard and his audience had surely known the real Adalbert and rightly feared his power and influence. But his two-dimensional caricature fitted Nithard's polemical purposes of demonising the leading figures of the opposition to Charles and Louis, and thus not only assuring his audience of the justice of its cause but also flattering its sense of self-worth by presenting its opponents as formidable but wicked and vulnerable. While Nithard demonised Adalbert, he did not ascribe his behaviour to the devil's inspiration, as writers such as the Astronomer did, in his account of risings against Louis

---

[69] *AF* s.a. 841, p. 32, tr. Reuter, p. 19; for Thegan, Matfrid was the 'incentor omnium illorum malorum', a phrase stemming from the Bible, Thegan *c.* 55, p. 250, with Tremp's comment at p. 251, n. 303.

[70] E. Freise, 'Der Einzugsbereich der Klostergemeinschaft von Fulda', in K. Schmid *et al.*, eds., *Die Klostergemeinschaft von Fulda in früheren Mittelalter*, 3 vols. (Munich, 1978), II, 3, pp. 1204–16 (Fulda), p. 1142 n. 754, p. 1215 (Würzburg), and pp. 1213 n. 1146, 1215 (Reichenau); see also G. Althoff, 'Über die von Erzbischof Liutbert auf die Reichenau übersandten Namen', *FMS* 14 (1980), pp. 219–42, at 233–5, 238–9.

the Pious.[71] Nithard's Adalbert had failed to adhere to the code of approved behaviour for the Christian Carolingian aristocracy: he abused the gift of his restored bodily health; he abused his privilege as a counsellor to urge fratricide. Nithard's fixing of his negative image for posterity showed the consequences of failing to live up to the code: Adalbert was engulfed in catastrophe that was personal (death in battle against Louis the German) and public (he left only, at least for Nithard and his readers, a bad reputation). This text was thus a mirror for the aristocracy as well as for princes, though as it went on, its castigating of political vices ceased to be balanced by accounts of political virtue.

All this needs to be stressed because we need to remember that the categories of Nithard's historical writing and understanding were not those of modern historiography. Nithard gives us no sense of the political dilemmas posed for Adalbert by the determination of Louis the German to build a separate kingdom in the east. Nor is he interested in Adalbert's links with great churches such as Fulda, Mainz and Würzburg; he probably did not know about these links in any detail. But his picture is not simply partial. It distorts the logic of Adalbert's historical position. As Janet Nelson has pointed out, Nithard, and other writers writing after the battles of 841, knew that slaughter was on the agenda of the great conflict that broke out in 840, but historical actors such as Adalbert did not.[72] In the crisis years of Louis the Pious' reign, 830 and 833–4, great set-piece battles with kings were a looming possibility but had not actually taken place. A figure such as Adalbert would surely have assumed that the traditional dramas of threats and manoeuvres, not battles, would resume in 840. Of course, this was a gamble on Adalbert's part, but as such it was far removed from the near-psychotic craving for violence attributed to him by Nithard. One does not need to turn to clerical writers for distortion of the priorities and motivations of the secular aristocracy.

The ruling dynasty itself came to fare badly in Nithard's text. In the acid-bath of his disenchantment, even the figure of his patron Charles the Bald dissolves, not simply in the well-known sense that Nithard became disillusioned with Charles, but at a deeper level of the structure of his text.

---

[71] Astronomer c. 48, p. 472, and see also 45, p. 462, for diabolically inspired disturbances. On the devil in Christian historiography of the Carolingian era, D. Ganz, 'Humour as History in Notker's *Gesta Karoli Magni*', in E. B. King, J. T. Schaefer and W. B. Wadley, eds., *Monks, Nuns and Friars in Medieval Society* (Sewanee, TN, 1989), pp. 171–83, at 180.

[72] J. L. Nelson, 'Violence in the Carolingian World and the Ritualization of Ninth-Century Warfare', in G. Halsall, ed., *Violence and Society in the Early Medieval West* (Woodbridge, 1997), pp. 90–106, at 97–100.

Running through Nithard's work, for all that he composed it in sections and with a shifting agenda, is a miniature royal biography, a biography of Charles. We do not know for certain whether Nithard had read any of the contemporary royal biographies. He gives the hour of Charlemagne's death and he may have taken this from Einhard's *Life of Charlemagne*, though this is hardly conclusive proof that he was familiar with that text.[73] As for the biographies of Louis the Pious, it is unlikely that Nithard had read Thegan's *Deeds of the Emperor Louis* and, as we have seen, it is more likely that he and the Astronomer were using common sources than that he had read the latter's account of Louis' reign.[74] While we cannot be certain that he was unaware of these texts, we can surely be confident that it was not necessary for him to have read them in order to grasp what made a royal biography. The aristocracy knew that the rhythms of the royal life-cycle, the birth, maturing and death of the ruler, were fundamental factors in the shaping of political life. Contained within Nithard's overall historical narrative is a mini-narrative, a biography consisting of a survey of the milestones in the life of a male ruler.

Nithard tells his audience of Charles' birth, his being entrusted in childhood to a great magnate for guidance, his being given weapons and a crown as a mark of his coming of age.[75] Nithard tells us of the boy's formation in the arts of being a man. As a youth, Charles displays skill in wielding the lance, just as his father was said to have done, while his horsemanship probably had its roots in the early training in riding and the use of weapons that Einhard saw as the hallmark of the active boyhood of the Frankish elite, including its royal family.[76] Nithard gives a brief physical description of Charles (and of Louis the German), highlighting his fine physical and moral qualities. This is a shorthand version of the descriptions found in Einhard and Thegan, and the stress on physical strength and on social and public virtues is again masculine.[77] Finally, at the very end of the text, Charles marries, a key episode in the life of a

---

[73] Nithard I, 1, p. 4; cf. *VK c.* 30, p. 35.
[74] On the distribution and reception of Thegan's text, E. Tremp, *Studien zu den Gesta Hludowici imperatoris des Trierer Chorbischofs Thegan*, MGH Schriften 32 (Munich, 1988), pp. 99–168; Thegan's text, like Einhard's, was edited by Walahfrid in the early 840s, Tremp, pp. 112–28. On Nithard and the Astronomer, see n. 41, above.
[75] Nithard I, 2, p. 8, I, 3, p. 10, I, 6, p. 26.
[76] Nithard III, 6, p. 112; see Thegan on the skills of Louis the Pious, Thegan *c.* 19, p. 200; and, in general, *VK c.* 19, p. 23. For the young Louis the Pious being equipped with boyish weapons, see Astronomer *c.* 4, p. 294.
[77] Nithard III, 6, pp. 110–12; compare this with *VK c.* 22, pp. 26–7, and Thegan *c.* 19, p. 200.

The world, the text and the Carolingian 73

king, and Einhard, Thegan and the Astronomer paid due heed to it in their royal biographies.[78]

In Nithard's account, however, these milestones do not mark a stately progress towards kingly glory. They punctuate a story of crisis, a royal life-cycle gone badly wrong. The stages of Charles' life trigger discord and conflict. His birth leads to dispute and power struggles in the royal family; the bond of godparenthood is too feeble to restrain Lothar from trying to disinherit or injure Charles; Bernard of Septimania fails to act as a good role model for the young Charles and no lasting bond of *nutritor* and *nutritus* is established between them; Charles' coming of age and gaining of weapons and crown takes place in a context of conflicting claims among the royal family.[79]

Initially, Nithard must have intended this picture to serve his original polemical purpose, i.e., to justify Charles' claims to a throne. This picture, which is that of Books I and II, was designed to show that Charles was hard done by. Notoriously, Nithard's aims changed as he continued to write, and Books III and IV were not part of his original conception.[80] We must therefore beware of imposing a unity on the text. But the text ended up as one of four books. That is how it has been transmitted to us. That is how Nithard finished it and he finished it by self-consciously referring back to its beginning in his evocation of Charlemagne's reign as a golden age.[81] This was more than a mere 'flourish of literary symmetry'.[82] At the end of his work, Nithard looked back to its beginning. He thus came to visualise his work as forming a whole; indeed, in referring back to the beginning he was actively seeking to give his work retrospective unity, a unity that meant that the later stages of the work now shadowed the earlier ones. If the preface to Book I ascribed villainy to Lothar alone (in its reference to Charles's 'persecution at the hands of your brother [Lothar]'), the preface

---

[78] Nithard IV, 6, p. 142; *VK* c. 18, pp. 21–3; Thegan c. 4, pp. 178–80; Astronomer c. 8, pp. 306–8, and c. 32, p. 392.
[79] Birth and power struggles: Nithard I, 3, p. 8; failure of godparenthood, II, 1, p. 38, and 2, p. 40, III, 3, p. 92; Charles and Bernard: I, 3, p. 10, II, 5, p. 50, III, 1, pp. 82–4, Charles's coming of age, etc.: I, 6, p. 26.
[80] Nelson, 'Public *Histories*', pp. 208–9, 212, 225.
[81] Nithard IV, 7, p. 144, which explains the gloomy significance of Charlemagne's death, as part of its tight reference back to I, 1, p. 4, and which, in its evocation of Charlemagne as ideal king, echoes other references to Charlemagne, I, 2, p. 4, IV, 2, p. 120; see also his preface to Book IV, which he labels as a 'fourth book', i.e., as a part of a larger whole, and in this preface Nithard deploys the same language as his preface to Book I to describe his task as author: 'facta ... stili officio memoriae mandare', p. 116; cf. p. 2: 'gestas stili officio memorie traderem'.
[82] Nelson, 'Public *Histories*', p. 225.

to Book III referred in more general terms to a bad reputation of 'our family', the Carolingian family.[83]

Nithard's account in Book IV of the next milestone in Charles' young life unfolded under this sign of discontent. This was Charles' marriage. Einhard, Thegan and the Astronomer generally depicted the marriage of their protagonists in positive terms, highlighting the noble ancestry of the king's wife, or going on to list the children of the marriage and thus highlighting its dynastic success.[84] There are some exceptions to this; Thegan, for example, omits any reference to the birth of Charles the Bald in his account of Louis the Pious' marriage to Judith, though he emphasises that Judith was nobly born.[85] In comparison with such accounts Nithard is strikingly terse. He gives the name of Charles' bride, Ermentrude, and that of her parents, but distinguishes none of them by a noble epithet, and he fails to mention here that Ermentrude's father had been a count, or that he died in Louis' service in the crisis of 833–4. In fact he had mentioned all this earlier in his *Histories*, but he chooses not to refer back to that. Instead, he launches another attack on Adalhard, who was Ermentrude's uncle, and in doing so he refers back again to the reign of Louis the Pious as an era when self-seeking magnates such as Adalhard harmed the public good and dominated a weak ruler.[86] Nor does he go on to refer to any children of Charles and Ermentrude. Such children would not have been born when Nithard finished writing, but Nithard's omission of reference to any future offspring seems to be part of his terse disapproval of the union (contrast this with Notker of St Gall's later expressions of hope for dynastic continuity in a historical text written for a Carolingian monarch).[87] Nithard takes care to place Charles' wedding in a harsh and sterile winter landscape from which any prospect of spring is glaringly absent, just as the public order descends into chaotic self-seeking. He ends his *Histories* with a description of a lengthy winter and a lunar eclipse, and eclipses portended disturbance in the body politic.[88]

Much of this gloom stemmed from Nithard's own situation. He had lost out in the redistributing of properties and offices that accompanied the making of the treaty of Verdun in 842–3. We cannot therefore assume that Nithard's testimony is representative of the attitudes of Charles'

---

[83] Nithard, preface, p. 2; III, preface, p. 78.
[84] *VK* c. 18, pp. 21–3; Thegan c. 4, pp. 178–80; Astronomer c. 8, pp. 306–8, and c. 32, p. 392.
[85] Thegan c. 26, p. 214.   [86] Nithard IV, 6, p. 142; and see I, 5, p. 20 for Ermentrude's father Odo.
[87] Notker, *Gesta Karoli* II, 11 and 14, pp. 68, 78.
[88] Nithard IV, 6–7, pp. 142–4; compare Einhard on solar and lunar eclipses as signs of Charlemagne's approaching end, *VK* c. 32, p. 36; see also Astronomer c. 31, p. 388, and c. 62, pp. 544–6.

followers, let alone of the secular aristocracy as a whole. His articulateness, his literary skill, and his high-minded anger at the failure of kings and great magnates to live up to appropriate standards of public behaviour may have made him a member of the awkward squad; it is tempting to think that strong views strongly held may not be the mark of a successful courtier. But Nithard was not an isolated figure. His narrative showed ideals being challenged and failing, but these were the same ideals that occupied his lay contemporaries such as Dhuoda and Adalhard. This means that he wrote a language that could be understood, even if what he said in it was extreme. Janet Nelson argued persuasively in 1985 that Nithard's Book IV was so pessimistic and hostile to Charles the Bald that it could not have been written for him, but she argued even more persuasively in 1993 that it was precisely because Nithard had specific contemporary points to make that he envisioned Charles and his court as an audience.[89] We have seen that Nithard came to conceive of his work as a whole, and so, although its meaning had changed, it could retain its character as a public work. He wrote in no isolated vacuum; he was anxious to communicate, though it is unlikely that his text in fact circulated at all widely. As cousin of Charles the Bald, Nithard criticised the grounds for the former's marriage, just as another cousin of another Charles had done some generations previously, when Adalhard, future abbot of Corbie, had questioned the validity of Charlemagne's abandonment of his Lombard wife and subsequent marriage to Hildegard.[90] Adalhard had fallen into disfavour because of this, but he had returned to the great king's good graces. Nithard's untimely death cut short whatever career he could have gone on to have at Charles' court.

Nithard was offering his contemporaries a bleak vision of the contemporary political scene. But, despite his idealising of the reign of Charlemagne, Nithard was no mere *laudator temporis acti*. His picture of Adalbert, of Adalhard, of Bernard, of a host of faithless magnates, of Lothar, of Louis the Pious' weakness, of the wrong path Charles seemed to be taking, all this was not in fact simply a picture of a world collapsing. It was a picture of a world in crisis, but it was also an account of positive values in action in contemporary history, values ranging from complex ones

---

[89] Nelson, 'Public *Histories*', p. 225; Nelson, 'History-writing at the courts of Louis the Pious and Charles the Bald', p. 440.
[90] Paschasius Radbertus, *Vita Adalhardi* c. 7, *PL* 120, col. 1511. My thanks to the participants at Kalamazoo for their comments on an earlier and sketchier version of this paper. My gratitude to Patrick Wormald for inviting me to participate in the 'Lay Intellectuals' project is only part of my immense debt to him.

of good rule and the public weal to the simpler, more straightforwardly heroic ones of taking care to leave a good name to posterity. As such it was a call to action. Its vision of what had gone wrong in the past was such an intense one that it could serve as a warning for the future. The content of Nithard's text showed clearly the role of *force majeure* and bad faith in the Carolingian political world. But the sheer fact of the *Histories*' existence suggests something of the sophistication of that world. He was a public intellectual.

CHAPTER 5

Eberhard of Friuli, a Carolingian lay intellectual

Paul J. E. Kershaw

Eberhard, margrave of Friuli, was not a man who needed to learn about war from a book.[1] As a loyal ally of Lothar, it is highly probable that he served alongside him at that most traumatic of Carolingian battles, Fontenoy, in June 841, and certain that he played his part in the diplomacy that followed its carnage.[2] Several years later, in response to the Arab attack upon Rome in autumn 844, Lothar and his son Louis II organized the funding of firmer urban defences for Rome, the so-called Leonine City, and despatched an expeditionary force against the *inimici Christi*, the 'Saracens and Moors' of the Italian south.[3] The force was split into three *scarae*, each of which fell under the command of a number of *missi*.[4] The names of these field commanders were carefully listed in three columns at the close of the council's

---

[1] For Eberhard's life and family see C. La Rocca and L. Provero, 'The Dead and Their Gifts: The Will of Eberhard, Count of Friuli, and his Wife, Gisela, Daughter of Louis the Pious (863–864)', in F. Theuws and J. L. Nelson, eds., *Rituals of Power from Late Antiquity to the Early Middle Ages*, The Transformation of the Roman World 8 (Leiden, 2000), pp. 225–80; H. Krahwinkler, *Friaul im Frühmittelalter: Geschichte einer Region vom Ende des fünften bis zum Ende des zehnten Jahrhunderts*, Veröffentlichungen des Instituts für österreichische Geschichtsforschung 30 (Vienna, 1992), pp. 245–66; I. Fees, 'Eberardo', *Dizionario Biografico degli Italiani* (Rome, 1993), 42, pp. 252–5. All three offer comprehensive references to earlier studies. E. Dümmler, 'Fünf Gedichte des Sedulius Scottus an den Markgrafen Eberhard von Friaul', *Jahrbuch für vaterländische Geschichte* 1 (1891), pp. 167–88, remains valuable.
[2] Nithard IV, 3, p. 124. Fontenoy's impact is discussed by J. L. Nelson, 'The Ritualisation of Violence in the Ninth Century', in G. Halsall, ed., *Violence in Early Medieval Society* (Woodbridge, 1997), pp. 90–107; and see also her 'The Search for Peace in a Time of War: The Carolingian *Brüderkrieg*, 841–843', in J. Fried, ed., *Träger und Instrumentarien des Friedens im Hohen und Späten Mittelalter*, Vorträge und Forschungen 43 (1996), pp. 87–114.
[3] W. Hartmann, ed., *Die Konzilien der karolingischen Teilreiche 843–859*, MGH Conc. III (Hanover, 1984), no. 12, *c*. 9, pp. 133–9, 'Sarracenos et Mauros'; on which see L. Dupraz, 'Le capitulaire de Lothaire I, empereur, De expeditione contra Sarracenos facienda, et la Suisse romande (847)', *Zeitschrift für Schweizerische Geschichte* 15 (1936), pp. 241–93, at 250–92. Carolingian activities in southern Italy in the late 840s are analysed by B. M. Kreutz, *Before the Normans: Southern Italy in the Ninth and Tenth Centuries* (Philadelphia, PA, 1991), pp. 26–35; G. Musca, *L'emirato di Bari 847–871* (Bari, 1978), pp. 15–31. On Rome's defences see K. Herbers, *Leo IV. und das Papsttum in der Mitte des 9. Jahrhunderts: Möglichkeiten und Grenzen päpstlicher Herrschaft in der späten Karolingerzeit*, Päpste und Papsttum 27 (Stuttgart, 1996), pp. 135–52, with extensive references.
[4] *Konzilien*, no. 12, *c*. 13, pp. 138–9.

text.⁵ Eberhard's name stood at the head of the *prima scara*'s roster, a position that strongly suggests that it fell to him to spearhead the expeditionary force's drive into Arab-dominated territory. The campaigns that followed and the complex negotiations between the warring Lombard duchies of Benevento and Salerno, if not decisive in arresting Arab activity in southern Italy, showed at least that in the mid-ninth century the Carolingians could campaign effectively south of Rome. Eberhard's prominent place in the expeditions against the Arabs of southern Italy would be fêted in poetry in his lifetime, remembered after his death at his and his wife's foundation, the Picard monastery of Cysoing, and pass into the collective identity of his family, the so-called Unruochings.⁶ His son, Berengar, future king of Italy, would allude to it in his own actions and ideology.⁷

Eberhard held lands across the Carolingian territories, and succeeded in retaining them across the division of 843: no small achievement.⁸ Some came from his father, Unruoch, an intimate of Charlemagne in the later years of the emperor's life, presumably passing to Eberhard when Unruoch withdrew from secular life to the cloister of St-Bertin, where he was to die in 853.⁹ Other holdings came with his marriage to Gisela, the daughter

---

⁵ *Konzilien*, no. 12, c. 13, p. 139: 'In prima scara sunt missi: Ebrardus...' For the other *missi* see Krahwinkler, *Friaul*, pp. 255–6. For the *scara*'s place in Carolingian warfare, G. Halsall, *Warfare and Society in the Barbarian West, 450–900* (London, 2003), pp. 54, 76, 150, 152; B. Bachrach, *Early Carolingian Warfare: Prelude to Empire* (Philadelphia, PA, 2002), pp. 80–2, 191–5.

⁶ Kreutz, *Italy*, pp. 27–40. As the resting place of relics of Pope Calixtus I (217–22), Cysoing itself symbolised Eberhard's relationship with Rome, *Translatio S. Calixti Cisonium*, ed. O. Holder-Egger, *MGH SS* xv (Hanover, 1887), pp. 418–22. His military achievements in the south are described, c. 3, p. 419: 'Nam sepe adversum Ismahelitas atque Agarenos, qui se Sarracenos gloriantur, dimicans contraque Numidarum ac Maurorum sevissimos populos resistens fortiter, non modicum ex ipsis reportaverat triumphum.' On the identification of the Arabs with Ishmael and Hagar see J. V. Tolan, *Saracens: Islam in the Medieval European Imagination* (New York, 2002), pp. 10–14, 71–104. Rome would, in turn, preserve some memory of Eberhard, see John VIII's letter to Berengar of April 878, ed. E. Caspar, *MGH Epp.* VII, 2 vols. (Berlin, 1912–28), no. 74, pp. 69–71, at 69.

⁷ B. Rosenwein, 'A Gift-Giving King', in *Negotiating Space: Power, Restraint and Privileges of Immunity in Early Medieval Europe* (Ithaca, 1999), pp. 137–55, at 142, citing A. A. Settia, 'Églises et fortifications médiévales dans l'Italie du nord', in his *Chiese, Strade e Fortrezze nell'Italia Medievale Italia Sacra*, Studi e documenti di storia ecclesiastica 46 (Rome, 1991), pp. 81–94.

⁸ On Eberhard's landholding after 843 see R. Le Jan, *Famille et pouvoir dans le monde franc (VIIe–Xe siècles): Essai d'anthropologie sociale* (Paris, 1995), p. 74 (map); P. Geary, *Phantoms of Remembrance: Memory and Oblivion at the End of the First Millennium* (Princeton, NJ, 1995), pp. 48–9; S. Airlie, 'The Aristocracy', *NCMH* II, pp. 431–50, at 436. However, for Eberhard's loss of at least some holdings in northern Austrasia later in the ninth century see La Rocca and Provero, 'The Dead', p. 265; P. Grierson, 'La maison d'Evrard de Frioul et les origines du comté de Flandres', *Revue du Nord* 24 (1938), pp. 241–66, at 442, both discussing I. de Coussemaker, ed., *Cartulaire de l'abbaye de Cysoing et de ses dépendances* (Lille, 1883), no. 3, p. 7 (hereafter *Cysoing*).

⁹ R. Hennebicque-Le Jan, 'Prosopographica neustrica: Les agents du roi en Neustrie de 639 à 840', *La Neustrie* I (1989), pp. 231–69, at 257.

of Louis the Pious and Judith, around 836.[10] Eberhard had particular responsibility for overseeing Friuli, one of the Carolingians' most sensitive frontiers. This was historically charged territory. It had been the base for the Avar campaigns of the 790s, and was the doorway to the Slavic lands of Istria and Dalmatia, territories caught between the Carolingians and Byzantium which came increasingly under Frankish cultural and political dominance in the course of the ninth century.[11] Bitter experience had taught Carolingian kings that such a key zone demanded a capable leader.[12] Eberhard's appointment as margrave of Friuli, and his leading position in the southern Italian campaigns of the later 840s show that he was seen as such by both Louis the Pious and, later, by Lothar. Their opinion was shared by the anonymous author of the *translatio* of Calixtus' relics to Cysoing, writing in the late 860s.[13] From his northern Austrasian perspective, Eberhard was a man expressly associated with the defence of these far Carolingian frontiers: a *marginalis miles* on the *limes*.[14]

---

[10] On Eberhard's landholding see La Rocca and Provero, 'The Dead', pp. 235–8, 245–9; Grierson, 'Identity', pp. 437–61; Dümmler, 'Fünf Gedichte', pp. 171–2.

[11] Krahwinkler, *Friaul*, pp. 148–58. On Carolingian influence beyond Friuli see J. Osborne, 'Politics, Diplomacy and the Cult of Relics in Venice and the Northern Adriatic in the First Half of the Ninth Century', *EME* 8 (1999), pp. 369–86, at 382–6; *Croatia in the Early Middle Ages: A Cultural Survey*, ed. I. I. Supičić (London, 1999), pp. 117–37, 169–75, 197–204, 239–45, with substantial treatments of the archaeological and epigraphic evidence for Frankish influence along the Dalmatian coast; D. Obolensky, 'The Balkans in the Ninth Century: Barrier or Bridge?', *Byzantinische Forschungen* 13 (1988), pp. 47–66, at 63–6; J. V. Fine, *The Early Medieval Balkans: A Critical Survey from the Sixth to the Late Eleventh Centuries* (Ann Arbor, MI, 1983), pp. 248–6. On the presence of Croatian ruling family names in the Cividale Evangeliary see U. Ludwig, *Studien zu den transalpinen Beziehungen der Karolingerzeit im Spiegel der Memorialüberlieferung: Prosopographische und sozialgeschichtliche Untersuchungen unter besonderer Berücksichtigung des liber vitae von S. Salvatore in Brescia und des Evangeliars von Cividale* (Hanover, 1991), pp. 218, 221–5.

[12] On the military failure and subsequent dismissal of an earlier *dux* of Friuli, Balderic, for failing to prevent a Bulgar incursion see *ARF* s.a. 828, p. 174; Krahwinkler, *Friaul*, pp. 192–7. For Carolingian frontiers see J. M. H. Smith, '*Fines imperii*: The Marches', *NCMH* II, pp. 169–89, with references; K. F. Werner, '*Missus - marchio - comes*: Entre l'administration centrale et l' administration locale de l'empire carolingien', in W. Paravicini and K. F. Werner, eds., *Histoire comparée de l'administration (IVe–XVIIIe siècle)*, Beihefte der Francia 9 (Munich, 1980), pp. 191–239.

[13] S. Lorenz, 'Papst Calixt I (217–222): Translationen und Verbreitung seines Reliquienkultes bis ins 12. Jahrhundert', in K. Herbers, H.-H. Körtum and C. Servatius, eds., *Ex ipsis rerum documentis: Beiträge zur Mediävistik. Festschrift für Harald Zimmermann* (Sigmaringen, 1991), pp. 213–32, at 221–6. On the Frankish appropriation of Roman relics more generally see J. Osborne, 'The Roman Catacombs in the Middle Ages', *Papers of the British School at Rome* 53 (1985), pp. 278–328, esp. 292–5; P. J. Geary, 'The Ninth-Century Relic Trade: A Response to Popular Piety?', in J. Obelkevich, ed., *Religion and People, 800–1700* (Chapel Hill, NC, 1979), pp. 8–19.

[14] *Translatio S. Calixti* c. 3, p. 419. Ninth-century Carolingian frontier culture is assayed by E. J. Goldberg, '"More Devoted to the Equipment of Battle than the Splendor of Banquets": Frontier Kingship, Martial Ritual, and Early Knighthood at the Court of Louis the German', *Viator* 30 (1999), pp. 41–78, at 45–6.

It was, however, a book aimed at teaching the rudiments of military organisation and tactics, Vegetius' late antique manual of military science, the *Epitoma rei militaris*, that Hartgar, bishop of Liège, sent to Eberhard some time after his return from southern Italy.[15] The gift is indicative of an ongoing closeness between the bishopric of Liège and Eberhard's family, a relationship documented in Sedulius' poetry and probably grounded in their landholdings in Condroz and Hesbaye, close to Liège and within the diocese of St-Lambert.[16] Vegetius' text was prefaced in the manuscript by a dedicatory poem written in Hartgar's *persona* but composed by Sedulius Scottus, the Irish *peregrinus* who by the late 840s was well established as the house poet of the episcopal *familia* of St-Lambert.[17] Sedulius was clear why Hartgar's choice of this late antique military manual made an appropriate gift for Eberhard. 'Whatever of the art of war the world knows anywhere in its orb', he wrote, 'here are all contained in [these] new treasures.'[18]

Eberhard's career made him a man with proven knowledge of the art of war in the world and so the *Epitoma* was a suitable gift. Several years earlier Freculf of Lisieux had presented a copy to Eberhard's brother-in-law, Charles the Bald, a royal association that may well have heightened the gift's appeal to both donor and recipient.[19] This was not, as we shall see, the first time that

---

[15] On the text of Vegetius available to Eberhard see V. Von Büren and J. Meyers, 'Quelques poèmes inédits de Sedulius Scottus dans le Codex Vaticanus Latinus 4493?', *Bulletin du Cange* 57 (1999), pp. 53–110, at 53–71. For the wider question of Vegetius' reception in the early Middle Ages see M. D. Reeve, 'The Transmission of Vegetius's *Epitoma rei militaris*', *Aevum* 74 (2000), pp. 243–354, esp. 249–73, building upon the findings of C. R. Shrader, 'A Handlist of Extant Manuscripts Containing the *De Re Militari* of Flavius Vegetius Renatus', *Scriptorium* 33 (1979), pp. 280–305. See also Bachrach, *Warfare*, pp. 84–132, and P. Richardot, *Végèce et la culture militaire au moyen Âge (Ve–XVe siècles)* (Paris, 1998), pp. 43–5, 77–8, 86, 195.

[16] La Rocca and Provero, 'The Dead', p. 246; Dümmler, 'Fünf Gedichte', p. 172. On Carolingian Liège see S. Tada, 'The Creation of a Religious Centre: Christianization in the Diocese of Liège in the Carolingian Period', *JEH* 54 (2003), pp. 209–27, A. Dierkens, 'La Christianisation des campagnes de l'Empire de Louis le Pieux: L'example du diocèse de Liège sous l'épiscopat de Walcaud (*c.* 809–*c.* 831)', in *Charlemagne's Heir*, pp. 309–29, with references.

[17] Sedulius Scottus, *Carmina*, ed. I. Meyers, *CCCM* 107 (1991), no. 53, pp. 90–1 (hereafter *Carmina*). The argument of Von Büren, 'Quelques poèmes', pp. 67–9, that the donor of the book and poem was Hincmar not Hartgar seems unwarranted. On Sedulius Scottus' continental career, see D. N. Dumville, *Three Men in a Boat: Scribe, Language and Culture in the Church of Viking-Age Europe* (Cambridge, 1997), pp. 28, 39–46; cf. P. Godman, *Poets and Emperors* (Oxford, 1987), pp. 155–65, 167–70.

[18] *Carmina* 53, pp. 90–1, at p. 90, ll. 17–18: 'Quicquid belligerae mundus sapit artis in orbe,/ Hic in thesauris condita cuncta novis.' My translation differs somewhat from that in E. G. Doyle, *Sedulius Scottus: On Christian Rulers and the Poems*, Medieval and Renaissance Texts and Studies 17 (New York, 1983), at pp. 149–50. For commentary see R. Düchting, *Sedulius Scottus: Seine Dichtungen* (Munich, 1968), pp. 158–61.

[19] *Ad Epistolas variorum supplementum* no. 4, ed. E. Dümmler, *MGH Epp.* v (1898–99), pp. 618–19, discussed by M. I. Allen, *Freculfi Lexoviensis Episcopi Opera Omnia, Prolegomena, Indices* (Brepols, 2002), pp. 25–53, discussing dating and purpose at 25–8.

Eberhard acquired a work of which another copy had already been presented to a member of the royal house. The rest of Sedulius' dedicatory poem, however, belied any awareness of Eberhard's military experience, as his attention was drawn to the more sensational elements of the manual: *ballistae*, battering rams, scythed chariots and war elephants. The directing of Eberhard's eye to these passages, presented as a set of vivid images rather than sections of text, hints that Sedulius may have sought to guide him through an illustrated copy.[20] Was the volume intended to have a practical application, beyond its immediate function of reminding Eberhard of his loyal friends in Liège? Perhaps so. Siege warfare was a major part of the Franks' campaigns in the urbanised Italian south, and characteristic of Frankish warfare in Islamic territories more generally.[21] Moreover, since Abûl Abbas arrived in Aachen in 802, the gift of Hârûn al-Rashîd, elephants may well have been associated in some Carolingian minds with Muslim military power.[22] More specifically, Vegetius numbered amongst the users of war elephants the Numidians, a people that classicising Carolingians, including the author of the *Translatio Sancti Calixti*, identified with the Arabs of southern Italy.[23] We know nothing of Eberhard's immediate response to the gift. However, in the will he was to have drawn up with his wife Gisela in 864 a *liber rei militaris*, surely the same book as Hartgar's gift, was bequeathed to Unruoch, the couple's eldest surviving son.[24] If Vegetius' text held questionable utility for a seasoned *miles* such as Eberhard, he himself seems to have seen it as a text capable of teaching valuable lessons about warfare to his less experienced *primogenitus*, heir to his frontier lands.[25]

The *Epitoma* was far from being Eberhard's only book: no fewer than sixty-three volumes, each allotted to one of their eight children, are listed in

---

[20] For example, *Carmina* 53, ll. 5–8: 'Triplex bellorum hic splendidus ordo coruscat/Milibus armigeris martia bella ciens./Hic tuba terribili sonitu clangore remugit;/Praecipites scopulos carroballista serit.'

[21] See, for example, Ermoldus Nigellus' account of Louis the Pious' siege of Barcelona, in Ermold, pp. 26–47, ll. 302–571. Early medieval siege warfare is discussed more generally by Halsall, *Warfare*, pp. 223–7; cf. J. Bradbury, *The Medieval Siege* (Woodbridge, 1998), pp. 31–7. For Sedulius' praise of Eberhard's involvement in siege warfare see *Carmina* 39, p. 69, lines 25–8.

[22] ARF s.a. 802, 810, pp. 117, 131; p. E. Schramm and F. Mütherich, *Denkmale der deutschen Könige und Kaiser* (Munich, 1962), I, pp. 78–9; M. Borgolte, *Der Gesandtenaustausch der Karolinger mit den Abbasiden und mit den Patriarchen von Jerusalem*, Münchener Beiträge zur Mediävistik und Renaissance-Forschung 25 (Munich, 1976), pp. 46–61, 76–95.

[23] See above n. 14.   [24] *Cysoing* no. 1, p. 3.

[25] *Cysoing* no. 1, p. 1: 'Primogenitus namque noster Unruoch volumus ut habeat quicquid in Langobardia et in Alamannia de proprietate habere videmur…', La Rocca and Provero, 'The Dead', p. 256. For contemporary perceptions of Vegetius' practical value, see Hrabanus Maurus' dedicatory letter to his epitome (for Lothar II) of the work's opening section, ed. Dümmler, *MGH Epp.* III, no. 57, pp. 514–15, at 515. For the text of Hrabanus' 'quaedam capitula de disciplina Romanae militiae', see E. Dümmler, '*De procinctu Romanae militiae*', *Zeitschrift für deutsches Alterthum* 15 (Berlin, 1872), pp. 443–5.

his and Gisela's will, making it the largest recorded Carolingian book collection in lay hands, albeit only visible in the plans for its dispersal.[26] The existence of these books, kept in the household chapel, has meant that in many scholars' eyes Eberhard and, more recently, Gisela herself, have been included in the select group of learned Carolingian layfolk.[27] There is room for caution. In the ninth century the possession of books no more made a man learned than the possession of weapons made him a warrior, something the poet Ermoldus Nigellus sheepishly admitted when recounting his own hapless participation in the Breton campaigns of the mid 820s.[28] Unlike Einhard, Angilbert or Nithard (in whose presence he must, on occasion, have found himself), Eberhard has left us no writings that earn him automatic admission to the learned's ranks.[29] Indeed, the will apart, only a single piece of text survives that might be attributed to him. Written on the lower right-hand corner of the last folio of an eighth-century double psalter (Vatican MS Reg. Lat. II) amidst a number of later pen-trials are the words 'Evvrardus. s(ubscripsi?)', in a stiff and deliberate cursive.[30] Some scholars at least have accepted it as Eberhard's autograph, identifying this as the same psalter passed on in the will to Unruoch.[31] To suggest that this was Eberhard using a legal subscription to serve as a statement of ownership is to place a greater weight on this evidence than it can safely bear. Nevertheless, the conjunction of an assertion of legal

---

[26] P. Riché, 'Les bibliothèques de trois aristocrates laïcs carolingiens', *Le Moyen Age* 69 (1963), pp. 87–104, at 97–101, first drew attention to the significance of this document; see also R. McKitterick, *The Carolingians and the Written Word* (Cambridge, 1989), pp. 245–8. Both offer discussions of the books listed, with further references. There is a French translation in P. Riché and G. Tate, *Textes et documents d'histoire du Moyen Age, Ve–Xe siècles* (Paris, 1976), II, pp. 414–16. The book-list is printed by G. Becker, *Catalogi Bibliothecarum Antiqui* (Bonn, 1895), 12, pp. 29–30, omitting, however, the parts of the will listing the ten liturgical books.

[27] La Rocca and Provero, 'The Dead', pp. 234–40, make the case for the will's joint character.

[28] Ermold, p. 154, ll. 2016–8, and see below, p. 88.

[29] See the comments of Ganz and Airlie, above, pp. 37–50, 51–76.

[30] See E. A. Lowe, *Codices Latini Antiquiores: A Palaeographical Guide to Latin Manuscripts Prior to the Ninth Century*, 11 vols. (Oxford, 1935–71), I, no. 101; A. Wilmart, *Bibliothecae Apostolicae Vaticanae* (Vatican, 1938), pp. 26–30, at 29–30; L. Suttina, 'La sottoscrizione del marchese Eberardo in salterio della sua biblioteca', *Memorie Storiche Forogiuliesi* 8 (1912), pp. 300–3 ('una mano poco sicura'), with plate; and also A. Wilmart, 'Psautier de la Reine n. II: Sa provenance et sa date', *Revue Bénédictine* 28 (1911), pp. 341–76, and G. Morin, 'La provenance du psautier de la Reine et du "Missale Francorum"', *Revue Charlemagne* 2 (1912), pp. 17–29. On the group of manuscripts to which this codex belongs, see D. A. Bullough with A. Harting-Correâ, 'Text, Chant and the Chapel of Louis the Pious', in Bullough, *Carolingian Renewal: Sources and Heritage* (Manchester, 1991), pp. 241–71, at 246, 262–3; R. McKitterick, 'The *Scriptoria* of Merovingian Gaul: A Survey of the Evidence', in H. B. Clarke and M. Brennan, eds., *Columbanus and Merovingian Monasticism*, BAR International Series 113 (Oxford, 1981), pp. 173–207, at 194.

[31] Wilmart, *Bibliothecae*, p. 30; Suttina, 'Sottoscrizione', p. 303; but cf. the contrary view of Morin, 'Provenance', esp. pp. 17–19.

authority and a work of personal devotion might just capture something of Eberhard's relationship to the world of learning.

The Unruoching book collection is a familiar fixture in several accounts of Carolingian lay culture. It has, however, usually been viewed in isolation from the other evidence for Eberhard's relationship with the world of learning. My intention here is to break that quarantine, examining not only Eberhard's books but also the other evidence for his links to learning and to the learned: Sedulius Scottus (if not, perhaps, the pen-shy Hartgar), Lupus of Ferrières, Hrabanus Maurus and, most intriguingly, Gottschalk of Orbais. Eberhard also had dealings with Anastasius *bibliothecarius*, though as these seem to be based more upon imperial involvement in papal politics than intellectual interests *per se*, they are passed over here.[32] These relationships were nourished by the gift of books, poems and letters, many of which offer insights into their authors' perceptions of Eberhard. They also reveal something of the strategies which these intellectuals adopted to engage with him. Unlike Hartgar's, such strategies were not always ones of ingratiation. In this chapter, I am as much interested in the construction of the image of the learned Carolingian layman in the minds of contemporary ecclesiastics as I am in the recoverable realities of Eberhard's actual intellectual interests. Above all, what I want to suggest is that there is a discernible coherence linking these fragments of evidence, and that that coherence is best understood as a reflection of Eberhard's own intellectual concerns.

The *Epitoma* dedication was one of five poems composed by Sedulius for Eberhard and Gisela as a couple, or for Eberhard alone. For the couple Sedulius composed a *planctus* lamenting the death of their first-born son, also called Eberhard.[33] He followed it with a poem celebrating the subsequent birth of a new heir, Unruoch.[34] The portraits of Eberhard and Gisela in these *carmina* amount to miniature exercises in representing the ideals of the Carolingian *vita coniugalis*.[35] The remaining two poems concentrated upon Eberhard alone. They stressed his martial prowess, and frequent victories against the Franks' numerous pagan neighbours.[36] The first, written like the Vegetius dedication, in the wake of the campaigns in southern Italy, praised Eberhard who, with 'blazing helm', 'glorious

---

[32] Herbers, *Leo*, pp. 214–24; R. Davis, ed. and trans., *The Lives of the Ninth-Century Popes (Liber pontificalis)* (Liverpool, 1995), pp. 104–5.
[33] *Carmina* 37, p. 65.   [34] *Carmina* 38, pp. 66–7.
[35] K. Heene, *Legacy of Paradise: Marriage, Motherhood and Women in Carolingian Edifying Literature* (Berlin, 1997), pp. 61–113; P. Toubert, 'La théorie du mariage chez les moralistes carolingiens', *Il matrimonio nella società altomedioevale*, Settimane Spoleto 34 (Spoleto, 1977), pp. 233–85.
[36] *Carmina* 53, pp. 90–1; 67, pp. 109–10.

breastplate' and 'flashing sword', was an Aeneas-like *pius heros*, casting down proud Arabs.[37] The second, almost certainly later, poem celebrated Eberhard's return to Austrasia from the south. Here, however, Eberhard's arms and armour bore symbolic weight. Eberhard was armed by Christ himself. His sword and shield represented salvation, his breastplate faith and his helmet hope.[38] He was a Pauline *miles Christi* whose deeds outstripped those of Hector or Achilles. Only Gideon, wrote Sedulius, called by God to deliver the Israelites from the invading Midianites, presented an apt comparison with Eberhard.[39]

Such modulation between Virgilian motifs and Frankish Israelite self-identification places Sedulius' poetry firmly in the tradition of Carolingian panegyric.[40] It also served to place Eberhard in a specifically Friulian context, for it evoked an earlier scholar's image of an earlier margrave: Paulinus of Aquileia's treatment of Heiric of Friuli as a Christian warrior in his *Liber exhortationis*.[41] Like Paulinus, Sedulius envisaged his subject as a warrior in both spiritual and physical senses, struggling for earthly victories with earthly weapons, but seeking simultaneously to triumph over sin and temptation through the cultivation of virtue. Jean Meyers has made a compelling case for Sedulius' very careful selection of words, phrases and allusion, and his 'tailoring' of poems for their particular recipients, based upon his assessment of their ability to recognise and enjoy their textual echoes and borrowings embedded in the poem. In Meyers' persuasive formulation, Sedulius' poems were, in effect, invitations to cultural complicity.[42] If Meyers is correct to see this level of thought at work in Sedulius'

---

[37] *Carmina* 39, ll. 5–16, pp. 68–70.   [38] *Carmina* 67, ll. 15–16, p. 109.

[39] *Carmina* 67, lines 17–18, p. 109. For the counterpoint of Aeneas and St Paul in Carolingian thought, and its roots in Arator's *De Actibus Apostolorum*, see H. Kessler, 'An Apostle in Armor and the Mission of Carolingian Art', *Arte medievale* 2 ser. 4 (1989), pp. 17–41, at p. 29. Paul's *miles Christi* (Ephesians 6: 10–17) is discussed in its ninth-century context by E. Sears, 'Louis the Pious as *Miles Christi*: The Dedicatory Image in Hrabanus Maurus's *De laudibus sanctae crucis*', in *Charlemagne's Heir*, pp. 605–28, at pp. 617–18.

[40] The literature on these issues is vast, but entry points include L. Nees, *A Tainted Mantle: Hercules and the Classical Tradition at the Carolingian Court* (Philadelphia, PA, 1991), pp. 42–3, n. 45; Godman, *Poets*, pp. 75, 82–8, 146, and M. Garrison, 'The Franks as the New Israel: Education for an Identity from Pippin to Charlemagne', in Y. Hen and M. Innes, eds., *The Uses of the Past in: the Early Middle Ages* (Cambridge, 2000), pp. 114–61, at 148–54. For Sedulius' blending of Virgilian motifs with those of Scripture see D. M. Kratz, *Mocking Epic: Waltharius, Alexandreis and the Problem of Christian Heroism* (Madrid, 1980), pp. 1–13.

[41] Paulinus, *Liber exhortationis* c. 20, *PL* 99, cols. 212–14, 'miles spiritalis et terrenus'. Regrettably, A. De Nicola, 'Sancti Paulini Patriarchae Aquileiensis *Liber exhortationis*: Editio critica', *Atti e Memorie della Società Istriana di Archeologia e Storia Patria* 101 (2001), pp. 187–214, edits only chapters 1–9 of the work.

[42] Simpson, 'Sedulius', p. 26; J. Meyers, *L'art de l'emprunt dans la poésie de Sedulius Scottus* (Liège, 1986), esp. pp. 201–4.

poetry, Sedulius' portrait of Eberhard carried a double message. Explicitly it praised him as a warrior, yet in its allusions to classical texts and scripture, it flattered Eberhard the learned layman, at home with his Virgil and the historical books of Scripture, capable of tracing Sedulius' web of allusion.[43]

Hartgar's gift was not the first book Eberhard received whose contents sought to meet the demands of secular life. In the 830s Lupus of Ferrières compiled a collection of laws for him, prefaced with two poems.[44] In the first, Lupus made it clear that the compilation was the result of Eberhard's initiative; 'Eberhard had this book of laws written.'[45] Whilst Sedulius was to praise Eberhard's *martius ardor*, Lupus, as befitting a dedication to a book of law, focused upon his *prudentia*:[46] 'Whoever loves knowledge of all cases that the laws concern, and wishes himself to seem lucid as a judge to all, will eagerly and longingly explore it with eyes and mind.'[47] Lupus proceeded to draw Eberhard's attention to its contents, a series of illustrations of the various peoples of the empire, Salic and Ripuarian Franks, Lombards, Alamans and Bavarians, each of which preceded the texts of their respective law-codes.[48] These were followed by portraits of Charles with Pippin of Italy, and Louis the Pious with Lothar. Their respective capitularies followed.[49] All commentators agree that this was a volume intended to have a practical purpose.[50] At points Lupus even reordered and rubricated the codes in order to facilitate easy referencing.[51] Moreover, as Patrick Wormald has pointed out, the addition of legislation of Louis II

---

[43] For a comparable use, see the view of Garrison, 'The Study of Emotions in Early Medieval History: Some Starting Points', *EME* 10 (2001), pp. 244–7.
[44] O. Münsch, *Der Liber legum des Lupus von Ferrières*, Freiburger Beiträge zur Mittelalterlichen Geschichte 14 (Frankfurt-am-Main, 2001) now provides a full edition and commentary, and gives a profile of Eberhard at pp. 57–63; Wormald, *Making*, pp. 30–63, discussing the manuscripts at 54–6; H. Mordek, *Bibliotheca capitularium regum Francorum manuscripta: Überlieferung und Traditionszusammenhang der fränkischen Herrschererlasse*, MGH Hilfsmittel 15 (Munich, 1995). Hubert Mordek made a case for linking Lupus' work with the negotiations of Louis and Lothar, and with Eberhard's marriage to Gisela (836), 'Frühmittelalterliche Gesetzgeber und *iustitia* in Miniaturen weltlicher Rechtshandschriften', *La giustizia nell'alto Medioevo (secoli V–VIII)*, Settimane Spoleto 44 (1995), pp. 997–1052, at 1047–8.
[45] Ed. K. Strecker, *MGH Poet.* IV (Berlin, 1923), p. 1059, ll. 1–2, 'heros librum conscribere fecit,/ Evrardus prudens prudentibus omnia vexit'.
[46] 'Martius ardor', *Carmina* 67, l. 7, p. 109. On the virtues in Carolingian thought, S. Mähl, *Quadriga Virtutum: Die Kardinaltugenden in der Geistesgeschichte der Karolingerzeit* (Cologne, 1969).
[47] Ed. Strecker, p. 1059, ll. 3–5: 'Quisquis amat cunctas legum cognoscere causas/Arbiter et clarus vult omnibus ipse videri,/Hunc avidus cupiens oculis a<ni>moque requirat.' The translation cited is Wormald's, *Making*, p. 32.
[48] Mordek, 'Gesetzgeber', pp. 1035–49, with plates.   [49] Mordek, *Bibliotheca*, pp. 256–68.
[50] Wormald, *Making*, pp. 54–6; F. Bougard, *La justice dans le royaume d'Italie de la fin du VIIIe siècle au début du XIe* (Rome, 1995), pp. 47–8; McKitterick, *Carolingians*, pp. 39–40.
[51] Wormald, *Making*, pp. 32–6.

from 865 in the two surviving manuscripts of this so-called *Liber legum*, in one case preceded by Louis' legislation of the 850s, suggests it was kept to hand by Eberhard and periodically 'up-dated' to retain its utility in a society, northern Italy, where a knowledge of written law was widespread.[52] With its geographic span, and functional format, this was just the type of book the young Eberhard might have wanted when taking his place as a participant in a political culture created by the very rulers who stared back at him from the *Liber*'s pages, and as a landowner whose disparate lands were tenanted by people living under the laws that the book contained.

The *Liber legum*'s images of fathers and sons as legislators and judges are suggestive. It is worth considering their associations in Eberhard's own life. Wormald has rightly stressed the exceptional character of his request for a lawbook from Lupus, seeing in it evidence of his closeness to the main currents of Carolingian *renovatio*: 'Were any layman likely to have taken on board the full ramifications of the Carolingian programme, it would have been he.'[53] One of the key reasons for this was his immediate family environment. Eberhard was born into a household that took Charlemagne's cultural goals and written prescriptions very seriously indeed. Unruoch was close to Charlemagne in the years after 800, witnessing his will, and playing his part, as would his son, in Frankish dealings with hostile neighbours. He kept Saxon hostages, and made treaties with the Danes.[54] He was also a vocal proponent of Carolingian *correctio*.[55] At Liège in March 806 Unruoch, together with several other *missi*, issued a letter to a number of local counts exhorting them to obey the orders of their bishop, Hartgar's predecessor Ghaerbald, observe the rights of the emperor, re-read their capitularies, judge impartially and keep the written admonition itself close to them as a reminder of their obligations.[56] The letter captures something of the tone of exasperation present in Charlemagne's own later capitularies, and with it something of Unruoch's commitment to his ruler's programme.[57] With the *Liber legum* to hand Eberhard would have been well placed to follow his father's

---

[52] *Making*, p. 55; C. Wickham, 'Lombard-Carolingian Italy, 700–900', in W. Davies and P. Fouracre, eds., *The Settlement of Disputes in Early Medieval Europe* (Cambridge, 1986), pp. 105–24, at 112–13.
[53] *Making*, p. 56.   [54] *ARF* s.a. 811, p. 134; *MGH Capit.* I, no. 115, pp. 233–4, l. 21.
[55] For the backdrop of this, see J. L. Nelson, 'The Voice of Charlemagne', in R. Gameson and H. Leyser, eds., *Belief and Culture in the Middle Ages: Studies Presented to Henry Mayr-Harting* (Oxford, 2001), pp. 76–88, at 77–8; P. Fouracre, 'Carolingian Justice: the Rhetoric of Improvement and Contexts of Abuse', *La Giustizia nell'alto medioevo*, Settimane Spoleto 44, 2 vols. (Spoleto, 1997), I, pp. 771–803.
[56] *MGH Capit.* I, no. 85, pp. 183–4; P. D. King, *Charlemagne: Translated Sources* (Kendal 1986), pp. 258–9; Dierkens, 'Christianisation', pp. 314–15.
[57] *MGH Capit.* I, no. 58, pp. 145–6; Nelson, 'Voice', pp. 80–1.

injunction. In his relations with the bishopric of Liège, in his dealings with *exterae gentes* and evident concern for written law, Eberhard was very much his father's son. So, too, his brother Berengar, whom Thegan, deploying a word he used sparingly, repeatedly labelled *sapiens*.[58] The third of Unruoch's sons, Adalhard, became abbot of St-Bertin in 844, where he oversaw the production of its polyptych, and, in 861, abbot of St-Amand.[59] Learning and practical wisdom were family matters for the Unruochings.

The possibilities of paternal influence lead us to issues of intellectual formation, and the question of Eberhard's education. The books examined so far, one on warfare the other on law, signal the demands Carolingian society placed upon men, like Eberhard, involved in Carolingian 'public' life, what his contemporary Hildemar of Civate called the '*schola humani servitii*'.[60] Such demands shaped the time and effort laymen could invest in learning.[61] Life-cycle also played its part. Youth and old age offered themselves as times when laymen could devote sustained time to learning.[62] During adult life the time available for study of any sort could be short, and the demands made upon a layman distracting. Einhard's account of Charlemagne listening to 'histories, or the deeds of the ancients' whilst eating, and keeping his wax tablets in his bedroom, 'so that if he had any free time he might accustom his hand to forming letters' hints at this.[63] At its worst the demands of lay life could lead a layman to ponder whether it was even possible to live a good Christian life.

Alcuin composed his work on virtues and vices for another marcher lord, Wido, to calm precisely such fears.[64] Sedulius Scottus saw something of

---

[58] Thegan cc. 54, 58, pp. 248, 254. P. Depreux, *Prosopographie de l'entourage de Louis le Pieux (781–840)* (Sigmaringen, 1997) 45, pp. 131–2.
[59] *Le polyptyque de l'abbaye de Saint-Bertin (844–859)*, ed. F. L. Ganshof, F. Godding-Ganshof and A. de Smet, Mémoires de l'institut national de France, Academie des inscriptions et belles-lettres 45 (Paris, 1975). Nelson, *Charles the Bald* (London, 1991), pp. 176–8. On St-Amand see R. McKitterick, 'Carolingian Book Production: Some Problems', *The Library* 6 (1990), pp. 1–33, at pp. 14–29.
[60] M. de Jong, 'Growing up in a Carolingian Monastery: Magister Hildemar and his Oblates', *JMH* 9 (1983), pp. 99–128, at p. 114, citing Hildemar of Corbie/Civate, *Expositio regulae S. Benedicti*, in R. Mittermüller, ed., *Expositio regulae ab Hildemaro tradita et nunc primum typis mandata* (Regensberg, 1880), p. 66.
[61] *VK c.* 25, p. 30. See also Alfred's lament that when he was the right age and had the time to study there was nobody to teach him, *VA c.* 25, p. 21.
[62] Thegan *c.* 7, pp. 184–6, on Charlemagne's contemplation of a withdrawal from public life in old age see P. Dutton, 'Beyond the Topic of Senescence: The Political Problems of Aged Carolingian Rulers', in M. Sheehan, ed., *Aging and the Aged in Medieval Europe*, Selected Papers from the Annual Conference of the Centre for Medieval Studies, University of Toronto (Toronto, 1990), pp. 75–94, discussing such retirements at pp. 90–1.
[63] *VK c.* 26, p. 32.
[64] Alcuin, *De virtutibus*, PL 101, cols. 613–38. See M. Alberi, '"The Better Paths of Wisdom": Alcuin's Monastic "True Philosophy" and the Worldly Court', *Speculum* 76 (2001), pp. 896–910, at 909–10.

this pressure at work in Eberhard's life. Youth was the time when Eberhard had applied himself to study. In his poem celebrating the young Unruoch's birth, he exhorted the newborn infant to follow his father's example:

May the mellifluous teachings of Christ flower in your soul, in the tablets of your heart let holy wisdom shine. Thus did your father, mighty in the sword's use, drink in youth from the nourishing streams of holy wisdom.[65]

At the core of this evocation of the scriptural image of the *tabulae cordis* lay the notion that boyhood was the formative time for learning, when virtues could be inculcated, life-long patterns formed and Christian values internalised.[66] A few years earlier, Dhuoda had made the same point to her son William, citing *Ecclesiasticus*: 'The things that thou hast not gathered in thy youth, how shalt thou find them in thy old age?'[67] For men like Eberhard, childhood could not be devoted entirely to study for it was also a time when the study of holy wisdom had to be balanced with the study of war craft. 'If this age is passed without exercise and training, the body will soon become slow', observed Hrabanus Maurus in his own treatment of Vegetius' early chapters on recruitment and training, pinpointing the need for intense military preparation for the youth of the Carolingian elite.[68]

The balance between learning and the activities demanded by membership of Hildemar's *schola humani servitii* was hard to strike. Ermoldus recorded the young Charles the Bald's wish to follow his father on the hunt thwarted by his mother and his *pedagogus*.[69] Ermoldus, as we have already seen, was a far from effective soldier. His account of his own failings on the battlefield ends with the mockery of Pippin of Aquitaine, whose dismissal reveals something of an implicit sense of the tensions between learning and the active life: 'Give up your weapons, brother. Love learning more!'[70] Learned laymen such as Eberhard sought to bridge

---

[65] *Carmina* 38, pp. 66–7, ll. 25–8: 'Florescant animo melliflua dogmata Christi,/In tabulis cordis sancta sophia micet./Sic tuus ensipotens genitor puerilibus annis/Almae sophie sacra fluenta bibit.' For Sedulius on Eberhard's reliance upon Peter of Pisa's description of Charlemagne in his *planctus* on the young Lothar's death in 778, see Düchting, *Sedulius*, p. 47.

[66] Proverbs 3: 3; II Corinthians 3: 3. [67] Dhuoda, *Manuel* III, 5, p. 156.

[68] Dümmler, 'De Procinctu', 3, p. 444, discussed by J. L. Nelson, 'Ninth-Century Knighthood: The Evidence of Nithard', in C. Harper-Bill, C. J. Holdsworth and J. L. Nelson, eds., *Studies in Medieval History Presented to R. Allen Brown* (Woodbridge, 1989), pp. 255–66, repr. Nelson, *The Frankish World* (London, 1996), pp. 75–87. On the larger issue of Carolingian military training see Bachrach, *Warfare*, pp. 84–131.

[69] Ermold pp. 182–5, ll. 2399–407, discussed by R. McKitterick, 'Charles the Bald (823–77) and his Library', *EHR* 95 (1980), pp. 28–47, at p. 30. P. Wormald, 'The Uses of Literacy in Anglo-Saxon England and its Neighbours', *TRHS* 27 (1977), pp. 95–111, at 98.

[70] Ermold p. 154, ll. 2018–19: 'Pippin hoc aspiciens risit, miratur et infit:/ "Cede armis, frater; litteram amato magis".'

Eberhard of Friuli

both worlds. Nithard, who stood against Eberhard at Fontenoy, was well acquainted with the rigours of military training and the realities of warfare, and wrote about both in allusive Sallustian prose.[71] That both men had fathers who were participants in the court culture of Charlemagne's reign is probably not a coincidence. This ability to excel in learning and on the battlefield was a powerful ideal in Frankish panegyric, in large part precisely because it ran counter to reality. Heiric of Auxerre, for example, praised Charles the Bald because every day he participated in 'the scholarly no less than the military disciplines'.[72] Charles's own pursuit of holy wisdom was, at least in part, an attempt to emulate the ideal of the *rex doctus* represented by his grandfather.[73] It was an ideal that Eberhard, a member of the royal family by marriage to a Carolingian princess, a rare event in the earlier ninth century, may also have had cause to consider.[74]

Lupus' *Liber legum* was not the only book Eberhard requested. In the mid-840s he had asked Hrabanus Maurus for a copy of his heavily numerological collection of twenty-eight *carmina figurata*, *De laudibus sanctae crucis*.[75] Hrabanus happily acquiesced to the request: 'I have sent the work', he wrote to Eberhard: 'have it read to you.'[76] *De laudibus* was a prestige text in circulation at the highest level of Carolingian society. In the 830s a copy had been presented to Louis the Pious, perhaps at his

---

[71] Nithard's participation in and account of warfare is explored by Halsall, *Warfare*, pp. 1–5, 6–8, 178–80. The influence of Sallust on Nithard is signalled by J. L. Nelson, 'Public *Histories* and Private History in the Work of Nithard', in Nelson, *Politics and Ritual in Early Medieval Europe* (London, 1986), pp. 195–238, at p. 201, n. 24, citing the comments of David Ganz, and has been examined in depth by Matthew Gillis of the University of Virginia, to whose unpublished research I am indebted.
[72] Ed. L. Traube, *MGH Poet.* III, p. 429, translated and discussed by P. Godman, *Poetry of the Carolingian Renaissance* (London, 1985), p. 57. On this passage see also J. L. Nelson, 'Charles le Chauve et les utilisations du savoir', in D. Iogna-Prat, C. Jeudy and G. Lobrichon, eds., *L'école carolingienne d'Auxerre* (Paris, 1991), pp. 37–54, repr. Nelson, *Rulers and Ruling Families in Early Medieval Europe* (Aldershot, 1999), ch. 7, at pp. 39–41.
[73] W. Diebold, '"Nos quoque morem illius imitari cupientes": Charles the Bald's Evocation and Imitation of Charlemagne', *Archiv für Kulturgeschichte* 57 (1993), pp. 271–300.
[74] J. L. Nelson, 'Women at the Court of Charlemagne: A Case of Monstrous Regiment?', in Nelson, *Frankish World* (London, 1996), pp. 199–222, at 237–41, on Charlemagne's policy of keeping his daughters at court partly to prevent 'excessive dispersal of Carolingian blood' (p. 241). I must thank Valerie Garver for drawing my attention to the wider significance of Eberhard's and Gisela's marriage.
[75] Text: M. Perrin, *Rabani Mauri, In Honorem Sanctae Crucis*, CCCM 100 (1998), and his commentary, 'Il "Liber sanctae crucis di Rabano Mauro". Testo-immagine-contesto (Bern, 1999); Perrin, 'Hrabanica: Hrabans *De laudibus sanctae crucis* im Spiegel der neueren Forschung', in G. Schrimpf, ed., *Kloster Fulda in Der Welt der Karolinger und Ottonen*, Fuldaer Studien 7 (Frankfurt-am-Main, 1996), pp. 493–526, provides on overview of recent work on the poem; also H. Spilling, *Opus Magnentii Hrabani Mauri in honorem sanctae crucis conditum: Hrabansbeziehung zu seinem Werk*, Fuldaer Hochschulschriften 18 (Frankfurt-am-Main, 1992).
[76] *MGH Epp.* v, no. 42, p. 481: 'opusculum vobis transmisi … coram vobis legere faciatis'.

re-coronation at Metz in early 835.[77] Other manuscripts were sent to a number of leading figures and foundations, including St-Martin at Tours, St-Denis and the pope.[78] The Fulda monks Aschrich and Hruodpert, charged with the delivery of *De laudibus* to Rome, had stayed with Eberhard on their journey, and it may have been this encounter that led him to despatch a messenger to Fulda to ask Hrabanus for a copy of his own.[79]

There are signficant resonances between Hrabanus' poem and what we have seen so far of Eberhard's intellectual profile. As Celia Chazelle has recently noted, Hrabanus' poems gave striking poetic and visual form to the familiar image that Sedulius deployed in his poetry, the Pauline *miles Christi*.[80] The well-known dedicatory image of the manuscript of *De laudibus* presented to Louis the Pious, and incorporated into subsequent copies of the work, showed its royal recipient as a nimbed Roman military officer, helmeted, wearing a breastplate, clasping a cross-staff, supporting a shield, and with a *paludamentum* draped over his shoulder.[81] The text that ran over the image revealed that Louis' armour, like Eberhard's in Sedulius' poem, carried symbolic meaning. Louis' helmet, bestowed by Christ, represented salvation, his shield represented faith, his breastplate justice.[82] That Eberhard himself requested a copy of *De laudibus* is noteworthy, hinting that Eberhard saw himself, as the communities of Liège and Cysoing were to see him, as a soldier of Christ. Indeed, it may well be that it was an awareness of precisely this sense of self that Sedulius sought to play to in his poetry.

A final piece of evidence supports the notion that Christian warrior-hood occupied a special place in the Unruoching household. Amongst Eberhard's and Gisela's possessions was a piece of the True Cross, mounted in a gold crown. Clearly a valuable possession, it was left in their will to Unruoch.[83] The relic was a point where martial achievement fused with Christian *cultus*. It had been the focus for a sub-Constantinian cult of Christianised imperial triumph at the Frankish court from the later eighth century onwards. Louis had himself possessed such a crown, and had given

---

[77] C. Chazelle, *The Crucified God in the Carolingian Era: Theology and Art of Christ's Passion* (Cambridge, 2001), pp. 130–2.
[78] Ferrari, *Liber*, pp. 23–5; Perrin, *In Honorem Sanctae Crucis*, pp. xii–xxiii.
[79] Ep. 42, p. 481. See also *AF* a. 844, p. 35, tr. Reuter, p. 23.
[80] Chazelle, *Crucified God*, pp. 137–8.   [81] Sears, 'Louis', pp. 611–12.
[82] Perrin, *In Honorem Sanctae Crucis*, A5, pp. 10–11, with prose explanation, A6, at 13–16; Sears, 'Louis', p. 619.
[83] *Cysoing* no. 1, p. 2: 'coronam auream cum ligno Domini'.

pieces of the Cross to Louis the German, Charles the Bald, Lothar and Gisela.[84] Eric Goldberg has argued that the cult of the Cross took on a central role in the devotional and ritual life of Louis the German's court, a household given over, like Eberhard's, to warfare on and beyond the Carolingian frontiers.[85] The presence of the relic, and the request for Hrabanus' poem, indicates that the Cross may have occupied a comparable position within the devotions of the Unruoching household in Friuli, in addition to underlining the degree to which Eberhard's cultural interests were in step with those of the Carolingian courts.

It was conflict of a different sort, the predestination debate, which had spurred Hrabanus to write the letter which carried the allusion to Eberhard's request for the *De laudibus*. At its centre stood Gottschalk of Orbais. The son of a Saxon nobleman, he had entered Fulda as an oblate around 814, and first came to prominence when, at the council of Mainz in 829, he argued for his release from his monastic vows and the restitution of his patrimony.[86] Founded upon legal technicalities and a claim of coerced entry to the order, Gottschalk's argument for release found support from some members of the synod, but resulted not in his release but in his relocation, first, to Corbie and then Orbais. It also seems to have earned him the lasting ire of Hrabanus Maurus, his abbot at Fulda, and long-standing opponent. At some unspecified point, Gottschalk was ordained as a priest and began a period of travel that, by about 845–6, had led him south of the Alps, and to Rome.[87] At this time Gottschalk began to propound his theories on *gemina praedestinatio*, twin predestination, sparking a theological controversy that would engage many of the leading minds of the mid-ninth century.

Eberhard's part in this affair was small but, for present purposes, significant. Around 845–6, Gottschalk travelled to Friuli, finding safety and support with Eberhard. Why Eberhard gave his patronage to Gottschalk is a question not readily answered. Whilst the predestination dispute had yet to fully ignite by the mid 840s, Gottschalk was already a notorious figure, something Eberhard, well connected as he was, must have known. There is some evidence that twin predestination had become an issue in

---

[84] Goldberg, '"More Devoted"', pp. 61–2.   [85] Goldberg, '"More Devoted"', pp. 56–73.
[86] M. de Jong, *In Samuel's Image: Child Oblation in the Early Medieval West* (Leiden, 1996), pp. 77–91 on Gottschalk's career, with references to earlier studies. See also D. Ganz, 'The Debate on Predestination', in Gibson and Nelson, eds., *Charles the Bald*, pp. 283–302; D. E. Nineham, 'Gottschalk of Orbais: Reactionary or Precursor to the Reformation', *JEH* 40 (1989), pp. 1–18; K. Vielhaber, *Gottschalk der Sachse* (Bonn, 1956).
[87] Ganz, 'Predestination', pp. 287–8; Vielhaber, *Gottschalk*, pp. 19–21.

north-eastern Italy as early as 840. That year, Hrabanus, in a letter to Noting, bishop of Verona, a close associate of Eberhard, recalled the latter's concerns about heretics teaching predestination, and his request to Hrabanus for a collection of *sententiae* from Scripture and the Fathers with which he could refute their teachings.[88] If the date of this letter is correct, it is not impossible that already by the 840s Eberhard and others in northern Italy were sympathetic to Gottschalk's teachings. By the mid-840s he was certainly sympathetic enough to offer the *monachus gyrovagus* material support. In this context it is worth noting that amongst the books in the Unruoching chapel was the *Enchiridion*, a text that contained one of what John Rist has termed Augustine's more 'casual' statements on predestination, and one that carried the possibility of being read in support of twin predestination.[89] There may, therefore, have already been some pre-existing familiarity with the Augustinian underpinnings of Gottschalk's conception of twin predestination, and perhaps an independent basis for sympathy towards it. Did Gottschalk's teachings appeal to a sense of martial fatalism, or had Eberhard's experiences in battle by the late 840s, and the continued threat of the Arab presence to the south, sharpened Eberhard's interest in life's larger questions? Eberhard's near-contemporary, Alfred was, after all, to emerge from the Viking wars with a sustained interest in fate, and his own thoughts on *godcunde foretiohhung* (divine predestination) and the soul's immortality.[90] Hrabanus could certainly conceive of martial and metaphysical interests co-existing. The epitome of Vegetius that he gave to Lothar II accompanied

---

[88] Hrabanus Ep. 22, ed. Dümmler, *MGH Epp.* III, p. 428; the text is at *PL* 112, cols. 1530–53. The dating of Hrabanus' letter to Noting discussed by Vielhaber, *Gottschalk*, pp. 18–20.

[89] Augustine, *Enchiridion ad Laurentium de fide et spe et caritate*, ed. E. Evans, *CCSL* 46 (1988), 26:100, p. 103. On this passage, and its 'ambiguous reference to "double predestination" *in some sense*' (author's italics) see J. Rist, *Augustine: Ancient Thought Baptized* (Cambridge, 1994), pp. 269–83, esp. pp. 269–70 and G. Bonner, 'The Desire for God and the Need for Grace in Augustine's Theology', *Atti del Congresso Internazionale su S. Agostino nel XVI centenario della conversione*, Roma, 15–20 September 1986 (Rome, 1987), pp. 203–15. For Augustine's actual teachings on predestination see M. Lamberigts, 'Predestination', in *Augustine Through the Ages: An Encyclopedia*, ed. A. D. Fitzgerald (Grand Rapids, MI, 1999), pp. 677–9, with bibliography.

[90] D. R. Pratt, 'The Political Thought of Alfred the Great' (Ph.D., Cambridge University, 1999), pp. 299–310, now published in revised form as *The Political Thought of King Alfred the Great* (Cambridge, 2007); F. Anne Payne, *King Alfred and Boethius: An Analysis of the Old English Version of the Consolation of Philosophy* (Madison, 1968), pp. 78–108. The relationship of Alfred's interests and the predestination debate would repay closer study. For the influence of one of its participants, Eriugena, upon Alfredian thought see M. Treschow, 'Echoes of the *Periphyseon* in the Third Book of Alfred's *Soliloquies*', *Notes and Queries* 40 (1993), pp. 281–7. The connections between Alfred and Eberhard, and the points where their worlds overlapped are brilliantly mapped by A. Scharer, 'Alfred and the Continent' (forthcoming), whom I wish to thank for sharing his unpublished work with me.

a work on the nature of the soul.[91] Eberhard played host to Gottschalk at a time when the terms on which a *miles* might enter the gates of Heaven were particularly open to question. It was within precisely this context of the campaigns for Rome's defence of the later 840s that Pope Leo IV promised automatic entry to the kingdom of Heaven for all who died 'for the truth of the faith, the salvation of the soul and the defence of the homeland of Christ'.[92] In very different ways Gottschalk and Leo offered paths to eternal life that veered away from the route conventionally preached in the Carolingian world. Gottschalk's teachings denied the relevance of the sacramental, penitential and ethical apparatus of the Church. Leo's offered a channel to salvation founded upon one primary act, death in defence of Rome.

Eberhard and Gottschalk may also have had common interests. Eberhard's commission to Lupus shows a man with a keen interest in law. Gottschalk's arguments against his oblation based upon due process and personality of the law suggest that he, too, was something of a legist. His obsession with salvation resonates with Eberhard's interest in Hrabanus' *De laudibus*, and its extended treatment of the salvific powers of the Cross, whilst differing radically in content. Whilst some laymen strove to be learned, the learned Gottschalk strove to be lay. Had he been fully successful in reversing his oblation and reasserting his identity as a Saxon nobleman rather than a *servus Dei*, might Gottschalk have come in some way to resemble Eberhard with his lands, weapons, books and family? He certainly shared with Eberhard an interest in martial matters. He spent time with the Croatian *dux* Tripmir on campaign against the Byzantines and, in a discussion of oracles and *praescientia*, offered a rare Carolingian allusion to the beasts of battle.[93] Before armies clashed, Gottschalk observed, crows, kites, vultures and eagles followed those men whom they perceived in advance would be wounded, butchered or slain.[94] Might this have been the kind of example he drew upon when discussing predestination with his warrior host Eberhard?

---

[91] See above, n. 25; for the text of *De Anima*, *PL* 110, cols. 1109–21.
[92] Herbers, *Leo*, pp. 120–7, with extensive references (text at p. 120).
[93] R. Frank, 'Did Anglo-Saxon Audiences Have a Skaldic Tooth?', *Scandinavian Studies* 59 (1987), pp. 338–55, noting at 348 other Carolingian allusions to animals on the battlefield, and at 349 offering examples drawn from OE and ON of birds as 'choosers of the slain'. On this theme in Old English literature, see M. S. Griffith, 'Convention and Originality in the Old English "Beasts of Battle" Typescene', *ASE* 22 (1993), pp. 179–99, 185, 189–90; A. B. Rooth, *The Raven and the Carcass*, Folklore Fellows Commmunications 186 (Helsinki, 1962), pp. 210–18, 227–33; F. P. Magoun, 'The Theme of the Beasts of Battle in Anglo-Saxon Poetry', *Neuphilologische Mitteilungen* 56 (1955), pp. 81–9.
[94] D. C. Lambot, *Œuvres théologiques et grammaticales de Godescalc d'Orbais* (Louvain, 1945), p. 169.

Hrabanus was clear that the relationship of the two was that of pupil and teacher: *vester doctor* was his description of Gottschalk to Eberhard. In his dealings with Eberhard over his support for Gottschalk, Hrabanus found himself in the sensitive position of a churchman preaching orthodoxy to a layman whose power supported intellectual curiosity and nourished independence of thought. In their differing ways Eberhard and Gottschalk both raised questions about the relationship between learning and monastic control. Einhard, writing to one Vussin, pointed out the dangers of learning without discipline. Study, he reminded him, should serve a clear purpose, the formation of 'good habits'. 'Knowledge puffs up, but *caritas* edifies', cautioned Einhard, citing Paul's letter to the Corinthians.[95] Hincmar seized on the same verse when describing Gottschalk in a probable interpolation to Prudentius' entry for 849 in the *Annals of St-Bertin*.[96] As the author of a several exegetical works for Carolingian royalty, the role of authoritative *expositor* to the powerful was not novel for Hrabanus, but explaining the flaws underlying twin predestination was no easy task. Hrabanus' letter to Eberhard is characterised by a striving for lucidity and directness. 'Many air their opinions rashly but few really grasp these questions', admitted Lupus when, in early 850, he tried to explain twin predestination 'briefly, truthfully and clearly' to Charles the Bald.[97] Even then he concluded his letter with a tangible note of hesitancy, born from the fear of error, and its consequences.

Such hesitancy is less immediately apparent in Hrabanus' attack on the preaching of the man he dismissed as a *sciolus*.[98] He opened with a rhetorical question. Those who followed Gottschalk's teachings might say to themselves, 'Why is it necessary for me to work for my salvation and eternal life? For if I do good, but am not predestined for eternal life, nothing will lead me to it. If, however, God has predestined me to attain eternal life, and I do bad things, nothing will hinder me from attaining it.'[99] Gottschalk's teachings led men to disobey the teachings of the

---

[95] Einhard Ep. 57, *MGH Epp.* v, p. 138.
[96] *AB* s.a. 849, pp. 54–5, trans. Nelson, p. 67, with a discussion of Hincmar's probable authorship at n. 2.
[97] Lupus, *Correspondance* 78, pp. 22–36, at 24: 'quaestiones, quas audacter multi ventilant, intellegenter pauci capiunt, breviter, veraciter perspicueque dissolvam'.
[98] This letter is discussed *inter alia* by De Jong, *In Samuel's Image*, pp. 86–8; G. Schrimpf, 'Hraban und der Prädestinationsstreit des 9. Jahrhunderts', in R. Kottje and H. Zimmermann, eds., *Hrabanus Maurus: Lehrer, Abt und Bischof* (Wiesbaden, 1982), pp. 145–53, at 148–9.
[99] Hrabanus Ep. 42, p. 481, lines 33–36: 'Quid mihi necesse est pro salutate mea et vita aeterna laborare? Quia si bonum fecero, et predestinatus ad vitam non sum, nihil mihi prodest; si autem malum egero, nihil mihi obest, quia predestinatio Dei me facit ad vitam aeternam pervenire.'

Evangelists. They were socially destructive.[100] Hrabanus then moved on to a well-worn scholar's strategem, he questioned Gottschalk's grasp of the secondary scholarship, and in particular his use of Augustine. 'Your teacher', he told Eberhard, 'has excerpted testimonies in support of his position from the works of the most blessed and learned father Augustine.' But Augustine attacked the Pelagians when they spoke against God's grace. He was the defender of grace, Hrabanus observed, not the destroyer of the laws of faith.[101] He went on to give Augustine's definition of the distinction between predestination and prescience, driving home his initial point about Gottschalk's erroneous use of Augustine's authority by invoking it to support his own arguments. Hrabanus followed this with a series of extracts, not from Augustine himself, but from several of Prosper of Aquitaine's tracts in defence of Augustine's teaching on predestination, grace and free will.[102] Hrabanus' articulation of Augustine's actual teachings on these subjects *contra* Gottschalk relies heavily upon Prosper's, and reveals little of his own engagement with the *magister*'s thought.[103] It is in this dependence upon Prosper that we discern something of Hrabanus' own hesitancy in explaining, and refuting, predestination. Hrabanus moved to reject twin predestination through a series of related issues: God's desire to save all men, not merely a predestined few, the relationship of free will and evil, and the nature of original sin. Returning to the question with which he began, Hrabanus restated the importance of the sacraments and good works for the achievement of salvation, rejecting the complacency Gottschalk's teachings threatened to engender.

Having addressed the teachings, Hrabanus turned his attention to the teacher, expressing the same worries Einhard had voiced about the dangers of learning. Investigation and meditation upon the Holy Scriptures must be done cautiously and carefully. He who undertakes such study should try '"not to be more wise than it behoveth to be wise, but to be wise unto sobriety", according to the rule of faith'.[104] Hrabanus' letter closed with some basic images intended to drive home to Eberhard the dangers Gottschalk's teachings posed. Penetrating the mysteries of Holy Writ was,

---

[100] Ganz, 'Predestination', pp. 295–6.
[101] Ep. 42, pp. 481–2: 'Dicitur enim ipse doctor vester multa testimonia excerpsisse de opusculis beatissimi et doctissimi patris Augustini, quibus nititur suam sectam affirmare, cum memoratus pater et doctor catholicus, contra Pelagianos scribens, qui gratiae Dei contrarii predicatores fuerint, defensor eiusdem gratiae, non destructor recte fidei fuerit.'
[102] *Ibid.*, p. 482, ll. 4–11. On Hrabanus' use of Augustine see B. Blumenkranz, 'Raban Maur et Saint Augustin: Compilation ou adaption? À propos du latin biblique', *Revue du Moyen Age* 7 (1951), pp. 97–110.
[103] Ep. 42, pp. 482–6. [104] Ep. 42, p. 486, ll. 24–6, citing Romans 12: 3.

the margrave of Friuli was informed, like digging a pit. If one is dug, and it is then left uncovered, an ox or an ass might fall into it. Should this happen, the hole's digger would be held responsible for the cost of the unfortunate animal. In the same way, Hrabanus explained, the profound truths of scholarship should also be protected by those who investigate them, lest, like the ox or the ass, the less-learned Christian, the *parvulus in Christo*, or an unbeliever, should fall into error, and risk damnation. This blunt, bucolic image was not Hrabanus' own but was drawn from Gregory the Great's exegesis on Mosaic law in the *Moralia*.[105] Hrabanus made the point repeatedly that the higher levels of theology were not for everybody. Milk not meat was the fitting food for the 'little one in Christ'. Too much honey made one sick. The teacher had to pitch his lesson at a level appropriate for his listeners. He had also to be mindful of the danger he exposed them to by his revelations. Eberhard had to prevent Gottschalk from broadcasting his errors, from digging his metaphorical holes in the ground for others to fall into. 'Stop him', implored Hrabanus.[106]

Hrabanus' letter can be read as an extended warning to Eberhard not to delve too deeply into the world of higher learning and, indirectly, as a castigation of Gottschalk's willingness to share his learning, erroneous as it was, with those for whom such knowledge was inappropriate as well as dangerous. Hrabanus' directness, his reliance upon rhetorical questioning and deployment of a series of strikingly concrete metaphors, suggest that, in Hrabanus' eyes, Eberhard the powerful marcher lord was himself a *parvulus in Christo*, easily led astray. We cannot read this letter as any kind of reliable portrait of Eberhard's actual intellectual sophistication, of course, though it does cast striking light upon Hrabanus' assessment of it, and his concern about the dangers uncontrolled learning posed to the wider Christian community. Hrabanus was a man more used to seeing powerful laypeople as the passive recipients of his own tireless expositions of orthodoxy than as the active supporters of dissident thought.

Hrabanus' letter seems to have had some effect. Some time after it was received, Gottschalk quit Eberhard's household for the court of Tripmir of Croatia and to travel in pagan Slavic territory, a *peregrinatio* as individual as any other aspect of his career.[107] By 848, however, he was at Mainz,

---

[105] Gregory the Great, *Moralia in Job*, ed., M. Adriaen, CCSL 143A (1979), XVII, 38, pp. 872–3, discussing Exodus 21:33.
[106] Hrabanus Ep. 42, p. 487.
[107] *AB* s.a. 849 (see n. 96), trans. Nelson, p. 67; Vielhaber, *Gottschalk*, p. 21; Nineham, 'Gottschalk', pp. 2–3.

defending his position before a full synod. At this point, as far as we can know, Eberhard's link with his former *doctor* was severed. It is likely that it was this decision that led Hincmar, in a fragmentary letter preserved in Flodoard's *Histories*, to write to Eberhard, praising him for his devotion to God and commitment to the peace and unity of the Church.[108] Within the walls of his home as much as on the frontiers of the empire, Eberhard, it would seem, stood in Christianity's defence.

It is now time to examine the best-known body of evidence for Eberhard's learning, the collection of more than sixty books bequeathed in his joint will with Gisela.[109] This collection is often described as a library, though the will itself described them simply as 'the books of our chapel (*libri ... capellae nostrae*)', and it ought to be noted that it is far from clear that the volumes listed in the will were the total number of books available in the Unruoching household. Eberhard's copy of *De laudibus*, for example, is conspicuously absent.[110] Régine Le Jan has drawn attention to the books listed amongst the goods given by Eberhard's chaplain Walgar to Cysoing around 865, a list that included Bede's Commentaries on the Apocalypse and the Seven Catholic Epistles, Gregory's *Moralia in Job* and his homilies on Ezechiel, Isidore's *Liber officiorum*, as well as a number of liturgical volumes.[111] As chaplain, it would have fallen to Walgar to perform the readings for Eberhard's family and extended household and it is worth considering that his instructional responsibilities may have extended beyond the demands of the liturgical offices. Had Hrabanus' instructions that Eberhard have *De laudibus* read before him been followed, it is likely that the task would have fallen to Walgar, or someone very much like him.[112] Walgar also serves as a useful reminder that most of Eberhard's regular contacts with learned clergy would not have been with figures of Hrabanus' calibre. Even Noting, a man with whom Eberhard had frequent dealings, bishop of a city with cultural traditions as rich as Verona's, turned to Hrabanus for the patristic ammunition he needed to tackle

---

[108] *MGH Epp*. v, 69, pp. 36–7.
[109] La Rocca and Provero, 'The Dead', pp. 256–9; Riché, 'Bibliothèques', pp. 97–101; McKitterick, *Carolingians*, pp. 245–50.
[110] Spilling, *Opus Magnentii*, pp. 69–70, suggests that the MS of *De laudibus* in Turin, Bibliotheca Nazionale K.II. 20, is Eberhard's copy, on which see Perrin, *Sanctae Crucis*, p. xxxiii, n. 54 ('une hypothèse plausible, mais indémontrable').
[111] Le Jan, *Famille*, pp. 66–7; *Cysoing* no. 2, pp. 5–7.
[112] Compare with the role of *lector* played by a cleric in the household of another learned layman, *VA* 81, p. 67 and see the comments of M. de Jong, 'Old Law and New-found Power: Hrabanus Maurus and the Old Testament', in J. W. Drijvers and A. A. MacDonald, eds., *Centres of Learning: Learning and Location in Pre-Modern Europe and the Near East* (Leiden, 1995), pp. 161–76, esp. 164–6.

predestination. Like his episcopal contemporary Hartgar across the Alps, he knew his limits when it came to certain types of specialised learning, something that makes Eberhard's own interests the more impressive.

Whilst Riché gave plausible identifications for many of the works listed in the will, not all have been satisfactorily identified. The book entitled *Gesta Francorum* given to Berengar, for example, could refer to a number of works (or a compilation of several), as could the *Collectaneum* and the *Ordo priorum principum* bequeathed to Rodulph.[113] This vagueness is in itself suggestive, for it implies a degree of familiarity with the books on the part of those bequeathing and receiving them. These problems aside, the book-list is nevertheless illuminating. Its contents were divided unevenly between Eberhard and Gisela's eight children.[114] Unruoch, the eldest son and inheritor of Eberhard's key holdings in Italy and Alemannia, received thirteen of them, including a *Psalterium duplum*, a *Liber de lege Francorum et Ripuariorum et Langobardorum et Alamanorum et Bavariorum* and a *Liber rei militaris*. As we have already seen, all three can be plausibly identified: the psalter with the manuscript in the Vatican library that bears Eberhard's name, the law collection with Lupus' *Liber legum*, and the *Liber rei militaris* with Hartgar's gift of the *Epitoma*. At the other extreme, and last in the list of children, Gisela, a nun at San Salvatore Brescia, received just two books, one *De quattuor virtutibus*, to which I shall return, the other, Augustine's *Enchiridion*. The will's distribution of books was intended to help shape and sustain a further generation of Unruochings in their fulfilment of worldly commitments and cultivation of Christian virtues. To misquote Alfred, these were perhaps some of the works that Eberhard and Gisela felt it most necessary for their children to know. Some were also intended, like Hartgar's gift, as remembrances, but here of family not friends. Rodulph, for example, the future abbot of St-Bertin and St-Vaast, received the *Psalterium cum sua expositione* that Gisela herself had used, and the daily missal 'which we have always had in our chapel'.[115]

Rather than itemise the books, a task in any case undertaken by earlier commentators, what I want to do here is consider briefly some of their contents, highlighting some potential relationships with the themes encountered so far. Eberhard's and Gisela's books fall into several linked categories. First, liturgical and devotional works whose use either can be related to the offices of the household chapel or were for use in private devotion. These include Eberhard's and Gisela's *Bibliotheca*, gospel books,

---

[113] *Cysoing* no. 1, p. 4.   [114] *Cysoing* no. 1, pp. 2–3.   [115] *Cysoing* no. 1, pp. 2–3.

lectionaries, missals, a penitential and multiple prayer books, some of which were clearly prestige objects, decorated with gold and ivory, and listed in the will with the chapel's *paramentum*, rather than with the books themselves. The Psalter's key place in Carolingian lay devotion is signalled not only by the bequest of a psalter to each of Eberhard's sons, but also by the fact that they were listed first amongst the various individual bequests. The various sermon collections that Eberhard and Gisela divided amongst their children also fall into this category. Unruoch, Berengar and Rodolph all received a copy of the compilation known as the *De verbis Domini*, a widely diffused collection of Augustinian and Pseudo-Augustinian sermons on the Gospels and St Paul's epistles.[116] Two other sermon collections were listed in the will, designated by their opening texts. Unruoch received a volume beginning with *De Elia et Achab*, identified by Riché as Ambrose's *De Helia et ieiunio* ('On Elijah and Fasting').[117] His sister Judith received a book beginning with a sermon *De Ebrietate* ('On Sobriety'), falsely ascribed in the will to Augustine, but probably by Caesarius of Arles.[118] Significant resonances exist between the two sermons. Both, as their titles suggest, focused upon the dangers of drunkenness.[119] Caesarius criticised the heavy social drinking of his flock, and the violence and infidelity that followed in its wake. In *De Helia* Ambrose, like Caesarius, had targeted the danger of overindulgence, but expanded his thoughts into an extended meditation on the nature of fasting, the benefits of continence and the dangers of drunkenness through the citation of a sequence of biblical exemplars, good and bad. A martial theme runs through the whole work. Ambrose dwelt not only on the dangers of drunkenness in times of war and, implicitly, the need for self-discipline at such times, but he began the sermon by invoking an image of the Israelites who would sound the trumpet when they went into battle, in order that the Lord would remember and aid his people.[120] Ambrose

---

[116] P.-P. Verbraken, *Études Critiques sur les Sermons Authentiques de Saint Augustin*, Instrumenta Patristica 12 (Steenbrugge, 1976), pp. 218–25.

[117] Riché, 'Bibliothèques', p. 97; Ambrose, *De Helia et ieiunio*, PL 14, cols. 694–728, English translation and commentary in M. J. A. Buck, *S. Ambrosii de Helia et Ieiunio: A Commentary, with an Introduction and Translation*, Catholic University of America, Patristic Studies 19 (Washington, DC, 1929).

[118] Riché, 'Bibliothèques', p. 97; Caesarius Arelatensis, *Sermones*, ed. G. Morin, CCSL 103 (1953), 46, pp. 205–11, discussed by W. Klingshirn, *Caesarius of Arles: The Making of a Christian Community in Late Antique Gaul* (Cambridge, 1994), pp. 196–8.

[119] For Carolingian concerns about overindulgence, Nelson, 'Voice', p. 80, n. 27.

[120] Ambrose, *De Helia* c. 1, col. 697. See also cc. 9, cols. 707–8 (Holofernes and Judith), and 13, cols. 713–15 (pitfalls of drinking sessions waged like battles *before* battle proper is joined). Over a century later Ælfric would share with Eberhard the belief that the story of Judith and Holofernes held

paralleled the Israelites' battle with the Lenten fast: 'We must sound the trumpet, as if going forth to battle, in order to announce the day of solemnity', he observed, but noted that unlike the literal battles of David, 'our victory is the Cross of Christ, our trophy is the Paschal feast of Lord Jesus'.[121] It is hardly coincidental that this work was given by the man who also bequeathed a copy of *De laudibus* to the son who would inherit his land, his finest arms and armour, weapons and a fragment of the True Cross, and take his father's place as a *miles Christi*, defender of the eastern Carolingian *limes*. In the coherence of themes and images that these fragments reveal, we might begin to glimpse the thought of Eberhard of Friuli himself.

Sermon collections lead us to a second category of texts which includes the great bulk of those listed in the will, texts which addressed the cultivation of Christian virtues and right conduct. Issues of Christian self-knowledge were treated in the most sophisticated fashion in the copy of Augustine's *Enchiridion* left to Gisela, itself a work written in response to a layman's request for a handbook that explained key elements of Christian faith. Augustine responded with a treatment of faith, hope and love, and, as we have already seen, the workings of grace and free will. A number of texts addressed virtues and vices, several of which, like the *Enchiridion*, were originally written with a lay audience in mind. Alcuin's *De virtutibus et vitiis* of the 790s, listed simply as *Liber Alquini ad Widonem Comitem* and left to Judith, falls into this category. So, too, do the two copies of the *Liber de quattuor virtutibus* left to Unruoch and the younger Gisela. Riché identified this *Liber* as Martin of Braga's *Formula vitae honestae*, written around 570 at the apparent request of the Suevic King Miro, but intended, at least according to its author, less for the king and more for his courtiers.[122] It dealt with the four virtues, *prudentia*, *magnanimitas*, *continentia* and *justitia*, and the need for their balanced exercise. Martin placed heavy

---

valuable lessons for a warrior faced with *pagani* when he sent his prose adaption of the story to his neighbour Sigeweard of Asthall: B. Assmann, 'Abt Ælfrics angelsächsische Homilie über das Buch Judith', *Anglia* 10 (1888), pp. 76–104, discussed by S. S. Klein, 'Ælfric's Sources and his Gendered Audiences', *Essays in Medieval Studies* 13, Proceedings of the Illinois Medieval Association (1996), pp. 111–17, esp. 114–15; M. Clayton, 'Ælfric's Judith: Manipulative or Manipulated?', *ASE* 23 (1994), pp. 215–27.

[121] Ambrose, *De Helia* c. 1, col. 697: 'Canamus tuba, ut annuntiemus solemnitatis diem, simul nobis et certamen imminet, et victoria repromittur. Victoria nostra, crux Christi est: tropaeum nostrum, pascha est Domini Jesu.'

[122] Martin of Braga, *Formula vitae honestae*, ed. C. W. Barlow, *Martini Episcopi Bracarensis Opera Omnia*, Papers and Monographs of the American Academy in Rome 12 (New Haven, CT, 1950), pp. 236–50.

emphasis throughout upon these virtues' practical application, and in particular that of *prudentia*, giving advice on how and when to to speak, and how to judge: base your decisions on the truth, and do not be swayed by personal friendships, a point the elder Unruoch himself made in 806; and how to conduct oneself in war. Battle ought only to be joined, he cautioned, after a formal declaration of hostilities had been made, a bitter lesson for anyone associated with Lothar's cause at Fontenoy.[123] With its concern with correct behaviour, self-control, social conduct and the maintenance of right relations at court, Martin's *Formula* bears some superficial comparison with Dhuoda's advice to William.

Several other books listed in the will ought also to be considered in this category. The *Liber S. Augustini*, a book containing Augustine's letter to the priest Jerome on James 2: 10 ('And whosoever shall keep the whole law, but offend in one point, is become guilty of all') is also a treatise on the virtues and vices and the acquisition of wisdom. In his letter to Eberhard, Hrabanus quoted Gregory on the resemblance of scriptural study to digging a hole in the ground. Augustine began his letter by comparing humanity's post-lapsarian state to a man who had fallen down a well. How he got there, he reminded Jerome, was an issue of less importance than how he could get out.[124] The cultivation of Christian virtues was also a theme of Isidore's *Synonyma*, whose first book, an extended lamentation on sin, gave way in the second to a short guide on the pursuit of the Christian life, and the *Admonition to a Spiritual Son* ascribed to Basil of Caesarea.[125] Both were works evoked elsewhere for the lessons they taught laymen. 'Read the *Synonyma*', advised Dhuoda when discussing the need for William to cultivate discernment when choosing advisors, whilst Paulinus of Aquileia drew extensively in his *Liber exhortationis* upon pseudo-Basil's *Admonition*.[126] The *Liber Ephrem* given to Berengar may have been intended to serve a similiar

---

[123] *Ibid.*, 2–3, pp. 238–41.
[124] Augustine Ep. 167, ed. A. Goldbacher, *CSEL* 44 (1904), pp. 586–609.
[125] Isidore of Seville, *Synonyma de lamentatione animae peccatricis*, PL 83, cols. 825–66; *Die Admonitio S. Basilii ad Filium Spiritualem*, ed. P. Lehmann, Sitzungsberichte der Bayerischen Akademie der Wissenschaften 12 (Munich, 1955).
[126] Dhuoda, *Manuel* III, 6, p. 160; and see also Rosenwein, 'Gift-giving', pp. 150–1, on the relevance of Isidore's lessons for Berengar. For Paulinus' use of pseudo-Basil in the *Liber* see A. de Nicola, 'La dottrina spirituale del *Liber Exhortationis* di San Paolino di Aquileia', in G. Fornasir, ed., *Atti Convegno internazionale di studio su Paolino s' Aquileia nel XII Centenario dell' Episcopato* (Udine, 1988), pp. 35–118, esp. 37–8. This reliance gave rise to the belief that the pseudo-Basil had plagiarised Paulinus, *PL* 99, 211, as noted by M. A. Locherbie-Cameron, 'From Caesarea to Eynsham: A Consideration of the Proposed Route(s) of the *Admonition of a Spiritual Son* to Anglo-Saxon England', *The Heroic Age* 3 (2000) (www.mun.ca/mst/heroicage/issues/3/cameron.html). No pagination.

purpose.[127] Even works that seem at first to address issues of nature and the natural world were in fact directed towards the cultivation of Christian knowledge. The *Physiologus*, for example, the probable work described in the will as '*Liber bestiarum*', is primarily a collection of allegorical interpretations of animals and their characteristics, in effect, the lessons of Scripture and salvation taught by the examples of the natural world.

Sedulius Scottus' vision of Eberhard's boyhood studies was a poetic fiction, but many of the books in the adult Eberhard's household were works intended to foster precisely the kind of inner cultivation of *sancta sophia* Sedulius envisaged. The contents of these books reveal the Unruoching household as a place of stringent self-improvement, the moral and corrective drives of Charlemagne's *renovatio* shrunk to the scale of a single family. At first sight these guides in correct Christian *conversatio* may seem to stand in sharp contrast to Gottschalk's teachings which, as Hrabanus observed, rendered such striving redundant. But if the routes offered were different they shared a common terminus. What Gottschalk's teachings shared with the kind of Christian life that these texts sought to cultivate was their ultimate goal: salvation. It was the theme at the heart of Hrabanus' *De laudibus*, and it was the hope of aiding its attainment, rather than any concern with temporal remembrance, that lay behind the masses said for Eberhard and for others in the chapels of Cysoing, St-Gall, Pfäffers and San Salvatore Brescia.[128] What lay at the roots of much of Eberhard's engagement with the world of learning, whether through the collection and distribution of books, or the patronage of Gottschalk, was a characteristically Carolingian concern about entry to the heavenly kingdom.

If many of these texts were morally and ethically prescriptive a further set of texts, law-books, were prescriptive in a different sense. In addition to Lupus' *Liber legum*, we find a *Liber de constitutionibus principum et edictis Imperatorum* (perhaps, as McKitterick suggests, a copy of Ansegisus), a text of Lombard laws and a *liber Aniani* (Alaric's *Breviarium*). The presence of two recensions of Lombard law in the book-list are a reminder of Eberhard and his sons' north Italian responsibilities as judges and governors, and the prevalence of written law in the legal culture of ninth-century Italy.[129]

---

[127] For his writings used as 'guides to self-knowledge' by ninth-century readers, see D. Ganz, 'Knowledge of Ephrem's Writings in the Merovingian and Carolingian Age', *Hugoye: Journal of Syriac Studies* (http://syrcom.cua.edu/ syrcom/Hugoye) 2 (1998), par. 11, noting Ephrem's *De Compunctione Cordis* in Carolingian manuscripts containing works on virtues and vices.
[128] Ludwig, *Transalpinen*, pp. 29–31, 37–47–55, 164–6; Le Jan, *Famille*, p, 37.
[129] Wormald, *Making*, pp. 67–8.

'To suppose that their lawbooks had any other end in view is to dig one's own pitfalls', commented the present volume's editor, felicitously echoing Hrabanus.[130] As a work with the possibility of practical application, the Vegetius belongs in the same category as these law-books. So, too, does a work that Riché described as 'un livre de médicine', the *Physionomia Loxi medici*.[131] A Latin compilation drawn from the writings of Loxus *medicus*, Aristotle *philosophus* and Palemon *declamator*, this work set out the relationship between character and physical appearance, teaching lessons about the characteristics of various ethnic groups and animals, but also how one might assess character by appearance: what different types of hair or the movement of the eyes reveal about the personality of their possessor.[132] The *Physionomia* was not a book of law, but it was a guide to judging men.

This Italian perspective also serves as a context for a number of the other works listed. A copy of the *Liber pontificalis*, for example, has an obvious interest for any member of the north Italian Carolingian ruling class, and particularly one so closely identified with Rome's defence. The absence of Paul the Deacon's *Historia Langobardorum* from Eberhard's and Gisela's book-list has drawn comment, despite its early circulation to ninth-century Friuli.[133] The book-list, as we have already seen, was probably not comprehensive, but Paul's absence may also be explained by the fact that Eberhard's and Gisela's will carries tangible traces of the cultivation of a particularly Frankish sense of identity. The only other relic, apart from the True Cross, to warrant mention in the will was a phylactery containing relics of St Remigius, the apostle of the Franks.[134] Similarly, the will distributed no fewer than two copies of the *vita* of St Martin, one of the Franks' most favoured saints and the archetypal soldier of Christ, and a *Liber Isidori, Fulgentii, Martini episcoporum*. The relics of St Remigius and the lives of St Martin hint at the cultivation of a distinctively Frankish identity within Eberhard's household. St Martin appeared prominently in the *Versus de Verona*, composed during Pippin's

---

[130] *Ibid.*, pp. 54, 87–8. Hrabanus echoed Gregory, who himself evoked Pss. 7: 16, 9: 16 and 56/7.

[131] Riché, 'Bibliothèques', p. 100.

[132] *Anonymi de Physiognomonia liber*, ed. R. Förster, Scriptores Physiognomonici Graeci et Latini, 2 vols. (Leiden, 1893), with a discussion of manuscripts and transmission at 1, pp. cxxxi–clxxv (Eberhard's will cited at p. cxxxvii), and text II, pp. 1–145. P. Squatriti, 'Personal Appearance and Physiognomics in Early Medieval Italy', *JMH* 14 (1988), pp. 191–202, explores the presence of physiognomic thought in ninth-century north Italy.

[133] W. Pohl, 'Memory, Identity and Power in Lombard Italy', in *Uses*, pp. 9–28, at p. 25.

[134] P. Depreux, 'Saint Remi et la royauté carolingienne', *RH* 285 (1991), pp. 235–60.

stay in the city in the years around 800;[135] and there is evidence that the cult of St Martin was spreading through the northern Adriatic in the mid-ninth century as a result of Frankish missionary activity from Aquileia.[136] The Friulian marches also provide a context for understanding another book in the Unruoching chapel, Aethicus Ister's *Cosmographia*. This pseudo-geographical treatise, purporting to have been written by 'Jerome' and drawing upon the lost writings of one 'Aethicus Ister', was probably composed in the later eighth century, in Bavaria.[137] Its author drew upon Isidore, and in particular Orosius, to shape his idiosyncratic vision of the world.[138] The work has a strong eschatological component, and a sustained interest in the bizarre practices and transgressive behaviours of a range of peoples, both historical and mythological. Ian Wood has seen behind Aethicus' concern with 'the Other' a concerted effort to define alien peoples and their practices and to demarcate the border between civilisation and barbarity. Reflecting upon its possible audience, he noted that these concerns would have made it a work with 'continuing interest to all those who lived on an early medieval frontier'.[139] Its presence amongst Eberhard's books suggests that the same thought occurred to someone in the ninth century. More specifically, 'Aethicus' wrote from the perspective of Istria, a territory with which Eberhard was closely involved, and focused upon the Balkans and Asia. As much as the lawbook defined the peoples Eberhard governed, and the lives of St Martin evoked his family's Frankish identity, 'Aethicus' addressed the territories and their inhabitants, real and imagined, against whom Eberhard stood guard.

The subject of one of the books in the Unruoching chapel, Apollonius of Tyre, was a wealthy nobleman who, over the course of an eventful life, married the daughter of a king, fathered an educated daughter and possessed an impressive library.[140] It may be nothing more than coincidence

---

[135] Osborne, 'Politics', p. 384. On the *Versus de Verona* see G. V. B. West, 'Studies in Representations and Perceptions of the Carolingians in Italy 774–875' (Ph.D., University of London, 1998), pp. 137–9, with full references.

[136] Osborne, 'Politics', pp. 383–6; Z. Rapani, 'La costa orientale dell'Adriatico nell'alto medioevo', *Gli Slavi occidentali e meridionali nell'alto medievo*, Settimane Spoleto 32, 1 (1983), pp. 831–69.

[137] O. Prinz, ed., *Die Kosmographie des Aethicus* (Munich, 1993); I. Wood, 'Aethicus Ister: An Exercise in Difference', in W. Pohl and H. Reimitz, eds., *Grenze und Differenz im frühen Mittelalter* (Vienna, 2000), pp. 197–208, to which this paragraph is heavily indebted.

[138] N. Lazovsky, *The Earth is Our Book: Geographical Knowledge in the Latin West, ca. 400–1000* (Ann Arbor, MI, 2000), pp. 28–34.

[139] Wood, 'Difference', p. 200.

[140] E. Archibald, *Apollonius of Tyre: Medieval and Renaissance Themes and Variations* (Cambridge, 1991), pp. 9–26, with discussion of the Carolingian reception of the work at pp. 45–6, and text and translation at 112–75; and Archibald, 'Fathers and Kings in Apollonius of Tyre', in M. M. Mackenzie

that Eberhard and Gisela left their copy of the *Apollonium* to Engeltrude, their eldest daughter.[141] But it is more likely, as with many of the other books in the will, that the bequest was the result of careful reflection, perhaps even a hint of self-recognition. What emerges from even this cursory glance at this and some of the other books in the Unruoching chapel is a sense of the degree to which many of them relate to the particular character of Eberhard's active life. Learning mattered to him, as it would matter to Alfred of Wessex: another warrior against *pagani* who would also see the value of scholarship for those engaged in the *schola humani servitii*. As far as we can see, however, Eberhard, unlike his West Saxon contemporary, appears to have had little trouble successfully integrating the demands of secular life with a preoccupation with piety.[142] Anxiety was not the automatic outcome of a close adherence to the Carolingian ideals of the pious layman. As Sedulius well knew, Eberhard was very familiar with the art of war in this world, but he also possessed, as his books and his actions make clear, an awareness of the world beyond. In the last analysis, the image of the *miles Christi* was not simply a trope by which an Irish poet could praise a Frankish nobleman, it is also the key with which we can unlock the relationship of learning and lay culture in Eberhard's life.

Before he and Gisela divided their books they divided their lands and their moveables. For their three elder sons this latter category meant, before anything else, swords and armour.[143] Many of the books that the will subsequently divided were guides to the cultivation of an armoury of a different kind, virtues and Christian values, with which inner battles could be fought, and the demands of lay life – warfare, judgement, service at court – fulfilled in the proper moral manner. They were an armoury for participation in both physical and spiritual struggles, for it was through victory in those struggles that Eberhard, the defender of Rome, and in due time his children, might gain entry to the city of God.

---

and C. Roueché, eds., *Images of Authority: Papers Presented to Joyce Reynolds on the Occasion of her 70th Birthday* (Cambridge, 1989), pp. 24–40. *Making*, pp. 209, 210.

[141] *Cysoing* no. 1, p. 4.

[142] J. L. Nelson, 'Monks, Secular Men and Masculinity, *c.* 900', in D. M. Hadley, ed., *Masculinity in Medieval Europe* (London, 1999), pp. 121–42.

[143] Geary, *Phantoms*, p. 48. I wish to thank Celia Chazelle, Cyril Edwards, David Ganz, Eric Goldberg, Jinty Nelson and especially the late Patrick Wormald for their incisive comments and wise advice. The errors and flaws that remain that are mine.

CHAPTER 6

Dhuoda

Janet L. Nelson

Complimented by Captain Absolute on her intellectual accomplishments, Mrs Malaprop was well and truly flattered: 'Sir, you do me infinite honour! ... Few gentlemen nowadays know how to value the ineffectual qualities in a woman!'[1] Historians of the Middle Ages until not so long ago tended to be gentlemen, few of whom gave the impression of valuing – or even noticing – intellectual qualities in medieval women. To use 'intellectual' as a noun in the context of the Middle Ages is flagrant anachronism in the literal sense that the term itself is a nineteenth-century coinage. But anachronism, especially the flagrant sort, may justify itself by being provocative, that is, by destabilising orthodoxies. That is why Jacques Le Goff entitled his paean of praise to the scholars of the twelfth century *Les intellectuels au moyen âge*, and why Alain Boureau has recently discerned in the linking of the past with the present implied by Le Goff's title 'a key to the work's success and influence'.[2] In the preface to the book's second edition, Le Goff himself refused to define the term 'intellectual'.[3] I must

---

Patrick Wormald's invitation to speak about Dhuoda at Kalamazoo in 2000 spurred me to put her and her work in context. For that, and for all the years of inspiration and friendship, my gratitude to Patrick endures.

[1] Richard Sheridan, *The Rivals* (1775), Act III, Scene iii.
[2] J. Le Goff, *Les intellectuels au moyen âge* (Paris, 1957). See also A. Boureau, 'Intellectuals in the Middle Ages, 1957–95', in M. Rubin, ed., *The Work of Jacques Le Goff and the Challenges of Medieval History* (Woodbridge, 1997), pp. 145–55, esp. 146, stressing 'the vocation to universality' as defining the intellectual 'today as in the Middle Ages' in Le Goff's account.
[3] As noted by Dunbabin, 'Jacques Le Goff and the Intellectuals', in Rubin, ed., *The Work of Jacques Le Goff*, pp. 157–67, at 157, referring to pp. xvii–xix of Le Goff's 1985 introduction. (Boureau offers no comment on the refusal to define.) At pp. 157–8, Dunbabin helpfully infers 'the Platonic form' of Le Goff's 'intellectual': 'a self-made professional, a passer of examinations, <u>a member of a republic of letters</u>, a town-dweller, detached from aristocracy whether landed or business, identifying emotionally with artisans, <u>committed to communicating with a wider public</u> as well as to research, anti-clerical, anti-bourgeois, magnanimous to other scholars, <u>reasonable</u>, and <u>above all open-minded in his search for truth</u>'. Dunbabin comments: 'As one reads, the whiff rises up the nostrils of mingled Gauloises and roasting chestnut braziers on the Boulevard St Germain in the late 1950s.' For a gentle riposte to this, see Nelson, 'The Church and a Revaluation of Work in the Ninth Century?', *SCH* 37 (2001), pp. 35–43.

shoulder that task, though, because Le Goff's intellectuals were men (if not gentlemen) and not to be found before the twelfth century or outside its urban landscape. True, the noun 'intellectual' plays in some distinctive ways in the early Middle Ages, but there are still recognisable commonalities with the modern variety.

In Raymond Williams' *Keywords*, the noun 'Intellectual', especially in the plural form, is traced from pejorative usage in the nineteenth and much of the twentieth centuries, to its use 'now [i.e., in c. 1976] neutrally, and even at times favourably, to describe *people who do intellectual work and especially the most general kinds*' (my stress).[4] Intellectuals may be distinguished from 'specialists or professionals' (academics, for instance), implying that the intellectual has *'wider interests'*, and *a wider 'social function' in cultivating 'organised thought and learning'*. I have italicised the traits or criteria that in my view link the 'present' to the early medieval past.[5] Two further points should be added: the first is that an intellectual is self-consciously so: writes within a discourse, wears a badge; second, intellectuals' activity should be linked with another word, 'public', because 'intellectual', for me, denotes someone who positions him- or her-self so as to be read and heard, assumes a public role, addresses a public, considers, speaks and writes about matters of public concern, so, applies 'organised thought and learning' to what she or he proposes as the public good.[6] Pierre Bourdieu recently unmasked intellectuals' claims to be uniquely *dis*interested, but at the same time underlined their role in creating 'universes in which people have an interest in the universal', i.e., recognise the primacy of the collectivity, and *its* interests.[7]

Clearly, in Dunbabin's list, only the phrases I have underlined have relevance to the earlier Middle Ages. Yet her sustained critique of Le Goff's connection between urbanism and the emergence of his intellectuals opens the way to considering other intellectual-friendly environments, including that of an early medieval court.

[4] R. Williams, *Keywords: A Vocabulary of Culture and Society* (Glasgow, 1976), pp. 140–2, 'Intellectual'; cf. Williams' introduction, p. 22, on words and word clusters used in social and cultural discussion in terms of 'a shaping and reshaping, in real circumstances'.

[5] I put 'present' in inverted commas, partly because I am aware that *une vielle soixante-huitarde*'s use of 'intellectuals' is time-bound, partly because I sense that demotic pressures in late twentieth-century culture may well have resulted in the revival of the pejorative usage. (I am exploiting final editor's privilege to add that in the early twenty-first century, I am more aware than ever, thanks not least to Stefan Collini, whose lecture on Benda and 'the translation of the clerks' is now part of a searching book, *Absent Minds: Intellectuals in Britain* (Oxford, 2006), esp. pp. 499–501, that the word 'intellectual' is evolving still. I will stick, nevertheless, for present purposes, to the definition I offered at Kalamazoo in 2000.)

[6] I assumed some such criteria, but did not sufficiently address the definitional question, in 'The Intellectual in Politics: Context, Content and Authorship in the Capitulary of Coulaines, November 843', in L. Smith and B. Ward, eds., *Intellectual Life in the Middle Ages* (London, 1992), pp. 1–14, at 5–6 (reprinted in Nelson, *The Frankish World* (London, 1996), pp. 155–68, at 159).

[7] P. Bourdieu, 'Is a Disinterested Act Possible?', in his collection of essays, *Practical Reason: On the Theory of Action* (London, 1998), pp. 75–91, with quotation at 89 (translated by R. Johnson from

By the later ninth century, intellectuals were so well established you could joke about them: Notker the Stammerer's *opening* joke in the *Gesta Karoli* is about the two *Scotti*, Irishmen, incomparably learned in secular as well as sacred writings, who, finding themselves in a market where everyone else is selling, announce, 'wisdom for sale at our stall!' The market fortunately turns out to be not far from Charlemagne's court, indeed it sounds as if the market is at Aachen – and so the Irish strike a fine bargain: they are employed by Charlemagne as teachers of wisdom in return for being fed and clothed.[8] What, then, was the universe to which Carolingian intellectuals belonged and which they addressed? One answer would be 'the Church', but that was *too* universal, too shapeless, too abstract, a group to make much sociological sense. Ecclesiastical intellectuals lived *in saeculo*, in the world. At Charlemagne's court, Clement the Irishman taught *pueri nobilissimi, mediocres et infimi*, 'boys who were of the highest nobility, of middling rank, and of humble station'.[9] Over two and three generations an elite of lay and ecclesiastical teachers and life-long students was formed, driven by but not confined to the courts of kings and magnates. What Alcuin or Lupus or Hincmar have in common with Einhard or Nithard is a sense of shaping, and belonging to, new public universes that were political communities – and when the Carolingian world was riven as never before by conflict in 840–3, at least half a dozen writers (their works are still extant) were moved to comment, advise, justify and try to make sense of this personal and public and political débacle. Dhuoda was one of them.[10]

Raisons Pratiques (Paris, 1994)). For the role of Benda's *trahison des clercs* in shaping modern French views of the intellectual, see Stefan Collini's paper mentioned above, n. 5.

[8] Notker, *Gesta Karoli Magni*, ed. H. Haefele, *MGH SRG* n.s. 12 (Berlin, 1959), 1, 1, pp. 1–2. For the meaning of this story, including the scriptural allusion that provides the key, see D. Ganz, 'Humour as History in Notker's *Gesta Karoli Magni*', in E. B. King, J. T. Schaefer and W. B. Wadley, eds., *Monks, Nuns and Friars in Medieval Society* (Sewanee, TN, 1989), pp. 171–83. For the topography of Aachen, see Nelson, 'Aachen as a Place of Power', in M. de Jong and F. Theuws, eds., *Topographies of Power in the Early Middle Ages*, The Transformation of the Roman World 6 (Leiden, 2001), pp. 217–42.

[9] Notker, *Gesta Karoli* 1, 1, p. 2.

[10] Nelson, 'The Search for Peace in a Time of War: The Carolingian *Brüderkrieg*, 840–843', in J. Fried, ed., *Träger und Instrumentarien des Friedens im Hohen und Späten Mittelalter*, Vorträge und Forschungen 43 (Sigmaringen, 1996), pp. 87–114. P. Riché's edition, with French translation by B. de Vregille and C. Mondésert, of Dhuoda's book, as *Manuel pour mon fils*, Sources chrétiennes 225 (Paris, 1975) is still invaluable; but M. Thiébaux's new edition with English translation, *Dhuoda, Handbook for her Warrior Son: Liber Manualis* (Cambridge, 1998) is now the anglophone's version of choice. Both have substantial introductions. Unfortunately, neither has an index, and Thiébaux's select bibliography is all too select. C. Neel's translation, *Handbook for William: A Carolingian Woman's Counsel for her Son* (Lincoln, NE, 1991), has, again, no index, but the translation is lively and there is a valuable discussion of the historiography in the Introduction, pp. ix–xxviii, and also

But 'public' and 'political' should ring alarm bells here. For Dhuoda, the subject of this paper, author between November 841 and February 843 of a handbook of instruction for a noble layman, was a *woman*, and so by definition lay. In the Carolingian world, did her sex not exclude her from the political, the public, the universe of assembled lords great and small? That question presented me with a double task – for my subject is a woman as a lay *intellectual*: I need to show, first, how Dhuoda avoided taint by gender-association, in other words, how, as a woman, she plausibly claimed to offer wisdom to men without thereby seeming to subvert a natural hierarchy, but second, more important, I need to ask if Dhuoda, after all, was not only a mother, not only a wife, not only a domestic advisor, but someone addressing a wider audience on public concerns, creating, in Bourdieu's phrase, a universal interest.

First, then, did Dhuoda establish her own authority as an advisor? Yes. Dhuoda's claim was based, in large part, on her maternity, which underlined her lay status, and made her an embodiment of carnality, but which nevertheless gave her a legitimate, authoritative voice, acknowledged within her patriarchal world.[11] It is certainly true that Dhuoda saw herself, like her children, as subject to the authority of a husband who was *dominus et senior*, and her cutting-and-pasting of biblical statements on parental authority often omitted occasional references to mothers, leaving the impression that parental meant paternal. Yet patriarchy depended on mothers, as well as, obviously, on fathers. Mothers, like fathers, had parental rights as well as obligations. Their children owed them a debt, and honour. Dhuoda is in fact the only moral writer of the Carolingian period who stood on a parental platform.[12] Alcuin, Paulinus, Hrabanus, and especially Jonas, said some similar things about parental authority; but they were not parents; and neither, so far as we can tell, were Einhard or

---

in the Addendum to the paperback reprint of 1999, pp. 155–63. S. A. Stofferahn, 'The Many Faces in Dhuoda's Mirror: The *Liber Manualis* and a Century of Scholarship', *Magistra. A Journal of Women's Spirituality in History* 4 (1998), pp. 91–134, is a valuable critical survey: I am grateful to Steve Stofferahn for sending me a copy. My thanks also go to Rachel Stone whose fine doctoral thesis, 'Masculinity, Nobility and the Moral Instruction of the Carolingian Lay Elite' (Ph.D. University of London diss., 2005), on Carolingian masculinity will soon, I hope, be published.

[11] See Nelson, 'Les femmes et l'évangelisation', *Revue du Nord* 68 (1986), pp. 471–85; Nelson, 'Women and the Word in the Earlier Middle Ages', *SCH* 27 (1990), pp. 53–78.

[12] For moral writers in this period, see H. H. Anton, *Fürstenspiegel und Herrscherethos in der Karolingerzeit* (Bonn, 1968), pp. 83–6, and *passim*; 'Introduction', in *Manuel pour mon fils*, ed. P. Riché, *SC* 225 (Paris, 1975), pp. 11–15, 24–32, and for their representations of women, see K. Heene, *The Legacy of Paradise: Marriage, Motherhood and Women in Carolingian Edifying Literature* (Frankfurt-am-Main, 1997), and J. M. H. Smith, 'Gender and Ideology in the Earlier Middle Ages', *SCH* 34 (1998), pp. 51–73.

Nithard.[13] It is no coincidence, then, that Dhuoda's work puts unique emphasis on progeny. She wrote for her son William, whom she addressed by name twenty-four times in all, in the book's title, in its epigraph, in its prefatory acrostic poem, and often in the text itself, as well as dozens more times when she called him simply 'son'.[14] 'Son, you will have [male] teachers who may teach you more and fuller examples of usefulness, but [they will not be] in a position equal to mine, with a heart of one burning in their breast, as I your mother (*genetrix*) [have], O my first-born son.'[15] *Genetrix*, as Marcelle Thiébaux points out, is a significant choice of word, being a fairly rare feminine form of *genitor*, 'engenderer' or 'bringer forth', rather than *mater*, which Isidore of Seville explained etymologically as derived from '*materia*, "matter" ... so called because from her something is made ... while the *genitor* is the cause'. Dhuoda's repeated preference for *genetrix* thus 'renounces passivity'.[16]

The maternal theme has rightly been very strongly stressed in all the modern commentaries (and there are now a lot).[17] Against this univocal emphasis, Pierre Riché, introducing his edition, reacted with just a trace of sharpness: 'Il ne faut pas se représenter Dhuoda simplement comme une mère aimante et faible. C'est une femme qui a mis toute sa force et sa fortune ... au service du chef de la famille ... Elle écrit un livre à la gloire de son mari.'[18] So, Dhuoda is to be appreciated as wife, espouser of *une religion de la paternité*. It is true that Dhuoda does present herself near her book's beginning as a wife joyfully obeying the orders of her *senior* and rejoicing in his triumphs,[19] and near the book's end, as a faithful custodian left in his stronghold of Uzès to manage his military support at the cost of incurring huge debts.[20] But her own wifely role, prerequisite to her maternity, is ancillary to it. Dhuoda, *mère aimante*, is anything but a

---

[13] J. M. H. Smith, 'Einhard: The Sinner and the Saints', *TRHS*, 6th ser. 13 (2003), pp. 55–78, at 58, with n. 10, considers the possibility that Einhard had a son, but to my mind the evidence is slim.

[14] Dhuoda addresses William by name in *Liber Manualis*, ed. Thiébaux (hereafter referred to as *LM*) I, 1, 3, 4, 5, 7, pp. 60, 62, 64, 68; II, 3, p. 78; III, 1, 2, 7, 8, 10 (twice), pp. 86, 88, 104, 106, 112, 116; IV, 8 (twice), pp. 148, 154; IX, 4, p. 214; X, 2, pp. 220–2; XI, 2, p. 238. See also six further references in the prefatory material at pp. 42, verse inscription, 44–6, prologue, 46–8.

[15] *LM* I, 7, p. 70: 'Fili, habebis doctores qui te plura et ampliora utilitatis doceant documenta, sed non aequali conditione, animo ardentis in pectore, sicut ego genetrix tua, fili primogenite.'

[16] Thiébaux, *LM*, 'Introduction', p. 28, with reference to Isidore of Seville, *Etymologiae*, ed. W. M. Lindsay, 2 vols. (Oxford, 1911), IX.5.3.

[17] P. Dronke, *Women Writers of the Middle Ages: A Critical Study of Texts from Perpetua (+203) to Marguerite Porete (+1314)* (Cambridge, 1984), ch. 4, 'Dhuoda', is superb. R. McKitterick, *The Carolingians and the Written Word* (Cambridge, 1989), *passim*, provides essential context for Dhuoda's work, and see also Heene, *The Legacy of Paradise*, pp. 269–74.

[18] Riché, 'Introduction', *Manuel*, p. 27.   [19] *LM*, preface, p. 50.   [20] *LM* X, 4, p. 226.

mère faible. Her protestations of weakness are *captationes benevolentiae*, gender-inspired topoi, yet, at the same time, symptoms of a deeply felt sense of *human* dependence on God. Dhuoda's maternity is not only the psychological mainspring of her work, it authorises her to write *verba salutis*, and so to feminise the roles of adviser-intercessor and encourager: she is her son's *oratrix* and *ortatrix*.[21] Perhaps in a generous reference to a female entourage which, given her husband's frequent absences, might have been especially important to her, she presents herself as a woman 'of the frail sex, living unworthily among worthy women': this combines humility topos with affirmation of these particular *dignae*.[22] Dhuoda's likening of her moral *speculum* for her son's scrutiny to the mirror used by 'some women' as a beauty aid to please their husbands *in seculo* appropriates an old simile, transposing familial relationships, while defying and transcending gender in a nicely self-conscious touch of irony ('as in my joke').[23] Dhuoda locates herself not just in her relationships to her son, and to her husband, but very firmly and repeatedly within the family, as it reproduced itself through time, down the generations. Dhuoda espouses not so much *une religion de la paternité* as one of *parenté*, parenthood and kinship.[24]

Dhuoda's authority has other roots as well. Her playing out of the advisory role in her own writing is stunningly confident. Not only is she up to date with Carolingian moral thinking about the validity of the lay way of life: Dhuoda goes beyond any of her near-exact contemporaries Nithard, Jonas and Hincmar, in spelling out the demands of God and the world while affirming that they can be harmonised. According to

---

[21] *LM* I, 7, IV, 8, pp. 68, 148 (*ortatrix*); IX, 5, p. 214 (*oratrix*).
[22] *LM*, prologue, p. 46. Cf. the citation of Matthew 15: 27 (the story of the woman who asked Jesus to drive demons from her daughter) at *LM* I, 2, p. 60, where Dhuoda evokes, in her quest for understanding of God, not the Gospel's *catelli* (puppies) snaffling crumbs under the master's table but, *inter catulos*, an importunate little female puppy (*importuna catula*). Worth noting here are both the exegetical references explored at length by M. A. Mayeski, *Dhuoda: Ninth-Century Mother and Theologian* (Scranton, NY, 1995), pp. 65–92, and a change of gender which is self-referential as well as self-deprecating, and also, surely, meant to make William (and any other reader) smile?
[23] *LM*, prologue, p. 48. It should be said that in the same sentence, Dhuoda evokes, parallel to mirror-using women, young persons' enthusiasm for dice, and urges William to pay her book close attention *velut in speculis atque tabulis ioco*. Thiébaux's translation, following Riché, *Manuel*, p. 81, misses the reference to a joke; but Neel, *Handbook*, p. 5, picks it up neatly.
[24] The kinship theme is highlighted by J. Wollasch, 'Eine adlige Familie des frühen Mittelalters: Ihr Selbstverständnis und ihre Wirklichkeit', *Archiv für Kirchengeschichte* 39 (1957), pp. 150–88; C. B. Bouchard, 'Family Structure and Family Consciousness among the Aristocracy in the Ninth to Eleventh Centuries', *Francia* 16 (1986), pp. 639–68; and R. Le Jan, *Famille et Pouvoir dans le monde franc (VIIe-Xe siècle): Essai d'anthropologie sociale* (Paris, 1995), pp. 35–6, 54–5, 77.

Michael Wallace-Hadrill, the programme of spiritual exercises she offered William 'might have strained a monk'.[25] That is a statement that seriously underestimates the prayerfulness of the Carolingian lay elite and of Carolingian rulers themselves.[26] Dhuoda may have taken her cue from Alcuin's handbook for a layman, *Virtues and Vices*, but she affirmed with a force and consistency essayed, or risked, by no other Carolingian moralist, that a life of Christian mindfulness was compatible with the life, and the lifestyle, of a layman, and a layman at a Carolingian court.[27]

One passage in this quite substantial book (though Dhuoda characteristically calls it a little one) illuminates Dhuoda's method and intent more clearly, I will even say more brilliantly, than any other. Book VII, 1 stands out as a key point in the book's structure[28] – does so unmistakeably, I think, if you read the whole book from beginning to end, in Latin, at one go, as I did when I started to write this chapter. Dhuoda herself says, 'to see what is going on in this book, read the chapter headings';[29] and all three manuscripts give chapter headings (though they don't wholly coincide), both as a separate list at the beginning, and within the body of the work. They were clearly part of the author's original design. Book VII, 1 is headed, uniquely, *Admonitio singularis utilissima*. Now, unfortunately, this particular heading is attested only in one of the three manuscripts.[30] Nevertheless, Dhuoda clearly intended this passage as a discrete section, in fact as bridge between what she conceived as the book's two parts: at the end of the prologue, she says she will deal with *utrumque negotium*, that is, pleasing the *saeculum* and pleasing God (or as she rephrases it in the next

---

[25] J. M. Wallace-Hadrill, *The Frankish Church* (Oxford, 1983), p. 286; cf. Nelson, 'Monks, Secular Men and Masculinity c. 900', in D. M. Hadley, ed., *Masculinity in Medieval Europe* (London, 1999), pp. 121–42, at 128.

[26] In *LM* II, 3, p. 76, Dhuoda quotes from the Rule of Benedict 52, 4, on how to pray 'non ... in longa pertrahendi verba, sed in summo et brevi affectu'. On the distinctive *Sitz im Leben* of private prayer in this period, see now S. Waldhoff, *Alcuins Gebetbuch für Karl den Grossen*. Liturgiewissenschaftliche Quellen und Forschungen 89 (Münster, 2003), pp. 32–42; and Nelson, 'The Carolingian Cult of the Cross and the Civilising Process', forthcoming.

[27] See G. W. Olsen, 'One Heart and One Soul (Acts 4: 32 and 34) in Dhuoda's "Manual"', *Church History* 61 (1992), pp. 23–33, at 30–1; Nelson, 'Was Charlemagne's Court a Courtly Society?', in C. Cubitt, ed., *Court Culture in the Early Middle Ages* (Turnhout, 2003), pp. 39–57; Nelson, 'Did Charlemagne Have a Private Life?', in D. Bates, J. Crick and S. Hamilton, eds., *Writing Medieval Biography, 750–1250: Essays in Honour of Frank Barlow* (Woodbridge, 2006), pp. 15–28. Anton, *Fürstenspiegel*, barely mentions Dhuoda, but at p. 87, n. 52, he indicates her place in the development of 'eine christliche Adelsethik'.

[28] *LM* VII, 1, pp. 190–1. [29] *LM* X, 1, p. 218: 'Et quid ibidem gerantur, lege capita versorum'.

[30] It is not in MS 'B', and there is a gap at this point in MS 'N', so it is only attested by the late copy P. In the list of chapters that follows the preface, this chapter is entitled: 'De gemina nativitate sciendum', *LM*, p. 54.

line, 'being useful in the *saeculum* and pleasing God').³¹ In VII, 1, Dhuoda picks up this dual theme.

Like Augustine in *The City of God* (and though Dhuoda's scale is very much smaller than Augustine's, I would defend the comparison), Dhuoda starts with a clearly stated structure, and reminds the reader of it. She says that she has served her son up to now as his *ordinatrix*, the one who puts him in rank (an apt military metaphor – lost, and, alas, totally misrepresented, in Thiébaux's 'governess'), one who organises him, as regards *temporalia*, so that he can advance confidently and calmly while he lives *in militia actuali*, on active service, and is concerned with worldly office, but now, and from now on, she is going to continue to admonish (*ammonere*) him on how to advance to the highest level the service of his soul (*militia animae*). This makes her a mother twice over: once for his body, the second time, for his soul (*mens*), and the result will be that he is reborn every day in Christ.

> For a Christian person experiences two births: physical and spiritual. But the spiritual is nobler than the physical. In the human race the one cannot subsist profitably (*utiliter*) without the other. And in order that the physical and the spiritual may accord more worthily (*dignius*), someone says: [they are those] "with which and without which we cannot live". And although the meaning turns in another sense in that passage as originally written, I want you to accept it in the way I say, because of the clear reasons [for interpreting it as referring to] different things.

The New Testament notion of being born again was amplified by Augustine in his *Commentary on John* (and elsewhere) into an idea of *duae nativitates*.³² Where St Paul had seen a conflict between flesh and spirit, requiring the believer to crucify the flesh,³³ Dhuoda saw tension but the necessity of coexistence, and ultimately a kind of harmony. To convey this she looked to another source than the Apostle: in Dhuoda's mind, and at precisely this point, Augustine met Ovid. Riché followed the scribe of MS B in misreading the abbreviation for *aliquis* as that for *Apostolus* ('apls', as opposed to MS P's 'aqs', with superscript 'i' over the 'q'), yet failed to find the quotation in St Paul. Peter Dronke pointed out in 1984 that the *aliquis* was Ovid, and that Dhuoda here alludes to his lines to his beloved in the *Amores*: 'Aversor morum crimina, corpus amo. *Sic ego nec sine te nec tecum vivere possum. With or without you, life's impossible*)' (Dronke cites

---

³¹ *LM*, prologue, p. 48.
³² John 3: 5–7; Augustine, *Sermo* 121, 4, *PL* 38, 679; *Tractatus in Johannem* 11, 6, *CC* 36, 113–14.
³³ Galatians 5: 16–24.

Lee's rather free translation).³⁴ Compare Dhuoda on spiritual birth and fleshly birth: 'Cum quibus et sine quibus vivere non possumus' ('We cannot live with these, but neither can we live without them'). Note the extra force and subtlety of *vivere* in *her* context. Dhuoda clearly is not citing Ovid's tag at second-hand, for she knows its sense, she says, 'in the passage as originally written'. Furthermore, she offers her own interpretation of it, and tells her son to accept that.³⁵

Dronke rightly pointed out that the passage 'casts new light on Dhuoda's intellectual adroitness'. It certainly does. But still more can be said. The passage occurs in VII, 1, that is, at the fulcrum of the whole work, where Dhuoda distinguishes its two parts, and two *militiae*, two types of service, of body and spirit. The carnal birth can be useful, but it needs to be completed and transcended by the second, spiritual one. This is the theme of the rest of Book VII. Spiritual birthing goes on in the Church every day – and women as well as men do it: the mothers of martyrs, who encouraged sons to martyr themselves, did it; but *tunc et nunc et semper*, 'then and now and ever again', many do it *per Evangelium*, whether through preaching or – and this is evidently an allusion to herself and mothers in general – through the example of their *conversatio* of good works. This is how second birth comes about, then.³⁶ 'Hitherto I have been your *ordinatrix* as to your secular life; now, your mother a second time and in another sense, I admonish your soul, *ut in Christo cotidie renascaris* ('that you may be reborn again in Christ every day'), and so that, though this body is mortal, you can escape spiritual death and live eternally with God.'³⁷

The rest of Book VII, then Books VIII and IX, explain how this is to be achieved by reading and prayer. Dhuoda has intimate knowledge of the *libelli precum*, books of private prayer, and has already ensured that her son has this knowledge too. He is to exercise it daily, on behalf of family, king and counsellors, and all ranks and orders of the *res publica*. Private prayer is also public prayer. Dhuoda also urges close attention to the spiritual

---

³⁴ Dronke, *Women Writers*, p. 46, with the translation of Ovid's *Amores* by G. Lee (London, 1968), III, xi b, l. 7. Lee translates the preceding line: 'I adore your face and abhor your failings', where a more literal version might be: 'I scorn the offences of your behaviour [but] I love your body.'

³⁵ 'Et licet aliter in loco volvatur sensus, pro certis differentium causis, ego volo ut ita teneas sicut fateor.' Thiébaux's translation, p. 191, of this, as of the whole chapter, captures Dhuoda's meaning better than other translators. I draw on hers while offering my own: 'And although the meaning of this in the passage as originally written may be unrolled otherwise [than I offer here], and there are certain reasons for the differences, I want you to grasp it just as I bear witness to it [here].' For Ovid in Carolingian manuscripts, see R. J. Tarrant, 'Ovid', in L. D. Reynolds, ed., *Texts and Transmission: A Survey of the Latin Classics* (Oxford 1983), pp. 257–84.

³⁶ *LM* VII, 3, p. 192.   ³⁷ *LM* VII, 1, p. 190.

meanings of numbers which enhance prayer.³⁸ It seems, then, that Dhuoda's (and others') *conversatio operum bonorum* is to be the model for her son's. The word *conversatio* was important in monastic tradition, of course, but Charlemagne in a late capitulary had applied it to a reformed life for lay persons as well as ecclesiastics.³⁹ Alcuin, *Virtues and Vices*, is surely another source for Dhuoda in the key passage VII, I. Alcuin told his lay addressee, Count Guy, at the end of his work: 'Do not let the quality of lay conduct and secular way of life frighten you, as if you cannot enter the gates of heaven if you live that way. There is no difference there [in heaven] between who the layman might be and who the cleric in the life of this world.'⁴⁰ Compare VII, I's opening phrase, *Qualitas temporalium*, and Dhuoda's later reference to the *conversatio* of good lay models, including herself. This is really the gist of Dhuoda's whole work. She picks up a new theme in Carolingian spirituality for those *in saeculo*; and in developing that theme she makes a strong claim to originality.

Dhuoda has nothing to say about warfare, though she repeatedly refers to her son's service at the king's court with his young fellow-warriors (*comilitones*, another Pauline term,⁴¹ but Dhuoda, as ever, uses it in a quite specific sense). She has *much* to say about patriarchal families, about the Old Testament patriarchs' service in the marriage bed as a model for her son's own future.⁴² She looks forward to her son's marriage and to his

---

³⁸ *LM* VIII, 1, p. 196.
³⁹ *MGH Capit.* 1, no. 71, pp. 162–3: a reform agenda can be agreed by lay and ecclesiastical participants at an assembly in 811, says Charlemagne, *si diligenter conversationem coram discutere voluerimus*. See Nelson, 'The Voice of Charlemagne', in R. Gameson and H. Leyser, eds., *Belief and Culture: Studies in the Middle Ages. Studies presented to Henry Mayr-Harting* (Oxford, 2001), pp. 76–88.
⁴⁰ Alcuin, *De virtutibus et vitiis*, PL 101, col. 638: 'Nec te laici habitus vel conversationis saecularis terreat qualitas, quasi in eo habitu vitae coelestis januas intrare non valeas. Ubi non est distinctio, quis esset in saeculo laicus vel clericus.' Cf. St Paul, Philippians 3: 20, on *conversatio in coelis*, which Dhuoda cites in *LM* III, 10, p. 114. Cf. below, p. 116. See also Nelson, 'The Native Tradition 4: Alcuin', in *Pluscardine Benedictines* 138 (Pluscarden, 2005), pp. 34–40, which I wrote, alas, in ignorance of M. Alberi, '"The Sword which you Hold in your Hand": Alcuin's exegesis of the two swords and the lay *Miles Christi*', in C. Chazelle and B. Van Name Edwards, eds., *The Study of the Bible in the Carolingian Era* (Turnhout, 2003), pp. 117–31, who puts admirably some points similar to mine. I am very grateful to Abbot Hugh of Pluscarden Abbey for his invitation to think harder about Alcuin, and also for friendship and inspiration over the many years since he was an undergraduate at King's College London.
⁴¹ Philemon 1: 2.
⁴² *LM* IV, 6, p. 144: the *doctores* have not excluded the compatibility of marriage and what is sacred, as in the case of the patriarchs *qui in thoro coniugatorum militantes mundum in Christo cor studuerunt servare*, 'who doing service in the marriage-bed applied themselves to keeping a heart pure in Christ'. Thiébaux's little mistranslation, 'who soldiered *against the world* within the bonds of marriage and served Christ with a pure heart', runs counter to Dhuoda's message here and elsewhere. Cf. III, 3, p. 90, IV, 2, p. 130 (on the *iocunditas filiorum*), IX, 4, p. 214.

offspring.[43] She is clear and calm on the subject of sexuality within marriage. Though she ends her book foreseeing her own imminent death, when she began it, she had looked forward to the possibility of more children of her own.[44] She has much to say about concern for the *pauperes* and *humiles*, and the need for the young noble to conceal his nobility 'in poverty of mind' (*in paupertate mentis*), she uses more than once the phrase *fraterna compassio* and insists on a kind of natural equality, she is strong on almsgiving, and on the obligation of *maiores*, by which she means, she says, not just kings but *duces*, bishops and all *praelati*, to answer for the moral well-being of their *subditi*.[45]

In all this she is very practical. Not only are social duties set out in terms of action, the book includes a manual of conduct: of manners. Her son is told whom to talk to, whom to dine with, from whom, therefore, to learn how to behave, and from whom to hope for help. None of this is surprising, given his place *in militia actuali*. *Collationes in magna domo* ('conversations in a big house' such as the palace) were Dhuoda's recommended sources and contexts of instruction, the means of improving a lad's *conversatio* in both the modern and early medieval senses.[46] At one level, much of Book III is about how to make friends and influence people – even though Dhuoda's theme is class duty as well as class conduct.

Much of what Dhuoda says is derivative, especially on the moral side. In fact, whole sections are made up of chains of biblical citations, apparently from memory, and the added-on Book XI is entirely borrowed from a tract on the use of the psalms attributed to Alcuin. But such traits are absolutely characteristic of these Carolingian intellectuals, just as the psalms are at the heart of personal prayer. Riché chides Dhuoda's repeated use of *quasi*, as in *quasi potentes*, *quasi florentes*, as a sign of poor style. Not so – for there is (as Riché himself notes) a much broader Augustinian context, the *Commentaries on the Psalms*, counterposing the seeming (*quasi*) and the true: Dhuoda has a whole chapter about this, and she points out that the Book of Job is based on it.[47] Riché picks up in Book I, 6, an interesting instance of adynaton, that is, the trope of impossibility transcended (the poet's love will survive though

---

[43] *LM* III, 3, p. 92.   [44] *LM* II, 3, p. 80.
[45] *LM* III, 10, pp. 108–16 (which ends with an Augustinian echo in the idea of *conglutinatio dilectionis*, cf. Augustine, *Annotationes in Iob* 38, PL 34, 879, 'ut Dominus ... cohaeret eis tamquam glutine charitatis'), IV, 8, 9, pp. 148–63. On these chapters, Olsen, 'One Heart and One Soul', is particularly helpful.
[46] *LM* III, 9, pp. 106–8.
[47] *LM* V, 1. Riché, *Manuel*, chastises at 'Introduction', p. 43, and notes the Augustinian inspiration at pp. 262–3, n. 2.

seas run dry; divine power can override nature). Riché does not exhaust the interest of the passage. Dhuoda's thought takes off from Psalm 103: 2 where the psalmist imagined the Lord *extendens caelum sicut pellem*, 'who stretchest out the heavens like a curtain' (I quote the Authorised Version (Ps. 104: 2)). But Dhuoda then creates something that is quite her own. Taking up the literal meaning of *pellis* as skin or hide, she transforms the psalmist's verse into: 'si polus et arva in modum cartis membranae extensae per aera essent…' – 'if heaven and earth were extended through the sky like a charter on a spread-out sheet of parchment' – and then pursues the image: 'atque [si] ipsi orbi cultores cuncti, nascentes in mundum, ob ingenio humanitatis augmentum omnes fuissent scriptores, de initio usque nunc, quod est contra naturam impossibile, comprehendi non valerent Omnipotentis magnitudinem.'[48] Surely that is a writerly conceit? And surely Dhuoda is conscious of herself here as a writer, belonging to a rarified group? Dhuoda, elsewhere in her book, sees herself as someone with *regiminis cura*, an expert in *conversatio*, her son's *ortatrix, oratrix, ordinatrix*, someone knowledgeable in the writings of *articulatores*, experts in the lore of numbers.[49] The idea that she was derivative to the point of plagiarism can be stood on its head: in Dhuoda's culture, what you signalled thus was mastery of a shared *scientia*. You placed a quote from Ambrosius Autpertus here, an echo of Smaragdus there, and a verse from Prudentius in a context so unexpected that Karl Strecker completely failed to notice it and spent some time reconstructing Dhuoda's 'correct' text.[50] This lady was more learned than she has been given credit for. Did that make her an intellectual? Yes of course it did – in Carolingian terms – just as Chinese intellectuals were so because of (not despite) their assimilation of Lao Tze and Confucius, an assimilation so thorough that even the merest allusion would be picked up by others similarly trained and socialised.

But – and I want finally, squarely to address my second question about audience and intent – was Dhuoda also an intellectual in Raymond Williams' sense, in Bourdieu's sense, in *our* sense? Dhuoda's reading, according to Riché, was wholly religious.[51] Yet as we have seen, she had read pagan as well as Christian authors, and at least one pagan poet as well

---

[48] *LM* I, 6, pp. 66–8. I slightly adapt Thiébaux's translation: 'and if all earth's inhabitants born in the world from the beginning until now were – through some increase of human wisdom, an impossibility contrary to nature – writers, they would not be able to capture the grandeur … of God'.
[49] *LM* VI, 4, p. 186.
[50] Ambrosius Autpertus: *LM* IV, 6, p. 142; Smaragdus *LM* IV, 3, 7, pp. 132, 147; Prudentius: *LM* III, 10, p. 116, and see Riché, *Manuel*, pp. 182–3, n. 3.
[51] Riché, *Manuel*, 'Introduction', p. 37.

as some pagan grammarians. Further, she had a strongly positive interest in the secular world of the court: indeed it is the parts in Book III about how to get on *in domo magna* that seem most strikingly original by comparison with Alcuin or Jonas. Conversely, they remind me of Adalard and the *De ordine palatii*.⁵² What both works present is not just knowledge but know-how: *scientia* – which comes not just from books but also from life-experiences. In Dhuoda's case, those experiences might be thought to have equipped her with the licence of the freelance, the provincial, the outsider. Wallace-Hadrill imagined her 'tucked away on a hillock in the Midi',⁵³ and even though Uzès, where Dhuoda tells us she was writing, was not that far off the beaten track, it was no more than a regional political centre.

Uzès, though, was not where Dhuoda's view of the world, and of herself, had been shaped.⁵⁴ Listen to what she herself wants William to remember: she and William's father, Bernard, were married in 824 at Aachen, not, *pace* Riché, 'dans la chapelle' but *in palatio*, which *could* mean the big church there but that is not what Dhuoda wanted to stress.⁵⁵ I think she is laying claim here to time spent at court. And since she herself declares her own nobility, I wonder if she was one of that crowd of noble girls (as well as women) that congregated at Aachen, at Charlemagne's court (though Dhuoda was presumably very young when Charlemagne died in 814), and, after Charlemagne's daughters and cousin had been expelled, was then reconstructed by Louis the Pious. If so, she could have known Adalard in the mid-820s, might even, like Hincmar, have read the *De ordine palatii* 'while a young person in the palace' (*dum adolescens in palatio*).⁵⁶ She was also surely acquainted with the Empress Judith, that

---

⁵² The *De ordine palatii* was 'reissued' by Hincmar in 882, and in the standard modern edition is attributed to him, *Hincmarus de ordine palatii*, ed. T. Gross and R. Schieffer, *MGH Fontes iuris germanici* (Berlin, 1980), although Hincmar firmly credited it to Adalard, whose text he said he had seen *in palatio* in the 820s, prologue, p. 34. For the attribution of the core text to Adalard, and a date (probably) late in the reign of Charlemagne, see Nelson, 'Aachen as a Place of Power', pp. 226–32; also B. Bachrach, 'Adalhard of Corbie's *De ordine palatii*: Some Methodological Observations', *Cithara* 41 (2001), pp. 3–34, rightly criticising Nelson's earlier views on the *actualité* behind parts of the text. I am very grateful to Bernard Bachrach for sending me an offprint of his inimitably thought-provoking paper.

⁵³ Wallace-Hadrill, *The Frankish Church*, p. 286 (cf. the review by Nelson, *JEH* 37 (1986), pp. 322–8, at 327). Wallace-Hadrill here sums up Dhuoda's work, not unsympathetically, as 'Carolingian introspection at its best'.

⁵⁴ Dhuoda is sometimes depicted (typically by southerners) as a southerner by origin, but I can see no evidence for that assumption. As Riché, 'Introduction', *Manuel*, pp. 21–3, observes, her name is Germanic and well documented in northern parts.

⁵⁵ *LM*, preface, p. 48; cf. Riché, 'Introduction', p. 17.

⁵⁶ *De ordine palatii*, Hincmar's Prologue, p. 34.

patron of poets and serious educator of *her* son.[57] That one mention of Aachen in the *Liber Manualis*, strategically placed in the first sentence of Dhuoda's preface, establishes her credentials as a courtier in the palace of Louis the Pious in the years when the little Charles the Bald (born 823) was beginning to attract attention.[58] Further, it seems likely, since Bernard was Louis's godson, influential at court probably from 824, and certainly from 829 when he was appointed chamberlain until 830 when he fell from grace,[59] that some of Dhuoda's early married life was spent at Aachen. Thus, when she wrote for William about life at court in the *magna domus*, she was not imagining it, but remembering it. The Carolingian *aula* of the 820s was her palace of memory.[60] *In domo magna ut est illa ... collationes conferuntur multae*. She imagined wherever it was that William now was, in Charles the Bald's *aula*, as somewhere like the Aachen she had known.

Dhuoda did not forget. Nor, finally, did she write only for William. She says quite explicitly at the beginning of the book, and repeats the point, again symmetrically, at the end, that she writes for a court audience: she addresses William with a little courtly flourish, *tua iuventutis nobilitas*, 'as if I were with you', and also 'all those to whom you may show this book and have them read it too'.[61] Her envoi invokes the thoughts and prayers of 'whoever may read this book that you are reading'.[62] I think she sees those *comilitones* in her mind's eye, *quasi praesens*. She writes for them, and through them for king and counsellors. The fact that no fewer than three manuscripts of this work survive (that is one more than survives of Geoffroi de Charny's fourteenth-century *Book of Chivalry*) is some kind of indication that it did not remain a private work, nor ever was conceived as merely that. Gender did not preclude Dhuoda's writing for a public, nor

---

[57] See E. Ward, 'Agobard of Lyons and Paschasius Radbertus as Critics of the Empress Judith', *SCH* 27 (1990), pp. 15–25, and see now Ward, 'The Career of the Empress Judith' (University of London Ph.D. dissertation, 2003); also A. Koch, *Kaiserin Judith: Eine politische Biographie* (Husum, 2005). What Dhuoda thought of the allegations about her own husband's adultery with Judith was something she kept to herself. She might have been forearmed if she had read *De ordine palatii*, section 360, p. 72, on the *honestas palatii*, which pertained 'ad reginam praecipue et sub ipsa ad camerarium'. Bernard had held the post of chamberlain in the critical year 829–30.

[58] Dhuoda mentions Charles, her son's king and lord, in positive terms appropriate to 841–3, in *LM* III, 4, 6, pp. 92, 100–2, but she may have known him since he was little.

[59] The fall was permanent, as it turned out. Bernard thereafter tried to build an alternative power-base in the region of Narbonne: Nelson, *Charles the Bald* (London, 1993), pp. 88–91, 102–3, and P. Depreux, *Prosopographie de l'entourage de Louis le Pieux* (Sigmaringen, 1997), pp. 137–9.

[60] I echo the title of a recent resonant paper by Stuart Airlie, 'The Palace of Memory: The Carolingian Court as Political Centre', in S. Rees Jones, R. Marks and A. J. Minnis, eds., *Courts and Regions in Medieval Europe* (York, 2000), pp. 1–20.

[61] *LM* I, 1, p. 58.   [62] *LM* x, 6, p. 228.

the transmission of her work. Her public platform, even *in absentia*, was built of maternity, nobility and experience.

Like Hincmar, she knew that a palace was not a building but the people who inhabited it.[63] Like Hincmar, and like those others she remembered – Adalard, Einhard, Nithard – that was the audience she aimed to write for, beyond her immediate concern for her own beautiful boy. Her theme was the way of living of *aulici* as a group: she wrote to stimulate their service to the *res publica*, and their devotion to the Carolingian dynasty. She herself, after all, had once been among courtiers.[64] She wrote, in short, not only as a mother for her son (and that repeated invocation of him is itself perhaps a bit of literary legerdemain), but as a would-be giver of a second birth in the mind and spirit to other women's sons. That is why, given this writer's talents, I would take a small bet that she was not ineffectual; more positively, it is why, in the end, Dhuoda, not despite but in part *because of* her gender, deserves the name of intellectual.

---

[63] Letter sent on behalf of the bishops assembled at Quierzy in 858, to King Louis the German and King Charles the Bald, *MGH Conc.* III, ed. W. Hartmann (Hanover 1984), no. 41, *c.* v, p. 412: 'The palace of the king is so called on account of the rational human beings who dwell therein, not on account of walls or courtyards that are insensible things.' For courtiers' consciousness of themselves as such even when they had left the court, see Airlie, 'Bonds of Power and Bonds of Association in the Court Circle of Louis the Pious', in P. Godman and R. Collins, eds., *Charlemagne's Heir* (Oxford, 1990), pp. 191–204, at 196.

[64] Maybe Hincmar did not mean his palace *homines* to include women; but there is plenty of evidence that there were women at Carolingian courts: see Nelson, 'Women at the Court of Charlemagne: A Case of Monstrous Regiment?', in J. C. Parsons, ed., *Medieval Queenship* (New York, 1993), pp. 43–61 (repr. in Nelson, *The Frankish World* (London, 1996), pp. 223–42), and Nelson, review of Depreux, *Prosopographie de l'entourage de Louis le Pieux*, in *Early Medieval Europe* 11 (2002), p. 285, for the absence of women, save Ermengard and Judith, from this otherwise marvellously rich compendium.

CHAPTER 7

Learned women? Liutberga and the instruction of Carolingian women

Valerie L. Garver

One evening early in the ninth century a Saxon noblewoman named Gisla stopped to spend the night at a monastery. She had been travelling on business, looking after her many estates, which were extensive and far-flung. During her stay at the monastery, one girl caught Gisla's eye. She seemed 'to stand out among the others in beauty and character', and furthermore was capable, deferential and talented.[1] After determining her origin, family and status, Gisla began to urge this girl, Liutberga, to come with her. Although Liutberga would already have taken her vows had she not been so young, Gisla managed to convince her to leave the monastery to live with her and be loved as one of her own daughters.[2]

This episode from the *Vita Liutbirgae Virginis* introduces one of the portrayals of instruction that appear throughout a text offering much advice about how women should treat each other and how they should behave. For example, Gisla became a mentor to Liutberga, taking up a role the author describes in a maternal manner. Just as she would have for one of her own daughters Gisla provided Liutberga with knowledge she later passed on to other women. The author, almost certainly a cleric who had some connection to Windenhausen, the religious house to which Liutberga eventually attached herself, surely meant that this *vita* should offer examples

---

For valuable comments on various drafts of this essay, I would like to thank Cristina Cervone, Abe Delnore, Paul Kershaw, Tom Noble, Anne Schutte, and especially Patrick Wormald from whose intellectual generosity I greatly benefited.

[1] 'ut virgunculam quandam forma vel ingenio ceteris coaetaneis suis', *Das Leben der Liutbirg c.* 3, ed. O. Menzel, *MGH SDM*, Kritische Studientexte III (Leipzig, 1937), p. 12, hereafter *VL*. Most scholarship concerning the *vita* has dealt with its date and the location of Liutberga's cell when she eventually became a recluse: O. Menzel, 'Das Leben der Liutbirg', *Sachsen und Anhalt* 13 (1937), pp. 78–89; W. Grosse, 'Das Kloster Wendhausen, sein Stiftergeschlecht und seine Klausnerin', *Sachsen und Anhalt* 16 (1940), pp. 45–76; *Das Leben der Liutberg: Die Geschichtsschreiber der deutschen Vorzeit*, ed. E. Witte (Leipzig, 1944); L. J. Samons II, 'The *Vita Liutbirgae*', *Classica et Mediaevalia* 43 (1992), pp. 273–86.

[2] 'in pari dilectione filiarum suarum omni tempore secum eam fore permansuram', *VL c.* 3, p. 12.

and counterexamples of appropriate female life to the women in that community but also perhaps more generally to other women. Examining the portrayals of instruction in the *vita* will reveal much about the kinds of knowledge the author thought aristocratic women transmitted among each other and the ways contemporaries understood instruction among women. By paying close attention to possible models and the points at which the text offers incidental detail it will be possible to suggest that this female instruction may reflect local or regional practices.[3] The *vita* furthermore depicts the relations among members of an aristocratic family. In addressing both instruction and family relations, it comments on subjects broached in studies of another Carolingian woman, Dhuoda.[4]

Yet the women depicted in the *Vita Liutbirgae* seem rather less learned than Dhuoda. The author of the *Vita* expected that women transmitted two broad categories of knowledge: household arts, the skills and knowledge necessary to supervise a home, and basic religious virtues and practices. Such instruction hardly qualified them as 'learned'. Rather, these categories of knowledge would have aided women domestically, particularly in raising children, running an estate, administering a convent, producing and keeping track of daily necessities such as textiles, and managing the resources over which they had control. Carolingian aristocratic and royal women provided

---

[3] Liutberga's *vita* displays gendered norms of Carolingian hagiography, recognised by Julia Smith, that must temper discussions of female sanctity for this period. However, the overall pattern of the life interests me less for the purposes of this study than the asides and details relating to female instruction that appear throughout the text: J. M. H. Smith, 'The Problem of Female Sanctity in Carolingian Europe *c.* 780–920', *P&P* 146 (1995), pp. 3–37. Scholars have argued that incidental details in hagiography can provide much information about the past, especially if they are mentioned in other contemporary sources and do little or nothing to prove a subject's sanctity: D. Weinstein and R. M. Bell, *Saints and Society: The Two Worlds of Western Christendom, 1000–1700* (Chicago, 1982), p. 13; P. Fouracre and R. A. Gerberding, *Late Merovingian France: History and Hagiography, 640–720* (Manchester, 1996), pp. 44–8. Ottokar Menzel pointed out that Liutberga's *vita* contained no claims that she was a saint and that it, therefore, could not properly be called a saint's life. In fact, no evidence for her veneration exists before the Renaissance. Since she was never formally canonised, some might not categorise her as a saint at all. *VL*, p. 3; Samons, 'The *Vita Liutbirgae*', pp. 282.

[4] P. Dronke, *Women Writers of the Middle Ages: A Critical Study of Texts from Perpetua (203) to Marguerite Porete (1310)* (Cambridge, 1984), pp. 36–54; J. Marchand, 'The Frankish Mother: Dhuoda', in K. M. Wilson, ed., *Medieval Women Writers* (Athens, GA, 1984), pp. 1–29; M. A. Claussen, 'God and Man in Dhuoda's *Liber Manualis*', in W. J. Shields and D. Wood, eds., *Women in the Church*, SCH 27 (1990), pp. 43–52; M. A. Claussen, 'Fathers of Power and Women of Authority: Dhuoda and the *Liber manualis*', *French Historical Studies* 19 (1996), pp. 785–809; the introduction to Carol Neel's translation of the text, *A Handbook for William: A Carolingian Woman's Counsel for her Son* (Washington, DC, 1991, repr. 1999); and the introduction to Marcelle Thiébaux's edition and translation of the same text, *Dhuoda, Handbook for her Warrior Son: Liber manualis* (Cambridge, 1998). Both modern English translations rely heavily upon P. Riché's annotated edition, with French translation by B. de Vregille and C. Mondésert, of Dhuoda's book, as *Manuel pour mon fils*, Sources chrétiennes 225 (Paris, 1975). See now Janet L. Nelson's chapter in this volume, above, pp. 106–20.

forms of instruction to others that remain at the margins of both the sources and modern scholarship, but their activities in this instruction were crucial to the strength and stability of their families and religious communities.[5] Unlike the learned texts of clerics which circulated among an elite minority, the ability of women to manage resources shrewdly, make decisions effectively, and look after their natural and spiritual families affected many individuals on a daily basis and must have been essential to helping sustain aristocratic society even if female actions in this regard remain in the background of contemporary sources. The differentiation between *sapientia* (scholarly knowledge focused on books) and *scientia* or *prudentia* (wisdom or knowledge that could extend into 'practical' spheres of life) is apt here.[6] Women learned a social competence from each other, which advanced their own interests and those of their families. Investigating such domestic 'learning' will extend understanding of Carolingian cultures beyond the more learned actions and works of other laity discussed in this volume and will further incorporate laywomen into the study of female education, which has focused mainly on religious women.[7]

Scholars may have not fully appreciated the information this text has to offer because of doubts about its reliability as a Carolingian source. Historical and textual questions once surrounded the *Vita Liutbirgae Virginis*, but a number of scholars, particularly Ottokar Menzel, whose 1937 edition caused a brief spate of scholarship on the *vita*, have established its historical origin. Menzel confronted the late dates of the manuscripts and made convincing arguments for a date closer to the death of the text's subject: the author claimed to have met Liutberga himself; certain linguistic errors the author makes are typical of pre-Carolingian and Carolingian usage; and proper names are Carolingian in form throughout the text.[8]

---

[5] Anneke Mulder-Bakker has argued persuasively that lay people continued to receive similarly informal educations through the central Middle Ages: A. B. Mulder-Bakker, 'The Metamorphosis of Woman: Transmission of Knowledge and Problems of Gender', *Gender and History* 12 (2000), pp. 642–64.

[6] *Ibid.*, pp. 644–5; see also Abels' chapter, below, p. 251.

[7] As scholars have increasingly acknowledged a lack of distinction between public and private, whether physically or conceptually, in the pre-modern West, they have also recognised the 'domestic' sphere as a subject integral to understanding society as a whole: J. L. Nelson, 'The Problematic in the Private', *Social History* 15 (1990), pp. 355–64, at 355–6, 363–4. Among those, not cited elsewhere in this chapter, who have argued that early medieval women, especially in the religious life, had opportunities to gain learning are M. P. Heinrich, *The Canonesses and Education in the Early Middle Ages* (Washington, DC, 1924); P. Riché, *Education and Culture in the Barbarian West: Sixth through Eighth Centuries*, trans. J. J. Contreni (Columbia, SC: 1976); J. M. Ferrante, 'The Education of Women in the Middle Ages in Theory, Fact, and Fantasy', in P. H. Labalme, ed., *Beyond Their Sex: Learned Women of the European Past* (New York, 1980), pp. 9–42. See also n. 45, below.

[8] *VL*, pp. 2–8; Samons, '*Vita Liutbirgae*', pp. 274–8, 283.

A charter dated 9 October 800 – 8 October 801 from Fulda, furthermore, records a donation that this Liutberga may have made.[9] Everything points to a date of composition shortly after her death, probably before 876.[10] The *vita* therefore doubtless offers information about ninth-century understanding of female instruction.

A near-constant theme in the *vita* is Liutberga's dramatic effect on Gisla's family and on others in the local community. Returning with Gisla to Saxony, she spent her time helping her patroness with 'women's work', travelling with her between estates and looking after the poor.[11] Eventually, Gisla's two daughters Bilihild and Hrothild founded and became abbesses of Windenhausen and Karlsbach respectively, while Liutberga remained with Gisla.[12] Her only other child, Bernard, inherited her estates. At Gisla's deathbed Bernard swore to care for Liutberga just as his mother had. Gisla urged Bernard to let Liutberga look after household matters for him and to heed her advice, 'because she was always trustworthy in all things for me'.[13] Bernard followed his mother's advice, and Liutberga became one of his most trusted and indispensable servants. Not only did she help him look after his estates and household matters, but also she had influence over each of his successive wives and helped look after his children.[14] When Liutberga told him she wished to lead a solitary religious life, Bernard did not feel he could deny such a reasonable and devout request, and he had a cell built for her at Windenhausen, where his sister Bilihild was abbess.[15] After gaining the permission and blessing of the local bishop and priests, Liutberga was enclosed in the cell, where she would spend the next thirty years leading an ascetic life of prayer and helping many others, especially through her instruction of girls and her care for and exemplarity to those in her community, particularly women.

The *vita* is full of information about Liutberga's education, her teaching, the sorts of knowledge women seem to have been expected to possess, and the ways they transmitted such learning. Lay and religious aristocratic women needed expertise in both household arts and basic devotional practices such as praying and reading psalms in order to look after their families well and to administer and provide necessities for their religious communities. Before

---

[9] *Urkundenbuch des Klosters Fulda*, ed. E. E. Stengel (Marburg, 1958), pp. 409–10. Liutberga was enclosed at Windenhausen, where her patroness Gisla's daughter Bilihild was abbess from 835–40 to 865–70, although evidence from the charter at Fulda indicates that Liutberga may have lived somewhat earlier than that or had a rather long life. Both Stengel and Menzel offer compelling reasons for their dating of Liutberga's *vita*, but since the difference between them is at most thirty years and quite possibly less, the lack of an exact date does not greatly affect this study.
[10] Samons, '*Vita Liutbirgae*', pp. 282–3.   [11] *VL* cc. 4, 6, p. 13: 'muliebria … opera' appear in *c*. 6.
[12] *VL c*. 2, p. 11.   [13] 'quia michi semper in cunctis fidelis extiterat', *c*. 7, pp. 14–15.
[14] *VL* cc. 8–10, pp. 15–16.   [15] *VL* cc. 14–15, pp. 19–21.

assuming these responsibilities, they required instruction. Many women mentioned in the *vita* were probably from wealthy and locally powerful families.[16] That Liutberga's social status, however, is never unambiguously stated has resulted in some disagreement about her background.[17] Yet evidence strongly indicates that she at least operated among the local elite. If wealth, influence and recognition as a member of the elite marked an aristocrat, then Liutberga was aristocratic. Her entrance into a monastery as a child, presumably as an oblate destined to become a nun, suggests that her parents or another sponsor were able to afford the usually necessary oblation offering.[18] Certainly, once Gisla became her patroness, Liutberga lived in an aristocratic family and interacted with some wealthy and influential women and men, and sometime after their arrival in Saxony Gisla furnished her with '*dignis honoribus*'.[19] If *honores* be taken here to mean land, this statement in the *vita* may have helped convince Edmund Stengel that a charter from Fulda recorded a substantial donation by this Liutberga.[20] But *honores* also imply status: Gisla may have provided Liutberga with high rank, not merely wealth. Furthermore, Gisla's admonition to Bernard that he look after Liutberga provides the context for this statement, and her emphasis upon her provision of these markers and her adoption of Liutberga bolsters her request that Bernard regard Liutberga as a sister.[21]

High birth may have been one reason Gisla thought so well of Liutberga. When they met, Gisla specifically asked about her family background:

[Gisla] began to ask who she was and where she came from, about her family and the rank of her kin. [S]he had answered all these things cleverly, discussing them in order and saying that she had parents in a place called Solazburg and discussing their ancestry and the nature of their rank and explaining her whole way of life…[22]

---

[16] Gisla's family was rich and powerful on an imperial level since her father, Hessi, had been a Saxon nobleman whom Charlemagne had rewarded richly for his loyalty: Samons, '*Vita Liutbirgae*', p. 278.
[17] D. Herlihy, *Opera Muliebra: Women and Work in Medieval Europe* (Philadelphia, PA, 1990), p. 88; L. B. Gray, '"Mighty in Appropriate Ways": Liutbirg, a Ninth-Century Life' (University of Vermont, MA dissertation, 1994), pp. 97–101. While Herlihy is convinced Liutberga had humble origins, Gray is less convinced and suggests a variety of explanations for the absence of any discussion of Liutberga's heritage.
[18] M. de Jong, *In Samuel's Image: Child Oblation in the Early Medieval West* (Leiden, 1996), p. 184. De Jong explains that the 'most important lacuna' in the history of the Carolingian oblation ritual is the lack of information about girls.
[19] *VL* c. 7, p. 15. [20] *Urkundenbuch Fulda*, pp. 409–10. See also n. 9.
[21] 'meam dilectam Liutbirgam, quam … adoptavi michi in filiam', *VL* c. 7, pp. 14–15.
[22] 'percunctari coeperat, quaenam esset aut unde originem duceret, quae natalium suorum atque condicionis professio. Haec ergo illi prudenti responsione per ordinem disserenti seque de loco, qui dicitur Solazburg, parentes habere dicenti indeque progenitam ac qualitatem condicionis exprimenti omnesque vitae suae conversationes exponenti…', *VL* c. 3, p. 12.

Since most Carolingian *vitae* mention that saints were well born, the author's omission concerning her background is highly unusual. The absence of such a description, however, need not mean that Liutberga was not well born. Recognition of high social status may have been necessary for Gisla's establishing such a relationship of patronage.

The author also describes Liutberga's manner in answering as 'prudens', demonstrating her practical wisdom at an early age, another reason that probably prompted Gisla to take Liutberga back to Saxony. A parallel but contrasting scene occurs in Liudger's *Vita Gregorii Abbatis*, written sometime just after 800. Relationships of patronage and the development of aristocratic bonds have been well established in the Carolingian world.[23] These episodes depict such relationships while suggesting differences in the knowledge and levels of learning thought appropriate for boys and girls. In the *Vita Gregorii*, the great Anglo-Saxon missionary Boniface first met Gregory, future bishop of Utrecht, on a visit to Pfalzel, where Addula, Gregory's grandmother, was abbess. Sitting around a table, Boniface, Addula, her *familia* including Gregory, and presumably some of Boniface's followers discussed Scripture. When they needed a reader, Addula had Gregory read aloud before their famous guest. Although Gregory could not explain the passage when Boniface requested that he do so, Boniface nevertheless found his reading remarkable, and Gregory's amazement at Boniface's subsequent exegesis of the passage he had just read was so great it caused him to forget both his kin and his land: he soon begged Addula to let him follow Boniface as his student so that he could discuss holy books with him.[24] In each *vita*, a youth impressed a future mentor: Boniface and Gisla recognised potential in Gregory and Liutberga. The repetition of certain hagiographic patterns, which often indicate the influence of certain *vitae* upon others, should dissuade scholars from reading too much into such passages, especially in this case, for Liutberga's and Gregory's *vitae* are both associated with the community at Fulda.[25] Certainly, the episodes

---

[23] Mayke de Jong discusses commendation and fosterage of boys to clerics in hagiography, including Gregory's case, noting that these relationships are depicted as being of an 'eminently personal nature', *In Samuel's Image*, pp. 214–16, quotation p. 216; S. R. Airlie, 'Bonds of Power and Bonds of Association in the Court Circle of Louis the Pious', in P. Godman and R. Collins, eds., *Charlemagne's Heir*, pp. 191–204; G. Althoff, *Verwandte, Freunde und Getreue: Zum politischen Stellenwert der Gruppenbindungen im früheren Mittelalter* (Darmstadt, 1990); Althoff, *Amicitiae und Pacta: Bündnis, Einung, Politik und Gebetsgedenken im beginnenden 10. Jahrhundert*, MGH Schriften 37 (Hanover, 1992).

[24] Liudger, *Vita Gregorii abbatis*, ed. O. Holder-Egger, *MGH SS* xv, i, pp. 67–8.

[25] I. Wood, *The Missionary Life: Saints and the Evangelisation of Europe, 400–1050* (Harlow, 2001), p. 19; on Gregory, pp. 107–15.

recall Jesus' calling of his disciples. This scene of a mentor noticing a possible student may result from the adoption of models from other *vitae* also connected to Fulda. Nevertheless, the two episodes also differ substantially enough that their details are revealing. In her *vita* Liutberga requires some convincing to leave with Gisla, whereas according to Liudger Gregory is eager to follow Boniface. Gregory has already become an adept reader when he meets Boniface while Liutberga attracts her mentor mainly through appearance and disposition. Gregory eventually studies books, and Liutberga learns how to manage domestic affairs. Thus, preparation may have helped young people establish a bond with a mentor, but those preparations were almost certainly different for boys and girls.

References to the instruction Liutberga must have received as a child at her community are rather vague, but clues in the text indicate some skills she learned there. When a demon wants to remind Liutberga that she has not always been as devout as she now is, he recalls that when she was a small child, she traded her broken needle for another girl's whole one during their communal work.[26] In the *Institutio sanctimonialum Aquisgranensis*, a rule for religious women composed at the Synod of Aachen in 816, two canons mention handiwork by members of the community.[27] Thomas Schilp has suggested that this handiwork referred to the copying of manuscripts rather than only to textile work, but surely the yearly allocation of wool and flax so that the *sanctimoniales* could make their clothes reveals it to have concerned textiles: the rule does not mention the provision of materials for manuscript production. Presumably their activities included spinning, weaving and sewing. Scholars have disagreed about how much domestic work the women actually did, since they had servants who may have done

---

[26] *VL* c. 28, p. 32. This episode is one of a number in the *vita* involving demons that seem to draw from the ideas and writings of Gregory the Great: C. Straw, *Gregory the Great: Perfection in Imperfection* (Berkeley, 1988), pp. 99–101. For sewing at religious houses in the sixth and seventh centuries, see G. Muschiol, *Famula Dei: Zur Liturgie in merowingischen Frauenklöstern* (Münster, 1994), p. 36. Einhard offers one of the best-known Carolingian references to textile work, Charlemagne's insistence that his daughters learn how to spin and weave wool: *VK* c. 19, p. 23. Also, the *Capitulare de Villis* and *Brevium Exempla* reveal many areas of work which Carolingian aristocratic women almost certainly helped supervise: *Capitulare de Villis. Cod. Guelf. 254 Helmst. der Herzog August Bibliothek Wolfenbüttel*, ed. C. Brühl (Stuttgart, 1971).

[27] For detailed examination of the *Institutio sanctimonialum* and its historical context see P. Heidebrecht and C. Nolte, 'Leben im Kloster: Nonnen und Kanonissen, Geistliche Lebensformen im frühen Mittelalter', in U. A. J. Becher and J. Rüsen, eds., *Weiblichkeit in geschichtlicher Perspektive: Fallstudien und Reflexionen zu Grundproblemen der historischen Frauenforschung* (Frankfurt am Main, 1988), pp. 79–115; and T. Schilp, *Norm und Wirklichkeit religiöser Frauengemeinschaften im Frühmittelalter: Die Institutio sanctimonialum Aquisgranensis des Jahres 816 und die Problematik der Verfassung von Frauenkommunitäten* (Göttingen, 1998). For the specific canons, see *MGH Conc.* II, ii, 10, 14, pp. 445, 448.

such work for them.²⁸ While the *sanctimoniales* may not have performed lowly labour such as cleaning, they undoubtedly engaged in textile work, labour appropriate for religious women because it minimised idleness and helped prevent the commission of some minor sins. Canon 10 of the *Institutio* directs that the *sanctimoniales* occupy themselves with handiwork, singing psalms and listening to sacred readings in order to prevent gossip and obscene stories and to keep themselves from becoming 'dulled from leisure'.²⁹ They probably also performed a valuable religious service by embroidering or sewing cloths for liturgical use. Surviving Carolingian church inventories frequently include textile pieces among lists of books and precious metal objects, indicating their material and spiritual worth.³⁰

Religious women doubtless participated in and at times supervised work essential to the outfitting and operation of their houses and attached churches, particularly the production of fine textiles. While such work did not merit extensive comment in Carolingian records, it was a vital aspect of daily life that benefited men and women alike. Efficient supervision and skilled understanding of these duties would have been traits that churchmen valued in nuns as much as laymen prized them in wives or an assistant like Liutberga. The household arts Liutberga learned almost certainly included sewing, embroidery and other textile skills.³¹ As a recluse, she continued to practise these arts, keeping hot coals and dyes in her cell, presumably to colour cloth.³² The church adjoining her cell would surely have been in need of vestments and other decorative and useful cloths, which she very likely furnished. Another ninth-century *vita*, the *De Sanctis Virginibus Herlinde et Reinula*, credits its subjects, two sisters who headed a religious community at Aldeneik, with fabrication of an altar cloth of rich materials.³³ Female correspondents of Boniface sometimes sent him

---

[28] *Institutio sanctimonialum* c. 13, p. 447; Heidebrecht and Nolte, 'Leben im Kloster', pp. 107–8; Schilp, *Norm*, pp. 83–4.

[29] *Institutio sanctimonialum* c. 10, p. 445: 'In monasteriis quoque positae non otio torpeant, non detractionibus et obscenis confabulationibus incumbant, sed aut psalmorum modulationibus aut manuum operationibus insistant aut certe divinis lectionibus aurem accommodent.'

[30] B. Bischoff, ed., *Mittelalterliche Schatzverzeichnisse* (Munich, 1967), 1, 12, 13, 15, 19, 27, 28, 33, 34, 49, 56, 65, 80, 82, 85, 89, 97, 107, 110, 117. Also see C. I. Hammer Jr, 'Country Churches, Clerical Inventories and the Carolingian Renaissance in Bavaria', *Church History* 49 (1980), pp. 5–17, at 9–13.

[31] For more information about embroidery, see M. Budny and D. Tweddle, 'The Maaseik Embroideries', *ASE* 13 (1984), pp. 65–96; M. Budny, 'The Byrhtnoth Tapestry or Embroidery', in D. Scragg, ed., *The Battle of Maldon AD 991* (Oxford, 1991), pp. 263–78.

[32] *VL* c. 22, p. 26.

[33] *De Sanctis Virginibus Herlinde et Reinula*, Acta Sanctorum Martii III, pp. 385–92, c. 12 at p. 388. The altar cloth described in the *vita* survives at Maaseik, but it was almost certainly produced in southern England in the late eighth century or early ninth century: Budny and Tweddle, 'Maaseik Embroideries', pp. 91–4.

gifts of vestments or other textile pieces. The letters indicate actual female provision of textiles to religious men, and the author of the *vita* portrayed his subjects both making and giving a rich liturgical textile. Association with textile work was a trope of virtue, but it also constituted a useful activity that others expected women to perform.[34] During her time serving Gisla and Bernard, Liutberga would almost certainly have overseen, if not participated in, the textile work of the household, conducted perhaps in a *gynaeceum* or *pisele*, a workshop where women participated in textile production.[35] Furthermore, Bernard's two daughters, Gisla and Bilihilt, could well have learned textile arts from Liutberga, whom they, along with their brothers and mother, Helmburga, so esteemed that they thought of her as a mother.

While the textile arts are clearly documented in the *vita* and may have been a primary concern of many women, the work attributed to Liutberga and Gisla also included estate management. Because she was a widow and she alone inherited her father Hessi's lands after the premature death of her brother, Gisla had to visit all her estates. Liutberga may have learned how to deal with the everyday affairs of the family lands from helping and watching Gisla. In many ways this is the most logical way such skills could be handed on, from mother to daughter, or from female patron to *protegée*.[36]

On her deathbed, Gisla urged Bernard to have Liutberga help him in these tasks, transmitting her maternal authority and responsibility to her student. Maternal authority provided Gisla and then Liutberga with substantial access to resources and influence over those around them, especially as the family was rather wealthy, but that authority also meant they needed both to model and to encourage right behaviour and actions in family members under their tutelage. Given the frequent absences required of Carolingian aristocratic men and of their presumably male stewards, a lord such as Bernard almost certainly would have required help from

---

[34] Many images of Mary with a spindle survive from across the Middle Ages because, according to apocryphal tradition, she was spinning wool at the Annunciation: G. Schiller, *The Iconography of Christian Art* (London, 1969, repr. 1972), I, p. 34.

[35] Herlihy, *Opera Muliebria* discussed the history of female textile workshops. A number of Carolingian texts mention *gynaecea* or *piseles*: for example, *Brevium Exempla* 7, 25, 30, 32, 36, ed. Brühl, pp. 50, 52–5; *Cap. de Villis* 31, 43, 49, ed. Brühl, pp. 58–60; *MGH Capit.* I, no. 125, *c.* 5, p. 236 (Olonna, Capitulare tertium, 822–3); *MGH Capit.* II, no. 293, *c.* 78, pp. 419–20 (Meaux, 15 July 845); and a document concerning a 735–7 donation by a Count Eberhard to the monastery at Murbach discussed in W. Levison, 'Kleine Beiträge zu Quellen der fränkischen Geschichte', *Neues Archiv* 27 (1902), pp. 331–408, at 385–6. Walafrid Strabo used *gynaeceum* as an example of a word of Greek origin used by his contemporaries, *De Exordiis et Incrementis Rerum Ecclesiasticarum c.* 7, *MGH Capit.* II, p. 481.

[36] P. Riché, *Les écoles et l'enseignement dans le Haut Moyen Age: Fin ve siècle – milieu du xie siècle*, 2nd edn (Paris, 1989), p. 292.

someone.³⁷ For example, while Bernard of Septimania went on campaign and travelled extensively on the emperor's business in the 820s and 830s, his wife Dhuoda stayed at their estate in Uzès.³⁸ Dhuoda mentioned her debts to William, indicating that she at least controlled some money and possibly had considerable control over the resources of the estate at Uzès.³⁹ Gisla died before her son Bernard married his first wife Reginhild, but rather than becoming the head of the family as one might expect, the *vita* relates that Reginhild remained subject to Liutberga's influence, as though in the role of the ideal daughter, during her short life: '[Reginhild] burned with such love for the venerable Liutberga that she was not easily led out of her sight for even a short time. With maternal precepts from Liutberga's conversation, she adorned her charming demeanour and her honest and upright nature with good morals, and she adorned her family each day with the great contributions of her generosity.'⁴⁰

Liutberga continued to help supervise Bernard's household after his second marriage to Helmburga. As Reginhild had, Helmburga and her children looked to Liutberga's maternal authority. 'Liutberga showed the vigour of customary loyalty and deepest love of great devotion to both the mother and the children that she was called mother (*genitrix*) rather than nurse (*nutrix*).'⁴¹ According to the *vita* Liutberga's maternal authority therefore rested upon more than her position in the family; age, experience and the concurrent ability to model for and instruct others allowed her to fulfil the responsibilities that came with such influence. Upon Liutberga's entry to the religious life, maternal authority may have passed to Helmburga, then the mother of six.⁴² Once she had become a recluse, Liutberga equipped her students with skills necessary for women in lay households, just as Gisla had trained her. Clearly mothers were not the sole educators of daughters.

---

³⁷ For the lord's required absences, *MGH Capit.* I, no. 50, *c.* 4, p. 137; for the steward's required absences, *Cap. de Villis* 5, 16, 20, pp. 56–7. The degree to which men were absent from their local areas for military service has been the subject of some debate, but surely many aristocratic men were at a minimum away during the summer campaign seasons: M. Innes, *State and Society in the Early Middle Ages: The Middle Rhine Valley, 400–1000* (Cambridge, 2000), pp. 151–6; B. Bachrach, *Early Carolingian Warfare: Prelude to an Empire* (Philadelphia, PA, 2001), pp. 202–43; G. Halsall, *Warfare and Society in the Barbarian West, 450–900* (London, 2003), pp. 55, 93–5, 145.

³⁸ Neel, *A Handbook*, pp. x–xi; Claussen, 'Fathers of Power', p. 804.

³⁹ Dhuoda, *LM*, ed. Riché x, 4, p. 352.

⁴⁰ 'Quae etiam erga venerandam Liutbirgam tanto fervebat amore, ut non facile ad tempus eius fraudebatur aspectibus; et veluti maternis ab eius colloquio documentis venustatis habitum et honestatis gravitatem moribus, generositatis suae prosapiem magnis quottidie profectibus exornabat', *VL c.* 8, p. 15.

⁴¹ 'Matri ergo necnon et filiis venerabilis Liutbirg solitae fidelitatis vigorem et summae devotionis intimum demonstravit amorem in tantum, ut illis genitrix potius quam nutrix diceretur', *VL c.* 9, p. 16.

⁴² *VL* cc. 8–10, pp. 15–16.

As mentioned earlier, household arts, particularly textile-related skills, were essential activities in female religious communities. The transfer of these skills took place in both secular and religious institutions. Anskar of Bremen sent 'beautiful young girls to her for the accomplishment of the divine work, in which she was continually engaged with great devotion. She educated them in psalmody and in craft works and freely permitted the educated ones to go either to relatives or to whomever they wished.'[43] Since these girls were allowed to go to whomever they wished, it seems clear that she had prepared them for work in secular households or to enter religious communities.[44] Certainly, young women would not have been allowed literally to go anywhere they wanted, but this passage implies some choice on the part of the women, perhaps in vocation, perhaps in marriage.

Liutberga also helped transmit basic religious knowledge to other women. Recitation or singing of psalms was an essential part of monastic life, but as Herbert Grundmann noted, aristocratic girls throughout the Middle Ages learned their psalms even if they were not bound for the cloister.[45] Liutberga's *vita* confirms his observation.[46] Learning to sing may have helped pass time and may have provided the girls with songs they could sing and enjoy without reproach. While keeping the students from impure thoughts, gossip and obscenity, singing also imparted religious lessons. Many songs, especially those taught to children, have a didactic purpose, but this case from Liutberga's *vita* along with Canon 10 of the *Institutio sanctimonialum* demonstrate that they equally related to preventing immoral thought and discussion while performing repetitive or potentially boring work.[47]

Mothers as well as religious women taught children the Psalms. In their ninth-century will, Eberhard of Friuli and his wife, Gisela, bequeathed numerous sacred books to their children, including two psalters specifically

---

[43] 'Cui ad divini operis implementeum, quibus illa iugiter summo inhaerebat studio, puellas eleganti forma transmiserat, quas illa et in psalmodiis et in artificiosis operibus educaverat et edoctas libertate concessa seu ad propinquos, sive quo vellent, ire permisit', *VL* c. 35, p. 44.

[44] I doubt that the girls were slaves or unfree textile workers as Gray and Herlihy have suggested, but rather local girls obliged to receive instruction from Liutberga for a time either by the bishop or their families and quite possibly both. Admittedly, their exact status is open to interpretation: Gray, '"Mighty in Appropriate Ways"', p. 82; Herlihy, *Opera Muliebria*, pp. 86, 89–90.

[45] H. Grundmann, 'Die Frauen und die Literatur im Mittelalter: Ein Beitrag zur Frage nach der Entstehung des Schrifttums in der Volkssprache', *Archiv für Kulturgeschichte* 26 (1936), pp. 129–61, at 134.

[46] *VL* c. 45, p. 44.

[47] See discussion of this canon above, p. 128 and n. 29. S. G. Bruce, 'Uttering no Human Sound: Silence and Sign Language in Western Medieval Monasticism' (Princeton University Ph.D., 2000), pp. 17, 30–31.

linked to Gisela. The presence of so many religious books in an aristocratic household underlines their significance in aristocratic spiritual life, but the psalters' specific link to Gisela may indicate that a mother had a special role to play in teaching the psalms.[48] Dhuoda's extensive knowledge of the psalter and her insistence in her handbook for William that he study it further indicate the psalter's importance among lay aristocrats.[49]

The Psalms were central to lay devotion in the ninth century. Alcuin and Dhuoda counselled Charlemagne and William to say the words of Psalm 69 to begin their first prayers of the morning followed by the *Pater Noster* and a series of other Psalms.[50] In *De institutione laicali* Jonas of Orléans urges regular prayer and cites examples from the Psalms, among other passages of Scripture, about appropriate times for prayer. Both Alcuin and Jonas quote two of the same Psalms concerning night prayers.[51] If lay men employed passages from Psalms for prayer and heeded the advice of psalms concerning prayer, aristocratic laywomen may similarly have heard and recited passages from the Psalms as part of their prayers.

Aristocratic lay women may have gained some understanding of Latin from learning the psalter, and that knowledge may have aided aristocratic women in looking after household, estate and religious house, as all of these institutions would have required the keeping of records, or at least an ability to understand records. Almost certainly, they would have reviewed records of financial transactions and production on their estates as outlined in the early ninth-century *Capitulare de Villis* and demonstrated in the inventories of royal estates from the same period in the *Brevium Exempla*. The information in the *Brevium Exempla* reflects the requirements of chapter 55 of *Capitulare de Villis*.[52] In fact, according to this capitulary, stewards were to keep various records and make reports to the king and queen, although it is unclear whether they were meant to deliver the reports in oral or written form.[53] The king and queen instructed the steward

---

[48] *Cartulaire de l'abbaye de Cysoing et de ses dépendences*, ed. I. de Coussemaker (Lille, 1886), no. 1; P. Riché, 'Les bibliothèques de trois aristocrates laïcs carolingiens', *Le Moyen Age* 69 (1963), pp. 87–104, at 97. See now Kershaw, above, pp. 98–9.
[49] Riché, 'Bibliothèques', p. 95.
[50] Alcuin, *Officia per ferias*, *PL* 101, 509–10; Dhuoda, *LM*, ed. Riché, 11, 3, p. 128; P. Kershaw, 'Illness, Power and Prayer in Asser's *Life of King Alfred*', *EME* 10 (2001), pp. 201–24, at 211.
[51] Jonas, *De institutione laicali* 1, 12, *PL* 106, col. 145; Alcuin, *Officia*, *PL* 101, col. 509: both quote Psalms 118: 55, 'Memor fui in nocte nominis tui, Domine', and 118: 62, 'Media nocte surgebam ad confitendum tibi'. See now Noble, above, p. 29.
[52] *Cap. de Villis* c. 55, p. 61.
[53] *Ibid.*, 30, 62, pp. 58, 61–2, for written records; 13, 25, 29, 31, 66, 69, pp. 57–8, 62, for reports of some kind.

each year to pay in a part of the royal revenue on Palm Sunday after he determined the total amount of revenue for that year.[54] Such statements indicate the existence of, or at least the desire for, written records or careful oral reports directed towards both male and female superiors. Aristocratic women would at least have been familiar with similar records for their estates. Given their responsibility for hospitality, some of them may have scrutinised reports concerning supplies and production on their estates just as the queen was meant to do for royal estates.

The central purpose of instruction in reading and possibly writing, however, was probably to provide women with knowledge of basic religious concepts, actions and behaviours. As Liutberga had done during her childhood, her students may have learned religious lessons not only at home but also from teachers at monasteries. While Liutberga's relatively frequent citation of Scripture owes much to the well-educated author of her *vita*, she, like Dhuoda, could have been familiar with Scripture and other religious texts. Given her reported intention to enter the monastic life, she may have been literate. She may also have heard sermons, frequently involving explication of a biblical passage, which were supposed to be delivered in a language lay people could understand.[55] Since Carolingian legislation urged regular preaching to the laity, aristocratic women may have heard sermons relatively frequently. An aristocratic woman named Pia regularly passed Liutberga's cell on her way to the attached church to hear mass.[56] Her name suggests that, for author and audience, she was an aristocratic 'every woman', an idealised pious female aristocrat who always heeded Liutberga's advice. Regardless of Pia's actual status, the author of the *vita* seems to prescribe regular church attendance through her example. *Florilegia* may have provided some aristocratic women with substantial knowledge about religious thought and traditions.[57] However, evidence in Liutberga's *vita* suggests a different kind of religious instruction that passed among women.

Dhuoda's handbook demonstrates the centrality of prayer in the family and the passage of a basic understanding of religious ideas and practices from mothers to children.[58] Liutberga's *vita* offers examples that bolster

---

[54] *Cap. de Villis* c. 28, p. 58.
[55] R. McKitterick, *The Frankish Church and the Carolingian Reforms 789–895* (London, 1977), pp. 80–114; T. L. Amos, 'Preaching and the Sermon in the Carolingian World', in T. L. Amos, E. A. Greene and B. M. Kienzle, eds., *De Ore Domini: Preacher and word in the Middle Ages* (Kalamazoo, MI, 1989), pp. 41–60.
[56] *VL* c. 35, p. 40.   [57] McKitterick, *Frankish Church*, pp. 155–83.
[58] Claussen, 'God and Man', p. 43; McKitterick, *Carolingians*, p. 226; J. L. Nelson, 'Women and the Word', in Shields and Wood, eds., *Women in the Church*, pp. 53–78, at pp. 69–70; M. Innes,

and expand upon this idea. Even while young and just beginning to serve Gisla, Liutberga gave alms generously, cared for the sick, orphaned and needy, and was pious in her actions.[59] The author depicts Liutberga as following her religious inclinations, and because he may have systematised and enhanced her early attainment of Christian virtues, he clearly offers her as an example of correct female behaviour, both for lay and religious women. No doubt Liutberga perfected her virtues by following Gisla's example. An exemplar of ideal aristocratic female accomplishments, Gisla was pious, performed many good works, led a religious life upon the death of her husband, built churches, gave alms and provided pilgrims with hospitality.[60] Thus, within the *Vita Liutbirgae*, various aristocratic female types appear, from the models of Gisla and Liutberga to female members of Bernard's family and other women in the local community who learned from them.

Instilling such values, an important part of the instruction mothers provided their children, was undoubtedly a prime objective of Liutberga's teaching. Aristocratic women served as models and teachers not just for girls but also for young boys, as the abbess Addula was for her grandson Gregory and Dhuoda was for her son William.[61] Just as Paulinus of Aquileia, Jonas of Orléans and Alcuin urged aristocratic laymen to look after the weak, give alms generously, and avoid gluttony and drunkenness, aristocratic women encouraged other women to lead a Christian life.[62] This is not to say that male writers ignored the role of women as religious models in the home. In fact, in his *De institutione laicali* Jonas discusses the example that a woman ought to set. He urges parents to practise great solicitude in looking after their household, as though they were shepherds looking after a flock.[63] He writes that a home of learning is a healthy one, and that children, once they reach the age of reason, ought to be taught about the sacred doctrine of faith, the mystery of baptism and the seven

---

'Keeping it in the Family: Women and Aristocratic Memory, 700–1200', in E. van Houts, ed., *Medieval Memories: Men, Women and the Past, 700–1300* (Harlow, 2001), pp. 69–70, 17–35.

[59] *VL* c. 4, p. 13.

[60] *VL* 2, p. 11. Gisla's use of family lands to found churches and to provide land for her daughters' convents (see n. 12 above) also anticipates the way Saxon widows of the Ottonian era used family lands for female foundations in part to ensure their own financial security and that of their daughters. Karl Leyser noted that such land use extended back to Carolingian Saxony. K. Leyser, *Rule and Conflict in Early Medieval Society: Ottonian Saxony* (London, 1979), pp. 63–73, particularly 63–5.

[61] *Vita Gregorii* c. 2, pp. 67–8.

[62] Paulinus, *Liber Exhortationis* cc. 5, 16, 18, 31, 36, 37, 53, *PL* 99, cols. 200–1, 209, 210, 227, 234–5, 236–9, 258–60; Jonas, *De institutione laicali* 1, 18, 20, 11, 5, 23, *PL* 106, cols. 156–8, 161–6, 177–9, 215–18; Alcuin, *De virtutibus et vitiis liber* cc. 3, 7, 17, *PL* 101, cols. 615, 617–18, 625–6.

[63] Jonas, *De institutione laicali* 11, 16, *PL* 106, 197.

Learned women? 135

gifts of the Holy Spirit.[64] Mothers had an integral part in instructing their children in living a moral, Christian life.[65] Jonas writes that both parents have a responsibility to teach about these matters, but mothers would have been with their small children more frequently than their husbands, whose frequent absences at war, on business either at court or on distant estates, and on hunts would almost certainly have limited their contact with their young children.

Hrabanus Maurus and Hincmar of Rheims echoed Jonas' encouragement of religious instruction by mothers.[66] No better example of this idea in action survives than Dhuoda's handbook for William. Women furthermore provided religious instruction to those in their *familia*. Gisla and Liutberga encouraged those around them to lead a religious life, and Addula mentored Gregory.[67] Gisela, wife of Eberhard of Friuli, may have used the religious texts she owned to set a similar example for members of her household. These examples indicate both the expectations and the actions of aristocratic women in providing religious instruction. Since her daughters became abbesses and, according to the *vita*, her son showed great religious devotion, the author gave 'proof' that Gisla successfully inculcated piety in her children. As mentioned earlier, Liutberga had a profound effect on Bernard's first wife, Reginhild, as well as his second, Helmburga. Liutberga helped other women to practise Christian behaviour and actions. Besides training Gisla's granddaughters in household arts, she almost certainly passed religious ideals on to them, too. Thus, women may have taught not only their children but also each other about Christian virtues.

In the *Opus Caroli regis*, Theodulf of Orléans, echoing Paul the Apostle's views on women and teaching, explained that while it is acceptable for a woman to teach by word and example in her home, it is not acceptable for her to teach in public places.[68] Following a list of forbidden activities, the author wrote that women were allowed to demonstrate their prudence and

---

[64] 'Salutaris disciplinae domus est...', *Ibid.* 1, 8, col. 134; for a description of what children should learn see col. 135.
[65] C. Atkinson, *The Oldest Vocation: Christian Motherhood in the Middle Ages* (Ithaca, 1991), pp. 64–100.
[66] J. M. H. Smith, 'Gender and Ideology in the Early Middle Ages', in R. N. Swanson, ed., *Gender and Christian Religion*, SCH 34 (1998) pp. 51–73, at 64–7. Also see K. Heene, *The Legacy of Paradise: Marriage, Motherhood and Women in Carolingian Edifying Literature* (Frankfurt-am-Main, 1997).
[67] Liudger, *Vita Gregorii* 11, pp. 67–8.
[68] *Opus Caroli regis contra synodum*, ed. A. Freeman, MGH Conc. 11, Supplementum 1, p. 389: 'Aliud est enim matremfamilias domesticos verbis et exemplis erudire, aliud antestibus sive omni ecclesiastico [ordini] vel etiam publicae synodo quaedam [inutilia] docentem interesse, cum videlicet ista, quae domesticos exhortatur, eorum et suum in commune adipisci cupiat profectum, illa vero in con[ventu] ventosae tantum laudi et solius arrogantiae ambiat appetitum.'

to set an example of living well.⁶⁹ Women ideally should demonstrate moral behaviour and practical knowledge within their communities, whether estates, religious houses or court: Liutberga's activities fit these guidelines well. She never formally taught anyone save the girls Anskar of Bremen sent to her religious community, but to all the women with whom she came into contact, she stood as an example. Before she withdrew to her cell, she was much admired by neighbouring aristocrats, both male and female, who praised her for her abilities and pursued her friendship.⁷⁰ As a recluse, Liutberga literally had a window to the outside world, through which she continued to have regular contact with other women besides her pupils and sisters. Among those were a girl whom she convinced to abandon her illicit lover, a woman whose babies died before baptism because of her own sin and the aristocratic woman Pia.⁷¹ While one might argue that the author of Liutberga's *vita* depicted her contact with a wide variety of women to show models and counterexamples of the female lay life and the sins associated with it, this portrayal nevertheless suggests that women could act as examples to one other. Liutberga's care extended into the community in general, as it surely could have for many aristocratic women, both lay and religious. In writing a *vita* that instructed women in proper behaviour and action, the author inadvertently revealed much detail about female instruction.

Setting a moral example and teaching basic religious precepts were essential in both lay and religious spheres. Liutberga's childhood education may indicate that some girls received this sort of instruction. In the *Institutio sanctimonialum*, one of the offices described is the *magistra* or teacher who was responsible for the young girls and women. Instruction would have included memorisation of the Psalms, instruction in *sacrae disciplinae*, and learning to read so that they could study scripture. The latter would surely have involved lessons in grammar. While ability to teach certainly mattered, it appears that leading an exemplary life was the more essential qualification for this office.⁷² This requirement recalls the same ideal of women acting as pious exemplars that Carolingian churchmen encouraged. Thus, clerics urged both religious and lay female aristocrats to set a moral example for others, but those same women passed on learning in rather concrete ways. The letter of a female pupil in the manuscript Düsseldorf B3 (f. 308v) confirms that women taught women in religious houses. The writer refers to

---

⁶⁹ *Ibid.*, p. 388: 'sed prudentiam et bene vivendi exempla permiserit...' ⁷⁰ *VL* c. 6, p. 14.
⁷¹ *VL* cc. 30, 31–3, 35, pp. 34–40, 40–2.
⁷² *Institutio sanctimonialum* c. 22, pp. 452–4; Schilp, *Norm und Wirklichkeit*, p. 73.

her *magistra*.⁷³ The kernels of actual practice revealed in prescriptive sources and *vitae* indicate that the ideal bore some relation to reality. The clerical sources cited here urged women to continue practices, often domestic or related to child-rearing, for which they had long been responsible, and these clerical injunctions almost certainly affected female instruction of others in right Christian behaviour and domestic tasks. The instructive purposes of these texts in no way vitiate this evidence. Rather they demonstrate that others encouraged this knowledge in both lay and religious aristocratic women because it allowed them to help educate those around them, particularly the younger female members of the two institutions in which they were primarily active: the religious community and the lay family.

Aristocratic laywomen had no possibility of devoting themselves exclusively to the study, reflection and contemplation that characterised the narrowly defined intellectual life. The household arts they learned and practised probably consumed a great deal of their time and energy, but at the same time these women appear to have been partly responsible for passing religious knowledge on within the household. The examples from Liutberga's *vita* suggest that they discussed religious issues among themselves. The women in Liutberga's *vita* possessed practical knowledge, wisdom, ideas, experience and skills useful to managing resources expertly and to developing advantageous social relations for themselves and their families. Carolingian aristocratic women undoubtedly possessed a social competence that included making rational decisions, shrewdly managing daily tasks, using often limited resources skilfully and looking after the material and spiritual needs of those around them. Even if this category of knowledge is not learned, it is certainly a form of instruction that deserves more attention.⁷⁴

Liutberga's *vita* suggests that Dhuoda was almost certainly not alone in her practical and religious knowledge. Education at a monastic community may have been relatively common for girls from wealthy or even not so wealthy families. Whatever their status, the expertise they gained and the religious instruction they received would have served them well in lay life. Furthermore, the *vita* depicts women in Liutberga's local community as having regular contact with the monastery to which her cell was attached, its church and Liutberga herself as well as with various men. Gisla appears

---

⁷³ McKitterick, 'Women and Literacy', in her *Books, Scribes and Learning in the Frankish Kingdoms, 6th–9th Centuries* (Cambridge, 1994), pp. 1–43, at 39–40.
⁷⁴ My dissertation, 'Carolingian Aristocratic Women and the Transmission of Culture' (University of Virginia, 2003) explores these issues in more depth.

to have travelled widely and been active in the business affairs of her estates. Liutberga conversed not only with the women I have mentioned but also with laymen, monks and even priests and bishops. Since the author expected that these women were not closed off from the world, he indirectly suggests to a modern reader that female transmission of knowledge was a regular part of Carolingian aristocratic lay life.

Unlike the intellectual exchanges of clerics, female learning took place in spaces and at times about which written sources reveal little.[75] Liutberga's *vita* has offered a glimpse of women possessing a vital social competence and transmitting it to other women. Some laywomen may have received instruction that was relatively similar to that of religious women, up to a point. The *scriptoria* of female houses and the sometimes rich learning of religious women meant they almost certainly received greater training in Latin, writing and understanding Scripture than their lay counterparts. However, both needed to learn certain female skills to provide either household or church with necessary textiles and other goods for daily use; both gained grounding in Christian virtues; and both probably learned psalms and basic religious lessons. Though not learned, the aristocratic laywomen in the *Vita Liutbirgae* participated in a form of learning that allowed them to affect their communities on a fundamental and daily basis and that can help broaden modern understanding of what learning could be in the Carolingian era.

---

[75] J. Contreni, 'The Carolingian Renaissance', in *NCMH* II, pp. 709–57, at 716–17, 720.

CHAPTER 8

Charles the Bald, Hincmar of Rheims and the ivory of the Pericopes of Henry II

Celia Chazelle

As far as we know, Charles the Bald, crowned king in 838 and emperor in 875 (d. 877), never produced a corpus of scholarly work comparable to that of his Anglo-Saxon contemporary Alfred the Great.[1] Nor do we have records of his comments on scholarly literature, such as appear to survive for Charlemagne through the Tironian notes written in the margins of the extant working copy of the *Opus Caroli regis* (*Libri Carolini*). That manuscript, it is generally accepted, must have been read in the king's presence during its preparation, and the notes probably record his reactions to its contents, along with perhaps those of his ecclesiastical advisers.[2] There is no indication of similar efforts to register his grandson's pronouncements during doctrinal deliberations.

Yet Charles was surely the best educated of the Carolingian rulers according to the measures recognised by the educated elites of his day. As Janet Nelson has observed, the extensive instruction he received in his early years under Walahfrid Strabo, more clearly documented than for other members of his family, taught Charles 'to look out on the world through a learned man's eyes'.[3] This experience and his desire to emulate his grandfather Charlemagne were fundamental to the devotion to scholarship he continued to demonstrate as an adult – by supporting ecclesiastical councils and legislation; by commissioning treatises to address theological controversies; and by his substantial patronage in other circumstances of the finest intellects of his day. Those activities also had political motives, of course; they helped affirm and enhance his prestige in the face of fragile relations with his brothers and their heirs and of his desire, unrequited during

---

[1] R. Abels, *Alfred the Great: War, Kingship and Culture in Anglo-Saxon England* (London, 1998), pp. 219–57. On Charles' letter-writing, J. L. Nelson, *Charles the Bald* (London, 1992), pp. 235–8.
[2] *Opus Caroli regis contra synodum* (*Libri Carolini*), ed. A. Freeman in collaboration with P. Meyvaert, *MGH Conc.* II, Supplementum I (Hanover, 1998), pp. 48–50, where the editor discusses the evolution of scholars' opinions on this issue.
[3] Nelson, *Charles the Bald*, p. 82.

most of his life, for the imperial throne. Nevertheless, the political context cannot negate the vibrancy of the intellectual environment that Charles fostered in his realm, especially at his court, and in which he was involved.

The conviction of Charles's entourage that he possessed significant scholarly acumen, Nelson has noted, is suggested by the poetical and prose texts addressed to him and composed in his honour, and by the sophisticated artistic expressions of thought associated with his court.[4] One such work of art is the focus of this article: the magnificent ivory dominated by a crucifixion scene now set into the cover of the early eleventh-century Pericopes of Henry II (Munich, Bayerische Staatsbibliothek, Clm. 4452; Figure 8.1). In line with the ninth-century development of *Fürstenspiegel* literature, including tracts written for Charles, the tablet should be counted among the artistic productions for this king that convey moral messages relevant to his position as Christian monarch, by setting forth models of virtues he should emulate and vices he should oppose. This was evidently also a purpose of the ivory covers of the Paris Psalter (Paris, BNF lat. 1152), a manuscript completed before 869 and possibly given by Charles to Metz cathedral in that year or soon thereafter, to mark his coronation as king of Lotharingia.[5] The Paris plaques, carved with scenes based on Psalms 56 (front cover) and 50 (back cover), invite comparison with Carolingian texts that refer to the psalmist David as an example of virtuous rule.[6] In the Prayerbook of Charles the Bald, produced 846–69, Charles is depicted kneeling before and thus imitating the crucified Christ's model of humility (Munich, Residenz, Schatzkammer, fols. 38v–39r), in the hope of sharing in the saviour's exaltation.[7] As William Diebold has demonstrated, the illuminations of the San Paolo Bible (Rome, S. Paolo fuori le Mura), a manuscript made for Charles in the late 860s or early 870s, offered him exemplars of both good and wicked governance. The king must have recognised some of the Old Testament leaders in the miniatures as paradigms of royal virtue, such as David and Solomon (fols. 93r, 188v), while he must have identified others with evil, such as Pharaoh and Saul (fols. 21v, 83v).[8] On the gable of Charles's ivory throne known as the *Cathedra Petri*

---

[4] *Ibid.*, p. 83, more generally pp. 82–5, 234–5.
[5] W. J. Diebold, 'Verbal, Visual, and Cultural Literacy in Medieval Art: Word and Image in the Psalter of Charles the Bald', *Word & Image* 8 (1992), pp. 89–99, esp. 96 and n. 51.
[6] See H. H. Anton, *Fürstenspiegel und Herrscherethos in der Karolingerzeit* (Bonn, 1968), esp. pp. 420–32 (on David).
[7] R. Deshman, 'The Exalted Servant: The Ruler Theology of the Prayerbook of Charles the Bald', *Viator* 11 (1980), pp. 385–417, esp. 385 (on the date), 391–3.
[8] W. J. Diebold, 'The Ruler Portrait of Charles the Bald in the S. Paolo Bible', *Art Bulletin* 76 (1994), pp. 6–18, esp. 12–14.

Charles the Bald, Hincmar of Rheims: the ivory of the Pericopes 141

Figure 8.1 Pericopes of Henry II, cover

(in St Peter's, Vatican), the struggle between goodness and iniquity is recalled through scenes of conflicts between angelic and mythological creatures; and Lawrence Nees has presented evidence that the tablets carved with Hercules' labours on the throne's base were commissioned by Hincmar of Rheims, Charles's advisor, to exemplify an arrogance rooted in classical paganism that the king should reject.[9]

---

[9] L. Nees, *A Tainted Mantle: Hercules and the Classical Tradition at the Carolingian Court* (Philadelphia, PA, 1991), esp. pp. 199–257. Cf. N. Staubach, *Rex Christianus: Hofkultur und Herrschaftspropaganda im Reich Karls des Kahlen* (Cologne, 1993), pp. 283–334. Staubach's analysis has significant merits, but

Full-length portraits of Charles appear in his Prayerbook (fol. 38v) and the San Paolo Bible (fol. 1r), and his bust is set in the midst of the combatants on the back of the *Cathedra Petri*. Although he is not represented on the Paris Psalter covers, the intention that he attend to their David imagery is evident from the illumination of Charles in the manuscript itself (fol. 3v), below an inscription linking him to two other models of excellence, the Old Testament king, Josiah, and the Christian Roman emperor, Theodosius (probably both I and II).[10] Aside from the Pericopes tablet, then, all the artistic productions mentioned either incorporate depictions of the Carolingian monarch or are attached to objects that do, making it clear he was part of their expected audience. The unambiguous references to Charles differentiate these objects from the plaque on Henry II's Book of Pericopes. No image clearly representative of a Carolingian ruler appears on the ivory, nor an inscription referring to one; and while the carving may have originally been produced for a manuscript containing such a portrait, this cannot be proven.

Despite the Pericopes tablet's lack of inscription or other identifying traits, however, it, too, was most likely made for Charles in broadly the same period as these other works, that is, approximately the third quarter of the ninth century. This hypothesis is supported, first, by the ivory's close stylistic and iconographic connections to the other ivories of the so-called Liuthard group with which it has been identified. In the view of some scholars, the Pericopes plaque is by the same hand as the Paris Psalter ivory (part of the same group) illustrating Psalm 50, and possibly the ivory illustrating Psalm 56.[11] Second, correspondences are evident between the Pericopes tablet and works in other media probably or certainly produced for Charles, and works made for other recipients during his reign. The flying angels above the crucifix on the Pericopes carving, for instance, recall the lower two angels (above the horizontal of the cross) on the second cover of the Lindau Gospels (New York, Pierpont Morgan Library).[12]

Nees' interpretation of the Hercules ivories generally seems to me based on a sounder understanding of the Carolingian intellectual context.

[10] On the ivories, K. Van Der Horst *et al.*, eds., *The Utrecht Psalter in Medieval Art: Picturing the Psalms of David* (Westrenen, 1996), pp. 202–3 figures 14a, 14b; also see Deshman, 'The Exalted Servant', pp. 404–12. On the illuminations of the Paris Psalter, Diebold, 'Verbal, Visual, and Cultural Literacy', pp. 89–99, and see p. 91 on the likely allusion to both Theodosius I and II.

[11] Differing views found in A. Goldschmidt, *Die Elfenbeinskulpturen aus der Zeit der karolingischen und sächsischen Kaiser, VIII.-IX. Jahrhundert*, (Berlin, 1914), 1, no. 41, p. 25; D. Gaborit-Chopin, *Elfenbeinkunst im Mittelalter*, translated from the French by G. Bloch and R. Beyer (Berlin, 1978), p. 189, Katalog 54, 55; 'The Utrecht Psalter in Medieval Art', p. 202, Katalog 14.

[12] J. Hubert, J. Porcher and W. F. Volbach, *L'Empire carolingien* (Paris, 1968), p. 257, fig. 236.

Charles the Bald, Hincmar of Rheims: the ivory of the Pericopes 143

Personifications of Oceanus and Terra with some similarities to the Pericopes ivory personifications (though not identical) appear in the Maiestas illumination of the Paris Sacramentary fragment (Paris, BNF lat. 1141, fol. 6r) and in the painting of the adoration of the lamb in the Codex Aureus of St Emmeram (Munich, Bayerische Staatsbibliothek, Clm. 14000, fol. 6r).[13] Also striking are the ties the Pericopes tablet shows to drawings in the Utrecht Psalter, a Rheims production (Utrecht, University Library, MS 32),[14] and to miniatures in the Drogo Sacramentary (Paris, BNF lat. 9428), completed at Metz probably in the few years before Drogo's death in 855.[15] Peter Lasko and Christian Beutler stressed the significance for dating the Pericopes ivory of its formal connections to the Utrecht Psalter, but since they assigned the latter to *c.* 820, they held that the ivory, too, must have been made during the reign of Louis the Pious (d. 840).[16] Yet while their assessment of the relation with the Psalter is accurate, as I have elsewhere contended, that manuscript is itself better regarded as an early production of the archiepiscopate of Hincmar, to whom Charles the Bald gave the see of Rheims in 845.[17] The parallels that can be discerned between the Pericopes ivory's composition and ideas espoused in treatises that Hincmar wrote for Charles in the 860s and early 870s, discussed towards the end of this chapter, again link the plaque to this king and his court.

As the foregoing remarks should also indicate, it is very unlikely the Pericopes ivory was a wholesale copy of an ancient work of art, a view Beutler argued that has recently been echoed.[18] The connections between

---

[13] W. Koehler and F. Mütherich, *Die karolingische Miniaturen*, 5: *Die Hofschule Karls des Kahlen* (Berlin, 1982), pls. 43b, 47; Hubert *et al.*, *L'Empire carolingien*, pp. 150, 154, figs. 138, 142.
[14] Facsimile of the Utrecht Psalter in Utrecht-Psalter: *Vollständige Faksimile-Ausgabe im Originalformat der Handschrift 32, Utrecht-Psalter, aus dem Besitz der Bibliotheek der Rijksunjiversiteit te Utrecht*, 2 vols., Commentary by K. van der Horst and J. A. Engelbregt (Graz, 1984). A digital facsimile is available online: http://vitrine.library.uu.nl/wwwroot/en/texts/Hs32.htm. The illustrations of the Utrecht Psalter were published twice earlier; the more accessible of the two publications is E. T. Dewald, *The Illustrations of the Utrecht Psalter* (Princeton, NJ, 1933).
[15] Drogo-Sakramentar, MS Latin 9428, Bibliothèque nationale, Paris, *Vollständige Faksimile-Ausgabe im Originalformat*, 2 vols., ed. F. Mütherich, Commentary by W. Köhler (Graz, 1974), on the date, pp. 13–17. F. Unterkircher, *Zur Ikonographie und Liturgie des Drogo-Sakramentars* (Graz, 1977), pp. 9–11, 18–19 favoured a date before 840, but he has not been generally followed.
[16] C. Beutler, '*Magna Mater* oder Christus: Die Entstehung der Kreuzigungsdarstellung', *Idea: Jahrbuch der Hamburger Kunsthalle* 4 (1985), pp. 19–41, at 20; Beutler, *Der Gott am Kreuz: Zur Entstehung der Kreuzigungsdarstellung* (Hamburg, 1986), p. 6. Cf. Peter Lasko, *Ars Sacra 800–1200*, 2nd edn (New Haven, CT, 1994), pp. 28–30.
[17] C. Chazelle, *The Crucified God in the Carolingian Era: Theology and Art of Christ's Passion* (Cambridge, 2001), 241–54; Chazelle, 'Archbishops Ebo and Hincmar of Reims and the Utrecht Psalter', *Speculum* 72 (1997), pp. 1055–77.
[18] Beutler, '*Magna Mater* oder Christus'; see H. Fillitz, 'Jerusalem oder Rom? Bemerkungen zu einem karolingischen Motiv', in *Sancta Treveris: Beiträge zu Kirchenbau und bildender Kunst im alten*

individual elements of its design, various illustrations in the Utrecht Psalter, miniatures in the Drogo Sacramentary, and disparate motifs in other ninth-century Carolingian productions, do not support such a conjecture. Rather, these diverse relationships suggest it is more logical to think the Pericopes ivory's designer, like other Carolingian designers and artists, sought inspiration for different details from multiple sources. Some may well have been antique works, but others were probably Carolingian productions like the Utrecht Psalter that were themselves directly and indirectly influenced by antique and early Christian Mediterranean artistic traditions. The designer of the Pericopes tablet likely selected, arranged, adapted and integrated his 'borrowings' from other works with forms of his own invention, in order to create a unified composition expressive of ideas important to him and the Carolingian milieu in which he worked.

Although advisors such as Hincmar certainly may have guided Charles when he first pondered the meaning of this Carolingian work of art, its designer probably considered him quite capable of grasping, on his own, the principal elements of its signification. The assumption that he would both appreciate and understand its basic message would have seemed supported by knowledge of the education he received from Walahfrid, his participation in church ritual and ecclesiastical affairs, his patronage of intellectual endeavours, and his perceived acquaintance with the Pericopes ivory's iconographic "vocabulary" from other artistic productions in which similar forms occur. Consequently, our own study of the plaque's complex imagery can give us some degree of insight into what Charles' learning was believed, by contemporaries like its designer, to encompass at the time of its production. In the broadest sense, judging from the ivory, this included familiarity with the New Testament, the liturgy, the main tenets of Christian orthodoxy concerning Christ's death and resurrection, some aspects of Carolingian exegesis of Scripture, and some elements of patristic thought and the pagan classical traditions it transmitted. In addition, I will try to show, the designer expected the king to be sensitive to certain strains in Carolingian ethics of rulership. Charles was not necessarily assumed to read doctrinal or exegetical writings on his own. But he must have been believed sufficiently well exposed to the contents of such texts, if not through his own reading then through preaching, oral instruction, informal

---

Erzbistum Trier, ed. M. Embach *et al.* (Trier, 1999), pp. 119–23, esp. 122; W. Telesko, review of *The Crucified God in the Carolingian Era*, *Speculum* 79 (2004), pp. 153–5, at 155. I am very grateful to Telesko for drawing Fillitz's study to my attention, though I cannot agree with him that it is persuasive.

discussions with learned men in his circle, and recitations like those of *The City of God* that Charlemagne supposedly enjoyed, to recall themes from them relevant to the ivory's design.[19]

In order to elucidate the ideas the Pericopes tablet might have suggested to Charles and been meant to suggest, we need to pay careful attention to its individual formal elements and their integration into the larger composition. This in part involves searching out possible visual and textual precedents and comparative material, in particular Carolingian artistic productions and writings that may clarify the meaning which specific details of the ivory likely possessed in the specifically Carolingian context in which it was created. Identifying pre-Carolingian analogies and potential models, such as those some scholars have sought in antique Mediterranean artistic productions, is in itself insufficient for determining the carving's signification for its ninth-century designer and his patron.[20] In terms of artistic evidence, in other words, priority should be given to how motifs similar to those on this ivory are used in other Carolingian artwork, and to differences that may indicate differences in meaning. Correspondingly, efforts to gain insight into the ivory's "message" from textual sources must consider which patristic and other writings were studied in Carolingian schools, how they were interpreted by Carolingian scholars, and what those scholars – particularly ones with whom the ivory's designer was possibly in contact – taught in their own right, both developing on and deviating from patristic traditions. Our focus, therefore, must be on evidence more or less contemporary with the ivory: not only formal theological treatises from this period, but biblical commentaries, liturgical materials and other writings in prose and poetry that can inform us about the plaque's ninth-century intellectual context. Although in the past the Pericopes tablet has sometimes been associated with the thought of John Scottus Eriugena, the most brilliant theologian to receive the patronage of Charles the Bald,[21] the approach just outlined more noticeably points to the influence of Hincmar of Rheims. One aim behind the ivory's design, I think, was similar to that which Lawrence Nees has ascribed to the carvings on the *Cathedra Petri*, arguing for Hincmar's involvement in that production, as well: to steer Charles away from sins associated with the pagan Roman empire and

---

[19] Einhard, *VK* c. 24, ed. O. Holder-Egger, *MGH SRG* (Berlin, 1911), p. 29. For another comparison, see P. J. E. Kershaw's discussion of Eberhard, in this volume, above, chapter 5.
[20] Cf. Beutler, '*Magna Mater* oder Christus'; Fillitz, 'Jerusalem oder Rom?', pp. 120–3.
[21] For example, A. Vandersall, 'The Ivories of the Court School of Charles the Bald' (Ph.D. dissertation, Yale University, 1965), pp. 132–6; O. K. Werckmeister, *Der Deckel des Codex Aureus von St. Emmeram: Ein Goldschmiedewerk des 9. Jahrhunderts* (Baden-Baden, 1963), pp. 78–80.

towards different ideals of conduct that Hincmar thought befitted a Christian ruler.[22]

The interpretation of the ivory I offer here is a slightly revised version of one I have proposed elsewhere.[23] Critical to my analysis, though, remains a proper understanding of the crowned figure (female) to the right of the crucifix, seated beneath a portico, dressed in a long decorated vestment and holding a disk with decorated rim. Since her identity has incited considerable debate,[24] before discussing her or the veiled woman standing in front of her and the portico, it is helpful to review the other pictorial elements about which there seems to be greater consensus.[25] In the uppermost tier of imagery, we see the hand of God emerging from a cloud between personifications of the sun and moon driving *quadrigae*. Below them a bearded Christ, dressed in the perizoma, hangs from a rough-hewn cross over which fly three angels. All three angels carry short staffs whose tops have broken off, making it impossible to determine their original appearance. The ivory is too worn to tell whether Jesus' eyes are open or closed, yet his dying is implied by his inclined head and slightly slumped body, its weight pulling down on his arms. To the far left of the cross (Christ's right) and just behind his field of vision stand five veiled women, those described in the synoptic gospels as watching the crucifixion from afar (Matth. 27: 55, Mark 15: 40, Luke 23: 49). Mary is probably at the front of this group, nearest Christ. Between her and the cross, Longinus lifts his spear to Christ's side (John 19: 34) while another veiled female raises a chalice to his side-wound. This is a personification of Ecclesia, who is similarly represented in several other Carolingian crucifixion images, among them the miniature for Palm Sunday in the Drogo Sacramentary (fol. 43v).[26] To the immediate right of the cross (Christ's left), stand Stephaton with the sponge-pole and an oversized vinegar vessel near his feet, and behind him John the evangelist (John 19: 26–27). The serpent at the cross's base, a common motif in crucifixion imagery associated with ninth-century Metz, Rheims and Charles' court, marks the composition's centre. Its twisted body appears to push down the undulating line of ground that divides the ivory's upper half from its

---

[22] Nees, *Tainted Mantle*, pp. 199–257.   [23] *The Crucified God in the Carolingian Era*, pp. 266–92.
[24] Compare e.g., Fillitz, 'Jerusalem oder Rom?'; Gaborit-Chopin, *Elfenbeinkunst im Mittelalter*, p. 189, Cat. 55; R. Melzak, 'The Carolingian Ivory Carvings of the Later Metz Group' (Ph.D. dissertation, Columbia University, 1983), p. 192; Vandersall, 'Ivories of the Court School', pp. 88–9.
[25] I offer a more detailed discussion of the ivory, and related imagery in the Utrecht Psalter and Drogo Sacramentary, in *The Crucified God in the Carolingian Era*, esp. pp. 239–92.
[26] Above, n. 15.

lower sections.[27] Below the reptile, the three women approach the empty, three-storeyed tomb that rises up into the area of the crucifixion, its entrance guarded by an angel (Matth. 28; Mark 16; Luke 24). Longinus' lance traverses the space between its dome and the crucified Christ, leading the viewer's eye from one to the other. Behind the sepulchre and half-concealed in the acanthus border are four soldier/guards; one or possibly two of them are sleeping (one supports his chin on his hand), while two crouch behind their shields yet seem to look out at the scene before them. Below the sepulchre, in keeping with Matthew 27: 52–53, a group of sarcophagi and tombs release four rising dead.

In the tablet's bottom left corner, a reclining personification of Oceanus (Ocean) holds a cornucopia, his right arm rested on an overturned vessel of water. Terra (Earth) occupies the right corner, a cornucopia in one hand and two snakes on her right arm, one with its head at her breast. The identity of the central female figure in this tier, seated on a backless throne, her body thrusting up into the area of the opening graves, has provoked some disagreement. A female appears between personifications of Oceanus and Terra at the base of the ivory cover of the Drogo Gospelbook (Paris, BNF lat. 9383), yet differences in her attributes pose difficulties for efforts to ascribe to both images the same signification.[28] In order to understand who she is on the Pericopes ivory, we need to turn to literary evidence. The most plausible interpretation was proposed by Otto Werckmeister, who argued that in this carving the figure represents the Temple as described in the *Carmen paschale* of the fifth-century poet Sedulius, a work widely known and frequently quoted by Carolingian writers. As Christ died, Sedulius states, 'that marvellous temple, filled with ancient religion, groaned like a sad foster-child and wept for her own creator, as she beheld the roofs of the great temple fall. When the temple veil rent she immediately showed her bare breast to all, signifying that the secret things within were now to be revealed to the gentiles and all future people of faith.'[29] In line with this text, the woman on the Pericopes plaque has one exposed

---

[27] The motif of the serpent beneath the cross may have its earliest appearance in the Drogo Sacramentary Palm Sunday miniature. I discuss this iconography in 'An Exemplum of Humility: The Crucifixion Image in the Drogo Sacramentary', in E. Sears and T. K. Thomas, eds., *Reading Medieval Images: The Art Historian and the Object* (Ann Arbor, MI, 2002), pp. 27–35, at 30–1.

[28] Fillitz rightly stresses the difficulties: 'Jerusalem oder Rom?', pp. 119–20, see fig. 2. Cf. Goldschmidt, *Elfenbeinskulpturen*, I, no. 83, pp. 46–7, cf. no. 41, p. 26.

[29] 'Tunc illud quoque templum mirabile, plenum religionis antiquae, maioris templi culmina cecidisse conspiciens, uelut alumnus tristis et ingemens proprium defleret auctorem, discusso protinus uelo nudum cunctis pectus ostendit, interiora scilicet euidenter arcana gentibus reseranda significans et populis fideliter adfuturis... .', Sedulius, *Carmen paschale* 5, CSEL x, ed. J. Huemer (Vienna, 1885),

breast and looks up towards the crucifixion of her creator, the cause of the Temple's fall. Her raised right hand seems to acknowledge the power descending from the hand of God, which her gesture mirrors, through the cross, the serpent, Christ's tomb and the resurrected mortals, and the transition it effected from the Old Law to the New. This interpretation seems supported by the formal parallel between her posture and that of the seated old man in the Drogo Sacramentary Palm Sunday miniature (fol. 43v), most likely a representation of Nicodemus who is similarly a reminder of the Old Testament that cedes authority at Christ's death.[30]

A few ninth-century images of Terra show a snake winding up one of her arms; but the Pericopes plaque is the only Carolingian depiction known to me in which a serpent suckles at Terra's breast.[31] Disagreement has been expressed concerning the meaning of this detail, as well,[32] but another textual source, in this instance a Carolingian tract, sheds some light. In Book 12 of *De rerum naturis*, written in 842, Hrabanus Maurus draws on Isidore's *Etymologiae*, Cassiodorus' exegesis of Psalms 23 and 84, and the *Clavis* of Pseudo-Melito to explain that Terra is both good and evil, and he associates the latter characteristic with the serpent. For its participation in the fall of Adam and Eve, God condemned the snake to 'eat' earth (Gen. 3.14), that is, the corruption of human nature, leading sinners into damnation.[33] In an early eleventh-century copy of *De rerum naturis*, at Montecassino, this idea is evoked by an image of Terra with loose hair and naked torso, an ox (symbol of goodness) and a snake at her breasts. The image, which may be based on a ninth-century exemplar, possibly reflects an artistic source for or parallel to the Pericopes tablet motif.[34] While the cornucopia that Terra holds in the Pericopes carving likely signifies the goodness of earthly bounty, then, the snake at her breast seems there, too, a reminder of her association with iniquity, as is perhaps also implied by her

---

p. 292, ll. 13–18, see pp. iii–xxv on the manuscripts used for this edition; Werckmeister, *Deckel des Codex Aureus*, p. 59.

[30] Chazelle, 'An Exemplum of Humility', pp. 28–30; Chazelle, *The Crucified God*, pp. 257–60.

[31] Compare e.g., Goldschmidt, *Elfenbeinskulpturen*, I, nos. 83, 85, 88; and the figure on the *Cathedra Petri*, Staubach, *Rex Christianus*, fig. 34, Nees, *Tainted Mantle*, fig. 18.

[32] Telesko, review of *The Crucified God*, p. 155.

[33] Hrabanus, *De universo libri viginti duo* 12.1, *PL* III, cols. 331–2. That the correct title of this work is *De rerum naturis*, not *De universo*, is discussed in E. Heyse, *Hrabanus Maurus' Enzyklopädie 'De rerum naturis': Untersuchungen zu den Quellen und zur Methode der Kompilation* (Munich, 1969), pp. 1–3.

[34] Montecassino, Archivio e biblioteca dell'abbazia Cod. 132, p. 294; facsimile in *Rabano Mauro, De rerum naturis. Cod. Casin. 132 [dell'] Archivio dell'Abbazia di Montecassino*, Commentary by G. Cavallo (Pavone Canovese, 1994). The two animals in the Montecassino image probably represent the clean and unclean animals. I am grateful for this insight to an unidentified member of the audience at my paper in Kalamazoo, MI, May 2000.

cowering position and fearful expression looking up at the crucifix, as if afraid of its power. Further, the designer of the Pericopes tablet may have wanted to associate both Terra and the Temple with the carnality of Babylon, overcome through Christ's passion: their semi-nakedness and the water that flows from Oceanus' overturned jug towards Terra's feet, and under those of the Temple, recall the description in Revelation 17 of Babylon as 'the great harlot who sitteth upon many waters', the naked 'mother of the fornications' and 'abominations of the earth'.[35]

Taken together, the features of the Pericopes ivory so far discussed express a broad nexus of Christian principles with clear parallels in Scripture, writings by Carolingian authors and some earlier texts known to them. In light of the complex web of beliefs articulated in this poetry and prose, as may already be apparent, it is impossible to assign the imagery a single, monolithic interpretation. Details can be related with one another formally and iconographically in ways that seem intended to suggest to Carolingian viewers (such as Charles) numerous lines of thought. I can only indicate a few additional aspects of this polysemy here. To begin, the endeavour should be noted on the ivory to recall the doctrine, grounded in John 3:14–16 and often mentioned in Carolingian theological writing, that redemption demands faithful contemplation of the crucified lord.[36] To some extent, of course, this doctrine is implicit in any artistic depiction of the crucifixion, particularly those that include groups of witnesses; but the Pericopes ivory gives it exceptional force, relative to other Carolingian works of art, simply by the number of witnesses portrayed. This becomes evident if we consider the illuminations in the Drogo Sacramentary for Palm Sunday (fol. 43v) and Easter Sunday (fol. 58r).[37] In the Palm Sunday miniature, a painting that shows significant formal ties to the ivory's crucifixion scene, the crucified saviour is attended by two angels,

---

[35] Revelation 17: 1: 'And there came one of the seven angels, who had the seven vials, and spoke with me, saying: Come, I will shew thee the condemnation of the great harlot, who sitteth upon many waters.' Verse 5: 'And on her forehead a name was written: A mystery; Babylon the great, the mother of the fornications, and the abominations of the earth.' Verse 16: 'And the ten horns which thou sawest in the beast: these shall hate the harlot, and shall make her desolate and naked, and shall eat her flesh, and shall burn her with fire.' Scriptural texts from the Douay-Rheims Version. Cf. Augustine, *De civitate Dei* 16.4, 16.17, 18.2, *CCSL* 47, ed. B. Dombart and A. Kalb (Turnhout, 1955), pp. 504–5, 522, 594.

[36] 'And as Moses lifted up the serpent in the desert, so must the Son of man be lifted up: That whosoever believeth in him, may not perish; but may have life everlasting. For God so loved the world, as to give his only begotten Son; that whosoever believeth in him, may not perish, but may have life everlasting.' Cf. nos. 21: 8–9. See Chazelle, *The Crucified God*, pp. 207–8, 260–6, 276–7, Chazelle, 'An Exemplum of Humility', pp. 29–31.

[37] Above, n. 15.

personifications of the sun and moon, Ecclesia, the seated old man who probably represents Nicodemus, the Virgin Mary, John the Evanglist and two dead rising from their graves. The sacramentary's Easter illumination shows the three women visiting the sepulchre, beside which two soldier-guards lie stunned or asleep. The Pericopes ivory, however, is remarkably crowded in comparison. Here we find the crucifixion beheld by personifications of the sun and moon (and, apparently, the animals drawing their vehicles), three angels, the five women in place of the Virgin alone, Ecclesia, Longinus and Stephaton, John, four mortals rising from their graves, the figure I have identified as the Temple, and Terra. At least two of the four soldiers behind Christ's tomb watch the women who approach from the other side;[38] and although Oceanus looks outward, his gaze, it seems, draws the viewer's own eye into the carving.

Second, Charles and educated members of his court circle would have understood the ivory to be replete with visual references to Christ's triumph by means of the crucifixion. The Carolingian designer has left no doubt that the passion led to resurrection, of the redeemer and all faithful, and to the conquest of sin and Satan, through the tightly interconnected motifs recalling these varied events. Though Christ is shown dying, the cross's rough-hewn form commemorates its origin as the tree of life in Eden that the blessed will behold in heaven, and therefore Jesus' role as the second Adam, important themes of Carolingian prayers for the *Adoratio crucis*, Easter and the feasts of the cross, as well as of ninth-century poems and liturgical and biblical commentary.[39] At the base of the cross, the snake's twisted body, poised at the midpoint between the areas of crucifixion and resurrection, also signals both evil's defeat to be completed at the end of time and the garden of paradise where sin made its first appearance. The cloths held by two of the angels above the crucifixion, and the hand the angel to the right lays on the cross, link the earthly realm of human mortality with the celestial realm of the divine omnipotence symbolised by the hand of God. The universality of the crucified and resurrected Christ's power, a concept stressed in innumerable Carolingian writings,[40]

---

[38] Matthew 28: 4 notes that all the guards became as though dead. The Pericopes tablet's iconography is not unprecedented, though. One guard watches the women at the tomb on the ascension ivory of c. 400 in Munich, Bayerisches Nationalmuseum, and in the Rabbula Gospels, Florence, Biblioteca Laurenziana, Cod. Plut. 1, 56, fol. 13; see C. Steigemann and M. Wemhoff, eds., *799: Kunst und Kultur der Karolingerzeit, Karl der Grosse und Papst Leo III. in Paderborn: Katalog der Ausstellung Paderborn 799*, 2 vols. (Mainz, 1999), II, p. 689, Fig. X.2; W. Braunfels, *Die Welt der Karolinger und ihre Kunst* (Munich, 1968), fig. 178; A. Kartsonis, *Anastasis: The Making of an Image* (Princeton, NJ, 1986), fig. 5.

[39] See *The Crucified God*, pp. 132–64.

[40] Ibid., esp. pp. 14–23, 132–42, cf. (on the thought of Hincmar and John Scottus Eriugena), 181–204.

is implied both by the ivory's combined allusions to creation and the last day and by the personifications of the sun, moon, Oceanus and Terra. Although the carving is divided into different levels, pictorial elements that break from one band into another strengthen this message of the passion's essential unity with the resurrection and the final victory of the eschaton: the empty sepulchre rising into the area of the crucifixion, the line traced by Longinus' spear from the tomb to Christ's side-wound, the serpent pushing down the ground that divides the two scenes, the lid of one opened tomb at the feet of the three Marys. The imagery's cohesion is strengthened, too, by the hand of God at the top mirroring the Temple's hand at the base, and by the downward gaze of the sun, moon and angels while the Temple and Terra look upward.[41]

Yet another prominent theme of the ivory is the connection between the passion and the eucharist. Like other Carolingian crucifixion images that show a chalice receiving Christ's blood, the ivory implies a doctrine of the eucharist's nature such as Hincmar and Paschasius Radbertus defended in the eucharistic controversy of the mid-ninth century. The wine or blood of the mass is the same liquid that flowed from the incarnate, crucified body, and the body of the sacrament (the bread) is therefore the same body that hung on the cross.[42] For Radbertus and Hincmar, the incarnate and eucharistic flesh and blood are also the food of the tree of life that the blessed and angels eternally consume in paradise.[43] Perhaps, as Werckmeister suggested, the three angels above the cross are partly meant

---

[41] The sepuchre on this ivory finds an interesting comparison in the frontispiece miniature of the St Petersburg manuscript of the *Visio Baronti*, a Rheims codex of *c*. 850: Russian National Library, cod. lat. Oct. v. I. 5, fol. IV. See Lawrence Nees, 'The Illustrated Manuscript of the *Visio Baronti* (*Revelatio Baronti*) in St. Petersburg (Russian National Library, cod. Oct. v. I. 5)', in *Court Culture in the Early Middle Ages*, ed. C. Cubitt (Turnhout, 2003), pp. 91–128, figs. 1–2.

[42] Paschasius Radbertus presents his doctrine of the eucharist in three writings: *De corpore et sanguine Domini*, written 831–3 and revised *c*. 843; and a letter to Fredugard and his commentary on the last supper in Matthew 26, both texts dating to the early to mid-850s: *De corpore et sanguine Domini cum appendice epistola ad Fredugardum*, CCCM 16, ed. B. Paulus (Turnhout, 1969); *Expositio in Matheo 26.26–29*, CCCM 56B, ed. B. Paulus (Turnhout, 1984), pp. 1288–98. The principal source for our knowledge of Hincmar's teachings is his treatise, *De cavendis vitiis et virtutibus exercendis*, written in the late 860s or early 870s but reflecting ideas expounded in more abbreviated form in some earlier works, among them his writings on the *Ferculum Salomonis* (see below, at n. 77). Hincmar was probably influenced by Paschasius: Hinkmar von Reims, *De cavendis vitiis et virtutibus exercendis*, MGH Quellen 16, ed. D. Nachtmann (Munich, 1998). See Chazelle, *The Crucified God*, pp. 209–25, 251–4; Chazelle (on Paschasius and his opponent, Ratramnus), 'Figure, Character, and the Glorified Body in the Carolingian Eucharistic Controversy', *Traditio* 47 (1992), pp. 1–36, with references to earlier literature.

[43] See Paschasius, *De corpore* 1, 7, 9, CCCM 16.19, 39, 54–5. Hincmar alludes to this idea in his 'third treatise' on predestination, drawing on Augustine, *De praedestinatione Dei et libero arbitrio*, PL 125, cols. 65–474, at 458D–459A. See also *De cavendis* 3.2, MGH Quellen 16.242–4.

to encourage thoughts of the mass prayer asking that an angel bear these consecrated elements to the heavenly altar;[44] and they may denote the celestial throngs who join the faithful in the mass's three-fold Sanctus hymn. Or perhaps they, or in particular the right-hand angel touching the crucifix, present it to the surrounding witnesses and the ivory's viewers for adoration, just as the clergy displayed the cross on Good Friday. An *ordo* in a later ninth-century northern French manuscript directs that three clergy sing the Sanctus as the cross is brought forward for the Adoration.[45] The cloths held by two of the angels possibly evoke the cross's ritual unveiling on Good Friday, a custom first mentioned in the same *ordo*. After the veiled cross had been set near the altar, the cloth was pulled away as *Ecce lignum crucis* ('Behold, the tree of the cross') was sung.[46] To a Carolingian audience, this ritual almost certainly brought to mind the tearing of the temple veil when Christ died, the episode that Sedulius links to the Temple's uncovering of her breast and that the Gospel of Matthew links to the quaking with which the earth gave up her dead (Matth. 27: 51–52).[47]

Moreover, the images of Stephaton, Longinus, Ecclesia and the crucified Jesus would have reminded Charles the Bald and his contemporaries that Christ's death and eucharistic body and blood are the sources of sin's purgation. A key motif for conveying this concept is the oversized pitcher near Stephaton, which some Carolingian exegesis identifies as a symbol of human wickedness.[48] This symbolism is also implied in the marginal illustration for Psalm 68: 22 of the ninth-century Byzantine Khludov Psalter (Moscow, Historical Museum, cod. 129, fol. 67r). In that image Stephaton, portrayed with Jewish features, stands with his vessel before the crucified Christ, while an adjoining painting shows iconoclasts who use an identical container to whitewash an icon.[49] The most distinctive Carolingian exegesis

---

[44] 'Supplices te rogamus omnipotens deus, iube et perferri per manus angeli tui in sublime altare tuum, in conspectu diuinae maiestatis tuae, ut quotquot ex hac altaris participatione sacrosanctum filii tui corpus et sanguinem sumpserimus omni benedictione caelesti et gratia repleamur', in *Sacramentaire grégorien*, 3 vols., ed. J. Deshusses (Fribourg, 1971–82), I, no. 13; Werckmeister, *Deckel des Codex Aureus*, p. 58.

[45] *Ordo* 31, *Ordines Romani: Les ordines romani du haut moyen âge*, 5 vols., ed. M. Andrieu (Louvain, 1931–61), III, pp. 491–509 (Paris, BNF lat. 9421).

[46] *Ordo* 31, Andrieu, ed., *Ordines Romani*, III, p. 498; see Gerhard Römer, 'Die Liturgie des Karfreitags', *Zeitschrift für katholische Theologie* 77 (1955), pp. 39–93, at 73–4.

[47] See above, n. 29.

[48] My thanks to Ilene Forsyth and Elizabeth Sears for pointing out to me the vessel's extraordinary size (oral communication, Kalamazoo, MI). See Paschasius Radbertus, *In Matheo* 27, *CCCM* 56B.1387–90; cf. *ibid.*, 1366–7; Hrabanus Maurus, *Commentariorium in Matthaeum* 8, *PL* 107, cols. 1142D–1143C.

[49] K. Corrigan, *Visual Polemics in the Ninth-Century Byzantine Psalters* (Cambridge, 1992), 30.

of the vinegar vessel occurs in the commentary on Matthew that Radbertus completed in the early 850s. Through passages from Jerome, Hilary and Ambrose, Radbertus associates the vinegar and gall with the corruption of Jews, unbelievers, and more generally human nature. Christ receives wine mixed with myrrh and vinegar mixed with gall when we believe he sleeps, not seeing our wrongs. But having assumed sinless human nature, he revealed that he would restore the immortality grown sour 'in the vessels of the human race'. Christ drinks from the cup of death in order to absorb the vices we should transfuse to him in baptism and penance, 'in order that our sins may be deleted on his cross and, through him, death absorbed in victory'. Transferred to his crucified body, human bitterness and corruption become the new wine that the lord and his followers drink in paradise.[50] These ideas clarify both the pitcher's size on the ivory, where it contains the sins of the entire human race, and its position.[51] Stephaton's sponge-pole guides the viewer's eye from the defeated serpent and the jug poised just above its tail to Christ's face, while Longinus' spear takes the eye from Christ down to Ecclesia and, below her, the empty tomb. The wine-based liquid in Stephaton's pitcher moves through the sponge to the crucified redeemer who provides the saving blood that pours into Ecclesia's cup. Drawing the vinegar of mortal wickedness into his innocent body, Christ dies bestowing the remedy of sin in the eucharistic blood received by the church, before he conquers death through his resurrection.

The foregoing analysis by no means exhausts the multivalence of the Pericopes ivory, but it gives an idea of the scope of the liturgical, exegetical and theological doctrine it could have recalled for an educated Carolingian viewer. In studying the plaque, I think, Charles was expected to recognise that it presented, in compact visual form, the essential corpus of Christian dogma taught to him by Walahfrid Strabo and later by churchmen in his court circle, among them Hincmar and John Scottus. One goal of its design was to encourage the king to remember that his hope to be saved rested on acceptance of this summary of faith. Now, though, I want to turn to the two figures on the ivory whom I have not yet discussed, the woman with the banner and the seated figure to the cross's right. In general, whereas the rest of the carving celebrates the divine victory over sin, death and the devil and the transition from the Old Testament to the New, these two details imply a concern to bring to mind certain ideals of Christian rulership,

---

[50] See above, n. 48.
[51] Compare the Utrecht Psalter illustration to Psalm 88 (fol. 51v), where the vessel has a similar size relative to the other figures in the scene, but motifs are differently arranged (above, n. 14).

deriving from Augustinian thought, that find their clearest contemporary expression in writings by Hincmar.

Scholars are generally in agreement that the standing woman in this group is a second image of Ecclesia. Despite damage to both this figure and the Ecclesia who raises the chalice, it seems probable they originally had the same dress and type of banner. That the seated figure just before the portico, too, is female is apparent from her beardlessness; male figures in the carving all seem to be bearded. That she is a personification of earthly territory, as other scholars have noted, is suggested by her tower-crown and disk, both attributes given to personified cities and regions in other Carolingian works of art. Although some towers on her crown are broken, the original form remains discernible; the closest comparisons known to me are the crowns worn by Francia and Gothia in the illumination of the enthroned Charles the Bald in the Codex Aureus of St Emmeram (Munich, Bayerische Staatsbibliothek, Clm. 14000, fol. 5v).[52]

Still, it is important to recognise how unusual is the motif on the Pericopes ivory relative to other Carolingian representations of personified regions. The seated woman to the far right of the crucifix on the cover of the Drogo Gospelbook (Paris, BNF lat. 9383) must have some formal connection with the woman on the Pericopes plaque, though the exact relation between the two works has yet to be determined. But a much more pronounced wall of towers springs from her veiled head, and she holds a banner and a knife, the latter detail probably identifying her as Jerusalem.[53] The Utrecht Psalter's drawing for Psalm 49, illustrating the earth's fullness (verse 12; fol. 28v), shows a personification of Terra in long robes and a differently styled crown, holding two wands, cornucopias and, on her lap, a disk or orb of approximately the same size relative to her body as the disk in the Pericopes carving. The Utrecht Psalter picture for Psalm 89 depicts a crownless Terra, seated with a globe or disk (fol. 53r).[54]

It is striking, however, that the best contemporary analogies to the combination on the Pericopes ivory of seated figure with crown, long vestment, disk and gabled portico are found not among Carolingian images

---

[52] Fillitz, arguing that the figure is Roma, contends this is not a tower crown ('Jerusalem oder Rom?', p. 119), but he overlooks the similar crowns in the *Codex Aureus* miniature; for a reproduction of the miniature see Diebold, 'Ruler Portrait', p. 8, fig. 2. The Pericopes ivory and *Codex Aureus* crowns clearly differ from those worn, for example, by Charles the Bald in his portraits, such as the *Codex Aureus* miniature and his carved image on the *Cathedra Petri*: Gaborit-Chopin, *Elfenbeinkunst*, p. 74, fig. 71.

[53] Goldschmidt, *Elfenbeinskulpturen*, 1, no. 83, p. 46; Melzak, 'Carolingian Ivory Carvings', pp. 68–70, 182, 191–2, with references to earlier literature.

[54] Above, n. 14.

Figure 8.2 Utrecht Psalter, illustration of Psalm 18

of personified regions (including Terra), but among those of kings. The Utrecht Psalter illustration to Psalm 18 (fol. 10v; Fig. 8.2) depicts a beardless crowned king in long vestment, possibly David, seated in a mandorla and holding a cross-staff and globe. Other pictures in the psalter show various princes, sometimes David, beneath or in front of gabled structures resembling the one on the ivory. The portico evidently functions in these drawings as a sign of authority, as does the triangular pediment over the head of Charles the Bald, holding an orb and sceptre, on the *Cathedra Petri*.[55] In the Utrecht Psalter illustration to Psalm 88 (fol. 51v), a crowned, beardless, long-robed David, enthroned beneath a gabled portico, impales an enemy at his feet. The illustration to Psalm 1 (fol. 1v) depicts the ungodly man as a prince, and those to Psalms 51 and 151 (fols. 30r, 91v) represent King Saul; in all three pictures the rulers wear long robes, hold swords and sit enthroned beneath or before gabled structures, accompanied by armed attendants.[56] Similarities are also evident between the Pericopes tablet

---

[55] See Nees, *Tainted Mantle*, p. 152 and plate 1.

[56] I discuss these images of wicked rulers in a forthcoming article, 'Violence and the Virtuous Ruler in the Utrecht Psalter', in F. O. Büttner and Jeffrey Hamburger, eds., *The Illuminated Psalter: Content, Function, and Decoration* (Turnhout, in press).

motif and David on a later ninth-century ivory in Florence. Bearded, crowned and dressed in long decorated robes, the psalmist sits on his throne flanked by attendants, a sceptre in his right hand and in his left a tiny version of the orb or disk. His body is in frontal view, and like the figure on the Pericopes ivory he turns his head to his right.[57] The most striking resemblances in Carolingian art, though, are provided by the portraits of Charles the Bald in the San Paolo Bible (fol. 1r) and Paris Psalter (fol. 3v). Both depict the crowned monarch in long decorated vestments, seated beneath a gable-roof structure, holding a fairly large sphere or disk, along with a sceptre in the Paris Psalter illumination. The orb or disk is decorated with his cross monogram in the San Paolo Bible and a cross symbol in the Paris Psalter. Smaller, unadorned spheres are held by the Louvre's bronze statuette of a mounted ruler, probably Charles the Bald though possibly linking him to Charlemagne (Paris, Musée du Louvre),[58] and by Charles the Bald on the *Cathedra Petri*.[59]

Although the spheres and disks in the images just surveyed differ in size and other details, they can generally be traced to pagan antique symbols of earthly dominion or rulership. The differences in appearance do not reflect discernible differences in significance.[60] Only four portraits of Charles the Bald are known in which he holds a version of this emblem: the Louvre statuette, the *Cathedra Petri* carving and the illuminations in the Paris Psalter and San Paolo Bible. Aside from the possibility that the Louvre bronze also represents Charlemagne, the orb or disk of rulership appears in no extant image of any other Carolingian ruler. Each of these four works clearly reflects Charles's long-lived desire for the imperial title and his efforts, in that context, to increase his authority in rivalry with other Carolingians and aristocrats. Prior to 875, the climax to this struggle occurred in September 869, when he was crowned at Metz as king of West Francia and Lotharingia and gave orders that he be called emperor, since he then controlled two realms. As already noted, the Paris Psalter, completed

---

[57] Florence, Museo Nazionale del Bargello; colour plate in Gaborit-Chopin, *Elfenbeinkunst*, pp. 69–70, fig. 65, see Kat. 62.
[58] See M. McCormick, 'Paderborn 799: Königliche Repräsentation – Visualierung eines Herrschaftskonzepts', in Steigemann and Wemhoff eds., *799: Kunst und Kultur der Karolingerzeit, Karl der Grosse und Papst Leo III. in Paderborn: Beiträge zum Katalog der Ausstellung Paderborn 799* (Mainz, 1999), pp. 71–81, at 77, Pl. 3; P. E. Schramm and F. Mütherich, *Denkmale der deutschen Könige und Kaiser I: Ein Beitrag zur Herrschergeschichte von Karl dem Grossen bis Friedrich II. 768–1250*, 2nd expanded edn (Munich, 1981), p. 267, pl. 58.
[59] Gaborit-Chopin, *Elfenbeinkunst*, p. 74, fig. 71.
[60] Schramm, *Sphaira, Globus, Reichsapfel: Wanderung und Wandlung eines Herrschaftszeichens von Caesar bis zu Elisabeth II* (Stuttgart, 1958), pp. 57–9.

before 869, may have been given to Metz to commemorate this event.[61] For the next few months Aachen was the seat of Charles' government, until Louis the German forced him to withdraw in early 870.[62] As Janet Nelson remarks, Hincmar used the coronation rite of 869 to stress the Frankish character of Charles' new position. But although the archbishop evidently believed that its Frankishness rendered Charles' kingship superior to the Italy-based *imperium* of Louis II, for which Hincmar implies his scorn, in Charles' opinion the ceremony at Metz brought him closer to the imperial crown, finally acquired in 875.[63] There is no textual evidence that Charles ever actually used the orb or disk as an attribute, yet it seems appropriate to think he adopted this symbol of authority, at least in his portraits, because of its connection with classical imperial Rome.

While the images of Charles the Bald holding the disk or globe are important for understanding the Pericopes ivory figure, however, another source that probably influenced this design, as well, is literary: the discussion of Tellus in Book 7.24 of *The City of God*. A passage that Augustine quotes from the classical author, Marcus Terentius Varro, describes Tellus as the 'Great Mother' goddess. Summing up in herself many of the Roman deities, according to Varro, she is portrayed seated to show she is motionless, carries a tambour (*tympanum*) that designates the world's disk, and has towers rising from her head to represent towns.[64] The passage from Varro is followed by Augustine's lengthy, vigorous condemnation of Tellus as a symbol of the temporal, carnal wickedness of pagan Rome, which Christians must spurn in order to pursue the truth leading to eternal life.[65] Given the closeness of Varro's account of Tellus to the Pericopes ivory figure, it is difficult to believe that educated Carolingian viewers of the plaque such as Charles, who was certainly familiar with *The City of God*, did not connect the image with this text, or that the passage did not occur to the ivory's designer as he planned the carving.

The figure on the Pericopes tablet, I think, should be broadly identified as Tellus, that is, a female personification of the Earth and worldly dominion or *imperium*. But only by keeping in mind Augustine's criticism

---

[61] Above, at n. 5.   [62] See Nelson, *Charles the Bald*, pp. 219–24.
[63] See Nelson, trans., *The Annals of St. Bertin* (Manchester, 1991), pp. 104 (863), 161–2 (869); Latin text in Félix Grat *et al.*, eds., *Annales de Saint-Bertin* (Paris, 1964), p. 96 (Année 863), pp. 162–3 (Année 869); Nelson, *Charles the Bald*, pp. 219–53.
[64] 'Eandem, inquit, dicunt Matrem Magnam; quod tympanum habeat, significari esse orbem terrae; quod turres in capite, oppida; quod sedens fingatur, circa eam cum omnia moueantur, ipsam non moueri', Augustine, *De civitate Dei* 7.24, p. 205.
[65] See *De civitate Dei* 7.24, 26, CCSL 47.205–8, see esp. 208, ll. 8–10.

of Tellus and, in conjunction, of the sins of the pagan Roman Empire – the sins of precisely this *imperium* – do I think it possible to understand the figure's more specific significance, her relation to the Ecclesia standing before her, or the hand Ecclesia lays on her disk. In my earlier discussion of the Pericopes carving, I argued that Ecclesia was pulling the disk away, but on further consideration it seems to me that the depiction does not support this interpretation. The best evidence for deciphering the gesture is provided by the comparable gestures of two other figures on the same tablet: Oceanus, who drapes an arm over his vessel and, a closer comparison, the flying angel on the right (above the crucifixion) who rests a hand on top of the cross. In neither instance is an object or the power it symbolises (for example, the power inherent in Christ's cross) taken from or bestowed on someone else. Rather, both gestures, though in particular the angel's, seem meant to highlight the significance of the object touched and indicate a connection with the figure touching it. The angel, as mentioned earlier, thus appears to demonstrate the bond between the crucifix and heaven and consequently heaven's participation in Christ's passion. Analogously, I suggest, Ecclesia's touch of the disk draws attention to this symbol of worldly power and reveals that a connection exists between her, the object or the authority it signifies, and the bearer of earthly rule to whom the disk belongs. Ecclesia does not remove the disk from the seated woman, nor does the Church transfer earthly power to her, a signification suggested by Hermann Fillitz but hard to reconcile with Carolingian ideas about ecclesiastical authority.[66] Instead, Ecclesia's gesture implies that the mundane authority designated by the disk must be wielded in cooperation with or in submission to the Church, the representative of Christ and the Christian faith. The idea that proper governance in this world depends on the Church's participation, and on Ecclesia's mediation of heavenly or spiritual power, seems reinforced by the positioning of the two figures. Standing immediately in front of the seated woman, Ecclesia blocks her view of the crucifix. Tellus is the only figure in this tier not allowed to behold Christ directly. In order to see the cross, receive the eucharistic elements created in the crucifixion, or exercise power in this world, she must turn to the Church.

This interpretation of Ecclesia and the seated woman elucidates the similarities between the latter and ninth-century Carolingian representations of rulers, especially Charles the Bald. If the Pericopes ivory postdates

---

[66] Fillitz, 'Jerusalem oder Rom?', p. 121; Ecclesia passes power to Roma.

the Paris Psalter, the San Paolo Bible, the *Cathedra Petri*, or any comparable images of Charles now lost, it is hard to think he or a member of his entourage would have failed to notice the resemblance to his portraiture. The decorated robes and gabled portico, not typically seen in Carolingian depictions of the personified Earth or cities and regions, and not called for by Varro's description of Tellus, most likely constitute details included by the plaque's designer deliberately in order to direct Charles' attention to the figure and help him find, in her, a mirror of his own comportment. The most reasonable explanation of this personification's very 'royal' appearance is that the designer sought to remind Charles that the symbols of governance in his own portraits, especially the disk, linked him to Tellus and, consequently, to the pagan Roman imperialism Augustine condemned. In so far as the king embraced such attributes, they risked undermining his rejection of the materiality and wickedness of the pagan past, unless, like the figure on this tablet, he wielded them and the mundane authority they represented in submission to the Church.

Even though the Pericopes ivory does not depict Charles himself, then, its iconography is thematically linked with those other artistic productions, from the third quarter of the ninth century, which seem intended to warn him away from sins associated with un-Christian rule and encourage him to govern according to Christian virtue. As seems true of the miniatures of good and evil kings in the San Paolo Bible, the painting of Charles before the crucifix in his Prayerbook, the Paris Psalter covers, the Psalter's portrait of Charles and the carvings on the *Cathedra Petri*, the Pericopes tablet sets forth a visual *Fürstenspiegel* meriting comparison with ninth-century written mirrors of princes that exhort royal and aristocratic audiences to virtuous behaviour.[67] In general terms, this literature reveals the influence of ideas about Christian kingship traceable back to Augustine and *The City of God*. Often the Carolingian authors present their teachings through quotations from Augustine, such as his discussion in Book v, 24 of *The City of God* of the happiness of Christian emperors.[68]

If the Pericopes tablet can be linked to any one Carolingian scholar's development on Augustinian thought, though, it is Hincmar's. As Nees has observed, the archbishop of Rheims was particularly suspicious of Charles' desire for the Roman imperial title, apparently worrying, along

---

[67] See Anton, *Fürstenspiegel*, pp. 132–356.
[68] Jonas, *De institutione regia* ends with this passage: *SC* 407, ed. A. Dubreucq (Paris, 1995), pp. 282–4. See Anton, *Fürstenspiegel*, pp. 216–17, and on Augustinian thought and its influence, pp. 47–8, 98–9; Nees, *Tainted Mantle*, pp. 77–109.

lines marked out by Augustine, that it reflected a misguided interest in the remnants of pagan antiquity.[69] One work by Hincmar revealing this attitude is his continuation of the *Annales Bertiniani*, where he describes the coronation of 869 and makes the earlier-mentioned reference to Louis II's *imperium*.[70] Moreover, he strenuously defended ecclesiastical power, especially episcopal, against perceived challenges from within Francia and from Rome;[71] and he expended enormous energy admonishing lay rulers, among them Charles the Bald. Two such treatises composed for Charles are *De cavendis vitiis et virtutibus exercendis*, written in the 860s or early 870s,[72] and *De regis persona et regio ministerio*, written about 873.[73] As a *Fürstenspiegel* in the strict sense, *De regis persona* discusses qualities directly pertaining to the royal office.[74] Hincmar draws on several Church fathers, mainly Augustine, to outline his conception of virtuous rule; the most important source is *The City of God*. True happiness, Charles is reminded, depends not on present glory but on how he prepares for eternal life, by governing with Christian piety, humility, charity and justice, avoiding unnecessary warfare, and seeking peace. *De cavendis vitiis* is a different type of work, a mosaic largely composed of scriptural, liturgical and patristic excerpts not narrowly concerned with earthly monarchy. The aim is to clarify for Charles the virtues necessary to all Christians desiring redemption and the cost to his soul of sin, in particular greed, presented as the source of the other vices.[75] The feature that most clearly sets this treatise apart from other moral tractates for Carolingian princes is the devotion of the last third to an exposition of the eucharist.[76] The archbishop elaborates a doctrine hinted at in the surviving fragments of his earlier poem and treatise, the *Ferculum Salomonis*, written for Charles c. 853–6,[77] that the mass liturgy and the eucharist, Christ's incarnate body and blood, are the foundation of the Christian faith and virtuousness in which the king must persevere. By rejecting sin, participating in the mass,

---

[69] Nees, *Tainted Mantle*, pp. 210–11, 243–5; see Nelson, *Charles the Bald*, pp. 220, 235–42.
[70] Above, n. 63.
[71] See my discussion in, 'Archbishops Ebo and Hincmar of Reims and the Utrecht Psalter', pp. 1068–70, with references to earlier literature.
[72] Above, n. 42. [73] *PL* 125, cols. 833–56. [74] Anton, *Fürstenspiegel*, pp. 286–7.
[75] See *De cavendis*, MGH Quellen 16.5. [76] *De cavendis* 3, MGH Quellen 16.226–266.
[77] Hincmar, *Carmen* 4.1, *MGH Poetae* III, ed. L. Traube (Berlin, 1896), pp. 414–15; *Explanatio in ferculum Salomonis*, *PL* 125, cols. 817–34. Additional verses discovered by Bernhard Bischoff are discussed in B. Taeger, ed., *Zahlensymbolik bei Hraban, bei Hincmar – und im 'Heliand'?: Studien zur Zahlensymbolik im Frühmittelalter* (Munich, 1970), pp. 144–92. See J. Devisse, *Hincmar, archevêque de Reims, 845–882*, 3 vols. (Geneva, 1975), I, pp. 54–59; A. Wilmart, 'Distiques d'Hincmar sur l'eucharistie? Un sermon oublié de S. Augustin sur le même sujet', *Revue Bénédictine* 40 (1928), pp. 87–98.

receiving the consecrated bread and wine in penitence, humility and faith, and recognising the power of the Church that alone grants access to the eucharist, Charles can hope to enjoy the inner vision of Christ that foreshadows the sight of the crucified and resurrected lord in heaven.[78]

Although the Pericopes tablet seems to respond to a diverse array of Carolingian intellectual currents, it is plausible to think Hincmar's ideas exerted particular influence on its design. We may even reasonably speculate, I think, that the archbishop helped plan the carving, in the hope it would encourage Charles the Bald to remember those Christian principles which Hincmar believed should restrain the ruler's delight in earthly power and its material embellishments. Yet the ivory's intricately interwoven allusions to biblical doctrine, liturgy, patristic thought, above all Augustine's, classical literature and ideals of statecraft, it should also be noted, reflect a view Hincmar shared with other members of Charles's court, as well, that this was a king exceptionally capable of appreciating sophisticated intellectual discourse. The tablet offers indirect yet rich testimony to the conviction of his entourage that, in Charlemagne's namesake and grandson, the Carolingians once more had a ruler devoted to Christian learning.

---

[78] Note, e.g., Hincmar, *De cavendis* 2.6, *MGH Quellen* 16.207–209 (Gregory, Bede); 3.1, 2, *MGH Quellen* 16.227–228 (Gregory); 3.2, *MGH Quellen* 16.244–245 (Augustine), 261 (Leo); cf. Hincmar, *Explanatio in ferc. Salom.*, *PL* 125, cols. 818B, 826C–827B. See *The Crucified God*, pp. 215–25.

CHAPTER 9

Problems of authorship and audience in the writings of King Alfred the Great

David Pratt

In the search for the lay intellectual in the early middle ages, West Saxon King Alfred 'the Great' seems an outstanding candidate. Whereas there are quite plentiful examples of laymen commissioning or receiving texts and manuscripts from ecclesiastical writers, Alfred takes his place among a far smaller group of laymen who are identified as actual authors of surviving literary texts. Yet with Alfred the existence of an identifiable corpus is complicated, as not for Einhard, Nithard or Dhuoda, by his status as king, which raises singular questions of the relationship between text and practice. Alfred's case bears comparison with other early medieval rulers variously associated with learned composition. A corpus of Latin hymns, poetry and hagiography survives in the name of the Visigothic King Sisebut (611/12–20).[1] Gregory of Tours reports that the Merovingian King Chilperic I (561–84) composed Latin poetry and liturgical items, and a single hymn attributed to him has chanced to survive.[2] Numerous Merovingian and Carolingian legal decrees are written from the perspective of the royal 'we'.[3] Jonathan Shepard has recently drawn attention to the implications of various theological works attributed to Alfred's near-contemporaries, the eastern Emperor Leo VI (886–912) and Tsar Symeon of the Bulgars (893–927).[4] In each case, these rulers might be thought to have gained considerable

---

[1] Noted by R. Gameson, 'Alfred the Great and the Destruction and Production of Christian Books', *Scriptorium* 49 (1995), pp. 180–210, at 195–6.
[2] Discussed by J. M. Wallace-Hadrill, *The Long-Haired Kings and Other Studies in Frankish History* (London, 1962), pp. 195–8.
[3] F. L. Ganshof, 'Recherches sur les capitulaires', *Revue historique des droits français et étranger*, 4th ser. 35 (1957), pp. 33–87, 196–246, at pp. 50–69; I. Wood, *The Merovingian Kingdoms, 450–751* (London, 1994), pp. 102–19, and J. L. Nelson, 'Literacy in Carolingian Government', in R. McKitterick, ed., *The Uses of Literacy in Early Medieval Europe* (Cambridge, 1990), pp. 258–96, repr. Nelson, *The Frankish World* (London, 1996), pp. 1–36; cf. also Nelson, 'The Voice of Charlemagne', in R. Gameson and H. Leyser, eds., *Belief and Culture in the Middle Ages: Studies presented to Henry Mayr-Harting* (Oxford, 2001), pp. 76–88.
[4] J. Shepard, 'The Ruler as Instructor, Pastor and Wise: Leo VI of Byzantium and Symeon of Bulgaria', in T. Reuter, ed., *Alfred the Great* (Aldershot, 2003), pp. 339–58.

political benefits from their status as royal authors, whether or not these rulers had in fact played the leading role being claimed for them in the actual process of composition. In each case also, additional doubt arises from the availability of ecclesiastical expertise, offering the most immediate potential for lay education in such 'royal' contexts, and therefore also raising at least a possibility of more complex processes of collective involvement, if not outright 'ghost-writing'.[5]

Needless to say, the issue of authorship itself occupies a problematic point of intersection between literary and historical modes of enquiry. One available response may be to approach the phenomenon of textual production in rather different terms. The very significance of individual involvement in constructing texts has been the subject of sustained questioning in certain spheres of literary criticism. Certainly, a potentially attractive feature of post-structuralist approaches from an early medieval perspective is the emphasis on the possibilities of authorial self-projection, the 'constructed' qualities of any resulting authorial image, and the concomitant dangers in accepting such representations straightforwardly as a reliable guide to the text itself, or its possible meaning.[6] As Mary Swan notes, modern notions of 'authorial control' are thrown into stark relief by the prevalence of anonymity among Old English poetry and prose.[7] This in turn raises particularly interesting questions about the unusual status of 'Alfred' as a named author, principally comparable only to the poet 'Cynewulf' and the later ecclesiastical writers Ælfric and Wulfstan within surviving vernacular literature. Of course, the precise role assigned to 'Alfred' is that of translator, rather than creator of a text *ex nihilo*, and thus as potential mediator of an existing Latin text. Yet even here, the extensive prefatory material attached to several of the 'royal' texts goes to some lengths to portray translation as a creative process, encapsulated by the ubiquitous formula 'sometimes word for word, sometimes sense for sense'.[8]

---

[5] Comparison might be drawn with approaches to such problems in an early modern context: e.g., B. Vickers, *Shakespeare, Co-Author: A Historical Study of Five Collaborative Plays* (Oxford, 2002), with review by J. Bate, 'In the Script Factory', *Times Literary Supplement* (18 April 2003), pp. 3–4. Cf. the correspondence of Elizabeth I, subject to revision from J. Guy, *'My Heart is my Own': The Life of Mary Queen of Scots* (London, 2004).

[6] Principally represented by M. Foucault, 'What Is an Author?', in D. F. Bouchard and S. Simon, eds., *Language, Counter-Memory, Practice: Selected Essays and Interviews* (Oxford, 1977), pp. 113–38; and R. Barthes, 'The Death of the Author', in his *The Rustle of Language*, trans. R. Howard (Oxford, 1986), pp. 49–55: both cited by M. Swan, 'Authorship and Anonymity', in P. Pulsiano and E. Treharne, eds., *A Companion to Anglo-Saxon Literature* (Oxford, 2001), pp. 71–83, at 72–4.

[7] Swan, 'Authorship and Anonymity', pp. 74–6.

[8] For this formulation see KL, p. 259 (n. 164). For its service among Roman and patristic writers in connection with a variety of translatory approaches, see R. Copeland, *Rhetoric, Hermeneutics, and*

'What is an author?' Foucault's oft-cited question raises at least the possibility of interpreting Alfredian authorship as an 'author-function' or strategy, deriving its greatest potency from such outward presentation, rather than from any particular facts lying behind its construction.

There is a striking correspondence between such theoretical and historical perspectives, in attaching caution to the precise testimony of texts attributed to the king; they also raise at least one possible means of coping with such problems, by leaving them conveniently unanswered. Such a solution has a number of attractions, not least as a means of generating findings apparently more resilient to scepticism. Foucauldian notions of 'author-function' seem particularly helpful in clarifying the potential distinctiveness of 'royal' output; there may be a certain rigour also in drawing some potential distinction between this authorial 'Alfred' and the king of the same name, if only because the two are so easily equated. What is striking about the extensive body of scholarship attached to the king's texts is the extent to which a strong identification of this kind has generally been assumed.[9] Despite occasional doubts by writers otherwise concerned to demythologise their subject, the 'royal' corpus has conspicuously failed to attract sustained scepticism.[10]

Many of the issues at stake here have recently been subjected to provocative questioning by Professor Malcolm Godden.[11] Precisely by leaving

---

Translation in the Middle Ages: Academic Traditions and Vernacular Texts (Cambridge, 1991), pp. 9–62; cf. also R. Stanton, *The Culture of Translation in Anglo-Saxon England* (Cambridge, 2002), pp. 73–8.

[9] Positive assessments from a wide variety of perspectives: D. Whitelock, 'The Prose of Alfred's Reign', in E. G. Stanley, ed., *Continuations and Beginnings: Studies in Old English Literature* (London, 1966), pp. 67–103, repr. in her *From Bede to Alfred: Studies in Early Anglo-Saxon Literature and History* (London, 1980), ch. 6; R. H. C. Davis, 'Alfred and Guthrum's Frontier', *EHR* 97 (1982), pp. 803–10, repr. in Davis, *From Alfred the Great to Stephen* (London, 1991), pp. 47–54, at 49, n. 1; J. Bately, 'Lexical Evidence for the Authorship of the Prose Psalms in the Paris Psalter', *ASE* 10 (1982), pp. 69–95, at 94–5; KL, pp. 28–35; J. L. Nelson, 'The Political Ideas of Alfred of Wessex', in A. Duggan, ed., *Kings and Kingship in Medieval Europe*, King's College Medieval Studies 10 (London, 1993), pp. 125–58, repr. in Nelson, *Rulers*, ch. 5, pp. 137–40; R. Abels, *Alfred the Great: War, Kingship and Culture in Anglo-Saxon England* (Harlow, 1998), pp. 219–57; cf. also A. P. Smyth, *King Alfred the Great* (Oxford, 1995), pp. 527–602.

[10] D. P. Kirby, 'Asser and his Life of King Alfred', *Studia Celtica* 6 (1971), pp. 12–35, at 33–5; cf. R. I. Jack, 'The Significance of the Alfredian Translations', *Australasian Universities Language and Literature Association: Proceedings and Papers of the 13th Congress* (Melbourne, 1971), pp. 348–61, reported by P. E. Szarmach, 'Introduction', in P. E. Szarmach, ed., *Studies in Earlier Old English Prose* (Albany, NY, 1986), pp. 1–14, at 2; J. Campbell, 'Asser's Life of Alfred', in C. Holdsworth and T. P. Wiseman, eds., *The Inheritance of Historiography, 350–900*, Exeter Studies in History 12 (Exeter, 1986), pp. 115–35, repr. in Campbell, *The Anglo-Saxon State* (London, 2000), pp. 129–55, at 147–8.

[11] M. Godden, 'The Player-King: Identification and Self-Representation in King Alfred's Writings', in Reuter, ed., *Alfred*, pp. 137–50; Godden, *The Translations of King Alfred and his Circle and the Misappropriation of the Past* (HM Chadwick Memorial Lecture 14, Cambridge, 2004); cf. also

the question of authorship open, and by focusing in the first instance on important features of the texts themselves – above all, their often problematic status as translations, exhibiting varying degrees of faithfulness towards their Latin source-texts, and the additional implications of those texts in dialogue form – Godden draws attention to the highly complex character of such translation processes, involving the mediation and manipulation of multiple voices and *personae*, in which the extent of 'royal' intervention is placed in doubt. His approach necessarily involves a wider range of issues than can be addressed directly here; what follows is a consideration of Godden's arguments in so far as they relate to the question of authorship.[12] The issues at stake pertain directly to the status of Alfredian 'royal' identity, and more generally to the interrelationship between literary criticism and historical enquiry.

The interrelatedness of this relationship provides an appropriate starting point. Cases of attributed royal authorship present particular potential for enquiry, and it is questionable whether this can be convincingly circumvented in any interpretational schema. If particular doubts are raised by such 'royal' attribution, then this places a particular premium on the need to develop some sort of position with regard to its status. Quite apart from the obvious contrast with anonymous texts, the most revealing comparison may be with 'Cynewulf', as a named author whose precise context remains uncertain. There can be no doubting the historical accessibility of Alfred the king, for all the problems involved in his reconstruction and recovery. Naturally in the case of the most extensive source, Asser's *Life*, one should heed the obvious questions raised by any royal biography, and by Asser's own status as an acknowledged helper in at least one 'royal' literary enterprise.[13] Yet if Asser's account is both retrospective and subjective, what needs stress is the extent to which the essential features of his portrait receive strong support from a wide variety of different sources.[14]

Godden, 'The Anglo-Saxons and the Goths: Rewriting the Sack of Rome', *ASE* 31 (2002), pp. 47–68, at 62, n. 53.

[12] Alfredian kingship and court culture receive wider treatment in my thesis, 'The Political Thought of Alfred the Great' (Ph.D. dissertation, Cambridge University, 1999), now published in revised form as *The Political Thought of King Alfred the Great* (Cambridge, 2007).

[13] See esp. recent discussion by P. Kershaw, 'Illness, Power and Prayer in Asser's *Life of King Alfred*', *EME* 10 (2001), pp. 201–21, at 201–3, 220–4, with references; cf. also Campbell, 'Asser's *Life of Alfred*', pp. 129–55; and M. Kempshall, 'No Bishop, No King: The Ministerial Ideology of Kingship and Asser's *Res Gestae Aelfredi*', in Gameson and Leyser, eds., *Belief and Culture*, pp. 106–27, at 107–8, 112, 122–3.

[14] This point emerges strongly from S. Keynes, 'On the Authenticity of Asser's *Life of King Alfred*', *JEH* 47 (1996), pp. 529–51. Even the account of Alfred's medical history, often seemingly its most problematic aspect, receives support from the survival of a list of remedies sent to the king,

Asser's *Life*, and the *Anglo-Saxon Chronicle* upon which it is partially based, acquire further significance when considered against the extensive body of surviving 'documentary' sources. Whatever allowances are made for the use of ecclesiastics as scribes and draftsmen, royal charters can be identified as providing snapshots of a king's behaviour, and these are supplemented in Alfred's case by such documents as his will and law-code, to say nothing of the evidence of coinage.[15] All this material provides excellent opportunities to detect agency, in significant measure, on the part of the king, and of locating this agency within the broader structures of West Saxon royal power. It matters enormously how far Alfred can be suspected to have pulled the strings within these structures, and how far his actions might have been guided by strings of their own. 'Literary' evidence undoubtedly poses its own problems, but this is no reason to exclude it from similar investigation; post-structuralist considerations of authority and power might themselves be cited as urgent grounds for situating such material within its wider political and cultural context.

One may now turn to the Alfredian evidence itself. The texts attributed to Alfred would seem to place his case above other early medieval examples of royal authorship, not only in terms of sheer scope, but also of the literary pretensions to which they aspire. It is the particular achievement of Janet Bately to have isolated a corpus of five substantial texts which are now held to be attributable in some sense to Alfred himself: the West Saxon translations of Gregory's *Regula pastoralis*, Boethius' *Consolatio philosophiae*, Augustine's *Soliloquia*, and the first fifty Psalms, plus the introduction to Alfred's law-book.[16] Four of these texts include attributions to Alfred of one kind or another, but the point to stress is the extent to which this material can be further distinguished as a single corpus, set apart from all other examples of contemporary vernacular prose. The texts in Alfred's name are written in early West Saxon dialect, so distinctions are only to be expected from contemporary Mercian texts, such as the translation of the *Dialogues* of Gregory the Great, attributed to Wærferth, bishop of Worcester, and the anonymous translation of Bede's *Ecclesiastical History*.

---

independently preserved in Bald's *Leechbook*: D. Pratt, 'The Illnesses of King Alfred the Great', *ASE* 30 (2001), pp. 39–90, 57–63, 67–81.

[15] S. Keynes, 'The West Saxon Charters of King Æthelwulf and his Sons', *EHR* 109 (1994), pp. 1109–49; Wormald, *Making*, pp. 118–25, 265–85, 416–29; M. A. S. Blackburn and D. N. Dumville, eds., *Kings, Currency and Alliances: History and Coinage of Southern England in the Ninth Century* (Woodbridge, 1998).

[16] See esp. J. M. Bately, 'King Alfred and the Old English Translation of Orosius', *Anglia* 88 (1970), 433–56; Bately, 'Lexical Evidence'; Bately, 'Old English Prose before and during the Reign of Alfred', *ASE* 17 (1988), pp. 93–138.

Attention therefore focuses on appropriate West Saxon comparanda, principally the translation of Orosius' *Historiae adversus paganos* and the 'common stock' of the *Anglo-Saxon Chronicle*. Even within this broader spectrum of early West Saxon, Bately shows that 'royal' texts can be further distinguished on grounds of lexical choice, supplemented by considerations of syntax and style.[17] The evidence of lexis deserves particular weight given the general availability of direct Latin equivalents, and Bately's distinctive features include cases of lexical variation as well as lexical consistency.[18] These correspondences seem especially strong given that the 'Chronicle' may itself be the work of several compilers, and can be firmly distinguished from the language and style of the Orosius.[19] Certain inconsistencies in usage can also be detected across the 'royal' corpus, together with the occasional appearance of words usually regarded as characteristic of Mercian dialect, but these are insufficient in Bately's view to undermine the case for common vocabulary.[20] Stylistically, the 'royal' texts bear the closest comparison with the Orosius, not least in the overall approach to translation, more heavily reliant on free paraphrase as opposed to the literal rendering of individual Latin sentences, generally adopted in Wærferth's translation and the Old English Bede.[21] Yet here too the 'royal' texts can be distinguished at micro-level by certain idiosyncracies of syntax and shared mannerisms.[22]

The crucial question, of course, is how far one might legitimately associate these distinctive features with the common involvement of a single individual. There can be no doubting Bately's case for the exceptional clarity and sophistication of the prose to which the king's name is attached; she presents a strong case also for regarding such stylistic unity as more than merely the product of 'standardisation' or 'common policy'.[23] Bately is accordingly convinced that behind this distinctive corpus 'there

---

[17] Bately, 'Lexical Evidence', esp. pp. 71–94. Bately's attribution of the Psalm translation receives further support from P. P. O'Neill in the introduction to his edition of *King Alfred's Old English Translation of the First Fifty Psalms* (Cambridge, MA, 2001), pp. 73–96.
[18] Bately, 'Lexical Evidence', pp. 90–3.
[19] See esp. J. M. Bately, 'The Compilation of the Anglo-Saxon Chronicle, 60 BC to AD 890: Vocabulary as Evidence', *PBA* 64 (1978), pp. 93–129, at 101–29; Bately, ed., *The Old English Orosius*, EETS, s.s. 6 (Oxford, 1980), pp. lxxxiii–vi.
[20] Bately, 'King Alfred and the Old English Translation of Orosius', pp. 452–3; Bately, 'Lexical Evidence', pp. 78–86.
[21] Bately, 'Old English Prose', pp. 118–38.
[22] Bately, 'King Alfred and the Old English Translation of Orosius', pp. 444–52; Bately, 'Lexical Evidence', p. 94. Cf. also syntactical similarities identified by E. M. Liggins, 'The Authorship of the Old English Orosius', *Anglia* 88 (1970), pp. 289–322, at 292–321.
[23] Bately, 'Lexical Evidence', esp. pp. 77–8.

was one mind at work (though probably never entirely on its own)', and given the evidence for contemporary attribution, she concludes logically enough that the unifying mind may have been Alfred's own.[24] This argument might be strengthened by the fact that the dialect of this corpus is essentially early West Saxon, which would have been the native tongue of the king himself, but not of any of the scholars whose help Alfred acknowledges in the Prose Preface to the *Pastoral Care*:[25] Plegmund was a Mercian, Asser a Welshman, Grimbald a Frank and John a continental Saxon. The distinctiveness of this 'royal' prose from other early West Saxon texts has already been noted.

As Bately has herself acknowledged, however, lexical analysis can only go so far, and her findings leave many questions unanswered.[26] Perhaps the greatest problem is that in lexical and stylistic investigations of this kind, the significance of any distinctive feature exhibited by the corpus attributed to Alfred is inevitably reduced by the nature of the surviving evidence. It has been insufficiently emphasised that the 'royal' texts are in fact the *only* examples of vernacular prose whose composition can be securely located within the king's own learned circle. This point cannot be explored in detail here, but problems posed by other contemporary texts have long been recognised, especially the *Anglo-Saxon Chronicle*, and the anonymous translations of Orosius and Bede. The only identifiable translator, Wærferth, is conspicuously absent from the list of helpers in the Prose Preface. In this light, it is perhaps not so surprising that the texts attributed to Alfred are stylistically distinctive. The available 'control experiments' are unsatisfactory, for there are no surviving vernacular texts demonstrably written by individual helpers.

Taken as a whole, the 'royal' corpus would seem to bear ample testimony to the cosmopolitan resources at the king's disposal. Carolingian influences have generally received the strongest emphasis in an Alfredian context, and it is accordingly important to recognise the input of 'Insular' expertise, together with the high degree of adaptation that is observable in most cases to local 'Alfredian' conditions. Mechthild Gretsch has noted that 'Mercianisms' within the 'royal' corpus must be judged carefully, given the considerable potential for incorporation of 'Mercian' vocabulary into

---

[24] *Ibid.*, pp. 94–5.
[25] *King Alfred's West-Saxon Version of Gregory's Pastoral Care*, ed. H. Sweet, EETS, o.s. 45, 50 (Oxford, 1871), p. 6.
[26] See esp. J. Bately, 'The Alfredian Canon Revisited: One Hundred Years On', in Reuter, ed., *Alfred*, pp. 107–20, at 111–12.

spoken early West Saxon, but it is difficult not to suspect some connection with the king's Mercian helpers, particularly given the greater prominence of this feature in 'royal' texts.[27] The influence of Irish learning may also be suspected in the 'royal' corpus, particularly in the exegetical introductions attached to the translation of the psalms, and the excerpts from Mosaic law in the law-book, which may well be dependent upon an Irish compilation of biblical law, the *Liber ex lege Moysi*.[28] These features lend significance to the Irish presence in the Alfredian royal household, and thus also to the possibility of input which may not have been explicitly acknowledged.[29] Yet in each case these influences need to be balanced against evidence suggestive of Carolingian expertise, in the concessions made towards the 'Gallican' text of the Psalter, and most definitively in the overall approach to law represented by the law-book introduction, which bears some clear relationship to attitudes available at contemporary Rheims.[30] Continental transmission may also be strongly suspected in the case of the Boethian and Augustinian source-texts, and the level of ambition involved in the translation of such texts needs to be judged against the quite impressive learning that has generally been detected in their execution.[31] At the least, these considerations raise the question whether the literary 'Alfred' should be regarded as a method of group composition rather than a single author, and indeed they have the additional effect of further weakening any interpretation dependent on 'standardisation' alone.[32] Yet at the far end of the spectrum, the possibility arises of an ultra-sceptical position, in which the distinctive features identified by Bately might be regarded as a collective 'court style' of high-register early West Saxon, with the king's own role left in doubt.

---

[27] M. Gretsch, 'The Junius Psalter Gloss: Its Historical and Cultural Context', *ASE* 29 (2000), pp. 85–121, at 98–106.
[28] P. P. O'Neill, 'The Old English Introductions to the Prose Psalms of the Paris Psalter: Sources, Structure, and Composition', in J. S. Wittig, ed., *Eight Anglo-Saxon Studies*, Studies in Philology 78, no. 5: Texts and Studies (Chapel Hill, NC, 1981), pp. 20–38; O'Neill, ed., *King Alfred's Old English Psalms*, pp. 23–6, 37–44; KL, p. 304, n. 2; Pratt, 'Political Thought', pp. 170–6, 199–206.
[29] *VA* 76, ll. 21–6, p. 60; *ASC* s.a. 891, *Two Chronicles*, ed. Plummer, I, 82.
[30] O'Neill, ed., *King Alfred's Old English Psalms*, pp. 32–4, 42; O'Neill, 'On the Date, Provenance and Relationship of the "Solomon and Saturn" Dialogues', *ASE* 26 (1997), pp. 139–68, at 162; Pratt, 'Political Thought', pp. 150–70; Wormald, *Making*, pp. 423–7.
[31] See esp. J. S. Wittig, 'King Alfred's Boethius and its Latin Sources: A Reconsideration', *ASE* 11 (1983), pp. 157–98; M. McC. Gatch, 'King Alfred's Version of Augustine's *Soliloquia*: Some Suggestions on its Rationale and Unity', in Szarmach, ed., *Studies*, pp. 17–46; Pratt, 'Political Thought', pp. 235–315, 316–56.
[32] For the case against such straightforward 'standardisation', see Bately, 'Lexical Evidence', esp. pp. 77–8.

There is of course an apparently respectable 'minimalist' position to which one might withdraw. This would be to argue that while the true extent of the king's personal involvement in these texts may be irrecoverable, it is at the very least inconceivable that Alfred would have allowed them to bear his name, if he had not first 'authorised' their contents. This position effectively bypasses the issue of authorship, placing greater emphasis upon Alfred's contemporary *image* as author, and it might also seem compatible with the post-structuralist approaches already outlined. Certainly Alfred's authorial image acquires significance in the context of the broader functions which the texts in his name were clearly assigned to serve. As has long been recognised, Alfredian 'royal' authorship needs to be seen in the context of wider cultural developments in the 880s and early 890s, primarily focused on the promotion of written vernacular prose, and principally ascribed to the king's own leadership and initiative.[33] Although conventionally described as an 'educational programme', a strong case has been advanced for emphasising the novelty of these developments, as an innovative process of aristocratic 're-education', centred upon the particular character of the Alfredian written vernacular, and the premium placed upon the ability to read.[34]

The implications of this cultural initiative warrant more attention than is possible here, and it must suffice to offer a brief review of its most striking features.[35] At the heart of these collective efforts lay a coherent attitude towards power itself, as a form of responsibility shared between the king and the leading ecclesiastical and secular nobility, in which the acquisition of divine knowledge or 'wisdom' was identified as nothing less than an indispensable and primary pre-requisite. In its fullest expression, language of this kind remained essentially restricted to the texts in the king's name, and in this sense Alfredian 'literary' innovation was entirely inseparable from such 'royal' political thinking. For all the emphasis generally placed on Carolingian precedent, there are strong grounds for identifying this language as distinctively 'Alfredian' in its implications and deployment. Alfredian 're-education' needs to be interpreted in the light of

---

[33] Whitelock, 'Prose of Alfred's Reign'; D. Bullough, 'The Educational Tradition in England from Alfred to Ælfric: Teaching *utriusque linguae*', Settimane Spoleto 19 (1972), pp. 453–94, repr. in his *Carolingian Renewal* (Manchester, 1991), pp. 297–334; KL, pp. 25–41; A. J. Frantzen, *King Alfred* (Boston, MA, 1986).

[34] P. A. Booth, 'King Alfred versus Beowulf: The Re-Education of the Anglo-Saxon Aristocracy', *BJRL* 79 (1997), pp. 41–66; cf. esp. Bullough, 'Educational Tradition', pp. 297–300.

[35] The following paragraph summarises some of my findings in Pratt, 'Political Thought'; cf. also Pratt, 'Persuasion and Invention at the Court of King Alfred the Great', in C. Cubitt, ed., *Court Culture in the Early Middle Ages* (Turnhout, 2003), pp. 189–221.

the precise terms in which it was justified, as a means of encouraging all those placed in positions of spiritual and secular authority to acquire divine wisdom, without which power would inevitably lead to greed and pride.[36] These priorities were reflected with equal precision in the range of audiences to which newly translated texts seem to have been directed. The translation of the *Regula pastoralis* was explicitly addressed to bishops, and the final chapter of Asser's *Life* implies no less strenuous efforts to inculcate wisdom among secular office-holders, identified as the king's ealdormen, reeves and thegns, with particular reference to their involvement in judgement and dispute settlement.[37] Parallels between the Prose Preface and Asser's remarks elsewhere reveal a further important audience, among youths apparently attached to the royal household in some way for the purposes of aristocratic and literate training.[38] Asser's characterisation of this body as a *schola* needs to be judged against the looser, corporate sense of the term. His account leaves little doubt that these youths were intended to supply a new cohort of literate office-holders, ready to replace their elders in due course, when the long-term process of 're-education' would finally be complete.

One can quite imagine how a 'minimalist' position might be developed on this basis. Alfred's status as a late beginner is repeatedly emphasised by Asser, and this image acquires further resonance when considered in the light of the parallel presentation of Charlemagne in Einhard's biography, certainly available within the immediate royal circle.[39] According to Einhard, Charlemagne had attempted to learn to write, but made little progress because he had begun too late in life: Alfred clearly surpassed this famous precedent, at least with regard to composition, as a lifelong enthusiast who eventually *did* manage to satisfy his ceaseless desire for wisdom when, according to Asser, he began in mid-life to translate from Latin into English, in order 'to instruct many others'.[40] It is Asser again who reveals the implications of such royal role-playing, in his final chapter. Current office-holders struggling to learn to read were expected to take heart from the king's own late start, while their children at the court *schola* were constantly reminded that such opportunities had been entirely denied a generation earlier, both to their parents and to the young Alfred himself,

---

[36] Pratt, 'Political Thought', esp. pp. 39–50, 67–70, 361–3, 31–75.
[37] *Ibid.*, pp. 50–60; *VA* c. 106, pp. 92–5.
[38] Pratt, 'Political Thought', pp. 31–4, 60–7; and p. 33, n. 121, for interpretation of *speda* as 'worldly means, prosperity', cf. Bullough, 'Educational Tradition', pp. 319–20, n. 12. *Alfred's Pastoral Care*, ed. Sweet, p. 6, ll. 6–15; *VA* c. 75, ll. 11–31, pp. 58–9.
[39] KL, p. 254, n. 139.   [40] *VK* c. 25, p. 39; *VA* cc. 88–9, pp. 73–5.

due to a lack of suitable teachers.[41] In this way, Alfred's image as a royal author, finally successful in his relentless pursuit of wisdom, functioned as a means of encouraging and persuading the lay and ecclesiastical nobles who constituted his primary intended audiences to imitate the king's own example. From this standpoint, Alfred's role need not necessarily have amounted to anything more than the 'authorisation' of vernacular texts which were to bear his name.

This 'minimalist' position seems superficially attractive; but in so far as it effectively sidesteps important questions of agency, it is important to emphasise the breadth of the basis for counter-argument. An initial point again proceeds from post-structuralist attention to authorial image. In an Alfredian context, authorship amounted to far more than 'authorization', and was presented to contemporaries in different terms.[42] It has been insufficiently stressed that the texts attributed to Alfred constitute in fact the *only* examples of projected authorial image among the vernacular texts generally associated with Alfred's reign. Wærferth's involvement in translating the *Dialogues* is only revealed by Asser.[43] Anonymity was ubiquitous, extending beyond translated texts, such as the Orosius or Bede, to include instances of more free-standing composition, such as the 'Chronicle' or the Old English *Martyrology*. The *Dialogues* are particularly significant given their explicit association with royal patronage, as is the anonymity of the 'Chronicle' given its availability to Asser. The important contrast is with the extensive prefatory material of the 'royal' corpus, in which the king's role as creative translator is prominently asserted.[44] There is no need to regard the Augustinian translation as problematic in this regard: the surviving preface lacks explicit reference to the king, yet the text itself seems to be acephalous, and there is a well-established first person in the opening as transmitted.[45] The only clear exception is the translation of the Psalms; even here there is no way of knowing whether prefatory material

---

[41] Pratt, 'Political Thought', pp. 24–5, 68–9; Pratt, 'Persuasion and Invention', pp. 193–4; *VA* c. 106, with cc. 22, 25 and 76, pp. 19–20, 21–2 and 92–5.

[42] Early modern comparison is again instructive, with widely varying uses of authorial representation, subject to particular scrutiny from a literary critical perspective within what has sometimes been termed the 'New Historicism': see esp. the seminal study by S. Greenblatt, *Renaissance Self-Fashioning: from More to Shakespeare* (Chicago, IL, 1980).

[43] *VA* c. 77, p. 62.

[44] See now A. Frantzen, 'The Form and Function of the Preface in Poetry and Prose of Alfred's Reign', in Reuter, *Alfred*, pp. 121–36; cf. also E. G. Stanley, 'King Alfred's Prefaces', *Review of English Studies* 39 (1988), pp. 349–64.

[45] *King Alfred's Version of St Augustine's Soliloquies*, ed. T. A. Carnicelli (Cambridge, MA, 1969), pp. 1–2; KL, p. 299 (n. 1); Gatch, 'Alfred's Version', pp. 23–4.

has subsequently been lost. The overall effect can only have been to reinforce the distinction between 'authorised' texts and those actually presented as the work of the king.

The significance of this distinction cannot be sufficiently emphasised; if its implications are equivocal in themselves, it is important that they are incorporated into debate. This point is of particular relevance given Professor Godden's recent contribution, on closely related questions of textual authority.[46] Godden's starting point is the degree of ambiguity involved in any project of translation, particularly heightened in the case of several of the Alfredian translations, including the versions of Boethius and the *Soliloquia*, characterised by instances of translatory freedom. Godden warns against any straightforward equation of the resulting utterances with any particular individual involved in translation, and he rightly draws attention to the considerable commitment shown within Alfredian texts to the status and historicity of original Latin authors. All these points are valid and important, yet Godden's argument as a whole takes insufficient account of the king's unique status as a named translator, and of the particular significance of this status from the perspective of potential aristocratic readers. Thus, to take the most complex examples, of 'royal' texts in dialogue form, both the Boethian and Augustinian translations might be likened to a nest of Russian dolls, involving multiple levels of fictive *personae*, nonetheless framed at the very least within prior awareness of the king's own authorial claims. This point is of particular importance given the distinctive style and lexical consistency that is exhibited throughout the 'royal' corpus. This additional layer of signification was entirely restricted to the texts attributed to the king. Indeed, this was surely one of the key features that made the Alfredian phenomenon of royal authorship so potentially effective. Considerations of historicity and invention must be situated very firmly within such exclusively 'royal' implementation of creative translatory identity.

The fundamental distinction between authorship and 'authorisation' has further implications from the perspective of intended audiences. Much hinges here on what might be regarded as a challenging and open question: to what extent were such claims accepted by targeted recipients of the 'royal' word? The central point is of course the exclusive significance of the king's authorial image, as a means of encouraging wisdom in others, and the premium that this might be expected to have placed upon

---

[46] Godden, *Misappropriation*.

the extended maintenance of this image, across the 'royal' output. The possibility arises of some ironic reception of the king's claims, perhaps encouraged by awareness of the involvement of scholarly helpers; the contribution of others is openly admitted in the Gregorian translation. Yet such possibilities need to be balanced against the testimony of Asser's *Life*, regularly attentive to the ambiguity of royal role-playing, in which personal involvement in translatory activity would seem to be unquestioningly endorsed.[47] These passages stand in contrast to the treatment of Alfred's mysterious illness, where the king's own impression of its severity seems subtly undermined.[48]

Nor is this contrast surprising, when one considers the wide array of learned activities otherwise ascribed to the king, many of which can only imply extensive aristocratic audiences: 'reading aloud from books in English and above all learning English poems by heart'; 'listening eagerly and attentively to Holy Scripture being read out by his own countrymen, or even ... in the company of foreigners'; and above all, the king's own role as a teacher within the *schola* of the royal household, such that 'he did not cease from personally giving, by day and night, instruction in all virtuous behaviour and tutelage in literacy' to the sons of his leading nobles.[49] It is conceivable of course that Asser's overstatement may conceal a greater element of exaggeration, but there can be no escaping the implications of this compelling portrait. Alfred's image as an author extended far beyond the written page, and can hardly be dissociated from all other aspects of the complex interaction of king and aristocratic audience, primarily conducted within the royal household. This point is all the more significant in a West Saxon context, where such contact seems to have been particularly intensive, with groups of thegns spending one month in every three with the king himself.[50] Overall, these considerations can only reduce considerably the parameters of any gap between authorial image and learned royal practice. At the very least, it is difficult to account for the very existence of the 'royal' texts had the king been unable to sustain this image whenever he was encountered in person.

The degree of equivocation hardly needs highlighting; the possibility arises of some revised 'minimalism', with emphasis placed on the king's ability to maintain such credibility through general familiarity with the texts at his disposal, rather than direct involvement in their fabrication.

---

[47] *VA* cc. 87–9, pp. 73–5.
[48] Pratt, 'Illnesses', pp. 74–7; *VA* cc. 74, ll. 64–70; 91, ll. 1–12, pp. 57 and 76.
[49] *VA* cc. 76, ll. 9–10, 26–9, 32–6, pp. 59–60.   [50] *Ibid.*, c. 100, pp. 86–7.

One must certainly bear this possibility in mind; it might be thought to receive some support from the element of dissimulation necessarily involved in any translation process. Yet one ought to ask how far this possibility might in turn be consistent with the apparently personal basis of Alfredian authorial appeal, in all its manifestations, and with the unique properties shared by the 'royal' corpus as a whole. Considerations of dissimulation are double-edged: parameters for the construction of these texts can only have been significantly restricted by the existing familiarity of the king himself to the eyes and ears of his aristocratic audiences, now to be mediated in textual form. Yet the translations that emerged did not merely bear the king's name in most cases, but were also endowed at a fundamental level by distinctive textual unity. One is entitled to ask how far these parameters could have been transgressed within such a consistent and exclusive enterprise of self-projection.

These arguments seem all the more significant when one considers the means by which such textual unity could have been maintained. Once again, it is Asser who provides the principal testimony, but with a degree of endorsement which has already been emphasised. Several details accord closely with well-documented continental examples of learned lay activity.[51] There are strong grounds for interpreting the quasi-miraculous occasion in 887, when the king 'first began through divine inspiration to read [Latin] and to translate at the same time, all on one and the same day', as some symbolic representation of the very onset of the 'royal' scheme of translation.[52] The attribution to St Martin's Day would be particularly appropriate, given Martin's memory as a martial saint who had achieved this status despite a distinct lack of learning, even described as *illiteratus* on one occasion in by his hagiographer.[53] It is tempting to detect a degree of irony in this association, but any point would seem to lie in the precise extent of the king's Latin competence, rather than any greater questioning of his distinctive contribution.

This impression emerges most clearly by comparison with the king's pre-existing learned abilities, which he is shown to have acquired in

---

[51] See esp. R. McKitterick, *The Carolingians and the Written Word* (Cambridge, 1989), pp. 216–20, 223–7, 244–52, 266–70; Pratt, 'Illnesses', pp. 40–9.

[52] *VA* cc. 87–9, pp. 73–5; KL, p. 28.

[53] Sulpicius Severus, *Vita Sancti Martini c.* 25, cf. *c.* 26: *Sulpice Sévère: Vie de Saint Martin*, ed. J. Fontaine, *SC* 133 (Paris, 1967), pp. 310–14. Martin's appearance here needs to be seen in the light of contemporary Carolingian ideals, and his role as a model for lay behaviour. See esp. Airlie, 'The Anxiety of Sanctity', pp. 381–3; cf. also *Notker der Stammler: Taten Karls des Grossen*, ed. H. F. Haefele, *MGH SRG* n.s. 12 (Berlin, 1959), 11, 11, pp. 68–9.

childhood and adolescence.⁵⁴ Asser's handling of the young Alfred's education is itself somewhat problematic, but basic familiarity with Latin grammar is strongly implied by his learning of the services of the hours, necessarily for celebrating the divine Office, together with 'certain psalms and many prayers'.⁵⁵ Alfred's resulting *libellus* of prayers might on this basis be regarded as a Latin counterpart to the book of vernacular poetry which he is reported to have received from his mother. Yet Alfred is also reported to have remained 'ignorant of letters (*illiteratus*) until his twelfth year, or even longer'.⁵⁶ *Illiteratus* usually denoted one unable to read or perhaps even comprehend Latin, but in Asser's hands the word seems more likely to imply an inability to read letters of any form, including the written vernacular.⁵⁷ As an adult King Alfred is portrayed reading aloud from books in English, while also encountering other books through oral recitation by his scholarly helpers.⁵⁸ Yet on one occasion Asser remarks that the king 'had not yet begun to read (*legere*) anything': any straightforward divide between Latin and vernacular literacy seems unlikely in view of earlier developments, and this formulation rather suggests some intermediate distinction between the ability to read simple and complex Latin texts.⁵⁹ It is in this context that one should consider the advance represented by the events of 887, apparently located within typical sessions of recitation. It is perhaps only to be expected that Asser should emphasise his own prominence in these reconstructed exchanges, to the implicit exclusion of other attested scholarly helpers.⁶⁰ What is striking is the high degree of initiative attributed to the king, in identifying particular passages of interest, and insisting on their copying for the purposes of written record, in a form designed to maximise the possibilities of his

---

⁵⁴ My interpretation differs in a number of respects from P. Wormald, 'Living with King Alfred', *Haskins Society Journal* 15 (2004, publ. 2006), pp. 24–39, who would place Alfred's first acquisition of literacy in 887. As Wormald's piece demonstrates, his interpretation remains equally compatible with the case for the king's personal involvement.

⁵⁵ *VA* c. 24, p. 21; cf. esp. KL, p. 239 (n. 46); S. Kelly, 'Early Anglo-Saxon Society and the Written Word', in R. McKitterick, ed., *The Uses of Literacy in Early Medieval Europe* (Cambridge, 1990), pp. 36–62, at 59–60; Pratt, 'Illnesses', pp. 63–4.

⁵⁶ *VA* c. 22, p. 20.

⁵⁷ Pratt, 'Illnesses', p. 64; H. Grundmann, '*Litteratus – illiteratus*: der Wandel einer Bildungsnorm vom Altertum zum Mittelalter', *Archiv für Kulturgeschichte* 40 (1958), pp. 1–66, at 36. Cf. *VA* c. 106, l. 42, p. 94.

⁵⁸ *VA* cc. 76, 77, 81, 88, pp. 59–60, 63, 67, 73–4.

⁵⁹ *VA* c. 77, l. 26, p. 63; cf. esp. Kelly, 'Early Anglo-Saxon Society', p. 60.

⁶⁰ Cf. the role in translation of Boethius ascribed to Asser by William of Malmesbury: expounding its meaning 'in clearer words', which the king himself then translated into English; the basis for William's claim remains uncertain: *WMGR* II, cxxii, 4, 1, pp. 190–1, and Thomson's commentary, II, 102.

own immediate perusal. The precise significance of the king's resulting *Enchiridion* or 'hand-book' warrants more attention than is possible here, but the potential implications of its status as a *florilegium*, assembled 'here and there from various masters', hardly needs emphasis in the context of creative 'royal' translation.[61]

Stylised representation, perhaps equivocal in itself, acquires further significance when set beside the testimony of the 'royal' texts themselves. Any attempt to recover compositional processes is necessarily fraught with difficulties, but again this is no reason to abandon it. Acknowledgement of 'Alfred' as authorial image invests significance in its particular means of construction. The status of these texts as translations, and the distinctive features of their execution, offer considerable potential for compositional reconstruction. What needs emphasis is the high degree of consistency between the general character of such processes, and the implications of Asser's depiction. Even at micro-level such consistency is impressive: grounds for accepting the participation of scholarly helpers have already been reviewed, and it is in this context that Bately's qualified case for a 'single mind' is so potentially significant, urging important limits on the parameters of collaboration.

These parameters are further limited when this distinctive output is compared with the varieties of Latin textuality on which it is ostensibly based. As Bately has emphasised, the 'royal' texts bear close comparison only with the version of Orosius in the degree of freedom adopted towards original source-texts, 'where close translation is less frequent than free paraphrase', as opposed to the Mercian *Dialogues* and Bede, where Latin sentence structures are frequently retained.[62] Bately herself suggests a connection with practices of recitation: the possibility of some significant oral element in composition is strengthened by considering the particular character of translatory departures, pursued to the greatest extent in the versions of Boethius and the *Soliloquia*.[63] There is a strong correlation between the wholesale recasting of large portions of these texts and their status as particularly ambitious monuments of late antique Latinity, largely complementary in their exemplification of Neo-Platonic theology, with the

---

[61] Pratt, 'King Alfred's *Handbook*' (article in preparation).
[62] Bately, 'Old English Prose', pp. 118–38, at 119, 125–31.
[63] *Ibid.*, p. 138. Aural effects in the Prose Preface to the Gregorian translation are persuasively emphasised by A. Orchard, 'Oral Tradition', in *Reading Old English Texts*, ed. K. O'Brien O'Keeffe (Cambridge, 1997), pp. 101–23, at 101–3; Bately, *Translation or Transformation?*; cf. also M. Godden, 'King Alfred's Boethius', in *Boethius: His Life, Thought and Influence*, ed. M. Gibson (London, 1981), pp. 419–24; Gatch, 'Alfred's Version'; Pratt, 'Political Thought', esp. pp. 357–64.

additional complexity of dialogue form.[64] Even without Asser's testimony, the degree of 'transformation' involved might be thought highly suggestive of some significant oral intervention, conveying the strong impression at least that literal translation of the Latin has formed merely the starting point for lengthy and inventive discussion of what the passage in question 'really means', and how this meaning might best be conveyed to aristocratic readers. Bately's case is again significant in supplying quite separate grounds for detecting a single vernacular mouthpiece.

With all this in mind, finally, one may consider the 'royal' texts at macro-level, and the extent to which their testimony may be situated within considerations of audience and context. Attention focuses on two closely related questions: the extent to which Alfred's image as an author might be thought to have received further support from their content and character; and the implications of any such supporting features for the logistics of construction. These questions seem especially significant given Alfred's exclusive status as named author, and the many distinctive features of the texts that bear his name. It is precisely this aspect of composition which receives insufficient attention in Professor Godden's recent emphasis on historicising and fictionalising tendencies within the 'royal' corpus.[65] There is no reason to minimise the possibilities of authorial intervention and representation in this case; on the contrary, such possibilities seem to acquire all the greater plausibility when considered against the exclusivity of authorship as a royal image. This factor in itself helps to explain the scholarly consensus in favour of such possibilities: until now, both historians and literary critics have generally stressed the extent to which these texts reflect a king-centred perspective, particularly in cases of translatory departure.[66]

These assumptions Godden has now thrown open to question. Focusing on the two translations in dialogue form, he raises an important question of how far the king himself may be speaking through their various *personae*, and again raises the problem that these *personae* can be handled as historical identities whose contemporary significance is then far from certain. In the translation of the *Consolatio*, the *persona* of 'Boetius' is presented historically as a royal counsellor who has fallen victim to the

---

[64] See esp. E. T. Silk, 'Boethius's *Consolatio philosophiae* as a Sequel to Augustine's Dialogues and *Soliloquia*', *Harvard Theological Review* 32 (1939), pp. 19–39.
[65] Godden, 'Player King'; Godden, *Misappropriation*.
[66] See above, p. 177, n. 63. Cf. also K. Otten, *König Alfreds Boethius*, Studien zur Englischen Philologie n. f. 3 (Tübingen, 1964), pp. 99–117.

wilfulness of wicked King Theoderic. Likewise, in the *Soliloquies*, efforts are made to give an historical orientation to the *persona* of 'Augustinus'. Not only does he reject marriage, as in the Latin: an addition appeals to his status as a faithful servant of the Emperor Theodosius I and of his son Honorius. Godden then interprets the handling of both these characters in terms which he considers to reflect the perceptions of a courtier, rather than a king. In his view, almost all the passages seeming to refer to kingship or lordship depend in fact upon appealing to the position of those in *service* to a king or lord. 'If we did not know already that a king was the author', he conjectures, 'we might well suppose that it was one of his associates at court.'[67]

The implications of this counter-factual are left unclear, and it should be noted that neither of these options seems very compatible with considerations of style and context. Godden's interpretation also focuses on these two *personae* alone, and one may debate its force against the 'royal' corpus as a whole. In the case of the translation of the *Regula pastoralis*, the figure of Gregory himself is all the more resonant in view of Gregory's own blurring of the boundaries between secular and spiritual authority – an ambiguity further heightened in translation.[68] In the law-book, meanwhile, the extensive excerpts from Old Testament law are shown as divine pronouncements spoken to Moses in his capacity as leader of all Israel.[69] Yet perhaps the most instructive comparison lies with the translation of the first fifty Psalms, an opportunity for 'royal' posturing exploited with particular immediacy.[70] The translation as a whole involves a sustained reconstruction of the *persona* of King David, established in the exegetical introductions with which each psalm is systematically equipped. The entire collection of psalms is attributed to David exclusively, without regard for traditions acknowledging additional participation by the sons of Chore and Asaph, and the mode of exegesis is heavily historical, giving particular prominence to the circumstances in which the psalm was composed.[71] Alfred's attested devotion to the Psalter has already been emphasised; in addition, the case has been argued elsewhere for situating this translation in the context of the king's conspicuous struggle against physical illness, and

---

[67] Godden, 'Player King', pp. 142–50.
[68] KL, p. 124; Pratt, 'Political Thought', pp. 76–107; Wormald, *Making*, pp. 428–9.
[69] Alfred's Laws Int. 1–49; F. Liebermann, *Die Gesetze der Angelsachsen*, 3 vols. (Halle, 1903–16), I, pp. 26–43.
[70] Pratt, 'Political Thought', pp. 191–234; 'Illnesses', pp. 85–9.
[71] O'Neill, 'The Old English Introductions to the Prose Psalms', pp. 26–38, esp. 35; Pratt, 'Political Thought', pp. 199–206.

for its particular significance in sustaining parallel symbolism with the struggle against Viking attack.[72]

There is already a case, in other words, for detecting exploitation of 'authority' figures within the 'royal' corpus. The question accordingly arises whether related processes might not be observed in the treatment of Boethius and the *Soliloquia*. In acknowledging the additional level of complexity arising from the dialogue form, such considerations are only enhanced by the two-way nature of the exchanges, all ultimately subject to compositional control. There may be dangers in focusing too closely on the status of the first-person speaker in each text, at the expense of their corresponding interlocutors. In both texts, the dialogue is effectively 'internal' in character, involving instances of ambiguous personification, respectively in the form of '*Wisdom* (Wisdom)' and '*Gesceadwisnes* (Reason)', and if pronouncements by both figures show strong signs of contemporary resonance on many occasions, they warrant particular attention for their additional didactic force.[73] Elements of historicity in both translations need to be considered against the rhetorical implications of such internal dialogue, as an appeal to the universal applicability of such experiences, achieved most directly through the voice of a first-person interlocutor.[74] Already central to the force of each Latin source-text, the effect of this conceit is further heightened in the handling of their translations.

Nowhere is this effect more apparent than in the opening chapters of the Boethius, amid a host of alterations and omissions amounting to imaginative recomposition. The opening of the text makes an important gesture towards historicity, by means of an historical introduction – though the story offers a singular reconstruction of the circumstances in which the *Consolatio philosophiae* came to be composed.[75] Gone are the rhetorical subtleties with which Boethius had vigorously defended his actions in Book I of the original: in the vernacular, Boethius is said to have explicitly plotted against the Ostrogothic king, with the aim of delivering

---

[72] Pratt, 'Illnesses', pp. 85–9.
[73] See esp. Frantzen, *King Alfred*, pp. 48–50; R. Waterhouse, 'Tone in Alfred's Version of Augustine's *Soliloquies*', in Szarmach, ed., *Studies*, pp. 47–85.
[74] For the significance of the dialogue form in both Latin texts see esp. Silk, 'Boethius's *Consolatio philosophiae*'; Gatch, 'Alfred's Version', pp. 20–1; T. F. Curley III, 'How to Read the Consolation of Philosophy', *Interpretation* 14 (1986), pp. 211–63, at 222–43.
[75] *King Alfred's Old English Version of Boethius: De Consolatione Philosophiae*, ed. W. J. Sedgefield (Oxford, 1899), 1, pp. 7–8. This introduction relies to some extent upon a prefatory series of short Latin *Vitae* of Boethius, which frequently accompanied the *Consolatio* in contemporary manuscripts. See Pratt, 'Political Thought', pp. 273–5.

the Romans into the hands of the emperor in the east. Boethius' plotting is justified within an original and coherent story of lordship and betrayal: the 'Caesar in Constantinople' is said to have been related by kin to the 'former lords' of the Romans – similarly described as 'the Caesars' – and Theodoric is portrayed as an 'unrighteous king' who has broken his promise to the Romans to uphold their 'former rights'. Yet considerations of historicity seem less prominent when the translation reaches the *Consolatio* itself. Almost every historical detail is conspicuously omitted from Book I, as if rendered superfluous by the story which has come before.[76] The very presence of an authorial Boethius is compromised and obscured throughout the translation. Although initially portrayed as first-person narrator, the identity of the historical Boethius is swiftly masked by that of his own mind: it is this new speaker, '*Mod* /Mind', who dominates the text as a whole, emerging as a character in its own right.[77] The implied universality of *Mod* can only have been further emphasised, paradoxically, by the inclusion of references familiar to contemporary aristocratic audiences; it is this quality which characterises the vernacular exploitation of the dialogue form.

The transformation of Boethius into *Mod* is accompanied by further reworking of the explanation for *Mod*'s downfall. In the original Book I emphasis on the injustice of Boethius' predicament is facilitated by lengthy sections of innocent protest, in which the prisoner rails against the apparent disorder of a world where his own efforts to secure Platonic philosopher-rulership have met with such conspicuous failure.[78] In the vernacular translation, by contrast, all sense of innocence is isolated in the historical introduction, and *Mod*'s downfall is portrayed as the result of his own guilt.[79] The new context is a further scenario of lordship and betrayal, but this time located more inclusively and universally in the internal relationship between *Mod* and *Wisdom*.[80] As Nelson observes, this transformation relies

---

[76] *Alfred's Boethius*, ed. Sedgefield, II–VI, pp. 8–14. Cf. *Anicii Manlii Severini Boethii Philosophiae Consolatio* i met. 1 – i met. 7, ed. L. Bieler, *CCSL* 94, 2nd edn (Turnhout, 1984), pp. 1–17.

[77] *Alfred's Boethius*, ed. Sedgefield, III, 1, pp. 8–9, for transition from narrator 'Boetius' to the *persona* of *Mod*. Cf. the subsequent return of 'Boetius' to designate the first-person in two isolated passages: x, p. 21 and xxv, 1–xxvii, 2, pp. 58–63.

[78] *Consolatio philosophiae*, ed. Bieler, i pr. 4, pp. 6–11.

[79] *Mod*'s guilt is rightly emphasised by Otten, *Alfreds Boethius*, pp. 22–6, 87; Frantzen, *King Alfred*, pp. 49–52; J. C. Frakes, *The Fate of Fortune in the Early Middle Ages* (Leiden, 1988), pp. 81–2, 105–6.

[80] *Alfred's Boethius*, ed. Sedgefield, vii, 1 – viii, pp. 14–19. Cf. *Consolatio philosophiae*, ed. Bieler, ii pr. 1 – ii pr. 3:2, pp. 17–21. For fundamental discussion of this section see esp. Otten, *Alfreds Boethius*, pp. 22–6, 87–8; Frakes, *Fate of Fortune*, pp. 81–110; Nelson, 'Political Ideas', pp. 144–5; Pratt, 'Political Thought', pp. 275–85, cf. 257–62.

in turn on ambiguous treatment of the divine interlocutor *Wisdom*: a masculine noun in Old English, it is here allowed to adopt the role of generous lord, 'a giver and lender of gifts'.[81] Some of these gifts are material, in the form of '*þa woruldsælþa* (worldly blessings)', simultaneously denoting physical goods and more general prosperity.[82] It is to *Wisdom* himself that *Mod* owes his former advantages, in the form of wealth and honour, 'both of which came from me when they were lent'.[83] Yet such 'worldly blessings' are only given in order to allow their use for the benefit of fellow men on earth, and in accordance with divine commandments.[84] *Mod* has effectively betrayed *Wisdom* by his actions, placing himself as a thegn under the alternative lordship of 'worldly blessings' themselves.[85] The entire exchange has the effect of attaching some justice to *Mod*'s loss of prosperity, through the related vices of pride and greed.

An initial point about these changes concerns their resonance in contemporary context. While clearly qualifying as one of the books 'most necessary for all men to know', the Latin *Consolatio* can only be regarded as a problematic text from the viewpoint of the targeted audiences for translation, all united by daily involvement in the holding of power, or the prospect of holding it in the future. In the Latin, Boethius' Stoic acceptance of his outrageous misfortune depended heavily upon an implied rejection of both wealth and power, together with all other aspects of material prosperity, arising from recognition of their status as deceptive and false goods.[86] Such an outlook had obvious force in the case of Boethius himself and comparable political reversals, but the implications would surely have been less clear for readers currently burdened with worldly responsibilities, or awaiting their future acquisition. It is just this problematic area which the vernacular alterations are effectively addressing, creating space for explicit acknowledgement of the possibilities of ethical action in the world, and indeed of the particular obligations arising from material prosperity itself, never distributed in vain.[87] In the

---

[81] Nelson, 'Political Ideas', p. 145.   [82] Frakes, *The Fate of Fortune*, pp. 109–10.
[83] *Alfred's Boethius*, ed. Sedgefield, VII, 3, p. 17, ll. 3–8. Cf. *Consolatio philosophiae*, ed. Bieler, II pr. 2:3, p. 19.
[84] *Alfred's Boethius* VII, 3, p. 18, ll. 14–16, vii, 5, p. 19, ll. 11–23; *Consolatio philosophiae* ii, pr. 2:10, pr. 3:1, pp. 20, 21.
[85] *Alfred's Boethius* II, p. 8, ll. 6–9 (for 'Boetius' as a *wrecca*, one placed in exile), III, 1, p. 8, ll. 21–3 (for 'Boetius' as *Wisdom*'s *þegn*), VII, 2, p. 16, lns 3–5, 24–8, and VII, 5, p. 19, lns 11–25 (for *Mod*'s acceptance of the lordship of *þa woruldsælþa*). Cf. *Consolatio philosophiae* I, met. 1, ll. 1–2, 1, pr. 1:11–12, II, pr. 1.17, II, pr. 3:1, pp. 1, 2, 18, 21.
[86] *Consolatio philosophiae* II, pr. 5 – II, pr. 7; Frakes, *Fate of Fortune*, pp. 45–9.
[87] Nelson, 'Political Ideas', pp. 144–5; Pratt, 'Political Thought', esp. pp. 268–98 and 310–13.

indispensability assigned to 'wisdom', and the dangers attached to pride and greed, these alterations encapsulate the coherent attitude towards power which has already been identified as the essential justification for Alfredian 're-education'.

In themselves, these alterations might seem insufficient to distinguish compositional input with requisite precision. The dependence on secular language and imagery deserves emphasis here, though it is questionable how far such concerns might necessarily be detached from the king's scholarly helpers, as ecclesiastics also variously entrusted with positions of responsibility. Account also needs to be taken of the lengthy addition to the translation later in Book II, where *Mod* explicitly delineates the 'tools and resources' pertaining to a king, in a passage often taken to represent Alfred's own vision of good kingship.[88] Professor Godden is willing to attribute this passage to Alfred himself, but wonders whether it might not represent an isolated intervention, with no wider implications for compositional control.[89] Yet the degree of congruence should at least be noted between this passage and earlier alterations. The attitude previously advocated towards power in general is now clearly being applied to the specific case of kingship. A king should never desire power, but, equally, he can never fulfil the duty thrust upon him, nor exercise 'virtue (*cræft*)', without possessing extensive material advantages: not least, effective personnel in the form of 'prayer-men, fighting-men and workmen', and whatever these three orders may need in land, gifts, weapons, food, ale and clothing.[90] The essential prerequisite for such royal power is again of course wisdom, 'because no man can bring forth any *cræft* without wisdom'.[91] There is a degree of coordination here pointing towards textual integrity. The notion of necessary resources is carefully prepared in a further addition explicitly drawing attention to the need for 'tools' in every *cræft*.[92] The prominence of lordship and gift-giving throughout strengthens the impression of an

---

[88] *Alfred's Boethius*, ed. Sedgefield, XVII, pp. 40–1; *Consolatio philosophiae*, ed. Bieler, II, pr. 7.1, p. 32.
[89] Godden, 'Player King', pp. 143–5.
[90] For fundamental discussion of this section see esp. Otten, *Alfred's Boethius*, pp. 30–4, 99–102; Frakes, *Fate of Fortune*, pp. 112–15; Nelson, 'Political Ideas', pp. 145–6; Pratt, 'Political Thought', pp. 285–98.
[91] For the important Alfredian concept of *cræft* see esp. P. Clemoes, 'King Alfred's Debt to Vernacular Poetry: The Evidence of *Ellen* and *Cræft*', in M. Korhammer et al., eds., *Words, Texts and Manuscripts: Studies in Anglo-Saxon Culture presented to Helmut Gneuss* (Cambridge, 1992), pp. 213–38, at 213–17, 223–38; cf. also N. G. Discenza, 'Power, Skill and Virtue in the Old English Boethius', *ASE* 26 (1997), pp. 81–108.
[92] *Alfred's Boethius*, ed. Sedgefield, XIV, 1, p. 30, ll. 7–10; *Consolatio philosophiae* II, pr. 5:15, p. 27.

integrated reworking of Boethian ethics, with the operation of kingship at its heart.

This relentless harnessing of the bonds of royal lordship provides an important context also for the handling of Augustine's *Soliloquia*. Once again, it is important to emphasise the wider rhetorical implications of this internal dialogue. As with the *Consolatio*, the force of the original *Soliloquia* had relied on the implicit appeal of its first-person interlocutor in exploratory philosophical discussion with 'Ratio', the personified faculty of reason. Already central to the Latin, this didactic quality acquires if anything greater prominence in the vernacular, as Ruth Waterhouse persuasively argues, enhanced by subtle adjustments emphasising complementary interaction between the speakers, and by a range of allusions to contemporary aristocratic life.[93] It is in this broader context that one should situate the treatment of the first-person interlocutor, initially identified as 'Augustinus', and his subsequent projection into positions of subordination and service. To this extent, Godden is right to emphasise such distinctive treatment, but this is no basis on which to assign compositional involvement. In any case account must also be taken of the important role accorded to the rational speaker *Gesceadwisnes*. The status of such subordination can only be regarded as ambiguous, initiated and encouraged by *Gesceadwisnes* himself in the immediate context of didactic exemplification.[94] Contemporary resonance in each case can hardly be denied: varying human competence in the pursuit of wisdom is explicitly likened to the degrees of intimacy available within a king's household.[95] The framework of royal lordship provides the context for several appeals to the force of loyalty, and for parallels involving the relationship between the king and his 'dear ones (*deorlingas*)'.[96] Any residual historicity seems compromised on this basis: even the addition referring to Theodosius and Honorius, rather fancifully presented as Augustine's 'worldly lords', must

---

[93] Waterhouse, 'Tone in Alfred's Version of Augustine's *Soliloquies*', esp. pp. 47–50, 60–80.

[94] Note the dependence upon simile and metaphor throughout the 'royal' corpus, also explored by S. J. Hitch, 'Alfred's *Cræft*: Imagery in Alfred's Version of Augustine's *Soliloquies*', *Journal of the Department of English (Calcutta University)* 22 (1–2) (1986–87), pp. 130–47.

[95] *Alfred's Augustine*, ed. Carnicelli, pp. 77, ll. 5–78, l. 2. Cf. Augustine, *Soliloquiorum libri duo* I, xiii 23: *Sancti Aurelii Augustini Opera: Sect. I Pars IV*, ed. W. Hörmann, CSEL 89 (Vienna, 1986), p. 35, ll. 3–7. Hörmann's text is reprinted with accompanying English translation by G. Watson, *Saint Augustine: Soliloquies and Immortality of the Soul* (Warminster, 1990).

[96] *Alfred's Augustine*, ed. Carnicelli, pp. 62, ll. 22–63, ll. 19, 87, ll. 18–89, l. 18 (this second passage occurs in the latter part of Book II, after the text of the original *Soliloquia* has effectively been abandoned), 94, ll. 2–6, 96, ll. 8–19, 96, ll. 19–97, l. 2 (all in Book III); Augustine, *Soliloquiorum*, ed. Hörmann I, v, II, pp. 18–19. Cf. inclusion of a 'prison (*carcern*)' in the earlier analogy with the royal household, p. 77, l. 19.

be judged against its position, late in Book II, after lordship itself has already been repeatedly described in suggestive contemporary terms.[97]

All these internal resonances acquire further significance when considered against the allusive preface.[98] As has long been recognised, the character of the preface needs to be seen in the light of the approach adopted towards the Latin *Soliloquia* as a whole, even exceeding the translation of Boethius in translatory freedom. Extensive portions of original text are either omitted or replaced; and whereas Augustine had left the *Soliloquia* unfinished at the end of Book II, leaving several questions unanswered, the vernacular 'translation' effectively 'completes' his work with a further section addressing the question of the soul's knowledge after death, to which Augustine himself had originally promised to turn.[99] The resulting 'Book III' draws at times on a further Augustinian text, *De uidendo Deo*, prominently mentioned at its opening, but more frequently proceeds along lines less obviously dependent upon any single source. It is no surprise then that this distinctive vernacular response should come equipped with a particularly extensive statement of compository justification, in which the implications of translation are suggestively compromised by an extended metaphor of physical construction. The problems associated with the opening lines have already been noted, but there are strong grounds for postulating a significant loss of text, including some initial identification of the king himself as speaker.[100] The resulting first person is heard describing his own actions in gathering timber, in the context of building-work on an aristocratic estate (*æt ham*). Yet there is no inconsistency in the speaker's subsequent subordination: the lord who emerges is clearly divine, and the evolving metaphor needs to be judged as an assertion of common cause with intended aristocratic audiences. The speaker himself claims to have progressed little beyond the sinking of some initial post-shafts, yet such modesty holds out the hope at least that he might one day be surpassed by others, better equipped to bring their *tunas* to fair completion.

What needs emphasis is the clear harnessing of aristocratic aspiration, from the very opening of the text, in this prominent assertion of authorial identity. It is on this basis that one should consider the subsequent

---

[97] *Alfred's Augustine*, ed. Carnicelli, pp. 88–9. Cf. Godden, *Misappropriation*.
[98] *Alfred's Augustine*, ed. Carnicelli, pp. 47–8.
[99] Gatch, 'Alfred's Version', pp. 33–7; see also Pratt, 'Political Thought', esp. pp. 330–46; Pratt, 'Persuasion and Invention', pp. 213–14.
[100] See esp. Gatch, 'Alfred's Version', pp. 23–4, 42–3 (nn. 32, 37), including personal correspondence with Whitelock.

exploitation of lordship through the utterances of *Gesceadwisnes*, all the more striking when prefaced in these terms. These appeals to the operation of lordship contribute significantly in themselves to the processes of recomposition and 'completion'. As has long been recognised, many of the departures from Books I and II of the *Soliloquia* amount to an effective rejection of the complexities of Augustine's dialectical reasoning, in favour of arguments frequently dependent on notions of testimony and authority.[101] Insufficient emphasis has been placed on the extent to which these arguments, along with several others, relate directly to *De uidendo Deo*.[102] In this respect at least, Godden's position could be pushed much further: there are good grounds for detecting a more consistent and overarching compositional agenda, amounting to wholesale revision of the Neo-Platonism of the *Soliloquia*, composed early in Augustine's career in 386, effectively reoriented and 'completed' in the light of mature Augustinian pronouncement in *De uidendo Deo* (*c*. 413).[103] The explicit citation of *De uidendo Deo* towards the end of Book II acquires new significance in this light, and there is no reason to regard the reference as ill-informed, still less as essentially misleading.[104]

The impact of *De uidendo Deo* is particularly striking in the case of arguments dependent upon testimony and authority. As a lengthy survey of the scriptural basis for man's perception of God, *De uidendo Deo* opens with treatment of the distinction between 'seeing' and 'believing', and of the fundamental role accorded to testimony in matters of belief.[105] When we see we are our own witnesses, but when we believe 'we are led to our assent (*ad fidem*) by other witnesses ... when signs are given by voices or by written words or by whatever proofs, so that, when these things are seen, unseen things are believed'.[106] Although principally focused on the testimony of Scripture, discussion is frequently informed by awareness of man's willingness to rely upon testimony of this kind in everyday matters, and it is this potent parallel which is deployed in a lengthy borrowing from *De uidendo Deo* towards the end of 'Book III'. 'Must I not necessarily do one of two things: either believe some men, or none at all?'; the ambiguous first person leaves little doubt which option must be accepted for, if

---

[101] *Alfred's Augustine*, ed. Carnicelli, pp. 100–1, 103, 105–6; Gatch, 'Alfred's Version', pp. 29–35.
[102] See esp. Pratt, 'Political Thought', pp. 330–52. Cf. Gatch's more sceptical assessment of its impact, 'Alfred's Version', pp. 35–7, largely followed by Godden, *Misappropriation*.
[103] Pratt, 'Political Thought', esp. pp. 330–4. [104] Cf. esp. Godden, *Misappropriation*.
[105] Augustine, *De uidendo Deo*, 2–11: *S. Aurelii Augustini Hipponiensis Episcopi Epistulae: Pars III. Ep. CXXIV–CLXXXIVA*, ed. A. Goldbacher, *CSEL* 44 (Vienna, 1904), no. CXLVII, pp. 275–85.
[106] *Ibid*. 8, pp. 281–2.

the latter, he would never know who constructed Rome, nor the identity of his father and mother, matters only known '*be gesegenum* (by report)'.[107] A very similar argument would have been readily available to the royal circle *via* Gregory's *Dialogi*, again arising from the acceptance of faith in matters which lie beyond trial and experience.[108] Not even an *ungeleafful man* lives *butan geleafan*, as Wærferth renders Gregory's words: he remains confident in identifying his father and mother, despite failing to witness either his conception or birth.[109] In each case, the argument depends upon appeal to facts which are known only indirectly, but could hardly be denied.

It is accordingly of the utmost significance that in Books I and II of the royal text such arguments should be deployed with specific dependence upon forms of testimony associated with earthly lordship. In Book I, it is testimony received in writing from one's lord, in the form of '*þines hlafordes ærendgewrit and hys insegel*, your lord's written message and his seal'; and *Gesceadwisnes* is depicted asking in astonishment 'whether you could say that you could not recognise him by this means, and could not thereby know his intention'.[110] In Book II, it is the oral testimony of one's lord, in the form of news relating to matters unheard and unseen, yet the implications are the same: 'there is no message (*spel*) so unbelievable that, if he said it, I would not believe him'.[111] The testimony of earthly lordship in turn provides the basis for faithfulness (*treow*), and for investing even greater love and trust in the 'higher lord', God himself, and in the truthfulness of his respective messengers, the Apostles, the Patriarchs and the Prophets, 'through whom God himself said what he wished to his people'.[112] There can be little doubt that these passages are to be understood in the context of Alfredian royal lordship. The appeal to a lord's *ærendgewrit and hys insegel* has long been interpreted as important evidence for the use of written letters associated with the impression of a seal, among several references suggesting significant royal use of such communication in the late ninth century.[113] As Keynes and Lapidge note, Asser reports his own

---

[107] *Alfred's Augustine*, ed. Carnicelli, p. 97, ll. 4–11; *De uidendo Deo* 5, pp. 278–9.
[108] Gregory the Great, *Dialogi* IV, 1–2: *Grégoire le Grand: Dialogues*, ed. A. de Vogüé and P. Antin, 3 vols., SC 251, 260 and 265 (Paris, 1978–80), III, pp. 18–22. Cf. *Bischof Wærferths von Worcester Übersetzung der Dialoge Gregors des Grossen*, ed. H. Hecht, 2 vols. (Leipzig, 1900–07), I, pp. 260–2.
[109] *Bischof Wærferths Übersetzung*, I, p. 262, ll. 14–24; Gregory, *Dialogi*, IV, 2, III, 22, ll. 1–10.
[110] *Alfred's Augustine*, p. 62, ll. 22–33; Augustine, *Soliloquiorum*, ed. Hörmann, I, v, 11, pp. 18–19.
[111] *Alfred's Augustine*, pp. 87, l. 18 – p. 88, l. 8. [112] *Ibid.*, pp. 88, l. 9 – p. 89, l. 18.
[113] F. E. Harmer, *Anglo-Saxon Writs* (Manchester, 1952), esp. pp. 10–13, cf. 1–10; S. Keynes, 'Royal Government and the Written Word in Late Anglo-Saxon England', in McKitterick, ed., *Uses of Literacy*, pp. 226–57, at 244–8.

receipt of 'letters' (*indiculos*) from the king, while in a further tantalising reference a legal dispute extending beyond Alfred's death is reported to have hinged at one point on the obtaining of an '*insigle* (lit. seal)' from the king's own grave.[114] Later usage suggests that the term could refer to a sealed document.[115] Contemporary resonances are equally paramount in the second passage, and the lord in question is introduced in similarly ambiguous terms. The value attributed to his oral testimony should be compared with Alfred's own reputation as a 'ueredicus dominus', initially emphasised by Asser in the suggestive context of recent West Saxon history, and a story told by the king himself.[116] The quality of truthfulness had wider implications in contemporary political thinking, specifically associated with the provision of justice in all its manifestations,[117] and Alfred's subsequent depiction as a *taediosus examinandae in iudiciis veritatis arbiter* ('painstaking judge in establishing the truth in judgements') acquires extra significance in this light.[118]

The implications of Alfredian 'truthfulness' surely need to be judged in these broader contexts. As Professor Godden observes, the very presence of arguments dependent upon testimony has interesting effects in passages of translatory departure; indeed, the possibility arises of detecting an element of irony in these passages when read in full awareness of this compositional process.[119] There is a playful quality to the references to Theodosius and Honorius, as Augustine's 'worldly lords', in terms which seem to imply a setting significantly later than the actual composition of the *Soliloquia* (386), in circumstances post-dating Theodosius' death (395).[120] Yet, as already argued, this isolated gesture is itself undermined by its late

---

[114] *VA* c. 79, ll. 36–9, p. 65; cf. two written lists, reported to have been presented to Asser in conjunction with the monasteries of Congresbury and Banwell, here described as 'epistolae': *VA* c. 81, ll. 15–27, pp. 67–8; S. Keynes, 'The Fonthill Letter', in *Words, Texts and Manuscripts*, ed. Korhammer, pp. 53–97, at 88–9.

[115] Harmer, *Writs*, pp. 12–13, 47; Keynes, 'Royal Government', p. 246.

[116] *VA* c. 13, ll. 31–5, cf. cc. 14–15, 37, ll. 12–22, pp. 12–14 and 28–9.

[117] See esp. Pseudo-Cyprian, *De duodecim abusivis saeculi* 9, ed. S. Hellmann, Texte und Untersuchungen zur Geschichte der Altchristlichen Literatur III.4 (1) (Leipzig, 1909), p. 51; quoted at length by Jonas of Orleans, *De institutione regia* 3, in A. Dubreucq, ed., *Jonas d'Orléans: Le métier de roi*, SC 407 (Paris, 1905), pp. 188–92, and by Hincmar of Rheims, *De regis persona et regio ministerio* 2, PL 125, cols. 835–6; also *Proverbia Grecorum* iv, 2, cited by D. Simpson, 'The "Proverbia Grecorum"', *Traditio* 43 (1987), pp. 1–22, at 17; quoted in Cathwulf's letter to Charlemagne, ed. E. Dümmler, *MGH Epp.* IV (Berlin, 1895), Epistolae variorum Carolo magno regnante scriptae no. 7, p. 503, and by Sedulius Scottus, *Liber de rectoribus christianis* c. 10, ed. S. Hellmann, *Sedulius Scottus*, Quellen und Untersuchungen zur lateinischen Philologie des Mittelalters 1(1) (Munich, 1906), p. 49.

[118] *VA* c. 105, cf. c. 106, pp. 91–5.   [119] Godden, *Misappropriation*.

[120] *Ibid.*; Pratt, 'Political Thought', p. 351, with 331–5; cf. Gatch, 'Alfred's Version', pp. 34–5; *Alfred's Augustine*, ed. Carnicelli, p. 103.

position in the text, when lordship itself has acquired far more immediate overtones.

What needs emphasis is the value of the vernacular translation as a text in its own right, to audiences largely unaware of its relationship to Latin sources. Augustine himself had characterised Book I of the *Soliloquia* as an attempt to explain 'what kind of man he ought to be who wishes to comprehend wisdom',[121] and this summary might equally be applied to the vernacular text as a whole, only further sharpened by the effects of its reconstruction. For example, the vernacular alterations have the additional effect of denying the full accessibility of wisdom in this life, providing a context in turn for the treatment of the after-life in 'Book III', as the time when all wisdom will at last be finally revealed.[122] Such alterations can hardly be dissociated from their rhetorical potential, as a means of encouraging those whose acquisition of wisdom may be especially partial. As *Gesceadwisnes* advises at one point, 'enjoy the wisdom that you have, and rejoice in the part that you *can* understand, and strive eagerly after more'.[123] The passages in question assume all the greater force in this context, providing further hope from the justified acceptance of divine revelation. Yet this vital argument in turn depends upon faith at once more immediate and mundane, implicitly vested in Alfred himself, through the certain recognition of his written messages, and his reputation as a 'truthful lord', carefully cultivated amid efforts to uphold justice and good judgement.[124] The case for wider reception of the vernacular text is only strengthened by selection of a message specifically received in the lord's absence, recognised by its form and written characteristics alone. The degree of reflexivity here hardly needs emphasis, and it is difficult to account for the very force of such effects if the king's own presence were not all too apparent in this artful harnessing of royal self-reference.

The issues at stake here encapsulate questions raised by the 'royal' corpus as a whole. These questions ultimately arise from the phenomenon of 'royal' authorship itself, but if the detection of agency is now the historian's prerogative, it should also be recognised as an obligation arising from the internal characteristics of the texts in the king's name, and from the implications of authorial image. The recovery of translatory processes

---

[121] Augustine, *Retractationes* 1.4; *Sancti Aurelii Augustini Retractationum Libri II*, ed. A. Mutzenbecher *CCSL* 57, (Turnhout, 1984), p. 14, ll. 1–11.
[122] Pratt, 'Political Thought', esp. pp. 337–42.
[123] *Alfred's Augustine*, p. 79, ll. 22–4; Augustine, *Soliloquiorum* I, xiv, 25, pp. 37, l. 20 – 38, l. 3.
[124] See esp. Waterhouse, 'Tone in Alfred's Version of Augustine's *Soliloquies*', p. 76.

acquires greater urgency in view of the king's unique status as a named translator, and the distinctiveness of the medium to which this name was prominently attached, united even at the fundamental level of lexis, syntax and style. The exclusivity of this 'royal' medium can only be considered in the broader context of Alfredian 're-education', and of the wider significance of the king's learned status, not only as an inspiration to aristocratic audiences, but also in some sense as a source of wisdom itself, conspicuously offered in distinctive 'royal' form. Alfred's attributed role as a teacher of literacy assumes particular significance given the high degree of personal contact within the royal household, and any irony attached to such posturing seems to have lain in the precise extent of the king's Latin competence, as opposed to the more general question of his compositional involvement. The input of scholarly helpers should be judged against the overall character of medium and message, otherwise consistent with a significant oral element in translatory processes.

The special properties of the 'royal' texts need to be situated in this broader didactic context, in the additional opportunities provided for the maintenance of authorial presence, over and above their status as translations. There is every sign that these opportunities were indeed exploited across the entire corpus, with a degree of sophistication well capable of adjusting to the variety of source-texts in question. The Boethian and Augustinian translations can hardly be excluded here; on the contrary, the intensity of such strategies in each case throws still further emphasis on their didactic potential, as sustained implementations of Neo-Platonic interiority. Far from reflecting the perceptions of a courtier, regular appeals to the obligations of lordship and gift-giving specifically relate to Alfred's own role as lord in the intimate environment of the West Saxon royal household, frequently projected implicitly through sophisticated manipulation of the dialogue form. Boethius' downfall is reinterpreted to offer lessons in the dangers of pride and greed, within an ethical framework entirely governed by such reciprocal obligations, and subsequently applied to the king himself, in his own position as giver of gifts and lord of men. Augustine's text receives nothing less than wholesale reconstruction, as a comprehensively mellifluous invitation to pursue divine wisdom, and the projection of lordship again supplies a vital tool of persuasion, even extending to the acceptance of revelation itself in supreme moments of reflexivity. There could be no more vivid demonstration of the extent to which the force of these texts depended upon the reception of their distinctive medium.

In Alfred's case, then, the special qualities of 'royal' expression strongly resist detachment from the king's person. On the contrary, the impression is of conscious self-projection, heavily dependent on authorial recognition. The overall effect is to restore confidence in the king's distinctive contribution, very far from ecclesiastical 'ghost-writing'. As a layman and a king, Alfred was uniquely placed within his scholarly circle to speak the language of kingship and lordship; there is every indication that in his case book-learning and composition supplied invaluable and highly effective means of exploiting these inherent kingly advantages. In practice as well as image, Alfred's learning actively incorporated the lay experiences of his secular aristocracy. Was Alfred unusual? The absence of direct Carolingian precedent seems only to strengthen the case for his exceptional involvement, in part the product of his own late education. Nor, finally, can one explain away the distinctiveness of the royal thought processes that the texts held so consistently open to view. To argue otherwise is to neglect the centrality of the relationship between authorship and audience, and the status of the texts themselves, as conduits of the king's uniquely manipulative truth.*

---

* This book's final passage to press coincided with the publication of a further piece by Malcolm Godden, 'Did King Alfred Write Anything?', *Medium Ævum* 76.1 (2007), 1–23. Offering a negative view, the article's grounds for doubt do not materially affect the case presented above, and indeed, many of its claims rely on assumptions and arguments which seem either problematic or contentious. I shall address the additional points now raised elsewhere.

CHAPTER 10

'Stand strong against the monsters': kingship and learning in the empire of King Æthelstan

Michael Wood

In the late 1120s William of Malmesbury recorded the 'strong current opinion' of King Æthelstan among the English people that no-one had ever administered the state *legalius vel litteratius* ('more lawfully or learnedly').[1] It is a big claim: but one William was especially well placed to judge, as the librarian of Æthelstan's favoured house. Taken literally, William's remarks would seem to say that the king was well remembered for having been particularly accomplished in Latin letters, but also for having taken a personal interest in the creation of English law, and in the principles and the enactment of justice. If true, the story would suggest Æthelstan was one of the more important lay intellectuals in Anglo-Saxon history, but until recently there has been very little to substantiate that opinion, apart from some intriguing hints gleaned by Armitage Robinson in 1922 from unconsidered trifles, burned manuscripts, gift inscriptions and relic lists.[2] In the last few years, however, a rather striking picture has begun to emerge, with studies of the king's books;[3] of Latin poems addressed to him;[4] of the role of his court circle in the intellectual foundations of the Benedictine reform;[5] and recently of the king's personal role in lawmaking[6] – offering a vivid picture of the king bombarding his councillors with his ideas on the law: a man, who, even if his ideas did not always work, was certainly intent on ruling *legalius*.

But in what way was Æthelstan learned, and how did he seek to rule *litteratius*? How did he use his learning in his kingship? To intellectuals of

---

[1] *WMGR* 1, p. 211.
[2] J. Armitage Robinson, *The Times of Saint Dunstan* (Oxford, 1923), pp. 51–80.
[3] S. Keynes, 'King Athelstan's Books', in M. Lapidge and H. Gneuss, eds., *Learning and Literature in Anglo-Saxon England* (Cambridge, 1985), pp. 143–201.
[4] M. Lapidge, 'Some Latin Poems as Evidence for the Reign of Athelstan', *ASE* 9 (1981), pp. 61–98.
[5] M. Gretsch, The *Intellectual Foundations of the English Benedictine Reform* (Cambridge, 1999), pp. 332–424.
[6] Wormald, *Making*, pp. 290–308.

the Carolingian age kingship and learning were inseparable. Kings engaged in scholarly debates, commissioned texts and translations, and surrounded themselves with scholars with whom they were on terms of cheery, and sometimes cheeky, *familiaritas*. I want to suggest that King Æthelstan saw himself as an intellectual and patron of scholars in the Carolingian style, and that he gathered round him a court school in the manner of his grandfather and the ninth-century Frankish kings – among them one of the great continental scholars of the age. More speculatively, I shall argue that the king's role was more than simply that of a donor of manuscripts, that his intellectual and spiritual interests may be the key to the political and intellectual revival of the second quarter of the tenth century, and that he was also the sponsor of one of the most important vernacular translations of the Anglo-Saxon period.

First, though, we should try to get an idea of the king's intellectual background. This might be thought a hopeless task, given the paucity of detail about the king's early life, but in fact there are some interesting pointers. The first is a poem. It comes from the last days of Alfred the Great and is addressed to a young prince in expectation of his future rule. Though short, the poem is full of nuance, and, it may be, psychological clues.[7]

> Little Prince, you are called by the name 'Sovereign Stone'.
> Look happily on this prophecy for your life.
> You shall be the 'noble Rock' of Samuel the Seer,
> Standing with mighty strength against the devilish monsters.
> Often an abundant cornfield foretells a fine harvest.
> In times of peace your stoniness will soften, for
> You are more abundantly endowed with the holy eminence
>   of learning.
> I pray that you may seek, and that God may grant, the promise
>   of your noble name.

The poem sets out our theme, the link between kingship and learning. The boy (who as we shall see was around five years old at the time) was apparently already to some degree literate in Latin. (And good for him, if he could read this poem: it is no mean feat to untangle the puzzle set by its author!) The poem tells us that the prince was 'abundantly endowed' with sacred learning; we may infer that he was already being educated in *utriusque linguae libri* (to use Asser's phrase of Alfred's

---

[7] Robinson, *The Times of St Dunstan*, p 69; For a translation and full commentary, see M. Lapidge, 'Some Latin Poems', pp. 81–3.

schools).⁸ It also tells us that he was being groomed for high office (like the young noblemen to whose education Alfred himself refers in his preface to the *Cura Pastoralis*).⁹ Also, if the poem's connection with the manuscript in which it is preserved is not fortuitous, it suggests that the boy may already have been encouraged to study Aldhelm's Latin, for the book's main text is the verse *De Virginitate*. Be that as it may, taken at face value the poem tells us that even at around five years old, the boy was on the road to becoming an intellectual.

The name of the young prince, by the way, is given to us by the puns on his name 'sovereign stone', 'noble rock' – and the joke about his 'stoniness'. But just in case we still haven't got it, the poem is an acrostic and the first letters of each line helpfully spell it out, though as a German-speaker would have rendered it: ADALSTAN.¹⁰ The line ends also spell the name of the poet: IOANNES, John the Old Saxon, one of Alfred the Great's circle of scholarly helpers in the 890s, and perhaps the boy's tutor. So, composed by one of Alfred's circle, written down in an early tenth-century English hand, the poem can hardly be about anyone other than Æthelstan the future king of Wessex, the man who was recently credited with being 'the founder of the medieval and modern English state'. Fittingly, the tale of the bibliophile king begins with a book.

The poem then seems to open ways into the king's literacy, his culture and contacts, and even to the role of the intellectual in early tenth-century England. The circumstances in which the poem was preserved offer us another clue. For though the poem seems to have been composed in the 890s when the boy was around five years old, it survives in a manuscript addition of the 930s when the king was in his forties. Bodleian Rawlinson C. 697 is a book with a very interesting history. It contains a Continental text of Aldhelm's *On Virginity* (with the *Enigmata* (*Riddles*), and Prudentius' *Psychomachia*); it was written in Germany in the third quarter of the ninth century; and it shares an East Frankish glossator with BL, Cotton Vespasian B.vi, a mid ninth-century north French copy of Bede's *De Temporum Ratione* which came to England at this time.¹¹

---

⁸ 'utriusque linguae libros': *VA c.* 75, p. 58. See D. A. Bullough, 'The Educational Tradition in England from Alfred to Aelfric: Teaching *utriusque linguae*', Settimane Spoleto 19 (1972), pp. 453–94, repr. in his *Carolingian Renewal: Sources and Heritage* (Manchester, 1991), pp. 297–334.
⁹ *King Alfred's Pastoral Care*, ed. H. Sweet (Oxford, 1871–2), p. 7.
¹⁰ On these spellings see Lapidge, 'Some Latin Poems' pp. 74–7.
¹¹ BL Cotton Vespasian B. vi, fols. 1–103, now attributed to St Denis, second quarter of the ninth century: see H. Gneuss, *Handlist of Anglo-Saxon Manuscripts: A List of Manuscripts and Manuscript Fragments Written or Owned in England up to 1100* (Tempe, AR, 2001), no. 384.

The presence in Rawlinson C. 697 of the acrostic by John the Old Saxon suggests the possibility that both books were brought to England by John himself.

It is intriguing, too, that the verses to young Æthelstan should have been entered into the back of a volume of Aldhelm; for we know that King Æthelstan considered the saint as his special patron, and both he and John the Old Saxon were later buried at the saint's shrine at Malmesbury. It may then be no coincidence that during Æthelstan's reign the study of Aldhelm's latinity was moved to the centre of the curriculum in Wessex, to become a major source of the intellectual revival in the second half of the tenth century. But the connections of the manuscript do not end there, for it was later annotated by two of Æthelwold's Aldhelm glossators (one of them perhaps Æthelwold himself?) and it also carries marginalia by 'Hand D' believed to be that of St Dunstan.[12] Containing a royal poem and with close links with two royal *protégés*, this clearly should be considered as a royal book. Perhaps it was originally given to the young prince with the poem entered on a blank leaf at the front, and treasured for nearly forty years; the poem could then have been recopied for the king at the back of the book when the frontispiece had become damaged or worn. On this reading, then, the book may contain Alfred's message to his grandson on the value of learning and the duties of kingship.

The gifting of books to young princes was common in ninth-century Francia, a ritual of kingship no less loaded with symbolism than the award of arms. Such books tended to be exemplary. As a boy Charles the Bald received Vegetius' *On Warfare* emphasising the military aspect of kingship, and also a special edition of Einhard, from his tutor Walahfrid Strabo, as a *speculum regis*.[13] Aldhelm's *On Virginity* is perhaps not the first gift which springs to mind for a Saxon prince of the Viking Age, a man who was remembered, later, by a court poet for having 'trampled on the barbarians and crushed their proud necks'. But there is evidence that Æthelstan deliberately remained unmarried; and that this went beyond political choice is suggested by a verse epitaph quoted by William of Malmesbury in his *Gesta Pontificum* which is based on Venantius Fortunatus and which closely resembles a passage in Wulfstan Cantor's

---

[12] On the Rawlinson annotators: T. A. M. Bishop, *English Caroline Minuscule* (Oxford, 1971), p. 2; Gretsch, *The Intellectual Foundations*, pp. 350–1, 368–70, and p. 333 for the possibility that the *Enigmata* in Rawlinson are English (as Bernhard Bischoff thought). Interestingly enough Rawlinson is the earliest manuscript of Prudentius' *Psychomachia* from England, and – with the exception of an eighth-century fragment – the earliest text of the *Enigmata* from England.

[13] J. L. Nelson, *Charles the Bald* (London, 1992), p. 84.

Narratio metrica on St Swithun from tenth-century Winchester. In this Æthelstan is saluted for his *munditia*: an extraordinary word to use of most early medieval kings, but one which alerts us to Æthelstan's peculiar brand of *pietas*, and perhaps to his particular concern for 'sacred learning'.[14] So the gift of the poem was no casual gift. It staked out the territory to be inhabited by this young ætheling.[15]

Now the other side of the coin, of course, was the giving of arms. More light is shed on the Rawlinson Aldhelm by a story told by William of Malmesbury.[16] Not long before he died, we learn, Alfred the Great invested his then only grandson Æthelstan with arms, presumably in a formal ceremony at court. Aged about five, the little boy was gifted with a sword and scabbard, a scarlet cloak and a jewelled belt, with 'an affectionate embrace' (or kiss – *gratiose complexus*?) in 'expectation of his future reign'. Now Alfred of course had experienced a similar life-event in Rome at roughly the same age, and perhaps in the Rawlinson poem's description of the young Æthelstan as a *triumvir* we are entitled to detect an echo of Asser's account of the Roman investiture of the young Alfred and even of Pope Leo IV's mention of 'the vestments of the consulate, as is customary with Roman consuls', if his letter-fragment is acceptable.[17] At any rate, it seems hard to avoid the conclusion that the Rawlinson poem and William's text are witnesses to the same story.

William's tale of Æthelstan's investiture with arms has often been dismissed as an anachronism. But there are close Carolingian parallels for the giving of cloak, belt and sword. Such things usually took place at the beginning of *adolescentia*, the onset of puberty, at the age of around fourteen. But if dynastic politics required more urgency, then such ceremonies might happen much earlier. According to the Astronomer, the young Louis the Pious was only three when he was invested with arms and set on a horse, to begin the *via regia* of Christian kingship.[18] William's

---

[14] William of Malmesbury, *Gesta Pontificum Anglorum*, ed. N. E. S. A. Hamilton, Rolls Series 52 (London, 1870), pp. 396–7. The old edition of Wulfstan Cantor's *Narratio*, by A. Campbell, is now superseded by the magisterial study of M. Lapidge, *The Cult of St Swithun* (Oxford, 2003), pp. 372–551.

[15] For a further (and complementary) possible context for Æthelstan's remaining unmarried, see Nelson, 'Rulers and Government', in *NCMH* III, pp. 95–129, at 103–4, and cf. S. Keynes, 'England, c. 900–1016', *ibid.* pp. 456–84, at 467–8.

[16] *WMGR* I, p. 211.   [17] *VA* c. 8, p. 7. See KL p. 69, and n. 19 (p. 232), with further references.

[18] Louis the Pious: Astronomer, *Vita Hludowici c.* 4, p. 294, and cf. *c.* 6, p. 300; Charles the Bald: *ibid.* c. 59, p. 526, but aged only 'hardly more than three', little Charles had been given miniature hunting weapons and told to use them, Ermold the Black, *In Honorem Hludowici Pii*, trans. P. Godman, *Poetry of the Carolingian Renaissance* (London, 1985), pp. 256–7; see R. Le Jan, 'Frankish Giving of Arms and Rituals of Power: Continuity and Change in the Carolingian Period', in F. Theuws and J. L. Nelson, eds., *Rituals of Power from Late Antiquity to the Early Middle Ages* (Leiden, 2000), pp. 281–309, at 283.

account should therefore be taken seriously. In a now controversial passage he says that this part of his narrative was derived from a lost poem: 'a certain obviously very old book' discovered only recently during the writing of his text.[19] Recently William's 'old book' has been written off as 'treacherous', 'dangerous' and even 'worthless as evidence'.[20] But this verdict urgently needs appeal. William says clearly that his source was a lengthy poem in the florid tenth-century English Latin style, which he has excerpted in a more 'familiar style' and close examination of his text suggests this was indeed the case. William's account is peppered with favourite words and phrases of the time; traces of hexameters are still visible in his prose, and his verse renditions even preserve common internal rhymes and line endings of the 'hermeneutic' style. The description of the king's coronation feast in particular has very close parallels with the banquet scene in Wulfstan Cantor's preface to the *Narratio metrica de Sancto Swithuno*, both passages being heavily indebted to the famous scene in the first book of the *Aeneid*.[21] Full justification of this argument must await detailed publication, but in the meantime, I believe it is certain that William did have a tenth-century manuscript in which he found this story. The lost poem described the king's *pueritia* and *adolescentia*, his coronation, battles and gift-giving, and perhaps ended with his funeral and a eulogy. One interesting feature of the *vita* was its insistence, perhaps against the king's detractors, that his succession had been legitimate. This was emphasised at several points: the investiture by Alfred; the terms of his father's will and testament; his father's care in his upbringing; his orthodox crowning by bishops and his acclamation by the nobility. It was in this context that the unknown author pressed the king's personal accomplishments, and in particular his literacy and learning, as further qualifications for kingship; as William tells it, an important message of the lost book was that Æthelstan 'had known letters' (*litteras illum scisse*).

In the section of William's account derived directly from the 'old book', there is significant detail to be gathered about the king's learning. As a boy, Aethelstan was sent to the court of his aunt Æthelflaed where he was placed *in documenta scholarum*. Here William gives us his source as a direct quotation, in what is evidently an abbreviated and modernised version of a

---

[19] WMGR I, p. 21.
[20] D. Dumville, *Wessex and England from Alfred to Edgar: Six Essays on Political, Cultural, and Ecclesiastical Revival* (Woodbridge, 1992), pp. 142–3.
[21] For a preliminary summary, see M. Wood, *In Search of England* (London, 1999), pp. 149–68. For Wulfstan's *Narratio*, see now Lapidge, *The Cult of St Swithun*, pp. 372–551.

tenth-century text, whose beginning was very likely also modelled on Venantius Fortunatus, a favourite author in tenth-century England:

> The royal line brought forth a noble progeny
> When a splendid gem lit up our darkness:
> Great Æthelstan, the country's glory, path of righteousness,
> The height of integrity, never swerving from the truth.
> At his father's command he was given to the learning of the schools.
> He feared strict masters with their rapping rods
> And eagerly imbibing the sweet honey of learning
> He did not spend the years of childhood childishly.
> Soon, dressed in the flower of young manhood
> He took up the study of arms, at his father's order.
> Nor did the demands of war find him wanting
> As later his kingship also showed ...[22]

This story of the king attending school has recently been dismissed as anachronistic, 'manifestly a flight of poetic fancy'.[23] But nothing in it would be out of place in a ninth-century continental biography, and even in William's cleaned-up version its latinity preserves strong echoes of the tenth-century Anglo-Latin style.[24] The lines about the strict *magistri*, which derive from Jerome, have parallels in Carolingian royal biography and also, for example, in the epigrams of a master to his pupil by Hibernicus Exul. Birching in fact was the rule in Carolingian schools of the ninth century, and in English ones of the tenth, as we can see in the colloquies of Ælfric of Eynsham and Aelfric Bata, and in a poem from St Æthelwold's circle.[25] The whole passage should then be seen in the light of Asser's account of the education of Æthelstan's father and aunt under

---

[22] *WMGR* I, p. 211; for parallels see, for instance, Venantius Fortunatus, *Opera Omnia*, ed. F. Leo, *MGH AA* (Berlin, 1881), IV, 6, 3, p. 134; 8, 5, p. 193, Appendix III (7), p. 280. These motifs were much imitated in the Carolingian era, for instance in Hincmar's poem on St Remigius, *MGH Poet.* III, ed. L. Traube (Berlin, 1896), p. 413 (*splendida lux nostras deseruit tenebras*).

[23] Lapidge, 'Some Latin Poems', p. 71.

[24] For close parallels to *WMGR* I, p. 212 (ll. 17–20 of his quotation), see e.g., Lapidge, *The Cult of St Swithun*, p. 378, from line 80, and esp. ll. 93–4; p. 390, l. 233; p. 392, ll. 239–40 and 249–50; the same trick is used in Wulfstan Cantor's *Breviloquium Omnium Sanctorum*, ed. P. Dolbeau, *Analecta Bollandiana* 106 (1988), p. 69; it is derived from Virgil's *Aeneid*, Book I, ll. 700 and 705. Cf. Venantius, *Carmina* III, 6, 3, *MGH AA* IV, pp. 85–137, at 134.

[25] For 'subjecting us to the birch rods' (*ferulis nos subdere privis*), see M. Lapidge, 'Three Latin Poems from Aethelwold's School at Winchester', *ASE* I (1972) pp. 130–1; the Hibernicus Exul epigrams are in *MGH Poet.* I, ed. E. Dümmler (Berlin, 1881), p. 403, and with English translation in P. Godman, *Poetry of the Carolingian Renaissance* (London, 1985), pp. 178–9; for a composite manuscript of Hibernicus Exul and Venantius in tenth-century England, see R. Hunt, 'Manuscript Evidence for Knowledge of the Poems of Venantius Fortunatus in Late Anglo-Saxon England', *ASE* 8 (1979), pp. 279–95, with an appendix by M. Lapidge.

certain *magistri* in the court *schola* of Alfred. William's source is surely describing something similar. The lost *vita* made Æthelstan's education central to his biography in the way the Carolingians did with their royal heroes. But where Asser tells a story of Alfred's learning acquired painfully in middle age, his grandson Æthelstan was literate from childhood. Indeed, Æthelstan perhaps was the first English king to be groomed from the start as an intellectual.

By background and education, then, Æthelstan was particularly well placed to do what his grandfather had hoped: to make real 'the England Alfred had dreamed'.[26] Had things fallen out differently, though, he might never have had the chance. After the death of his father and then his own half-brother Ælfweard in summer 924, Æthelstan was acknowledged as king by the Mercians some time between autumn 924 and summer 925. In Wessex, however, his right to succeed was disputed, and his crowning in September 925 was the outcome of a power struggle between different branches of the royal kin.[27] Not surprisingly then the first phase of his reign is entirely Mercian in character. His early charters grant land in the Midlands, his early acts of state take place in Mercia too, including the 926 royal marriage of the king's sister at Tamworth, not to mention the great council 'discussing the matter of allegiance' with exclusively Mercian bishops, earls and sixty other leading figures.[28] A summary of a lost charter from 925 or 926 also shows Æthelstan acting like a Mercian king in confirming the rights of St Oswald's, Gloucester, as per a 'pact of paternal piety' made with his foster-father and uncle, Æthelred, perhaps in 909 when St Oswald's remains were translated from Bardney.[29] Clearly the king's power-base – and his chief political *and* intellectual contacts – were Mercian.

By early 926 Æthelstan had received the allegiance at least of the English lands south of the Humber, and could call himself like his father

---

[26] [Michael Wood surmised that this was a quotation from J. L. Nelson, but she would like to credit it to Michael Wood! JLN]

[27] *Liber Vitae: Register and Martyrology of New Minster and Hyde Abbey*, ed. W. de G. Birch (London, 1892), p. 6; see now on this S. Keynes, *The Liber Vitae of the New Minster and Hyde Abbey, Winchester, Early English Manuscripts in Facsimile* (Copenhagen, 1996), pp. 19–22.

[28] ASC 'D', s.a. 926 ; cf. S. 392, 395, 396 and 397.

[29] G. Sayles, *Select Cases in the Court of King's Bench*, III, Selden Society Publications 58 (1939), pp. 140–2. Presumably the 'paternal pact' was made 'promoting the wishes' of Æthelstan's father, Edward: see C. Heighway, 'Gloucester and the New Minster of St Oswald', in N. J. Higham and D. H. Hill, eds., *Edward the Elder 899–924* (London, 2001), pp. 102–11, at 103, following M. Hare, 'The Documentary Evidence to 1086', in Heighway and R. Bryant, eds., *The Golden Minster: The Anglo-Saxon Minster and Later Medieval Priory of St Oswald at Gloucester* (York, 1999), pp. 33–46, at 34.

'King of the Anglo-Saxons'. But the rejection of his overlordship in Wales, Scotland and Northumbria in 927 led him to attempt to impose his rule over the whole of the mainland of Britain and led swiftly to the creation of a kingdom of England whose boundaries for the first time in history included all the lands of the *gens Anglorum* which had been described by Bede in the eighth century. It was a historic moment, as was recognised by a continental poet in the king's entourage in summer 927 who remodelled a poem to Charlemagne by Hibernicus Exul saluting *ista perfecta Saxonia* – this England 'completed' or 'made whole'.[30] By Easter 928, Æthelstan felt secure in his power and was acknowledged not only as king of the English but ruler of an *imperium* wider than any of his predecessors'.

Till that point Æthelstan looks rather like a ninth-century *Rex Anglorum*; coping with the fissile tendencies inherent in any early medieval state; negotiating the delicate politics of Wessex and Mercia; conciliating an extended royal kin, with prowling *æthelings* including his half-brother and heir apparent Edwin; keeping sweet the redoubtable and ambitious royal wife Queen Eadgifu, mother of three infant princes of royal blood. But now there comes a surprise, for which nothing has quite prepared us: a rush of ideas which bring about an extraordinary shift in the politics and culture of Late Saxon England. What follows is nothing less than a new political order with bold new aspirations. Its main expressions are both practical and ideological:

(1) New hegemonial gatherings and rituals of submission and tribute are held on festival days and witnessed by Celtic kings from all over Britain, often with upwards of a hundred bishops, earls and thegns.[31] At such assemblies law is enacted, land given, tribute taken and oaths of submission made to the king as 'father and lord': a visible demonstration of the West Saxons' rise to *imperium* over 'the whole world of Britain'.

(2) To go with the new politics comes a new diplomatic language. From 928, a central figure emerges in the court circle: a royal scribe, who until 935 will be the single person in charge of royal charters, hitherto produced by different people in various houses.[32] Æthelstan seems to have taken an unprecedented degree of control over this important

---

[30] W. Stevenson, 'A Latin Poem Addressed to King Aethelstan', *EHR* 26 (1911), pp. 482–7; Lapidge, 'Some Latin Poems', pp. 83–93.

[31] For a useful summary with maps see D. Hill, *An Atlas of Anglo-Saxon England* (Oxford, 1981), pp. 85–6.

[32] S. Keynes, 'The Charters of King Æthelstan (924–39), and the Kingdom of the English', *Bulletin of the John Rylands Library*, forthcoming.

royal activity. His writer – clearly one of the inner think-tank, and very likely a Mercian – aimed to express the king's love of high-flown titles, his sense of dignity, and even perhaps his intellectual pretensions. In language derived in part from glossaries, in part from Aldhelm, he worked to convey this new sense of a world in which, as a royal kinsman would put it, 'the fields of Britain were consolidated into one'.[33] One aspect of the royal clerk's experimentation was a new range of titles, sometimes using Greek words. In the charters written between 928 and 935 Æthelstan is now called *rex totius Britanniae*.

(3) Another sign of the new order is the coinage; the manner of its organisation reveals similar hegemonial ambitions, as does the king's title, echoing the charters: *Rex totius Britanniae*. Its roots lie in Edward's reign, but the Grately code specifies one coinage over the realm; buying and selling is to be confined to boroughs, regional variation is allowed but with strong central control over weight and silver content, and the king alone may have his name on the coins.[34]

(4) Another aspect of the revival to which very little attention has yet been paid is the restoration of sees which had ceased to function during the Viking wars. As yet our knowledge on this subject is very thin – many of Æthelstan's new intake of bishops cannot be placed, and in the East Midlands especially, much remains to be discovered. But in 929 in the province of York, for example, four suffragans appear, as had been the situation in the eighth century (Hexham, Lindisfarne, Whithorn and Mayo). It is uncertain precisely where the revived sees were, but three of the four suffragans are northerners attested elsewhere; and the possibility is worth bearing in mind that Æthelstan attempted to bring back Whithorn into the southern orbit in consequence of the pact made at Eamont in 927 with the kings of the Cumbrians and Scots on the suppression of paganism, presumably among the recent Norse-Irish settlers in Galloway – the fourth suffragan's name interestingly enough is Columbanus.[35] Æthelstan's role, as a Mercian scribe of 925 put it, is

---

[33] Æthelweard, *Chronicon*, ed. A. Campbell (London, 1962), p. 54: 'uno solidantur Brittannidis arva'. See the chapter of Scott Ashley, below, in the present volume.

[34] C. Blunt, 'The Coinage of Athelstan, 924–39: A Survey', *British Numismatic Journal* 42 (1974), pp. 35–160.

[35] S. 401 is spurious in its present form but the list of attestations clearly comes from an early source. P. Hill, *Whithorn and St Ninian: The Excavation of a Monastic Town, 1984–91* (Stroud, 1997), pp. 48–51 and 183–208 shows that the minster was restored in the mid/late ninth century after a mid-century destruction, and then demolished and replanned in the early tenth century, before *c.* 960. See too D. Howlett, *Caledonian Craftmanship: The Scottish Latin Tradition* (Dublin, 2000), pp. 143–5, 185–7, 194–5, for a summary of the twelfth-century relationship between Whithorn and York; Professor

now to be 'supervisor of the whole Christian household as far as the whirlpools of the *cataclismata*' that is, the 'vast ocean surges' of the western sea.[36]

(5) These ambitions are matched by another unifying trend, this time in sacred geography, in an effort to co-opt the important regional saints as national ones. There seems little doubt that this was a special interest of the king. At some point in the late twenties, perhaps at Easter 928, and in Exeter according to evidence from the eleventh century,[37] the king had a heaven-sent dream which led him to seek out the tales and relics of the saints of Britain and to commemorate them. We might connect this with a royal itinerary of 929 or 930 mentioned only by Roger of Wendover; in this year 'King Æthelstan decided to search out the relics of the saints of his kingdom in order to pray for God's grace.'[38] A neat piece of corroborative evidence is the famous account of Abbo of Fleury which describes the king interviewing an aged eye-witness to the martyrdom of St Edmund.[39] This is also to be dated around 929/30 when we know the young Dunstan (who later told Abbo the tale) was at court. It may be, therefore, that we should date the composition of the first layer of *The Resting-Places of the English Saints* to the same time. Though often considered to be Alfredian, as it stands the first part of the *Secgan* seems to be post-917, and was perhaps compiled soon after Æthelstan's translation of Edmund to Bury in *c*. 930. England, then, was to be a holy land once more: a land of saints, *sat deliciosa*, as Hrotsvitha would call it.[40]

(6) Finally, perhaps the most important and impressive sign of Æthelstan's new order, and of his intellectual ambition as king, is the law. Starting with Grately (928–9?) the king holds great lawmaking gatherings at

---

Rosemary Cramp, personal communication, detects a shift southwards in the connections of Whithorn's material culture in the tenth century.

[36] 'Cataclismata' is not 'cataclysms' as political upheavals. The word is glossed as *dodrantium/eogra* in several manuscripts; for example in a Phase II Æthelstan manuscript, British Library, Royal 7 D. xxiv, f. 52b, see A. S. Napier, *Old English Glosses, Chiefly Unpublished*, Anecdota Oxoniensia 4, pt. II (Oxford, 1900), p. 159, *cataclysmi = egores*; several manuscripts gloss *egor* as *dodrans*, 'flood, high tide' specifically with reference to the ocean, so the expression means 'as far as the Ocean surges'. The author was perhaps thinking of Aldhelm's letter to Heahfrith, *Aldhelmi Opera*, ed. R. Ehwald, *MGH AA* xv (Berlin, 1919), p. 489.

[37] Æthelstan's dream: *somnio ammonitus*, *WMGR* I, p. 228: a 'god-given idea', according to the Exeter Relic-list, *nyttwirdan gepanc*, P. Conner, *Anglo-Saxon Exeter* (1993), pp. 176–7.

[38] Roger of Wendover, *Flores Historiarum*, ed. H. O. Coxe (London, 1841), p. 387, s.a. 929.

[39] Abbo of Fleury, *Passio S. Eadmundi*, in M. Winterbottom, ed., *Three Lives of English Saints* (Toronto, 1972), p. 67.

[40] D. Rollason, 'Lists of Saints' Resting-Places in Anglo-Saxon England', *ASE* 7 (1978), pp. 61–93, esp. 63; Hrotsvitha, *Opera*, ed. H. Homeyer (Munich, 1970), p. 408.

which we can glimpse him discussing with his councillors the high ideals of early medieval kingship, and the grim reality on the ground.[41] The practical problems of law and order were immense, and in his stenographers' words the king sometimes tells us so himself: 'I am sorry my peace is so badly kept', he remarks, 'and my councillors say I have borne it too long...' The king's lawmaking councils also afford us interesting cases of his personal intervention in the making of law, for example in his raising the death penalty from twelve to fifteen on the grounds that to execute so many young people 'as he sees everywhere is the case, is *too cruel*'. This is just the kind of thing which is implied by William of Malmesbury's tale of a king remembered for his justice, and it is interesting that one of his direct 'quotes' from the lost *vita* twice mentions the king's just rule.[42]

Now these six strands suggest a rather impressive coherence of purpose. But are they a fortuitous series of events, on which we have imposed a pattern with hindsight? Was the creation of Æthelstan's England merely an opportunistic response to events? Or was there a plan? A 'vision thing', even? Here of course one has to admit we are reduced to conjecture, but it is hard to believe that the personality of the king himself was not at the heart of these developments. This is a learned ruler responding to a new political situation – a rule over a much larger and more racially and culturally mixed area than any of his predecessors: 'an English people diverse in customs, speech and dress' as a later tenth-century writer put it; a kingdom of all the English 'which prior to him his predecessors had held severally'.[43]

But to put those ideas into practice also needed literate intellectuals and scribes, administrators, bishops. It is when we come to the presence of foreign scholars in Æthelstan's court – as Armitage Robinson first noticed – that we get a real sense of a king who recruited and cultivated scholars just as Alfred and the Carolingian kings had done. Some of these new men were literary types, poets and hagiographers. It is remarkable to say the least, given the dearth of commemorative historical poetry in the whole period,

---

[41] Wormald, *Making*, pp. 290–308, 439–40. The quotation that follows is from V Æthelstan, prologue, and the new law on the age of capital punishment is VI Æthelstan, c. 12.1 (with a reference back to earlier debate on this subject in the context of II Æthelstan), to be consulted most conveniently in Whitelock, *EHD* I, pp. 422, 427, 417.

[42] *WMGR* I, p. 220: See on this the remarks of F. M. Stenton, *Anglo-Saxon England* (London, 1943), p. 352.

[43] Diverse customs: Lapidge, *The Cult of St Swithun*, pp. 408–9; 'severally': the Exeter Relic-list, Conner, *Anglo-Saxon Exeter*, p. 177.

that we have two surviving instances of court poets composing poetry for Æthelstan, both foreign: Petrus in 927, and the author of the Tiberius A. ii poem in 937–9. Others were experts in the liturgy (a fast expanding area of job opportunities in the tenth-century empire!); the special masses for St Cuthbert in Corpus Christi College, Cambridge 183, a volume gifted to the community in Chester-le-Street, for example, were written by a cleric from Flanders.[44]

Some, though, were working long-term in England, out in the field as bishops, especially perhaps in Northumbria, like the Columbanus who appears in 929, or the Benedictus who was with the king at Worthy 931 – this man was on the expedition to Scotland in summer 934, and inscribed the royal gift of BL, Otho B. ix with a verse panegyric to St Cuthbert at Chester-le-Street as 'Benedictus *Evernensicus*', that is, 'the Irishman'.[45] Perhaps Irish bishops had been brought in to help impoverished sees just as they were in Norman times in Lincolnshire and the north. These contacts start early. Mael Brigte mac Tornan, the coarb of Armagh, who presented the king with the Lambeth Gospels, died early in 927, so they were in touch at the very beginning of the reign; and no doubt Æthelstan had established other relationships before he became king, as he had, for example, with Radbod of Dol. A New Minster charter may perhaps list some of his personal group of scholars in 925.[46] *Werulf sacerdos* may just be the old Mercian scholar from Alfred's circle; with him, though, are three clerics with German names, Gundlaf, Hildewine and Waltere, and the Petrus who was in the king's chapel in July 927 in Northumbria whence he sent his poem back to the royal family at Winchester. Here too is a man called Dubliter; this Irish name occurs several times in Viking Age Irish annals, and always as a scribe, anchorite or bishop.[47] While it is possible all these men belong to the *familia* of New Minster, it seems conceivable, especially given the presence of Petrus, that we have here some of the king's court scholars.

---

[44] Lapidge, 'Some Latin Poems', pp. 92–3; C. Hohler, 'The Durham Services in Honour of St Cuthbert', in C. F. Battiscombe, ed., *The Relics of St Cuthbert* (Oxford, 1956), pp. 155–91, at 156–7; see too Gretsch, *Intellectual Foundations*, pp. 352–4.
[45] *Evernensicus*: see Wood, 'The Making of King Æthelstan's Empire', in P. Wormald *et al.*, eds., *Ideal and Reality in Frankish and Anglo-Saxon Society: Studies Presented to J. M. Wallace-Hadrill* (Oxford, 1983), pp. 250–72, at 255; and Keynes, 'King Æthelstan's Books', p. 172.
[46] S. 1417 (925 x 927?); see Keynes, *Liber Vitae*, pp. 19–20.
[47] S. Miller, *The Anglo-Saxon Charters of New Minster Winchester*, British Academy Charters 7 (Oxford, 2001), no. 9, with personal comment from David Dumville, and reference to 'Dublitir' in the *Annals of Tigernach* s.a. 736.

Such people set the tone of a reign international in its ambitions, none more so than the scholar who has only recently come to light in the king's court, Israel of Trier.[48] Later a European scholar of international fame, 'the last of the great Carolingian court scholars' as Bernard Bischoff called him, Israel was perhaps born not long before 900, and so was around the same age as the king. A follower of the school of Heiric and Remi of Auxerre, intellectual disciple of John Scottus Eriugena, we find him in England, Rome, the Rhineland and Francia. In Aachen, we overhear him in conversation with Salomon, a Greek-speaking Jewish ambassador from Constantinople;[49] at Verdun in the late forties he appears as a bishop with the Frankish court; later in Cologne he is the tutor of the brilliant young Bruno, brother of Otto I.[50] During his stay in England he was still in his thirties, not yet then perhaps a *magister*. But the recent rediscovery of Israel's English career is a salutary warning to the historian of Anglo-Saxon England that such an important figure well known to scholars of the intellectual history of tenth-century Europe could have escaped all mention in early sources for the Anglo-Saxon period. Well, almost all mention! Armitage Robinson picked up the mysterious reference in Corpus, Oxford, 221 to a scholar called Israel 'remarkably skilled in the Gospels' rubbing shoulders with an Irish bishop and – could it really be? – a Roman Jewish scholar 'in the house of King Æthelstan'.[51] It was Neil Ker who first put two and two together after noting his name in the Worcester grammatical treatise Q. 5 at the end of a very clever begging letter in verse to Robert of Trier from 'your Lordship's Israel'.[52] It is almost incredible that Israel's role in England had been missed for so long; especially given that Corpus 221 shows that the Irish Bishop Dubhinsi of Bangor met him in Æthelstan's court.

---

[48] On Israel, see J. Kenney, *Sources for the Early History of Ireland* (New York, 1929), p. 610; important on the German background is C. Selmer, 'The Origin of Brandenburg (Prussia), the St Brendan Legend, and the *Scoti* of the Tenth Century', *Traditio* 7 (1949–51), pp. 416–32, at 431–2 with references to Selmer's numerous other studies. On the manuscript tradition of the *grammatica*, see C. Jeudy, 'Israel le grammarien', *Studi medievali* 18 (1977), pp. 751–71. See also E. Jeauneau, 'Pour le dossier d'Israël Scot', *Etudes Erigeniennes* (1987), pp. 641–706; on the English connection, see M. Lapidge, 'Israel the Grammarian in Anglo-Saxon England', in H. J. Westra, ed., *From Athens to Chartres* (Leiden, 1992), pp. 97–114 (repr. in Lapidge, *Anglo-Latin Literature 900–1066* (London, 1993), pp. 87–104).

[49] Jeauneau, 'Pour le dossier d'Israël', *Archives d'histoire doctrinale et littéraire du Moyen Age* 52 (1985), p. 29, and 'Pour le dossier', *Etudes Erigeniennes* (1987), p. 663.

[50] Ruotger, *Vita Brunonis c.* 7, ed. I. Ott, MGH SRG n.s. 10 (Weimar, 1951), p. 8. In this light, the 'Israel Britto' said by Flodoard, *Historia Remensis Ecclesiae* IV, *c.* 34, ed. M. Stratmann, *MGH SS* XXXVI (Hanover, 1998), p. 426, to have been present at the Council of Verdun (947) can hardly be pressed as meaning 'Breton'.

[51] Robinson, *The Times of St Dunstan*, pp. 173–4 and frontispiece.

[52] Worcester Cathedral MS Q. 5 fol. 71v; personal communication, Veronica Ortenberg.

We now though have a picture of a scholar who later 'made Britannia famous throughout the world of the liberal arts'.[53] He is perhaps working in the Irish–Lotharingian tradition, not Breton as has been asserted recently. Ruotger, who knew him, is unlikely to be wrong here in calling him *Scottigena*: to the Germans he was Israel *Scottus*. To the Trier *familia*, too, he was 'a monk of this house'. So Israel was most likely one of the famous Irish of Lotharingia. He was brought to England, like Grimbald, to help the *renovatio*. He could have been recruited by Cenwald of Worcester who visited Trier at the end of 929, though a more intriguing possibility would be that he came as a monk of Trier after the reform of St-Maximin in 934.[54]

What brings Israel close to Æthelstan, indeed into his *domus*, as it says in Oxford, Corpus Christi College 221, is the presence of Greek liturgical material, which appears in some continental Israel manuscripts, in one of the most interesting books from tenth-century England: Cotton MS Galba A. xviii. There is good reason to think this was Æthelstan's own psalter,[55] and if it is, it is the only Anglo-Saxon royal book which bears comparison, in the interest of its additions, to manuscripts associated with Carolingian rulers. A ninth-century psalter from Rheims, its English material includes the early tenth-century metrical 'Hampson' calendar, and the series of beautiful fifth-century Romana Collects in an excellent text which was perhaps copied from an exemplar present in England since the seventh century.[56] In the 930s, at the end of the manuscript, a collection of Greek prayers was entered in accurate Greek in Latin letters with an Antiochene litany which, as Edmund Bishop first pointed out, came from Canterbury and was probably brought there by Theodore of Tarsus in the mid-seventh century.[57]

---

[53] The *Grammaticorum diadoche* of Gauzebertus is printed by W. Berschin, *Greek Letters and the Latin Middle Ages* (1988), pp. 123–5.

[54] At Trier (?the house of John the Old Saxon) he was remembered as 'a monk of this house'; we now know he wrote Latin poetry, ed. K. Strecker, *MGH Poet.* v (Berlin, 1923), pp. 501–2, 648, and see also D. Howlett, 'Five Experiments in Textual Reconstruction and Analysis', *Peritia* 9 (1995), pp. 1–50, at 46–8; a commentary on Porphyry of Tyre's Isagogue in BN lat. 12949, ed. C. Baeumker, *Frühmittelalterlichen Glossen des angeblichen Jepa* (Münster, 1924); a revision of the Remigian commentary on Donatus, *Ars minor*, as cited in W. Fox, *Remigii Autissiodorensis, In artem Donati minorem Commentum* (Leipzig, 1902), p. 11; and transmitted as series of doxographies from the school of Auxerre which appear in several English manuscripts as late as the fourteenth century, often alongside the Greek *liturgica* which turn up in Galba A. xviii, among them BL, Cotton Titus D. xviii.

[55] On Galba A. xviii, see R. Deshman 'The Galba Psalter', *ASE* 26 (1997), pp. 109–38; Dumville, *Wessex and England*, pp. 74–7 and 87–8; and Wood, *In Search of England*, pp. 169–88.

[56] A. Wilmart, *The Psalter Collects from Vth–VIth Century Sources*, ed. L. Brou, Henry Bradshaw Society 83 (London, 1949), pp. 174–227.

[57] E. Bishop, 'About a Prayer Book', in his *Liturgica Historica* (Oxford, 1918), pp. 144–5.

Galba's Greek prayers, which presumably were entered for the king's own use, came from the near-eastern roots of Christianity. So too, one would think, did the originals behind the cycle of paintings also added to the manuscript at this time, and presumably also for its royal patron. Their source, direct or indirect, was an early Christian Syrian painted book; their style, use of colour, iconography – and such telling details as the spindly flowers, letter forms and name tags – are shared by the Augustine Gospels at Cambridge, Corpus Christi College, and the Ashburnham Pentateuch. This makes it extremely unlikely that they derive from Carolingian prototypes, as the late Bob Deshman recently argued.[58] In particular, the Nativity (a cut-out now preserved as Bodley MS Rawlinson B 484, fol. 85r) and the Ascension (fol. 120v) are pure Syrian-Greek in style; their closest analogues are pictures in the Rabbula Gospels painted in 586 at Zagba in Mesopotamia, or the miniature Gospel scenes on a sixth-century Syrian

---

[58] For convenient illustrations, see K. Weitzmann, *Late Antique and Early Christian Book Illumination* (New York, 1977), pp. 136, 41–2, 44; and the facsimile of *The Rabbula Gospels*, ed. C. Cecchelli, G. Furlani and M. Salmi (Olten-Lausanne, 1959). For discussion, see F. Wormald, 'The Winchester School before St Aethelwold', in P. Clemoes and K. Hughes, eds., *England before the Conquest: Studies in Primary Sources presented to Dorothy Whitelock*, (Cambridge, 1971), pp. 305–13. Recently Deshman, 'The Galba Psalter', p. 110, n. 4, rejected Wormald's idea that the BL Cotton Titus D. xxvii, fol. 75v. crucifixion comes from the same cycle, because the depiction of St John with pen in hand is a tenth-century innovation. But this is to ignore the style of crucifixion with spindly flowers, name tags and studded frame which closely resembles the Galba cycle and its earlier sources; their dimensions are also identical, almost to the millimetre. The nativity was cut out opposite Psalm 1 at fol. 35v; paint rubbing in Galba on fol. 80r opposite Psalm 51 where we would expect a crucifixion shows that a picture was indeed removed here (see M. Wood, 'The Making of King Athelstan's Empire', pp. 250–72, at 268). That being so, it is clearly possible that the so-called Quinity at Titus D. xxvii, fol. 65v was also based on a picture removed from Galba: it shares the same name tags and use of a frame with little decorative circular studs with the Rawlinson Nativity and the Galba Ascension (an ancient style: the Codex Amiatinus *maiestas* makes similar use of a studded rectangular frame with a circular picture overlapping). The iconography of the Quinity, it has been argued, derives from the Utrecht Psalter. The only detailed discussion of the Quinity is E. H. Kantorowicz, 'The Quinity of Winchester', *The Art Bulletin* 29 (1947), pp. 73–85, which, for all its learning and ingenuity, misses the vital point that the picture with its depiction of Arius cannot be the invention of the Titus artist, but must derive from an earlier eastern model. The 'almost Nestorian christology' which perplexed Kantorowicz is a strong sub-current in insular Psalter exegesis which remarkably comes out in the Old English 'introductions' to the first fifty Alfredian psalms in the Paris Psalter: see J. W. Bright and R. L. Ramsay, 'Notes on the "Introductions" of the West-Saxon Psalms', *Journal of Theological Studies* 13 (1912), pp. 520–58; M. Laistner, 'Antiochene Exegesis', *Harvard Theological Review* 40 (1947), pp. 21, 26–7; and cf. M. Lapidge, 'The Career of Archbishop Theodore', in Lapidge, ed., *Archbishop Theodore: Commemorative Studies on his Life and Influence* (Cambridge, 1995), pp. 1–29, at 4–6. This (Theodoran?) exegesis on the Psalms, then, was still current or revived in England in the late ninth and early tenth centuries. Psalm 109 was at the centre of the debate on Arius in the Early Church and one would expect that the model behind the Titus picture was placed there in Galba. If so, the Quinity could be revealing about the intellectual interests of whoever owned the Galba Psalter in the second quarter of the tenth century.

relic shrine now in the Lateran. With their eastern connections one would imagine the source of these pictures too came with Theodore in the seventh century and was still available to artists in the court atelier of Æthelstan in the early tenth.

In a private book, one would expect that such material reflected the king's own tastes. The presence of Greek *liturgica* in the back of the psalter is also best explained by the king's intellectual interests; not that he necessarily knew any Greek (or at least, not more than a few words) but because the king was interested in having these testimonies to early eastern Christianity which provided an intellectual and spiritual link with Archbishop Theodore and Bede's 'happiest time'. Transliterated into Latin letters, the king would be able read them and speak them out aloud in his daily prayers, which of course would have included (as Asser says of the king's grandfather) recital of all the psalter. Galba A. xviii is a fascinating manuscript with very rich layers. With its obits for Alfred and his wife, the psalter collects, and the Greek prayers, we get a strong impression of the private devotion of the person who owned it. Its contents, too, fit with what we know about the king's passion for the Psalms – even in his charters, a number of which stipulate the singing of Psalms for his soul.[59] But like the Rawlinson Aldhelm, Galba's later history also closely links it to the king's protégés in the time of the Benedictine Reform. Galba's paintings were closely studied by the creators of the Benedictional of St Æthelwold, and Galba's Veneration of the Cross prayer is used in the *Regularis Concordia*.[60] This might suggest that when he was one of the king's intimates, Æthelwold had come to know the book well (perhaps while in the royal chapel, 935–9?), and renewed his association with it when it was among the king's *halidom* in the Old Minster in Winchester, where the book was later treasured.

Such speculations I hope give us some sense of the intellectual interests of Æthelstan's circle, and of the possibilities offered by surviving manuscripts to get us a little closer to the king himself. Let us now briefly turn to the evidence for the king in another guise as a lay intellectual, namely as a patron of letters. First, of course, Æthelstan certainly liked books: his painted portraits in Cambridge, Corpus Christi College 183 and the burned

---

[59] On the Psalter in tenth-century England, see Gretsch, *Intellectual Foundations*, pp. 6–41. The West Saxon Psalms translation was perhaps completed in Æthelstan's circle, Wood, 'The Making of King Æthelstan's Empire', p. 264. Alfred of course had always travelled with 'a book of psalms and hours in his bosom', *VA* c. 24, p. 21, and cf. cc. 76, 88, pp. 59, 73.

[60] *Regularis Concordia*, ed. T. Symons (London, 1953), pp. 42–44. On the Galba pictures as artistic inspiration, see R. Deshman, *The Benedictional of Æthelwold* (Princeton, NJ, 1995), pp. 21–4.

Cotton manuscript BL, Otho B. ix, both portrayed him presenting books as gifts. He is also unique among pre-Conquest rulers in that a number of books survive which we can connect with him. Recently these have been thoroughly explored by Simon Keynes, and there is no need to add anything further here, save to remark that four of them contain inscriptions that may have been dictated by the king himself and which may owe something to Milred's eighth-century collection of epigrams from Worcester. Many more Æthelstan books have not survived. Leland saw a group of five or six bearing the king's inscriptions in Bath for example, of which the magnificent Claudius B. v is the only survivor today.[61] Fragments of several tenth-century manuscripts in Exeter may be a remnant of the king's original donation.[62] Others may yet await identification. For example, could the *Liber Astrologicum* attributed to Æthelstan by Bale[63] perhaps be BL Harley 647, a splendid Carolingian *Aratea* with an added page in Phase II square minuscule which would have made a fitting gift for a would-be *imperator* who had himself depicted in his royal paintings in full Carolingian style?

But it is perhaps the newly commissioned books by English scribes working for the king which are most revealing in marking out the intellectual ambitions of the court. Following David Dumville's classification,[64] there is a shift in the choice of material which distinguishes the manuscripts of Phase II square minuscule, the developed court hand of the 930s, and which might form an interesting parallel to the new developments we have observed elsewhere. Loosely dated after the late twenties/930 watershed, these manuscripts seem to mark a change in direction, competence, style and vision from what had gone before. The revised dating of these suggests at present that there are around twenty or so surviving books or fragments from the 930s. We must remind ourselves of course that the English scale is very small compared with the powerhouses of Carolingian Europe. But, given that proviso, the haul is interesting: Amalarius (twice), Prosper, Aldhelm, Hrabanus Maurus, Alcuin's letters on the *via regia*, Virgil, Juvenal, Persius, Martianus Capella, Bede's *Life of St Cuthbert*. Taken as a whole this looks like a deliberate move forwards from the Alfredian phase of English learning. Though Alfred's translations were still being copied in

---

[61] A. Hall, *Commentarii de scriptoribus Britannicis* (Oxford, 1709), p. 160; see T. Williams, *Somerset Medieval Libraries* (Bristol, 1897), p. 35.
[62] Conner, *Anglo-Saxon Exeter*, pp. 171–209.
[63] J. Bale, *Illustrium Maiorum Britanniae Scriptorum ... Summarium* (Basel, 1559), p. 127.
[64] For the phases of this script, see the very helpful articles of Dumville, 'English Square Minuscule Script', *ASE* 16 (1987), pp. 173–8, and *ASE* 23 (1994), pp. 136–44.

the 920s and 930s, Æthelstan and his think-tank were trying to bring Carolingian learning into England. And again, if one had to guess, one would be inclined to see a plan behind it, a plan influenced by Carolingian ideas on the organisation of learning; and a plan driven in part perhaps by the king's own intellectual curiosity.

Some of the choices deserve further comment. Amalarius, for example, is often disparaged in modern times, but he was the object of a peculiarly English affection in the tenth century and this was no doubt because of his teaching method.[65] Allegorising the liturgy in this fashion is a mnemonic, a teaching aid in a memorising culture, as its author intended; and the interest in Amalarius, to judge by two surviving Phase II manuscripts, one of them of very high quality, might be a characteristic development of Æthelstan's circle. Another Carolingian author chosen by Æthelstan and his scholars was Alcuin. A beautifully produced (royal?) volume of the letters to Charlemagne in Phase I square minuscule, Lambeth 208, is the first English testimony to this central work on the *via regia*. The text derives from the Troyes exemplar made at the Carolingian court school. The book's date is still controversial, but it may date from Æthelstan's early adulthood, and it was subsequently gifted to Æthelstan's foundation at Bury. Then in Phase II minuscule, perhaps around 930, another copy was made by one of the king's royal scribes. Only a fragment of this survives in Chicago.[66] In terms of the king's own interest in these letters, it is fascinating that the same collection is recorded as prefacing an account of the deeds of Æthelstan in a thirteenth-century Glastonbury catalogue.[67] When we recall Æthelwold in the 950s at Glastonbury teaching the young *ætheling* Edgar about the *via regia* of Christian kingship, the association of a *vita* of Æthelstan with this Alcuin collection, in that same house, is to say the least tantalising. The lost manuscript with its accompanying glossary has all the appearance of a *speculum regis*. One might guess indeed that the lost volume discovered by William of Malmesbury was this very item: could it even have been prepared for the *ætheling* Edgar by his tutor Æthelwold?

---

[65] See now also C. A. Jones, *A Lost Work by Amalarius of Metz*, Henry Bradshaw Society Subsidia II (London, 2001).

[66] D. Ganz, 'An Anglo-Saxon Fragment of Alcuin's letters in the Newberry Library, Chicago', *ASE* 22 (1993), pp. 167–77.

[67] Printed by T. Hearne, *Johannis Glastoniensis Chronica*, 2 vols. (Oxford, 1726), II, p. 438; and by T. Williams, *Somerset Medieval Libraries*, p. 71 (MS Trinity College, Cambridge R. S. 33 fol. 103v); the first four items were evidently one book; in the manuscript a stop divides them from item five. On Æthelwold and the *via regia*, see *Vita Oswaldi*, ed. J. Raine, *The Historians of the Church of York*, 3 vols., Rolls Series 71 (London, 1879–94), I, p. 399.

Some of these commissions in the 930s, such as Cambridge, Corpus Christi College 183, or the BL, Royal Aldhelm, were probably books done to order and for a specific purpose.[68] We cannot always prove it, except where book inscriptions tell us, or where supporting evidence gives a clue, as, for example, with Cambridge, Corpus Christi College 183 which appears to have been made to be sent up to the community of St Cuthbert at Chester-le-Street after the king's visit to the saint in early July 934. But the connections between the scribes and artists of some of these books suggest we should always bear the possibility in mind. Scribal links are likely for example between Cambridge, Corpus Christi College 183, the BL, Royal Aldhelm and the Corpus Prosper: and similarly between the Boulogne Amalarius, Junius 27, and the Trinity Hrabanus Maurus; this last manuscript was closely copied from a Carolingian archetype from Fulda, and with its large format looks very much like a royal gift.[69] No doubt more work on these manuscripts will elucidate such questions.

So what can we draw from this kind of detail? Clearly with such a small circle of trained scribes the copying of a manuscript was a major investment, and no book was copied without a purpose. Æthelstan and his councillors were evidently attempting to broaden out English learning with Carolingian ideas. But two important intellectual currents at this time, which bore fruit in the later tenth century, look back to older insular models, and especially to Alfred. The first I have already alluded to in dealing with the king's psalter. The psalter was at the core of learning for early medieval people, with Alfred for example, as Asser tells us. One gets a strong impression that the psalter was at the centre of sacred learning for Æthelstan too. The king's love of psalmody is shown by the unusual stipulations on the recital of the Psalms in several of his charters, and as we have seen by the insertion of the rare and beautiful Romana psalter collects in Phase II minuscule into his private prayer-book. It was perhaps also at the king's behest that the vernacular translation of the Psalms begun by his grandfather was completed in his time. This important current of devotion, sacred study and glossing bore fruit in Æthelwold's Royal Psalter gloss.[70]

The second intellectual current centres on Aldhelm and Aldhelmian latinity. Again, the root of the king's interest must go back to his grandfather, who we are told revered Aldhelm as a poet in the English language.

---

[68] Gretsch, *Intellectual Foundations*, pp. 355–6, 359–67.
[69] Keynes, *Anglo-Saxon Manuscripts and Other Items of Related Interest in the Library of Trinity College, Cambridge* (Binghamton, NY, 1992), pp. 11–14.
[70] Gretsch, *Intellectual Foundations*, pp. 79–82.

But the fascination with Aldhelm's Latin surely comes out of Æthelstan's court and was very likely promoted by the king himself. Collections of Aldhelm glosses became the staple tools of learning during the Benedictine Revival: these go back to a large selection made in the second quarter of the tenth century and presumably in Æthelstan's circle.[71] The earliest testimony is BL Cleopatra A. iii, a collection of glosses in Phase II minuscule which must have been written soon after the end of the king's reign. This initial phase of Aldhelmian glossing lies behind the vocabulary of charters of Æthelstan A, and it may well be that it was under the king's tutelage that the young Æthelwold began his studies of Aldhelm, at a time when (as he later claimed to Wulfstan Cantor) he and the king were 'inseparable companions'.[72]

But the king's interest in Aldhelm and his works was evidently not solely an intellectual pursuit. William of Malmesbury tells us that Aldhelm was the king's personal saint; and he was buried close by him, as he had specified in his will, because to him there was 'nowhere more holy or desirable'.[73] As I hope to show elsewhere, Æthelstan reshaped the northern part of the Alfredian *burh* of Malmesbury into a Carolingian-style royal necropolis with a cluster of six or seven churches and chapels. The rebuilt St Mary's was a grand royal church which in the 1120s 'for decoration and magnificence was the finest of all ancient churches surviving in England'. As we have seen, Aldhelm's latinity emerges as a vehicle for the expression of royal ideology in the hands of 'Æthelstan A' from 928 in the charters, and one would have thought this must be connected with the king's own devotion to the saint.

These then were the ways in which a king who aimed to rule *litteratius* – 'in a more literate way' – could play his part in shaping the direction of the revival of learning towards the bigger goal of building a Christian society. But, finally, did the king actually commission literary works? It is one of the mysteries of Anglo-Saxon studies that no literary work has yet been securely dated in what was seen till only recently as a culturally barren gap between 900 and 950. There are many possibilities. One of the most interesting questions, namely the origin of the Old English poetic collections of the tenth century, was raised by Kenneth Sisam long ago,[74]

---

[71] *Ibid.*, p. 132.
[72] *Vita Aethelwoldi*, ed. M. Lapidge and M. Winterbottom, *Wulfstan of Winchester, The Life of St Æthelwold* (Oxford, 1991), pp. 14–15.
[73] *WMGR* I, pp. 396–7.
[74] K. Sisam, *Studies in the History of Old English Literature* (Oxford, 1953), pp. 61–108; 137–8.

though it has never been followed up since. Nor as far as I am aware has anyone examined the late medieval story that Æthelstan was responsible for bringing the text of Euclid into England.⁷⁵ Another case worth further investigation is the interesting poem known as Solomon and Saturn which has recently been connected with Æthelstan through an Irish reference to a 'High King of the English' who is said to have 'composed' a literary work connected with the *Pater Noster*.⁷⁶ The OE *Menologium* too, and its rather touching calendar of English piety, might reward further study, with its curious reference to the holy festivals 'now observed through the kingdom of Britain at the behest of the Saxon king'.⁷⁷ But in one important case it may now be possible to advance matters. John Bale, in his *Scriptores*, that mine of information about the destruction of manuscripts during the Reformation, says that the OE translation of the Gospels was commissioned by Æthelstan:⁷⁸

> *Teste* William of Malmesbury, this king ordered the translation of the Gospels from the purest founts of the Hebrews by certain Jews resident in his country who had been converted to Christianity for that purpose.

This extraordinary account, which surprisingly has occasioned no comment by OE scholars, is not known from any surviving work of William of Malmesbury. But Tyndale and John Foxe knew the story and Tanner in his *Bibliotheca Britannico-Hibernica* supplies a date: 930.⁷⁹ In a footnote, Tanner cites Bale and suggests that by the eighteenth century the relevant work of William was not then known. However, the source of Bale's story I believe can be narrowed down. The clue is offered by Tanner: in his footnote to the story Tanner suggests that Bale got it from Leland. Now in his notes later edited by Hearne, Leland says he saw at Malmesbury Abbey a copy of a work by William described as *libri quindecim de serie quattuor evangelistarum nullo*

---

⁷⁵ On Euclid: BL Royal 17 A. 1 fols. 2b–3; T. Heath, ed., *The Thirteen Books of Euclid's Elements*, 2nd edn (Cambridge, 1925), I, p. 95. This might perhaps be a Boethius, *De Geometria*, but note Trinity College Cambridge R 15.14 pt 1, an early tenth-century manuscript from northern France, which came to St Augustine's in the tenth century, and which includes material from Pseudo-Boethius, Cassiodorus – and Euclid *latinus*.
⁷⁶ B. O'Cuiv, 'St Gregory and St Dunstan', in N. Ramsay, M. Sparks and T. Tatton-Brown, eds., *St Dunstan: His Life, Times and Cult* (Woodbridge, 1992), pp. 273–97; C. D. Wright, 'The Irish Tradition', in P. Pulsiano and E. Treharne, *A Companion to Anglo-Saxon Literature* (London, 2001), pp. 360–1.
⁷⁷ *Menologium*, ed. E. V. K. Dobbie, *Anglo-Saxon Poetic Records* VI (London, 1942), p. 55.
⁷⁸ J. Bale, *Illustrium Maiorum Britanniae Scriptorum ... Summarium* (Basel, 1559), p. 127.
⁷⁹ Tanner, *Bibliotheca Britannico-Hibernica* (London, 1748), p. 267.

non genere carminis: a versified version of the Gospels.[80] William is not known as an author of poetry, but the same reference appears in Leland's *Commentarii de Scriptoribus Britannicis*.[81] This work is now lost or unlocated, though it is not impossible that it remains to be discovered. In the introduction to such a work William may well have mentioned earlier English versions of the Gospels, and one would expect that this is the source of the tale repeated by Tyndale, Foxe, Bale and Tanner. Unless a manuscript turns up, this is not capable of proof, of course, but it seems most likely that William is cited by Bale from this work.

But where did William get this story? We may never know, but as we have seen, his lost source, the mysterious 'very old book', gave prominence to Æthelstan's education and might well have mentioned his literary patronage too. Bale's story fits with Æthelstan's well-attested interest in the Gospels: at least ten Gospel manuscripts were imported from abroad in his time, four of which carry inscriptions as his gifts. Moreover, we now have Professor Liuzza's work on the stemma and sources of the OE translation, which it turns out was done not from one Latin text but with reference to a small collection of Gospel books.[82] Intriguingly, all but a handful of the variants in the OE version are found in a small group of manuscripts from Canterbury:

Lambeth 1370, the MacDurnan gospels; given by Æthelstan to Christ Church (in or soon after 925 x 927?).
BL Royal I A. xviii, of Breton origin: another Æthelstan gift.
BL Add. 40618: restored at Canterbury by the deacon Edward before 931 (if he is the man of that name who became a bishop in that year).
BL Royal I E. vi (lavishly restored in Æthelstan's reign with purple pages).

The pattern here is suggestive: this cluster of manuscripts, some with specific Æthelstan connections, had all found their way to Canterbury by around 930. The approximate date is hinted at perhaps by Add. 40618: the deacon Edward had left Canterbury by 931. A working hypothesis would be that the translation was done by a team under Archbishop Wulfhelm at Canterbury in around 930, the date given by Tanner in the eighteenth century, conceivably from William's lost source. Liuzza opts for

---

[80] J. Leland, *Collectanea*, ed. T. Hearne, 6 vols. (London, 1770), III, p. 157.
[81] J. Leland, *Commentarii de Scriptoribus Britannicis*, ed. A. Hall (Oxford, 1709), p. 196.
[82] R. Liuzza, *The Old English Version of the Gospels*, 2 vols., Old English Text Society (Oxford, 2000), p. 49.

a date around 960, but the translation has no features of the standardised West Saxon of the reformers. The earliest manuscript is eleventh century, by which time the text had clearly gone through revisions; but its language links it to Alfredian West Saxon with some Mercian features, as Madeleine Grunberg's earlier analysis of St Matthew suggested.[83] A date around 930, then, would fit the available evidence very well. The impetus no doubt was the Alfredian translations, indeed Alfred may even have had such a work in mind, as the *Liber Eliensis* suggests.[84] In that case, Æthelstan would again be fulfilling his grandfather's plan, in a commission which recalls the ninth-century vernacular Gospel versions done on the Continent for the likes of Louis the German. It would be a fitting task for a Christian ruler who saw sacred learning as a central part of his *ministerium regis*.[85]

So there are some of the lines of approach which have opened up recently on learning in the reign of Æthelstan. 'He is at the beginning of so many developments', Sisam wrote to Stenton in the New Year of 1944, following the publication of *Anglo-Saxon England*.[86] We can see now that he was right. Out of often unpromising and fragmentary evidence, a picture of Æthelstan is beginning to emerge which does indeed evoke the king described by William of Malmesbury, a ruler whose intent was to rule both *litteratius* and *legalius*. And it is perhaps only our lack of a contemporary biographer, an Asser, or a Thegan, which prevents us from seeing the extent to which his personality and interests dominated his time. Compared with Carolingian kings and intellectuals, of course, the evidence is thin and the achievement appears small-scale: the books for example are nothing compared with the 7,000 manuscripts which still survive from Frankish houses from the ninth century alone. This may still make things seem provincial compared with the intellectual powerhouses of Carolingian Europe; just as the learning of the English elite might seem second-rate compared with the court scholars of Charles the Bald. But the achievement of that English elite was real and long-lasting. It was their vision of history, and their sense of dynasty, which I think provided their intellectual motivation in their kingship and deeds. Bede's narrative made

---

[83] M. Grunberg, *The West Saxon Gospels* (Amsterdam, 1967), pp. 367–8.
[84] *Liber Eliensis*, ed. E. O. Blake, Camden Society, 3rd ser. 92 (London, 1962), p. 54.
[85] As for Bale's story about Jewish translators, it could of course have arisen from a simple misunderstanding of Israel's name; but in a ninth-century context it would suggest scholarly helpers like the *hebraeus modernis temporibus* mentioned by Hrabanus Maurus and Paschasius Radbertus, or the source cited by the Remigian Genesis commentator. I hope to return to this question.
[86] Stenton's Anglo-Saxon England *Fifty Years On*, ed. D. Matthew (Reading, 1994), p. 122.

a particularly deep impression on the tenth-century empire-builders – and their hope, I am sure, was to reestablish his golden age, his 'happiest time' for the English people.[87] After the struggles of the late ninth century, and the decline of learning to which Alfred refers in his *Cura Pastoralis* preface, Bede gave these people the shape and meaning of their future: the providentially ordained conversion of the *gens Anglorum*, which offered the prospect of a new Israel; the need for exemplary *doctores* to guide the *gens*, of whom Theodore was clearly the first model; and running it all, Bede's Christian kings who kept the sacred law, sponsored sacred learning and were a terror to the *barbari nationes*.

So, let me end as I began, with the short poem written for Æthelstan when he was about five years old. On the little boy's shoulders lay the weight of his dying grandfather's dreams. The poet, you will remember, exhorted the boy to fight the devilish monsters, a phrase which reminds us not only of Beowulf, but also of the reflection of Æthelstan A' in 931 that this was a world 'surrounded by monsters'.[88] The poem's author expressed the hope that in times of peace Æthelstan's 'stoniness' would soften, and that he would be able to devote himself fully to sacred learning. But this never happened. Aethelstan's *imperium* overeached itself, as a later scribe noted: 'for none of the kings who came after attempted to take the *imperium* further than Æthelstan had done'.[89] The end of his reign was taken up with 'warfare and deeds', as Æthelweard remarked.[90] And towards the end he appears a hard-bitten king having to show all his nerve and *fortuna* in the desperate struggle of 937, with the background of wider threats that year to the *imperium christianum* of Europe, leading to the collapse of his alliances in 939. The king died still only about 44 in the October of that year, perhaps worn out by the acute physical (and one imagines psychological?) strains of his office; perhaps though weakened by the hereditary illness (Crohn's disease?) which had dogged his grandfather and which killed his half-brother Eadred. But his battles had guaranteed the *imperium* and the *pax* later enjoyed by successors, and his patronage laid the foundations for the intellectual revival in Benedictine Reform.

Looking back on Edgar's predecessors, Æthelwold later wrote that the best of them were 'mature in age, and very prudent, far-seeing in wisdom, and hard to overcome in any crisis'. He was surely thinking of his old patron, 'his flaxen hair beautifully twisted with gold braids', as Æthelstan

---

[87] Bede, *Historia Ecclesiastica*, ed. C. Plummer (Oxford, 1896), p. 205.   [88] S. 416.   [89] S. 731.
[90] Æthelweard, *Chronicon*, pp. 34, 54.

was later remembered.⁹¹ If we could ask the king himself to review the achievements of his life, I wonder whether he might not refer us to the treasured poem given that day forty years back in his grandfather's court, and say that he had done what the poem asked of him as a child. 'Gifted abundantly with the pinnacle of sacred learning', he had endeavoured to 'stand strong against the devilish monsters'.⁹²

---

⁹¹ O. Cockayne, *Leechdoms, Wortcunning and Starcraft of Early England*, 3 vols., Rolls Series (London, 1864–6), III, pp. 436–7 recalls *WMGR* I, p. 210, on Æthelstan's *sapientiae maturitas*; *WMGR* I, p. 214, refers to his braided hair.

⁹² Patrick Wormald invited me to deliver this paper at Kalamazoo and I would like to end by expressing my gratitude to him. We were undergraduates at the same time, and were both supervised as graduate students by Michael Wallace-Hadrill. Though my career led me far away from the academic world, over the years Patrick kindly encouraged me to stay involved in a subject he knew I loved. Like so many of his friends, colleagues and pupils, I will always remember his open-spirited generosity.

CHAPTER 11

The lay intellectual in Anglo-Saxon England: Ealdorman Æthelweard and the politics of history

Scott Ashley

Ever since the early twelfth century, when William of Malmesbury assessed Æthelweard's Latin prose style and decided that the less said of it the better, the ealdorman of the Western Shires, descendant of royalty and author of a chronicle of the English in Britain, has not made much impact on the history of intellectual life.[1] The destruction of the single manuscript of his *Chronicon* in the disastrous Cotton Library fire in 1731 – which also carried off Asser's *Life of King Alfred* and the *Battle of Maldon* – has infinitely complicated any re-evaluation by forcing scholars to rely on the edition of the Elizabethan antiquary, Henry Savile, errors and all.[2] It has proved impossible for Æthelweard to benefit from the patient labours of modern textual historians, who made so many works bloom afresh once the corruptions were pruned and variant readings grafted on. Faced with very real problems of understanding what the words on the page were trying to say, early twentieth-century commentators, following William, tended to focus on the issue of Æthelweard's style and, following William again, found it little to their taste. Even Alistair Campbell, who produced a new edition and translation in 1962, seemed to take a perverse delight in pointing out his author's mistakes, confusions and infelicities, and explicitly doubted whether the ealdorman was 'equal to original historical composition'.[3] But Campbell also began a new mood in the modest field of Æthelweard studies by demonstrating that there was artistry, of a sort, behind what Kenneth Sisam had dismissed as 'tortured prose'.[4] Seminal contributions from Michael Winterbottom and Michael Lapidge have forced us to recognise that the *Chronicon* is, in fact, a rather well-crafted example of

---

[1] *WMGR* I, preface, p. 14.
[2] For the history of the MS, see E. E. Barker, 'The Cottonian Fragments of Æthelweard's Chronicle', *Bulletin of the Institute of Historical Research* 24 (1951), pp. 46–62; *The Chronicle of Æthelweard*, ed. A. Campbell (London, 1962) (hereafter *Chron.*), pp. ix–xii; Wormald, *Making*, pp. 258–9.
[3] *Chron.*, p. xii.
[4] *Chron.*, pp. xlv–ix; K. Sisam, *Studies in the History of Old English Literature* (Oxford, 1953), p. 106.

tenth-century Latin literature. No longer do we follow Sir Frank Stenton in calling Æthelweard's taste 'deplorable'; instead, his style is referred to as 'hermeneutic'.[5]

But the suspicion remains among students of Anglo-Saxon England that Æthelweard possessed, at best, a second-class mind. Routinely described as the author of a Latin translation of a lost version of the *Anglo-Saxon Chronicle*, there seems to be a silent consensus that his work has little independent historical vision. Rather than being read for its own sake, it has usually acted as a gateway to other, richer things, first by those hoping to understand more about the history and transmission of the *Anglo-Saxon Chronicle*, more recently by scholars interested in reclaiming a role for women in the production of early medieval historiography, drawn by the dedicatory letters to his distant kinswoman, Abbess Matilda of Essen.[6]

Consequently, there has been little sustained thinking about what Æthelweard might have been trying to achieve, and even less about ways of relating it to his social, political and cultural situation as a member of one of the premier West Saxon families and patron of monastic reform. Due to the assumption that Æthelweard's intention was primarily to translate the Old English *Chronicle* for Matilda (and as yet no evidence exists to suggest whether his Latin text actually reached Essen), not enough attention has been given to his textual adaptations, additions and omissions, several of which are significant. If we now recognise that 'Æthelweard was in full control of his medium' in regard to style, there seems little reason *a priori* to deny him a disciplined and active historical mind.[7] While clearly indebted to Alfredian or post-Alfredian material, Æthelweard should be read less as a slave to his sources and more as a conscious manipulator of them; as a reviser putting older work into new forms and imbuing it with new significance, analogous to the way many monastic communities

---

[5] M. Winterbottom, 'The Style of Æthelweard', *Medium Ævum* 36 (1967), pp. 109–18; M. Lapidge, 'The Hermeneutic Style in Tenth-Century Anglo-Latin Literature', *ASE* 4 (1975), pp. 67–111 (repr. with additions in his *Anglo-Latin Literature, 900–1066* (London, 1993), pp. 213–23); F. M. Stenton, *Anglo-Saxon England*, 3rd edn (Oxford, 1971), p. 461; and A. Lutz, 'Æthelweard's *Chronicon* and Old English Poetry', *ASE* 29 (2000), pp. 177–214.

[6] L. Whitbread, 'Æthelweard and the *Anglo-Saxon Chronicle*', *EHR* 74 (1959), pp. 577–89; *Chron.*, pp. xvii–xxxvii; E. E. Barker, 'The *Anglo-Saxon Chronicle* Used by Æthelweard', *Bulletin of the Institute of Historical Research* 40 (1967), pp. 74–91; A. L. Meaney, 'St Neots, Æthelweard, and the *Anglo-Saxon Chronicle*', in P. E. Szarmach, ed., *Studies in Earlier Old English Prose* (Albany, NY, 1986), pp. 193–245; E. van Houts, 'Women and the Writing of History in the Early Middle Ages: The Case of Abbess Matilda of Essen and Æthelweard', *EME* 1 (1992), pp. 53–68; van Houts, *Memory and Gender in Medieval Europe, 900–1200* (London, 1999), pp. 69–70.

[7] Winterbottom, 'Style of Æthelweard', p. 118.

periodically refashioned the *vitae* of their patron saints.[8] If we expect early medieval intellectuals, whether lay or ecclesiastical, to be self-consciously original, then we are likely to be disappointed.

Equally, despite Æthelweard being identified as one of only a handful of lay literates known from Anglo-Saxon England and in spite of his turning up time and again in some of the major events of tenth-century England – from the crisis of Eadwig's reign to the negotiations after the defeat by the Vikings at Maldon – no systematic study has been published of the bases of his very real power, either in land or kindred.[9] This is important, because if his *Chronicon* is in large part the history of the West Saxon dynasty and hence – as a descendant of King Æthelred I – by his own estimation a kind of family history, we need to incorporate the actual historical evidence for his family connections and relationships into any reading of his work to understand fully the conditions under which it was produced.[10] Naturally, given the nature of this evidence, any prosopographical description of Æthelweard and his kindred must of necessity be tentative and remain in part speculative. Many of the suggestions will never go beyond the possible or, at most, the probable. Yet as Patrick Wormald noted, 'Speculation and loose ends are inseparable from the study of European protohistory.'[11] Both the significant additions Æthelweard made to the skeletal narrative he derived from the *Anglo-Saxon Chronicle* and his equally significant omissions seem charged with new and potent meaning when placed alongside the fragments of his political life that lie scattered through charters, wills and administrative documents, the recalcitrant detritus of a vanished social order. This study cannot hope to map fully the fiendishly complex and still largely unexplored terrain, but it might be able to erect a few signposts to orientate future explorers.

It may seem odd to include in this volume a tenth-century Anglo-Saxon nobleman writing in the dying hours of Carolingian rule in western Europe. Æthelweard abandoned his work sometime during the period 975–88

---

[8] Or as Ælfric translated and summarised the lives of the saints at the request of Æthelweard and his son Æthelmær, *Ælfric's Prefaces*, ed. J. Wilcox, Durham Medieval Texts 9 (Durham, 1994), esp. pp. 131–2.

[9] For the 'problem' of Æthelweard's literacy, see C. P. Wormald, 'The Uses of Literacy in Anglo-Saxon England and its Neighbours', *TRHS* 5th ser. 27 (1977), pp. 95–114, at 110; J. Campbell, 'England, *c.* 991', in his *The Anglo-Saxon State* (London, 2000), pp. 164–5.

[10] *Chron.*, pp. 1–2, 34, 38–9. For a finely judged discussion of what is known, see Wormald, 'Æthelweard (d. 998?)', *Oxford Dictionary of National Biography* (Oxford, 2004), I, pp. 432–3.

[11] P. Wormald, 'The Strange Affair of the Selsey Bishopric, 953–963', in R. Gameson and H. Leyser, eds., *Belief and Culture in the Middle Ages: Studies Presented to Henry Mayr-Harting* (Oxford, 2001), pp. 128–41, at 140.

The lay intellectual in Anglo-Saxon England 221

(most probably by 980) just as history transmuted the last descendants of those who had ousted the Merovingian *rois fainéants* into shadow-rulers themselves.[12] But time is relative and tenth-century England experienced the Carolingian Renaissance a century after the Carolingian kingdoms, with revivals in education, book production, art and architecture matching visions of 'imperial' kingship, lawmaking, government and monastic reform to parallel those found in Francia during the eighth and ninth centuries.[13] And it was Carolingian encouragement of Latin and vernacular education for the laity, refracted through the Alfredian project as described by Asser, that ensured there was at least one ealdorman in tenth-century England with pretensions to classical learning.[14] The England that determined Æthelweard's work can usefully be thought of as an outlier of the Frankish world that continued to move to Carolingian rhythms and perpetuate Carolingian structures long after the dynasty had disappeared in the east and south and entered its senility in the west.

Yet Æthelweard's writings also registered with some precision the fading of the descendants of Charlemagne from the European stage and the emergence of alternative cultural networks to replace their waning influence. His epistolary communications with Matilda of Essen about their shared West Saxon ancestry encapsulated the manifold exchanges between England and Ottonian Germany in the tenth century, the extent of which has only begun fully to emerge in recent decades.[15] Those new configurations in western Europe inevitably left their mark on the chroniclers of

---

[12] For the dating of the *Chronicon* see Whitbread, 'Æthelweard', pp. 584–5, favouring a date before 980; A. Campbell in *Chron.*, p. xiii, n. 2, preferred the latter part of the period 978–88. The former seems more likely because Æthelweard clearly stated that no Viking fleet has attacked Britain since the Battle of Brunanburh in 937, *Chron.*, p. 54; the *Anglo-Saxon Chronicle* 'C' and 'D', s.a. 980, ed. Whitelock, *EHD*, p. 232, recorded that Viking raids were renewed in that year. Campbell's *terminus post quem* is based on the assumption that the final chapter headings for Edward the Martyr's and Æthelred II's reigns are strictly contemporary with the extant ending in 975, which must remain unproven: Barker, 'Cottonian Fragments', pp. 54–6.

[13] A classic statement of this theme is D. A. Bullough, 'The Continental Background to the Tenth-Century English Reform', in his *Carolingian Renewal: Sources and Heritage* (Manchester, 1991), pp. 272–96; Wormald, *Making*, consistently stresses how the 'political culture of the first English kingdom was European' (p. 30), and in particular, Carolingian; T. Reuter, 'Introduction: Reading the Tenth Century', in Reuter, ed., *NCMH* III, *c. 900–c. 1024* (Cambridge, 1999), p. 9.

[14] McKitterick, *Carolingians*, ch. 6; KL, p. 110.

[15] See, for example, S. Keynes, 'King Æthelstan's Books', in M. Lapidge and H. Gneuss, eds., *Learning and Literature in Anglo-Saxon England: Studies Presented to Peter Clemoes on the Occasion of his Sixty-Fifth Birthday* (Cambridge, 1985), pp. 143–201; J. Campbell, 'England, France, Flanders and Germany in the Reign of Ethelred II: Some Comparisons and Connections', in his *Essays in Anglo-Saxon History* (London, 1986), pp. 191–207; K. Leyser, 'The Ottonians and Wessex', in his *Communications and Power in Medieval Europe*, 1, *The Carolingian and Ottonian Centuries*, ed. T. Reuter (London, 1994), pp. 73–104.

the times. Revolutionary changes in the matrix of social and political power came in the wake of external invasion and crisis in the Carolingian regime, demanding new forms of history to legitimate, explain and sometimes criticise new kinds of rule. The monastic, clerical and lay literates fulfilled their accepted role by producing them.[16]

Given Æthelweard's potential links to continental exemplars via Essen, as well as the prominent role taken by his family and himself in the court politics of Anglo-Saxon England from at least the reign of Eadwig (955–9), this chapter argues that his *Chronicon* is a self-conscious response to the rise of new forms of power in tenth-century England, a political as well as a literary act akin to those of near-contemporaries such as Widukind, writing from the great Saxon monastery of Corvey.

That a monk and a layman could engage in similar work should keep us alert to anachronistic oppositions between secular and sacred forms of writing or experience. But we should also not be shy of recognising that someone like Æthelweard did indeed have different interests and concerns from those in the cloister that might affect the nature of his writing; hence the importance of some kind of biographical understanding to set alongside a purely textual one. We should also not be shy of using words like 'intellectual' to describe early medieval lay people. Unlike their modern counterparts, early medieval thinkers could never adopt a stance of disengagement from institutions of social and political authority. To have access to the skills and technologies of literacy or to the sources of authoritative orality in the Carolingian world marked an individual out as a member of a tiny elite; and to be part of the elite, lay or ecclesiastical, meant identification with the sources of established power, whether they be located in court, local office, church or monastery. While none offered – or would have had the tools to offer – a disinterested critique of the institutional or personal bases of power itself, they could be critical of contemporary manifestations of that power; witness, for example, Einhard and Nithard from among those discussed in earlier chapters of the present volume. Intellectuals were more than merely 'learned' people; they actively participated in shaping the values and ideologies of their societies and of mediating them to its members, at all levels of the social hierarchy. This organizing and directing quality, evident in the lives as well as the literary remains of the individuals in this book, marks them out as a certain type of 'intellectual'.

---

[16] The classic statement is M. Bloch, *Feudal Society*, trans. L. A. Manyon (London, 1961), esp. ch. 3. For a recent and characteristically stimulating attempt to understand these changes, see R. I. Moore, *The First European Revolution, c. 970–1215* (Oxford, 2000), esp. pp. 39–44.

The word is applicable to the early Middle Ages as long as we remember that we are describing people less akin to the idealised *philosophe*, meditating on abstract ideas, than to the Victorian public moralist, working to disseminate certain kinds of ethical and cultural models into society. The focus in this chapter is on the questions one individual living in an England caught between a sub-Carolingian and a post-Carolingian identity could ask about the near and distant past, on the choices he made and the factors determining why he may have made them. But if these help us to reach a better understanding of the roles a lay intellectual might have had in later Anglo-Saxon England and, perhaps by acting as a foil to the figures of the Carolingian noontide that occupy most of this book, continental Europe too, then that seems ample justification for taking Æthelweard seriously.

Patrick Geary has called the end of the first millennium an 'age of forgetting', in which 'Ruling dynasties began to deal with the problem of tidying up the often messy memory of their rise to power.'[17] Yet if the decades around 1000 AD witnessed the climax, the origins of these exercises in genealogical hygiene are surely to be found in the Carolingian eighth and ninth centuries, beginning with the efforts of the *Annales Regni Francorum* to shape the untidy elevation of the Pippinid clan into something approaching manifest destiny.[18] These interconnections between memory, kinship and power were at the heart of Æthelweard's historical vision, concerns which place him in a continuum with otherwise very different figures in this book, Einhard, Nithard, Dhuoda and, particularly, Alfred. Indeed, while the correspondence with Matilda provided the occasion for his surviving work, both his prefatory letters and the *Chronicon* reflect a vivid personal commitment to the history of the West Saxon royal dynasty with which Æthelweard strongly identified himself as a descendant of King Æthelred I (866–71), fourth son of King Æthelwulf of Wessex and elder brother of Alfred himself.[19] This commitment to the memory of his own kinsmen was, nevertheless, accompanied by the 'forgetting' and 'tidying up' characteristic of Carolingian and post-Carolingian historiography that proved as central to Æthelweard's project as any found on the continent. As we shall see, the fourth book of his chronicle, dealing with the years from the death of Æthelwulf in 855 to the death of Edgar in 975, came to be

---

[17] P. Geary, *Phantoms of Remembrance: Memory and Oblivion at the End of the First Millennium* (Princeton, NJ, 1994), p. 27.
[18] For a recent discussion, see R. McKitterick, 'The Illusion of Royal Power in the Carolingian Annals', *EHR* 115 (2000), pp. 1–20.
[19] *Chron.*, pp. 2, 38–9.

structured around a systematic omission of all events that questioned the distribution of power within the royal kindred that had prevailed since the reign of Alfred. It carefully avoided the three great internal crises of the West Saxon royal family in favour of a narrative of genealogical continuity and the peaceful passing of the crown from ruler to heir. The revolt of Æthelwold, who allied with the Vikings of the Danelaw to challenge the accession of Edward the Elder, disappeared from the record, even though the Battle of the Holme (902), at which Æthelwold was killed, did not. The murky transition from Eadwig to Edgar between the years 957–9 was presented as a seamless one, while the most contentious succession of all, fought out between the supporters of Edward the Martyr and Æthelred II from 975 to 978, seems to have stopped Æthelweard's work dead in its tracks. Despite the existence of headings referring to putative chapters on the murder of Edward and the deeds of Æthelred, the extant *Chronicon*'s fourth and final book ends with the passing of the noble King Edgar.

That Æthelweard almost certainly had a personal interest in all three of these challenges to the solidity of the royal kindred suggests that the silence surrounding them in his work may have been more than a purely editorial decision. As one of Æthelred I's two (known) sons, Æthelwold may well have been Æthelweard's direct ancestor; he was at least a blood relation. King Eadwig probably married Æthelweard's sister Ælfgifu, a connection that was still provoking controversy among monastic circles four decades later. And while the exact patterning of alliances remains unclear, both Æthelweard and his family were closely involved, through ties of kinship and patronage, with each of the opposed factions that coalesced around the sons of Edgar in 975. Reading Æthelweard's *Chronicon* in the light of his role as an active member of a major noble family complicates understanding of both its form and content. It draws attention to the way his textual choices interacted with questions of power and authority while demonstrating that the work was as engaged in the Anglo-Saxon political landscape as it was tailored for the abbess of Essen.

Despite Æthelweard's royal connections, there is almost no direct evidence for his immediate ancestors, including his father.[20] Nevertheless, what is clear is that by the middle decades of the tenth century, when they first begin to assume a historical presence, the family was in a position of

---

[20] One candidate is Ælfgar 'the king's kinsman in Devon' who died in 962, *ASC* 'A': A. Williams, *Land, Power and Politics: The Family and Career of Odda of Deerhurst*, The Deerhurst Lecture 1996/67, p. 24, n. 34; another might be Edmund, ealdorman of the Western Shires *c*. 949–64: C. R. Hart, *The Early Charters of Northern England and the North Midlands* (Leicester, 1975), pp. 331–2.

real power. For there is some evidence to suggest that in 956 the new King Eadwig married Æthelweard's sister, Ælfgifu, implying that they were already a weighty presence in the kingdom and able to offer support to the nascent regime.[21]

Æthelweard's earliest attestations at the royal council date from the mid-960s and he seems to have died of natural causes in 998 or soon after.[22] It is probably a reasonable guess that he was born somewhere around 950; his family's intimate connection with the court and access to the intellectual traditions of Winchester during Æthelweard's boyhood may certainly go some way towards explaining his subsequent development as a lay literate. Whatever the truth of these obscure matters, some sort of alliance with Eadwig was remembered with pride by Æthelweard in later years as his *Chronicon* makes a particular effort to give a positive interpretation of the king, noting that his good looks won him the nick-name 'All-fair': 'He held the kingdom continuously for four years, and deserved to be loved.'[23] This representation of Eadwig provides a useful counterpoint to that more familiar to historians, derived from monastic texts friendly to Edgar and especially from B's *Life* of Dunstan, which tells of a foolish and contemptible youth, remembered largely for bedding during his own coronation feast not only Ælfgifu but her mother Æthelgifu as well.[24] If Michael Lapidge's dating of the *Life* to the first part of the decade 995–1005 is correct, it is possible that Æthelweard could have seen it; since Æthelgifu was almost certainly his own mother too the reaction must have been worth witnessing.[25]

These monastic sources, which stress the malign influence of Æthelgifu over Eadwig, when allied to Æthelweard's evident affection for the king, and his family's privileged relationship with the throne during the mid-950s, have been interpreted as evidence that an 'Æthelweardian connection' was deliberately built up in opposition to a section of the political establishment inherited from the previous reigns of Edmund and Eadred.[26] The

---

[21] This identification of Queen Ælfgifu as Æthelweard's sister was first suggested in *Anglo-Saxon Wills*, ed. D. Whitelock (Cambridge, 1930), p. 119, and has been accepted by most historians since; for one dissenting voice, see C. R. Hart, 'The Will of Ælfgifu', *The Danelaw* (London, 1992), pp. 455–65, at 464.
[22] Barker, 'Anglo-Saxon Chronicle', p. 85; S. Keynes, *The Diplomas of King Æthelred 'the Unready', 978–1016* (Cambridge, 1980), p. 192, n. 139.
[23] *Chron.*, p. 55.
[24] *Memorials of St Dunstan*, ed. W. Stubbs, Rolls Series 63 (London, 1874), pp. 32–4.
[25] M. Lapidge, 'B. and the *Vita S. Dunstani*', in N. Ramsey, M. Sparks and T. Tatton-Brown, eds., *St Dunstan: His Life, Times and Cult* (Woodbridge, 1992), pp. 247–59, at 247 and n. 2.
[26] Most clearly in B. Yorke, 'Æthelmær: the Foundation of the Abbey at Cerne and the Politics of the Tenth Century', in K. Barker, ed., *The Cerne Abbey Millennium Lectures* (Cerne, 1988), pp. 15–26,

exile to Flanders of Dunstan, the reforming abbot of Glastonbury, and the declining influence of Æthelstan Half-King, the powerful ealdorman of East Anglia, has been directly related to the rise of Ælfgifu's kinsmen at court from early 956.[27] Although the absence of any clear candidate for Æthelweard's father suggests that the immediate family was always somewhat marginal to events, it is undoubtedly the case that several individuals claiming kinship with them did directly benefit from royal patronage, none more so than the brothers Ælfheah and Ælfhere, the former becoming ealdorman of Central Wessex in 959, the latter ealdorman of Mercia in 956.[28] Yet the tensions this palace revolution generated fractured the regime of Eadwig just a year later, as the *ætheling* Edgar was raised to the kingship of Mercia and Northumbria in circumstances that are still shrouded in mystery. Archbishop Oda of Canterbury divorced Ælfgifu from her royal husband 'because they were too closely related', as the *Anglo-Saxon Chronicle* put it.[29] In the absence of any evidence for more recent consanguinity, we must assume that it was Ælfgifu's descent from Æthelred I that aroused the ire of Oda and the reforming lobby in the Church, although that would derive from an extremely rigorous interpretation of canon law, inviting the suspicion that factional rivalries were involved in the archbishop's action.[30] Eadwig died in 959 without heirs and Edgar assumed the throne of a reunited English kingdom, 'crowned to rule, an admirable king' in Æthelweard's words.[31]

There seems a curious disjunction between this association with political conflict and the conspicuously loyalist quality of the fourth book of Æthelweard's *Chronicon*. He ironed out the awkward question of Edgar's messy rise to the throne, stating without qualification that Eadwig had ruled for four years and implying that his authority had remained unchallenged throughout England. This can be thought of as a pro-Eadwig analogue of the 'B' and 'C' versions of the *Anglo-Saxon Chronicle*, which implied that Edgar had become king of the Mercian kingdom in 957

---

at 16–17; and Barker, 'Æthelwold and the Politics of the Tenth Century', in Yorke, ed., *Bishop Æthelwold: His Career and Influence* (Woodbridge, 1988), pp. 65–88, at 76–7.

[27] For example, N. P. Brooks, 'The Career of St Dunstan', in Ramsey *et al.*, *St Dunstan*, pp. 1–23, at pp. 15–16; C. R. Hart, 'Athelstan "Half-King" and his Family', *The Danelaw*, pp. 582–5.

[28] A. Williams, '*Princeps Merciorum gentis*: The Family, Career and Connections of Ælfhere, Ealdorman of Mercia, 956–83', *ASE* 10 (1982), pp. 143–72, at 147–57.

[29] ASC 'C' and 'D', s.a. 957; P. Stafford, *Unification and Conquest: A Political and Social History of England in the Tenth and Eleventh Centuries* (London, 1989), pp. 47–50.

[30] However, N. P. Brooks, *The Early History of the Church at Canterbury* (Leicester, 1984), pp. 224–7, warns us against simply assuming Oda was a personal enemy of Eadwig.

[31] *Chron.*, p. 55.

in unexceptional circumstances. Æthelweard was certainly not averse to adding local colour and knowledge to his chronicle, so the painstakingly bland non-partisan and consensual quality is striking at this point, almost as if his writing aimed at mediating between the competing memories of the two kings, scrupulously giving each their due, while concentrating on the maintenance of the fabric of royalty rather than its frayed edges.

This narrative mediation takes on social significance when the identity of Æthelweard's maternal kindred is taken into account. Hart has suggested that the most economical way to explain the recorded descent of the estate of Risborough in Buckinghamshire is to assume that Æthelgifu, mother of Ælfgifu and quite possibly of Æthelweard himself, was the sister of Æthelstan Half-King.[32] If this identification is accepted then the Half-King was a significantly closer relation of Ælfgifu than men like Ælfheah and Ælfhere. While such uterine bonds were coming under pressure from the transition to agnatic lineages across western Europe in the tenth century, there is no reason to believe that the marriage of Eadwig to the niece of the Half-King should not have strengthened the latter's immediate position, rather than weakening it. Indeed, given the difficulty of identifying Æthelweard's father, it seems possible that the Half-King was in practical terms Ælfgifu's most important living relative in 956.[33] From this perspective, Eadwig's reign looks less like the ousting of one faction by another, than the fracturing of a single 'king's kindred' for reasons that are probably much more complex and visceral than we have direct access to through our problematic narrative sources.[34] Rather than contributing to divisions within the kingdom, Æthelweard and his kin may have experienced the confused loyalties characteristic of extra-legal dispute settlement that may have encouraged them to exert a mediating influence between the Half-King, his sons and followers, and Ælfheah and Ælfhere of Mercia and

---

[32] Hart, 'Will of Ælfgifu', pp. 460–2, although Hart would not accept the association between Ælfgifu and Æthelweard: see above, n. 21.

[33] A. Wareham, 'The Transformation of Kinship and the Family in Late Anglo-Saxon England', *EME* 10 (2001), pp. 375–99, esp. 385–90, argues that patrilineages were already the preferred kinship model in the mid tenth century, though the balance between preference and pragmatism needs further study.

[34] A point also made by C. Wickham, *Problems in doing Comparative History*, The Reuter Lecture 2004 (University of Southampton, 2005), pp. 23–5. Hart, 'Athelstan "Half-King"', pp. 569–70, notes that the Half-King was likely to be part of a cadet branch of the West Saxon royal family and was certainly the foster-father of the *ætheling* Edgar (p. 579). The importance of claims to royal kinship is stressed by Wormald, 'Strange Affair of the Selsey Bishopric', pp. 137–8. For more details on the royal kindred and the interconnections of the nobility, see R. Fleming, *Kings and Lords in Conquest England* (Cambridge, 1991), pp. 22–39.

their kinsmen and supporters.[35] It was thought proper in Anglo-Saxon England that ealdormen would intervene in disputes as arbiters.[36] Seen in this light, Æthelweard's historiographical strategy of dissolving any suggestion of conflict within the royal kindred in the wider panorama of admirable rulers peacefully devolving royal authority through the generations seems less the product of an unoriginal mind than the activities of a natural mediator and diplomat continued by other means.[37]

During the last decade of Edgar's reign an Æthelweard *minister* who can fairly confidently be identified as the future chronicler began to witness royal charters and was awarded the title of *discifer* or steward in the early 970s.[38] His first definite appearance as ealdorman was in a charter of 977 from King Edward the Martyr, granting him extensive lands in Cornwall.[39] This document assumes a wider importance when we come to interpreting Æthelweard's response to the violence that accompanied the years 975–8, once more centring around the rivalries of Ælfhere of Mercia and the family of the Half-King, now represented by his son, Ealdorman Æthelwine of East Anglia. Again, Æthelweard's kindred have been implicated as partisans of Ælfhere, Queen Ælfthryth and those who supported the succession of her son, Æthelred.[40] The only direct evidence for this, however, is Ælfgifu's will, with its benefactions to Ælfthryth and one of her sons, unnamed in the document.[41] One piece of circumstantial evidence perhaps lies in the fact that as the daughter of Ordgar, ealdorman in the south-west from 964–71, Ælfthryth and her kin had been near-neighbours of Æthelweard in Devon. They were also possibly related through marriage.[42] But, as under Eadwig, other links of kinship and patronage probably cross-cut these local loyalties. If the suggestion made above that Æthelweard's mother and the Half-King were siblings is

---

[35] 'Not infrequently intervenors were people caught in the middle, bound to both sides': W. I. Miller, *Bloodtaking and Peacemaking: Feud, Law, and Society in Saga Iceland* (Chicago, IL, 1990), p. 265.

[36] S. Baxter, 'The Leofwinesons: Power, Property and Patronage in the Early English Kingdom' (D.Phil. thesis, University of Oxford, 2002), pp. 105–7.

[37] For Æthelweard's career as a negotiator in the 990s, see *ASC* 'C', s.a. 994; S. Keynes, 'The Historical Context of the Battle of Maldon', in D. Scragg, ed., *The Battle of Maldon. AD 991* (Oxford, 1991), pp. 81–113, at 103–7.

[38] Barker, 'Anglo-Saxon Chronicle', p. 85; C. R. Hart, *The Early Charters of Eastern England* (Leicester, 1966), pp. 172, 174; S. 782, 792.

[39] S. 832, trans. Whitelock, *EHD* no. 115, I, pp. 566–7.   [40] Yorke, 'Æthelmaer', pp. 17–18.

[41] Whitelock, *Anglo-Saxon Wills*, p. 120, identified Edward the Martyr as the unnamed *ætheling*; but since the gift to Ælfthryth follows immediately, one of her own sons, either Edmund (d. 972) or Æthelred, seems at least as likely as her step-son Edward.

[42] Ælfthryth was the wife of Æthelwold, the Half-King's son, from 956–62 before marrying Edgar: Hart, 'Athelstan "Half-King"', pp. 584, n. 57, 589. If Æthelgifu was indeed the Half-King's sister, then Ælfthryth would have been Æthelweard's cousin by marriage.

in unexceptional circumstances. Æthelweard was certainly not averse to adding local colour and knowledge to his chronicle, so the painstakingly bland non-partisan and consensual quality is striking at this point, almost as if his writing aimed at mediating between the competing memories of the two kings, scrupulously giving each their due, while concentrating on the maintenance of the fabric of royalty rather than its frayed edges.

This narrative mediation takes on social significance when the identity of Æthelweard's maternal kindred is taken into account. Hart has suggested that the most economical way to explain the recorded descent of the estate of Risborough in Buckinghamshire is to assume that Æthelgifu, mother of Ælfgifu and quite possibly of Æthelweard himself, was the sister of Æthelstan Half-King.[32] If this identification is accepted then the Half-King was a significantly closer relation of Ælfgifu than men like Ælfheah and Ælfhere. While such uterine bonds were coming under pressure from the transition to agnatic lineages across western Europe in the tenth century, there is no reason to believe that the marriage of Eadwig to the niece of the Half-King should not have strengthened the latter's immediate position, rather than weakening it. Indeed, given the difficulty of identifying Æthelweard's father, it seems possible that the Half-King was in practical terms Ælfgifu's most important living relative in 956.[33] From this perspective, Eadwig's reign looks less like the ousting of one faction by another, than the fracturing of a single 'king's kindred' for reasons that are probably much more complex and visceral than we have direct access to through our problematic narrative sources.[34] Rather than contributing to divisions within the kingdom, Æthelweard and his kin may have experienced the confused loyalties characteristic of extra-legal dispute settlement that may have encouraged them to exert a mediating influence between the Half-King, his sons and followers, and Ælfheah and Ælfhere of Mercia and

---

[32] Hart, 'Will of Ælfgifu', pp. 460–2, although Hart would not accept the association between Ælfgifu and Æthelweard: see above, n. 21.

[33] A. Wareham, 'The Transformation of Kinship and the Family in Late Anglo-Saxon England', *EME* 10 (2001), pp. 375–99, esp. 385–90, argues that patrilineages were already the preferred kinship model in the mid tenth century, though the balance between preference and pragmatism needs further study.

[34] A point also made by C. Wickham, *Problems in doing Comparative History*, The Reuter Lecture 2004 (University of Southampton, 2005), pp. 23–5. Hart, 'Athelstan "Half-King"', pp. 569–70, notes that the Half-King was likely to be part of a cadet branch of the West Saxon royal family and was certainly the foster-father of the *ætheling* Edgar (p. 579). The importance of claims to royal kinship is stressed by Wormald, 'Strange Affair of the Selsey Bishopric', pp. 137–8. For more details on the royal kindred and the interconnections of the nobility, see R. Fleming, *Kings and Lords in Conquest England* (Cambridge, 1991), pp. 22–39.

their kinsmen and supporters.³⁵ It was thought proper in Anglo-Saxon England that ealdormen would intervene in disputes as arbiters.³⁶ Seen in this light, Æthelweard's historiographical strategy of dissolving any suggestion of conflict within the royal kindred in the wider panorama of admirable rulers peacefully devolving royal authority through the generations seems less the product of an unoriginal mind than the activities of a natural mediator and diplomat continued by other means.³⁷

During the last decade of Edgar's reign an Æthelweard *minister* who can fairly confidently be identified as the future chronicler began to witness royal charters and was awarded the title of *discifer* or steward in the early 970s.³⁸ His first definite appearance as ealdorman was in a charter of 977 from King Edward the Martyr, granting him extensive lands in Cornwall.³⁹ This document assumes a wider importance when we come to interpreting Æthelweard's response to the violence that accompanied the years 975–8, once more centring around the rivalries of Ælfhere of Mercia and the family of the Half-King, now represented by his son, Ealdorman Æthelwine of East Anglia. Again, Æthelweard's kindred have been implicated as partisans of Ælfhere, Queen Ælfthryth and those who supported the succession of her son, Æthelred.⁴⁰ The only direct evidence for this, however, is Ælfgifu's will, with its benefactions to Ælfthryth and one of her sons, unnamed in the document.⁴¹ One piece of circumstantial evidence perhaps lies in the fact that as the daughter of Ordgar, ealdorman in the south-west from 964–71, Ælfthryth and her kin had been near-neighbours of Æthelweard in Devon. They were also possibly related through marriage.⁴² But, as under Eadwig, other links of kinship and patronage probably cross-cut these local loyalties. If the suggestion made above that Æthelweard's mother and the Half-King were siblings is

---

³⁵ 'Not infrequently intervenors were people caught in the middle, bound to both sides': W. I. Miller, *Bloodtaking and Peacemaking: Feud, Law, and Society in Saga Iceland* (Chicago, IL, 1990), p. 265.
³⁶ S. Baxter, 'The Leofwinesons: Power, Property and Patronage in the Early English Kingdom' (D.Phil. thesis, University of Oxford, 2002), pp. 105–7.
³⁷ For Æthelweard's career as a negotiator in the 990s, see *ASC* 'C', s.a. 994; S. Keynes, 'The Historical Context of the Battle of Maldon', in D. Scragg, ed., *The Battle of Maldon. AD 991* (Oxford, 1991), pp. 81–113, at 103–7.
³⁸ Barker, 'Anglo-Saxon Chronicle', p. 85; C. R. Hart, *The Early Charters of Eastern England* (Leicester, 1966), pp. 172, 174; S. 782, 792.
³⁹ S. 832, trans. Whitelock, *EHD* no. 115, I, pp. 566–7.   ⁴⁰ Yorke, 'Æthelmaer', pp. 17–18.
⁴¹ Whitelock, *Anglo-Saxon Wills*, p. 120, identified Edward the Martyr as the unnamed *ætheling*; but since the gift to Ælfthryth follows immediately, one of her own sons, either Edmund (d. 972) or Æthelred, seems at least as likely as her step-son Edward.
⁴² Ælfthryth was the wife of Æthelwold, the Half-King's son, from 956–62 before marrying Edgar: Hart, 'Athelstan "Half-King"', pp. 584, n. 57, 589. If Æthelgifu was indeed the Half-King's sister, then Ælfthyrth would have been Æthelweard's cousin by marriage.

admitted as a possibility then Æthelweard and Æthelwine may have been cousins. More certain is the fact that as a recipient of significant Cornish estates in 977 the ealdorman of the Western Shires was clearly thought to be a loyal supporter at court only a few months before the young king's killing.

As in the crises of Eadwig's rule, the disputes of 975–8 appear less the clash of two discrete kindreds than the breakdown of a single 'king's kindred' and an attempt to re-negotiate the balance of power within it. Although it looks less likely than it once did that Edward's murder in 978 was the result of a conspiracy centred around Ælfthryth and Ælfhere with the aim of securing the throne for Æthelred, the attacks on monastic property and the scramble to recover lost land were clearly aligned with struggles for power within the kindred between Ælfhere and Æthelwine.[43] Even if Æthelweard's apparent difficulties in continuing his *Chronicon* beyond the death of Edgar were not motivated by direct embarrassment over the guilt of his 'party' in the death of Edward, questions surrounding the killing and the ambiguous roles played in it by the higher nobility may still have affected him. Although neither text is contemporary or disinterested, Byrthferth's *Life of St Oswald* did specifically accuse Æthelred's thegns – including a royal *discifer* – of stabbing the king, while the 'D' version of the *Anglo-Saxon Chronicle* claimed that the dead king's kinsmen would not avenge him and 'wished to blot out his memory on earth'.[44] If the last extant chapter headings that refer to Edward and his murder ('De regimine Eaduuerdi regis et de nece ipsius') are indeed Æthelweard's own, then the prospect of narrating these events may well have strained to the limit his basic desire to represent tenth-century English dynastic history as consensual and unproblematic.[45] For Æthelweard to have supported the idea that Æthelred assumed the throne without violence – even if only by casting a veil of silence over the whole affair – would have been tantamount to denying those who had supported Edward's succession. A strong, albeit not watertight, case can be made that in the shape of Æthelwine and his sons these supporters of Edward were also Æthelweard's kinsmen. Yet to have written that Edward had been

---

[43] See S. J. Ridyard, *The Royal Saints of Anglo-Saxon England: A Study of West Saxon and East Anglian Cults* (Cambridge, 1988), pp. 44–50, 154–69.

[44] *Historians of the Church of York and its Archbishops*, ed. J. Raine, Rolls Series 71 (London, 1879), pp. 448–9; M. Lapidge, 'Byrthferth and Oswald', in N. P. Brooks and C. Cubitt, eds., *St Oswald of Worcester: Life and Influence* (London, 1996), pp. 64–83, at 79–80, prudently warns against accepting too many of Byrhtferth's details as historical fact; *ASC* 'C' and 'D', s.a. 978.

[45] *Chron.*, p. 34.

deliberately killed would have been to cast doubt on the new regime of Æthelred, on whom Æthelweard depended for political and material patronage, and would have raised some awkward questions about the guilt of the royal thegns. There is no evidence to contradict the statement of the 'D' *Chronicle* that Edward's death went unpunished; Æthelred appears to have inherited the elite of his father and half-brother unchanged.[46] Personal anxiety may also have played a part. As a royal kinsman who had received extensive lands in Cornwall and most probably his ealdormanry from Edward, Æthelweard must have been one of those who felt some pressure to honour his dead lord in an age acutely attuned to the value and fragility of heroic loyalty.

It is in the nature of much of early medieval history that definitive provable links between the conditions of production for our surviving texts and the events they themselves narrate are lacking. However, at the very least, Anglo-Saxon historians need to consider whether Æthelweard was much more closely entwined in the events that abruptly ended his chronicle than a purely literary reading of his work would suggest. By 1014 Archbishop Wulfstan of York was preaching that the death of Edward had cast a long shadow over England; four decades earlier Æthelweard could well have found his pen frozen by its chill.[47]

The fourth book of Æthelweard's *Chronicon* dealing with tenth-century England is the tidiest defence we have of the West Saxon dynasty's right to rule England and the throne-worthiness of each ruler of that dynasty from Æthelwulf down to Edgar. That those historical purposes are never made explicit does not mean that they are not there; historians in the early Middle Ages devoted little time to philosophical or methodological exegesis. The strategies of all intellectuals, lay or otherwise, in the Carolingian era found common ground precisely in their aversion to the constructed, provisional and contingent aspects of experience. They knew, as Patricia Crone has noted, that 'all societies work best if their rules are felt to be self-evident, inescapable and effortless'.[48] For Æthelweard and many others that entailed deliberate amnesia, a purposeful forgetting of the kin-strife and antagonism that constituted the murky underside of each glorious reign and the equally purposeful remembering of a natural order. Not that he was always silent about the violence that accompanied dynastic politics; his poetic embroidering of the story of the 786 Cynewulf–Cyneheard feud precisely at the moment when the conflict of kinship and lordship arises

---

[46] Keynes, *Diplomas*, p. 175.   [47] *ASC* s.a. 978, Whitelock, *EHD* I, pp. 230–1; cf. *Chron.*, pp. xi–xii.
[48] Crone, *Pre-Industrial Societies* (Oxford, 1989), p. 118.

The lay intellectual in Anglo-Saxon England 231

deserves closer scrutiny in the light of his own experiences.[49] But that act of regicide was two centuries old and insulated from the actualities of the present.

Despite some characterisations which have portrayed Æthelweard as a kind of armchair antiquarian, picking over the bones of ancient history for their own sake, his imagination was always attuned to the present-day implications of his writing.[50] Geary's 'tidying up' of dynastic history is just as central to the narrative of Æthelweard's earlier books, although the sources of legitimation and authority are subtly different, with ecclesiastical patterns more clearly visible in places. Indeed, it has not perhaps been adequately appreciated how Æthelweard's essentially secular interpretative scheme takes on significant providential undertones at different points in his *Chronicon*. Sacred and secular chronologies jostle each other for space in the opening pages, before the latter asserts its dominance. But at times of heightened emotion, such as the accession of Ecgberht to the throne of Wessex or the victory at Brunanburh, Christian notions of time return to challenge purely worldly forms of order. James Campbell has drawn attention to the fact that Æthelweard was committed to the still relatively new term *Angli* to describe the ethnic – as opposed to the ecclesiastical – composition of the Anglo-Saxon kingdoms, to the extent that he coined the term 'West English (*occidentales*)' to describe the inhabitants of Wessex, an ethnographic neologism expanded to those of Essex, Sussex and eventually the Danelaw ('North English').[51] In doing so Æthelweard unexpectedly took on the mantle of successor to Bede by expanding the monk of Jarrow's vision of a single Church of the *gens Anglorum* in Britain to encompass the secular sphere more fully and complete the 'Anglicisation' of the Saxon peoples that had achieved renewed momentum under Alfred.[52] But the wider importance of all this lies in the transition of Æthelweard's vocabulary from 'Saxon', used of his pagan forebears, to 'English' – with all its overtones of Gregory the Great and missionary enthusiasm – which only becomes an active and systematic presence in his narrative after the conversion of Æthelberht of Kent.[53] Here following Bede's own decisive change in terminology in Book 1, chapter 23 of the *Ecclesiastical History*, the

---

[49] *Chron.*, pp. 22–4; cf. *ASC* 'A', s.a. 755; also Lutz, 'Æthelweard's *Chronicon*', pp. 181–4.
[50] *Chron.*, pp. xxxiv–vi. [51] Campbell, 'England, *c.* 991', p. 166; e.g., *Chron.*, pp. 18, 19, 21, 47.
[52] For the limits of Bede's *gens Anglorum* in the secular world, see N. P. Brooks, *Bede and the English*, The Jarrow Lecture 1999/2000, pp. 8–10; for Alfred, see S. Foot, 'The Making of *Angelcynn*: English Identity Before the Norman Conquest', *TRHS* 6th ser. 6 (1996), pp. 25–49.
[53] *Chron.*, p. 17; cf. p. 9, where it is explained that *Britannia* is now called 'Anglia' because it was conquered by *Angli*.

shift from 'Saxon' to 'English' was the way to mark the wider sense of ethnic redemption and transfiguration the Anglo-Saxons believed had been experienced at their entry into the Christian Church, symbolised in Old English re-tellings of the Biblical Exodus and memories of their own ancestral migration from the continent to Britain.[54]

Æthelweard promised Matilda at the beginning of his *Chronicon* 'wars and slayings of men and no small wreck of navies on the waves of ocean ... [and] the arrival of our ancestors in Britain from Germany'.[55] The first book did indeed offer a prose 'epic' of the *adventus Saxonum*, not uncritical of the savagery and heathenism of Hengest and Horsa, yet aware of their martial prowess and good fortune. This very un-Carolingian interest in the pagan and barbarian antiquity of Anglo-Saxon England gave the earlier parts of his chronicle as much the quality of a social and cultural charter for West Saxon rule as the later chapters directly concerned with contemporary kingship. Following the shape of the *Anglo-Saxon Chronicle*, but with greater narrative economy, Æthelweard's *Chronicon* proceeded to explain how the 'West English' arrived under Cerdic and Cynric, how they conquered the Britons and seized their lands and, by the third book, how their descendants came to be rulers of England.

But his was not a work of English or even 'West English' history except incidentally. It was a work of family piety and remembrance, and an assertion of kin relationships past and present. As he wrote to Matilda, it was 'the stock of our family' that provided the work with its dynamic force, and it was when tracing the descent of that stock that the most extreme forms of commemoration and forgetting entered his work.[56] The great set-piece act of remembrance both in the Alfredian *Anglo-Saxon Chronicle* and in Æthelweard's history was the genealogy of King Æthelwulf, a list of West Saxon rulers that has up to fifty generations back to Adam and Christ himself in the former, truncated to a still considerable thirty-two generations in the latter.

Æthelweard's recitation differs in several places from all extant versions of Æthelwulf's genealogy, though how many of the discrepancies of detail are due to alternative manuscript traditions, independent invention or personal knowledge on the part of the ealdorman is impossible to judge. However, given what we know of Æthelweard's sophistication as a historian

---

[54] Brooks, *Bede and the English*, p. 15; N. Howe, *Migration and Mythmaking in Anglo-Saxon England* (New Haven, CT, 1989); P. Battles, '*Genesis A* and the Anglo-Saxon "Migration Myth"', *ASE* 29 (2000), pp. 43–66.
[55] *Chron.*, p. 1. [56] *Chron.*, p. 38.

and stylist, it seems too easy to assume that his truncation of the royal genealogy simply reflects his mechanical copying of a lost early version of the *Chronicle*. If he, an ealdorman and self-styled descendant of West Saxon royalty, was unaware (or did not care) that the genealogies of the ruling house had been extended back to Adam and Christ for the best part of a century then historians need seriously to reconsider their ideas about how such texts circulated and functioned.

What must concern us immediately, though, is the shape of the genealogy, and in particular Æthelweard's treatment of the earliest ancestors of the West Saxon royal dynasty. His mythic story of the very first of these has ensured his work a place in medieval English literary history:

And this Sceaf arrived with one light ship in the island of the ocean which is called Skaney [*Scani*], with arms all round him. He was a very young boy, and unknown to the people of that land, but he was received by them, and they guarded him with diligent attention as one who belonged to them, and elected him king. From this family King Æthelwulf derived his descent.[57]

There is a clear relationship between this story of the foundling Sceaf and the origins of the Danish royal house in *Beowulf*, where Scyld son of Sceaf is said to have come as a child from over the seas.[58] While Æthelweard's belief that the water-borne founder of the dynasty was Sceaf himself rather than his son makes it unlikely that he relied directly on the surviving form of the poem, he may have had access to alternative versions in either written or oral form, or to an early king-list.[59] What is more important is that he found a space for the earliest origins of West Saxon – and hence English – kingship within a body of histories, circulating in a variety of forms, concerned with pagan Denmark. This was a remarkable claim to make in the tenth century, despite the role of the migration myth in Anglo-Saxon culture, in that it provided a clear alternative to the Alfredian ideology of Christian kingship that had extended the ancestral line into the Old Testament for the first time. Both the *Anglo-Saxon Chronicle* and Asser's *Life of Alfred* had lengthened the earlier West Saxon genealogies,

---

[57] *Chron.*, p. 33; cf. the use made of this passage by William of Malmesbury: *WMGR* II, 116, p. 176.
[58] For the sources of this story, see R. W. Chambers, *Beowulf: An Introduction*, 3rd edn (Cambridge, 1959), pp. 68–86. Despite its roots in Edwardian ethnology, there is still much to be gained from H. M. Chadwick, *The Origin of the English Nation* (Cambridge, 1907), pp. 269–302.
[59] For further discussion, see A. C. Murray, 'Beowulf, the Danish Invasions, and Royal Genealogy', in C. Chase, ed., *The Dating of Beowulf* (Toronto, 1981), pp. 101–11, at pp. 107–8; A. L. Meaney, 'Scyld Scefing and the Dating of *Beowulf* – Again', *Bulletin of the John Rylands Library* 71 (1989), pp. 7–40, at 13–20; R. North, *Heathen Gods in Old English Literature* (Cambridge, 1997), pp. 182–94; D. Anlezark, 'Sceaf, Japheth and the Origins of the Anglo-Saxons', *ASE* 31 (2002), pp. 13–46, at 19–21.

preserved in the late eighth-century 'Anglian Collection' and the so-called 'Genealogical Regnal List', by adding some two dozen extra generations back to Adam and by making Sceaf the son of Noah, born in the Ark.[60] Although Æthelweard's *Chronicon* followed the Alfredian extension of the genealogy back to Sceaf, it ignored all the biblical additions to the genealogy of Æthelwulf, placing the horizon of dynastic memory at those mysterious events on *Scani*. Ninth-century texts had sought to evoke an image of the West Saxon kings as biblical patriarchs. Whether through choice, his sources, or a mixture of the two, Æthelweard returned them to the harsher landscapes of the North Sea and Baltic coasts.

Although prestige of ancestry was usually associated with length of pedigree in Anglo-Saxon England, this truncation may have served the tenth-century nobleman's need for distinction more precisely than the universalist claims of the Alfredian genealogy. While the Old Testament provided a sacral quality to both Carolingian and English kingship, it also made clear that Adam and Noah were the common progenitors of all mankind. But ancestry can only provide historical justification for present inequalities of power when that ancestry is perceived as unique, as the transmission of charisma which other kindreds or individuals have never been able to access. By concentrating exclusively on the agnatic kindred running from Sceaf, Æthelweard more clearly distinguished both the royal lineage and his own from the rest of humanity. Moreover, if we are to think a lay intellectual culture might have existed in the early Middle Ages then attention should be paid to this revision of the genealogy of his ancestors.

The vision Æthelweard has left here is a resolutely secular one, breaking off his list precisely where ecclesiastical history was yoked to the heroic tradition. The suspicion that this move needs to be given more serious attention than it has hitherto received is confirmed when we look to the Continent, where concern with pedigree had also begun to develop among the lay aristocracy, the earliest surviving example being the genealogy of Count Arnulf I of Flanders produced in the monastery of St-Bertin by Witger during the 950s.[61] Arnulf's grandson and heir Arnulf II appears in

---

[60] See K. Sisam, 'Anglo-Saxon Royal Genealogies', *PBA* 39 (1953), pp. 287–348, at pp. 314–22; F. P. Magoun Jr, 'King Æthelwulf's Biblical Ancestors', *Modern Language Review* 46 (1951), pp. 249–50; T. D. Hill, 'The Myth of the Ark-Born Son of Noe and the West-Saxon Genealogical Tables', *Harvard Theological Review* 80 (1987), pp. 379–83; C. R. Davis, 'Cultural Assimilation in the Anglo-Saxon Royal Genealogies', *ASE* 21 (1992), pp. 23–36, at 28–32.

[61] *Genealogiae Comitum Flandriae*, PL 209, 929–31; J. Dunbabin, *France in the Making, 843–1180* (Oxford, 1985), pp. 71–2; E. Freise, 'Die "Genealogia Arnulfi comitis" des Priesters Witger', *FMS* 23 (1989), pp. 203–43.

Æthelweard's *Chronicon* as a great-great-grandson of Alfred the Great and it may well have been through his circle that the ealdorman became known to Abbess Matilda: the count was, Æthelweard wrote, *vicinus vester*.[62] Whatever the truth of this, Arnulf I was certainly as interested in length of descent-line as Æthelweard, and thanks to the fact that the count's grandfather Baldwin I had snatched Charles the Bald's daughter and married her in 862, the Carolingian royal house were annexed as his ancestors, albeit only affinal ones, with the shadow of the Merovingians beyond those again. But like Æthelweard, Witger preferred not to utilise biblical or ecclesiastical material in creating the pedigree – the auspiciously named St Arnulf of Metz is passed by without comment. By specifically locating current noble status solely in relation to wholly secular royal forebears, both Witger and Æthelweard offered a cultural model for aristocratic identity that might be regarded as 'lay'.

It has long been recognised that the interest in pedigree and kinship among *potentes* at the western end of the European continent during the tenth and eleventh centuries was a response to new forms of private power associated with crisis in the Carolingian imperial system from the 890s. Æthelweard's *Chronicon* paralleled the interests of his Frankish peers but was conceived in very different circumstances. While running the risk of gross simplification, we might characterise Francia as experiencing a decline in royal governance during the tenth century and a corresponding transformation of the Carolingian 'imperial aristocracy' into an assemblage of localised noble families organised as a series of regional hierarchies based on military power and landholding.[63] The English 'Grand Narrative' reverses that of the continent, being the story of the growth of ever more sophisticated and powerful forms of kingship and the integration of the regional centres into a single vertical hierarchy with the West Saxon crown at the top. Both the nobility and non-West Saxon royalty experienced this process. Throughout the eighth and into the earlier ninth centuries the royal genealogies and foundation legends of the Anglo-Saxon kingdoms were getting longer and more complex. From the reign of Alfred onwards the truncation and eventual obliteration of all dynastic and migration-era histories in the

---

[62] *Chron.*, p. 2; van Houts, 'Women and the Writing of History', pp. 66–7; Wareham, 'Transformation of Kinship', p. 388.

[63] The timing, extent and boundaries of these processes have been debated in a vast literature. For recent discussion, see T. Bisson, 'The Feudal Revolution', *P&P* 142 (1994), pp. 6–42; D. Barthélemy et al., 'Debate: the Feudal Revolution', *P&P* 152 (1996), pp. 191–223, and 155 (1997), pp. 177–225; Moore, *First European Revolution*, pp. 65–75. Wickham, *Problems in doing Comparative History*, offers, as its title suggests, a valuable comparative study of Francia and England.

Anglo-Saxon Chronicle except those of Wessex show an increasing intolerance towards alternative sovereignties, even historically eclipsed ones.[64] Despite an intriguing interest in Mercian history, Æthelweard's work is generally in the main West Saxon mould, concentrating overwhelmingly on the activities of the descendants of Cerdic, while clearly marginalising the important Northumbrian heroic tradition and ignoring the smaller kingdoms such as East Anglia or Essex altogether.[65] From this perspective, his comprehensive use of the ethnic label 'English' looks less about peaceful inclusion or anachronistic 'nationhood' than the cultural imperialism that accompanies a monopoly of effective violence.[66]

This structural situation has clear relevance for understanding Æthelweard's celebration of the rise of West Saxon and eventually English kingship in his *Chronicon*. As the dominant institution in tenth-century England, kings provided the central pillar around which a social memory of migration, conquest and final unification could be built. Æthelweard's genealogy of the West Saxon house grafted the charisma and order of antiquity onto the troubling and messy exercise of present royal power. What has been less often appreciated are the consequences for noble lineages of the survival of strong kingship in England, and especially for those such as that of Æthelweard, closely connected to royalty through kinship, marriage and favour. Unlike their continental contemporaries, the Anglo-Saxon higher nobility of the tenth century found their sense of dynastic identity eroded to nothing by the dominance of the royal lineage of Alfred. It is true that few continental genealogies were as long as that of Arnulf of Flanders; indeed, it is the shortness of aristocratic family memory by the twelfth century that most occupies historians of France.[67] But of Æthelweard's ancestors there is nothing *at all*, except his claim to be descended from Æthelred I, and this from a man with some expertise in the marriage strategies and relationships of kin in the senior royal

---

[64] A. Scharer, 'The Writing of History at King Alfred's Court', *EME* 5 (1996), pp. 177–206, at 180–1.

[65] *Chron.*, pp. 12–13, 24–5; cf. ASC 'A', s.a. 547, 560, 757. The Northumbrian genealogies of Ida and Ælle were finally expunged from 'A' at Christ Church, Canterbury, probably in the first half of the eleventh century. Æthelweard's interest in Mercia deserves closer attention, especially given his claim that Ealdorman Æthelred (883–911) was accorded the title *rex*: *Chron.*, p. 50; this is one of the main pieces of evidence for the downgrading of alternative royalty by Alfred; Barker, 'Anglo-Saxon Chronicle', pp. 82–5, 90–1, offers some suggestive starting-points.

[66] Cf. Foot, 'Making of *Angelcynn*', esp. pp. 32–7; P. Wormald, '*Engla Lond*: The Making of an Allegiance', *Journal of Historical Sociology* 7 (1994), pp. 1–24 (repr. in his *Legal Culture in the Early Medieval West* (London, 1999), pp. 359–82), is alert to the 'rough handling' (p. 15) that went with 'Englishness'.

[67] Bloch, *Feudal Society*, pp. 284–5.

lineage.[68] This extreme blocking of noble memory cannot be explained away by assuming – on slender evidence – that Æthelweard knew Matilda to be interested only in her own direct kin and tailored his account accordingly.[69] Despite the best efforts of a generation and more of students inclined to prosopography, no tenth-century member of the 'king's kindred' in England has been proved to be of genuine royal descent; all their empirically recoverable ancestries simply peter out within one or two generations at most. Whether these men did have a real blood-relationship with the West Saxon ruling dynasty or whether they were articulating what anthropologists call 'fictive kinship', the conclusion must be that the drive towards aristocratic lineage identity was compromised in tenth-century England. The evidence of Æthelweard's *Chronicon* encourages us to suspect that it was the hegemonic cultural presence of the Alfredian royal lineage that compromised it.[70]

We do not have access to the sense of family memory and identity possessed by Æthelstan Half-King, Ælfhere of Mercia or the other ealdormen and *ministri* gathered around the royal court, and that makes Æthelweard's testimony all the more valuable, both for what he tells us and what he neglects. That there was a systematic downgrading of cadet branches of the royal house paralleling that of the non West Saxon kingships by the lineage of Alfred from the late ninth century is undeniable.[71] By the mid-tenth century the sprawling and untidy West Saxon royal family of a hundred years before had been cleared out and cleaned up. There still existed those, like Æthelweard, who could claim kinship with royalty, but who were not classified as immediately 'royal' themselves. The exclusion from kingly charisma that process implied for Æthelweard and other noble kindreds was compensated for by inclusion within a sophisticated and heroic West Saxon 'epic' articulated in stories of the migration from Scandinavia and the wars against the Britons, culminating in the rise

---

[68] *Chron.*, p. 2; R. L. Poole, 'Burgundian Notes: I. The Alpine Son-in-Law of Edward the Elder', *EHR* 26 (1911), pp. 310–17, at 310–11.

[69] van Houts, 'Women and the Writing of History', p. 63.

[70] Baxter, 'The Leofwinesons', pp. 68–72, at 71, makes the interesting case that Æthelweard's account of Alfred's reign is a 'revisionist' one, giving greater praise for the achievements of the ealdormen and Edward the Elder than does the *Anglo-Saxon Chronicle*. The lavish praise offered Alfred on his death suggests that these revisions constituted less an alternative Æthelredian lineage memory of the reign than a plea for the importance of a reliable chain of command: *Chron.*, p. 51.

[71] J. L. Nelson, 'Reconstructing a Royal Family: Reflections on Alfred from Asser chapter 2', in I. Wood and N. Lund, eds., *People and Places in Northern Europe. 500–1600: Essays in Honour of Peter Hayes Sawyer* (Woodbridge, 1991), pp. 47–66, at 57–61 (repr. *Rulers*, chapter 3), collects the scraps of information known about some of Alfred's now obscure relatives.

of Wessex and the final triumph of Alfred, Edward the Elder and Æthelstan over the Vikings. Politically, the claims of these great noble clans on wealth, favour and high office were consolidated through their unique descent myth from Sceaf down to Æthelwulf, the royal *paterfamilias* whose wealth in sons made him the last ruler of Wessex in whom all members of the tenth-century 'king's kindred' could locate a common ancestry, real or fictive. Despite Æthelweard's boast to Matilda that he will tell the history of their family in ancient and modern times, by his fourth book he is telling the story of only one part of the family, that of Alfred and his heirs. The *Chronicon* is both evidence for and part of the process by which the lineage of Alfred achieved cultural hegemony as well as political supremacy in the new English kingdom by offering a glorious past in exchange for a subordinate present.

Æthelweard's position as an important mediator of this Alfredian invented tradition at the expense of his own semi-independent Æthelredian identity shows how powerful an imaginative hold it had over those it subordinated. But his youth had taught another, more pragmatic lesson about the dangers of advertising membership of a marginalised branch of the Ecgbertings. The reign of Eadwig had demonstrated that a claim on royal descent unaccompanied by a grip on royal power was a double-edged weapon which the wise avoided showing too readily, lest it be turned against them by their enemies. For had not his own sister most likely been divorced from the king in 957 'because they were too closely related'? Æthelweard's own grandchildren and those of his contemporaries were to be destroyed by Cnut because of their subversive status as the 'king's kinsmen' once a non-West Saxon regime ruled in England.[72] The aesthetic pleasure and functional utility associated with genealogical and dynastic hygiene are not to be separated from the brute facts of death and survival in the early Middle Ages.

The genealogy of the counts of Flanders produced by Witger was earlier referred to as a 'lay' vision of history. To modern eyes, the situation is complicated by the fact that these 'lay' aspects were accompanied by the efforts of its monastic author to represent his patron as a Christian hero and benefactor of the Church, ending his text with liturgical injunctions regarding prayers for Arnulf and his son Baldwin.[73] Yet Witger's promiscuous blending of secular and religious themes in his text is only one example from the early Middle Ages suggesting that 'lay' and 'ecclesiastical'

---

[72] See Fleming, *Kings and Lords*, pp. 39–52.   [73] Dunbabin, *France in the Making*, p. 72.

were less antagonistic and impermeable orders than complementary and overlapping identities. Issues of family patronage, audience and political context determined the tone of culture as much as personal status or institutional position. Holiness and the more earthly realities of ancestry, power and land went hand in hand in the early Middle Ages.[74] To be a layperson in the Carolingian world was more complex than being 'not-clerical' or 'not-monastic'. Reform was adjusting the boundaries of ecclesiastical and lay status with the aim of separating one from the other more clearly.[75] But by encouraging greater literacy and spiritual reflection among lay elites, while maintaining an engagement between the Church and the worldly environment of courts and kings, it only contributed to a blurring of the frontier between the two orders of society.

Turning to Æthelweard, we find that his concern with non-ecclesiastical history does not seem to have conflicted with writing for an abbess of a major Ottonian nunnery, or with his active support for spiritual learning and monastic reform in general. According to William of Malmesbury, Æthelweard refounded Pershore Abbey, although the act is usually associated with the charter of Edgar in 972.[76] Both Æthelweard and his son, Æthelmær, directed patronage to Ælfric at Cerne – which Æthelmær had refounded sometime around 987 – and were involved through the 990s in the production of the first series of *Catholic Homilies*, the translations of Genesis and the Book of Joshua, and in the *Lives of the Saints*.[77] A cogent case has been made for regarding their relationship with Ælfric as one of actively commissioning works helping them to incorporate monastic observances into their own lay devotions.[78] Æthelmær brought monks to Eynsham after his father's death and actually retired into the monastery for a number of years from 1005.[79] Æthelweard and Æthelmær have long

---

[74] I have learned much from J. Nightingale, *Monasteries and Patrons in the Gorze Reform: Lotharingia, c. 850–1000* (Oxford, 2001), esp. pp. 1–21; see also, Campbell, 'England, c. 991', pp. 162–7; J. M. Pope, 'Monks and Nobles in the Anglo-Saxon Reform', *Anglo-Norman Studies* 17 (1995), pp. 165–80.
[75] P. Stafford, 'Queens, Nunneries and Reforming Churchmen: Gender, Religious Status and Reform in Tenth- and Eleventh-Century England', *P&P* 163 (1999), pp. 3–35, esp. 6–8.
[76] William of Malmesbury, *De Gestis Pontificum*, ed. N. E. S. A. Hamilton, Rolls Series 52 (London, 1870); S. 786 (the charter itself may be spurious).
[77] *Ælfric's Prefaces*, ed. Wilcox, esp. pp. 9–13; P. Clemoes, 'The Chronology of Ælfric's Works', in Clemoes, ed., *The Anglo-Saxons: Studies in some Aspects of their History and Culture Presented to Bruce Dickins* (London, 1959), pp. 243–4; J. Hurt, *Ælfric* (New York, 1972), pp. 31–8. For the early history of Cerne: S. 1217; G. D. Squibb, 'The Foundation of Cerne Abbey', in *Cerne Abbey Millennium Lectures*, ed. Barker, pp. 11–14.
[78] M. McC. Gatch, *Preaching and Theology in Anglo-Saxon England* (Toronto, 1977), pp. 48–9.
[79] S. 911; C. A. Jones, *Ælfric's Letter to the Monks of Eynsham* (Cambridge, 1998), pp. 7–13, offers a recent discussion of the events at Eynsham in 1005.

been associated with both the production and possibly the donation of manuscripts, including the 'Exeter Book' of Old English poetry, a volume containing tracts by Bede and Augustine of Hippo (Lambeth MS 149) and perhaps a copy of Prudentius's *Psychomachia* (Cambridge, Corpus Christi College MS 23) donated by an Æthelweard to the abbey of Malmesbury.[80] Æthelmær's son-in-law, Ealdorman Æthelweard II (c. 1015–20), gave Lambeth MS 149 to an unidentified St Mary's abbey in 1018.[81] The male kindred certainly seem to have seen their spiritual welfare as bound up with the ideals of reformed monasticism.

Yet there are also undercurrents of more secular concerns. Both Cerne and Eynsham may have been *Eigenkirchen* (family churches) before they were 'reformed', perhaps as part of wider landholding and political strategies. This would make Ælfric as much the private chaplain of Æthelweard and Æthelmær as the independent object of their patronage.[82] Several of Ælfric's theological and moral themes, especially his interest in defending the rich from the strictures laid against them in the Christian tradition, have been related to his close personal involvement with men such as Æthelweard and his son.[83] A fellow south-westerner by birth, is it possible he might even have been their kinsman? Recent research has done much to uncover how normal such relationships were in the tenth and eleventh centuries. In an age before castles, such monasteries – reformed or otherwise – provided physical spaces for the maintenance of family identity, loyalties and material interests.[84] The religious activities of Æthelweard and

---

[80] The classic discussion is R. Flower, 'The Script of the Exeter Book', in *The Exeter Book of Old English Poetry*, ed. R. W. Chambers, M. Forster and R. Flower (London, 1933), pp. 87–90; see also P. W. Conner, *Anglo-Saxon Exeter: A Tenth-Century Cultural History* (Woodbridge, 1993), ch. 3, though his 'maximalist' thesis has not won general consent: cf. e.g., Wormald, *Making*, p. 223, n. 40; M. Lapidge, 'Artistic and Lay Patronage in Anglo-Saxon England', in his *Anglo-Latin Literature, 600–899* (London, 1996), pp. 46–7, and n. 31, suggests that the donor of the Prudentius does not have to be Abbot Æthelweard (c. 1033–43); a connection with the ealdorman would certainly go some way towards explaining William of Malmesbury's knowledge of the *Chronicon*.

[81] S. Keynes, 'Cnut's Earls', in A. R. Rumble, ed., *The Reign of Cnut: King of England, Denmark and Norway* (London, 1994), pp. 68–9, suggests Buckfast Abbey in Devon with which Æthelweard seems to have been closely associated.

[82] The fact that no full analysis of the lands of Æthelweard and Æthelmær has been undertaken makes a more definite view difficult. For the status of Cerne and Eynsham, see: M. Gelling, *The Early Charters of the Thames Valley* (Leicester, 1979), pp. 138–9; Yorke, 'Æthelmær', pp. 23–4; A. Crossley, ed., *Victoria County History of the County of Oxford*, XII (Oxford, 1990), pp. 103–4; Lapidge, 'Artistic and Lay Patronage', p. 89, n. 160; Jones, *Ælfric's Letter*, pp. 5–10. For the material remains of Eynsham, see A. Hardy, A. Dodd and G. D. Keevill, *Ælfric's Abbey: Excavations at Eynsham Abbey, Oxfordshire, 1989–92* (Oxford, 2003).

[83] M. Godden, 'Money, Power and Morality in Late Anglo-Saxon England', *ASE* 19 (1990), pp. 41–65, at pp. 64–5.

[84] Nightingale, *Monasteries and Patrons*, pp. 4–6.

Æthelmær need to be understood in terms of their lay concerns and *vice versa*. Their patronage of monastic reform was a complement in stone and plaster to the older man's chronicling of family memory with pen and ink.

Æthelweard's *Chronicon* is part of the last gasp of the heroic spirit in Anglo-Saxon England during its final century. In tune with the antiquarian poetic revival that saw the production of the four great Old English collections – the Exeter, Junius, Vercelli and *Beowulf* manuscripts – and the *Battle of Maldon*, the *Chronicon* is filled with nostalgia for a vanished northern world.[85] Æthelweard was moved, at least in part, by a world where *æthelings* washed up on the shores of Baltic islands, where warrior-kings with primeval ancestries seized land and ruled it through might and will, not by the quotidian reality of village reeves and wapentake reeves, hundred courts and taxation. While much current historiography expresses boundless admiration for Anglo-Saxon England the 'nation-state', Æthelweard's imagination ran in a different groove, in which – to use Weber's terminology – charisma eclipsed routinisation. If Æthelweard was indeed associated with the 'Exeter Book' and the preservation of such works as *Widsith*, *The Ruin*, *The Seafarer* and *The Wanderer*, then he may well have wondered with them, 'Where are those men? Where is the hoard-sharer? Where is the house of the feast? Where is the hall's uproar?'[86] And yet this longing for the sharp, heroic outlines of a vanished world was an acknowledgement of how far things had changed, both in the sphere of secular rule and in that of the monastic culture that did so much to shape it.

The fact that the boundaries circumscribing lay and religious remained open and permeable is not inconsistent with considerable intellectual energy being spent in an effort to distinguish more sharply between the two. Ælfric, who benefited so much from his connections with Æthelweard and his son, was one of the figures at the forefront of that effort. He attacked the old gods, about whom his patron seems to have been unusually knowledgeable, in *De Falsis Deis* (*c.* 995), denounced secular charms and practices as diabolic and sinful and questioned the love affair of both laymen and ecclesiastics with the pagan heroes, including perhaps even Sceaf himself.[87]

---

[85] Sisam, *Studies in the History of Old English Literature*, p. 99.
[86] *The Earliest English Poems*, trans. M. Alexander, 2nd edn (Harmondsworth, 1977), p. 72.
[87] *Chron.*, pp. xxiv, n. l, lix; A. L. Meaney, 'Æthelweard, Ælfric, the Norse Gods and Northumbria', *Journal of Religious History* 6 (1970), pp. 105–32; A. Orchard, *Pride and Prodigies: Studies in the Monsters of the Beowulf-Manuscript* (Cambridge, 1995), pp. 169–70. For the suggestion that the legend of Sceaf was undermined by the theological orthodoxy of Ælfric, see Anlezark, 'Sceaf, Japheth and the Origins of the Anglo-Saxons', pp. 45–6.

Over the course of the tenth century the revaluation of the secular past encouraged by a Bede or an Alcuin had begun to make greater inroads even into the hearts and minds of the new English aristocracy. The traditions of the heroic age were rapidly losing their lustre; as early as 900 the social elite seem to have abandoned names from secular Germanic legend for their children. The great poetic codices themselves witness these changes, in the difficulties the scribes had in understanding or sympathising with what they were copying, in the gradual transition from older works of legend and the heroic to poems more attuned to the new monastic ethos.[88]

It would have been impossible for Æthelweard to remain unaffected by this 'squeezing' of the secular in Anglo-Saxon culture. It might be significant that with his *Chronicon* completed sometime between 975 and 988, his careers as chronicler of the fading heroic past and as a pious lay patron of monasticism were chronologically sequential, not simultaneous. In the years after 993 Æthelweard became the senior ealdorman in Æthelred's kingdom, and as such was surely associated with the legislative activity and reform culture that imbued the years leading up to the millennium.[89] If we are to allow Æthelweard a mind as well as a purse, then we must at least consider what effects Ælfric's books may have had on this lay intellectual. Were they instrumental in turning his imagination away from Sceaf, Woden and Balder and towards the heroic traditions of Christianity?

Against the tendency of contemporary historiography to place gender and particularly the role of women centre-stage in the processes of social memory, it is perhaps what Robert Markus has termed the 'epistemological excision' of the secular from Christian discourse, affecting men and women equally, that needs greater attention.[90] Carolingian reform culture had already reduced memories of a Frankish 'deep past', genealogically connecting the present with its origins, down to the few ambiguous, contested and strictly localised references to 'Germanic' traditions that are regularly adduced as evidence for an interest in barbarian antiquity. As historians of the Carolingian era are beginning to realise, it is remarkable how little the ancestral pre-Christian world intruded on the consciousness of the

---

[88] For Anglo-Saxon naming patterns, see P. Wormald, 'Beowulf: the Dating Reassessed', in his *The Times of Bede: Studies in Early English Christian Society and its Historian*, ed. S. Baxter (Oxford, 2006), pp. 71–81. For the poetic corpus: J. Hill, '*Widsith* and the Tenth Century', *Neuphilologische Mitteilungen* 85 (1984), pp. 305–15; Conner, *Anglo-Saxon Exeter*, ch. 6.

[89] Keynes, *Diplomas*, p. 192; Wormald, *Making*, pp. 322–30, 442–4; could Æthelweard's knowledge of Old Norse have been useful in drafting the 'III Æthelred' law-code aimed at the Danelaw?

[90] See, for example, Geary, *Phantoms of Remembrance*, pp. 51–73; van Houts, *Memory and Gender*; R. Markus, *The End of Ancient Christianity* (Cambridge, 1990), p. 225.

sophisticated and historiographically literate court of Charlemagne and his heirs.[91] This process advanced furthest in the heartlands of Francia during the late eighth and ninth centuries, but affected all the areas touched by monastic and ecclesiastical reforming ideals, including Anglo-Saxon England.

On the one hand, Æthelweard's historical imagination seems little taken with the change. In its reworking of the West Saxon genealogical material in particular, but also in its basic ethos in general, the *Chronicon* is a secular work. But, on the other hand, there are significant markers of this pan-European shift in cultural values. It has already been noted how the shape of Æthelweard's thinking was influenced by the Christian redemptive scheme of Bede. Indeed, although most of the *Chronicon* has a secular flavour, its opening pages are indebted to biblical 'world history' in the style of Bede or Isidore. Even in the genealogies, Æthelweard was distinctly uncomfortable with the notion of pagan 'gods' among the ancestors of Anglo-Saxon kings. He stoutly condemned both ancient and modern offerings of sacrifice to Woden, originally merely a 'king of the barbarians', as heathenish superstition.[92] By including Woden among the ancestors of King Æthelwulf of Wessex, Æthelweard the layman was clearly drawn by the idea of finding ancient heroes among his own forefathers. But Æthelweard the ealdorman of the Christian kingdom of the English also knew (and seemingly before being told by Ælfric) that by doing so he was straining at the limits of religious orthodoxy.[93] The fusing of secular and sacred that characterised his subsequent career was both an immovable fact of early medieval life and a symptom of a society in the midst of radical change.

It was hinted at the beginning of this chapter that neither Æthelweard nor any inhabitant of the Carolingian world could be described as an *intellectuel engagé*, the sceptical, critical, often marginalised figure who tells uncomfortable truths to authority and society. There the idea of the public moralist was suggested as a useful alternative tradition. However, while this might help determine the social function of an Einhard, or even an

---

[91] A conclusion also reached by M. Innes, 'Teutons or Trojans? The Carolingians and the Germanic Past', in Y. Hen and M. Innes, eds., *The Uses of the Past in Early Medieval Europe* (Cambridge, 2000), pp. 227–49.
[92] *Chron.*, pp. 7, 9.
[93] On the contrasts between Ælfric's and Æthelweard's views of the old gods, see D. F. Johnson, 'Euhemerisation versus Demonisation: The Pagan Gods and Ælfric's *De Falsis Diis*', in T. Hofstra, L. A. J. R. Houwen and A. A. MacDonald, eds., *The Interplay between Christian and Traditional Germanic Cultures in Early Medieval Europe*, Germania Latina II (Groningen, 1995), pp. 35–69.

Alfred, the lack of a consistently moral dimension renders such a concept ultimately unsatisfactory as a description of Æthelweard's project. If we seek to define the essence of what Æthelweard was about, we are forced to reach for another term for which no exact equivalent exists in English, the *mythomoteur*, that individual who works to explain the place of the community in the world to itself, who explains that it *is* a community and not simply an atomised collection of kindreds or villages.[94] Utilising genealogical and typological stories that link past with present and make the one intelligible in the light of the other, the *mythomoteur* is the classic 'intellectual' for the early Middle Ages. Politically, ealdormen were powerful centripetal forces in tenth-century England. As a carrier of dynastic and lineage origins and of the 'epic' narrative of the fifth- and sixth-century migrations, as a mediator between problematic readings of the more recent past and as an advocate for an ideology of ordered royal succession over the clashes and confusions of kindreds and *æthelings*, Æthelweard also fulfilled his duties as ealdorman in a parallel imaginative sphere.

Surprisingly, even the use of such a non-English term as *mythomoteur* seems strangely apposite for the chronicler of the 'West English'. For if in contrast to much recent discussion, this history of Æthelweard has downplayed the importance of Matilda of Essen, that is a long way from reducing him to an insular figure. He knew some contemporary Greek, just conceivably learned directly from Continental visitors similar to Israel the Grammarian, the Breton scholar who sojourned at Athelstan's court, or Fredegaud of Brioude, who may well be the Frithegod of Canterbury who composed a *Life* of St Wilfrid in 1,400 'hermeneutic' Latin hexameters for Archbishop Oda.[95] Alongside the thematic similarities with Witger and his genealogy of the counts of Flanders, it was in Ottonian Germany that Æthelweard had his closest analogue, in the figure of Widukind of Corvey. Another *mythomoteur* of strong, single-lineage kingship, equally straddling the boundary between lay and monastic – though writing from the cloister to the outside world – Widukind created a history for another Matilda, of Quedlinburg, narrating the history of Saxons through the lens of the ruling dynasty, favouring a secular and barbarian origin for the people.

---

[94] The term was originally coined for early medieval Visigothic history: see J. A. Armstrong, *Nations Before Nationalism* (Chapel Hill, NC, 1982), pp. 129–67; A. D. Smith, *The Ethnic Origins of Nations* (Oxford, 1986), pp. 57–68, 229, n. 29.

[95] *Chron.*, pp. xlvi–xlviii; cf. Lapidge, 'Hermeneutic Style', pp. 135–9. M. Lapidge, 'Israel the Grammarian', in his *Anglo-Latin Literature, 900–1066*, pp. 87–104; and Lapidge, 'A Frankish Scholar in Tenth Century England: Frithegod of Canterbury/Fredegaud of Brioude', *ibid.*, pp. 157–81.

These general resemblances are partly the result of the similar contexts in which both works were written. But when added to Æthelweard's use of Widukind's favoured term *barbarus* in preference to the more usual 'heathen' or *paganus*, his considered avoidance of the ethnic label 'Saxon' – making his work complementary to the Continental *Historia Saxonum* – and his use of the Widukindian four-book structure, then we have some grounds for thinking that more might have passed between Germany and England than we now have evidence for.[96] Æthelweard and his *Chronicon* were formed by and in a European context as well as a local one, just like his greater forebears, Bede and Alfred. Together their work makes up the central triptych in the early history of 'Englishness', defining its nature while reminding us of the truth of the dictum passed down by that later *mythomoteur* of an imperial nation, Rudyard Kipling: 'And what should they know of England who only England know?'

---

[96] Some of these points are made in Campbell, 'England, France', pp. 194–5. The recent literary reading of Æthelweard by W. Jezierski, 'Æthelweardus redivivus', *EME* 13 (2005), pp. 159–78, appeared too late for me to be able to take account of its findings.

CHAPTER 12

Concluding

Richard Abels

'I cannot find anything better in man', King Alfred has St Augustine declare in his free rendition of the *Soliloquies*, 'than that he know, and nothing worse than that he be ignorant.'[1] As David Pratt shows, the sentiment and words were ultimately Alfred's own.[2] The image that Alfred and his biographer Asser wished to project was that of a Christian ruler who pursued wisdom as man's greatest good and regarded it as the *sine qua non* for good governance. Alfred's passionate devotion to learning was a public affair. He presented himself to his court as a model for emulation. He himself undertook the task of rendering (in his words) 'word for word or sense for sense' 'certain books which are necessary for all men to know'.[3] More than merely translating them, Alfred, through discussion and consultation with the clerical intellectuals of his court, transformed these works to enhance their timeliness and relevance and to reflect his own philosophical interests. Desiring his *witan* to be wise in more than name, King Alfred admonished his ealdorman, reeves and thegns, those who through God's authority and his own 'enjoyed the office and status of wise men', either to apply themselves to the study and application of wisdom or to relinquish their offices.[4] Alfred dreamt of an ambitious educational *renovatio* for the free-born males of his realm, and, at the very least, established a court *schola* in which his youngest children (and young grandson), along with the sons of nobility and 'a good many of lesser birth as well', would receive instruction in the liberal arts, so that they might be

---

[1] 'Forðam ic ne mæg nanwiht ongytan bætre on men þonne he wite, and nanwiht wyrse ðonne he nyte.' *King Alfred's Version of St Augustine's* Soliloquies, ed. T. A. Carnicelli (Cambridge, MA, 1969), p. 84; trans. H. H. Hargrove, *King Alfred's Old English Version of St. Augustine's* Soliloquies *Turned into Modern English* (New York, 1904), p. 36.
[2] See David Pratt in this volume, above, pp. 186–7.
[3] *King Alfred's West Saxon Version of Gregory's Pastoral Care*, ed. Henry Sweet, EETS, o.s. 45, 50 (London, 1871–72; rpt 1958), pp. 5–6 (Prose Preface); KL, p. 126
[4] *VA* c. 106 (p. 93); trans. KL, p. 110.

able to read and write in both Latin and English.⁵ Under Alfred, perhaps his children, and certainly his grandson Æthelstan, literacy and learning became a qualification for rule, whether ecclesiastical or secular.⁶

For Asser, Alfred was an English 'Solomon', a model Christian king who daily attended divine services and masses, avidly listened to Scripture readings, recited psalms and prayers, gave charity and alms to his subjects and foreign visitors alike, cherished his bishops, clergy, ealdormen, nobles, officials and associates, and never ceased from 'personally giving, by day and night, instruction in all virtuous behaviour and tutelage in literacy to their sons, who were being brought up in the royal household and whom he loved no less than his own children'.⁷ He was also, Asser assures us, a steady helmsman of the ship of state, guiding it through stormy seas, a great warrior victorious in nearly all his battles, a conscientious judge and ruler, and a student of the hunt so confident in his expertise that he was wont to instruct his falconers, hawk-trainers and dog-keepers on the finer points of their crafts.⁸

King Alfred is one of the nine lay intellectuals of the 'Carolingian world' featured in this volume. But what makes him so? The Readers for Cambridge University Press initially resisted the proposed title for this book. They pointed out that *The Lay Intellectual in the Carolingian World* combines three key problematics: the term 'intellectual' as applied to the learned of the early Middle Ages; the boundaries separating laity and clergy, and the types of wisdom and knowledge appropriate to each order; and the geographical and chronological contours of the 'Carolingian World'. Fair enough. The authors of the essays in this volume appreciate and address the difficulties presented by these terms. In doing so, they not only justify the book's chosen title but explore the nuances of and raise intriguing questions about each. What emerges is an understanding of how individuals as disparate as Alfred, Charles the Bald, Einhard, Nithard, Eberhard of Friuli, King Æthelstan, Ealdorman Æthelweard, Dhuoda and Liutberga can all be seen as lay intellectuals in a broadly conceived Carolingian world in which the English Channel was a conduit rather than a barrier for the

---

⁵ *VA* c. 75, p. 58; *King Alfred's Pastoral Care*, ed. Sweet, pp. 6–7; trans. KL, p. 126.
⁶ M. Wood, chapter 10, above, pp. 193–7.   ⁷ *VA* c. 76, pp. 59–60; trans. KL, p. 91.
⁸ *VA* cc. 42, 76, 91, pp. 32, 59, 77. For Alfred as scholar and philosopher, see R. Abels, *Alfred the Great: War, Kingship and Culture in Anglo-Saxon England* (London and New York, 1998), pp. 219–57, 309–17, and references at 341–42; A. P. Smyth, *King Alfred the Great* (Oxford, 1995), pp. 527–602; P. Wormald, 'Alfred', *The Oxford Dictionary of National Biography* (Oxford, 2004), 1, cols. 716–24. The published version (Cambridge, 2007) of D. R. Pratt's dissertation, 'The Political Thought of Alfred the Great' (Ph.D. dissertation, Cambridge University, 1999), advances our understanding of Alfred's political philosophy within the cultural context of his time.

transmission of ideas. Like Alfred, each of them, in his or her own way, pursued or promoted divine wisdom and shared an aristocratic ethos that admonished the lay elite to promote and exercise Christian wisdom and virtues in all their worldly activities, so that they might lead by word and example. Each shared, or at least wished to be seen as sharing, in the programmes of spiritual and educational *renovatio* that became the hallmark of Charlemagne's and, a century later, Alfred's reigns.

Who, then, is the 'lay intellectual' that emerges from these pages? The contributors agree on certain basic characteristics. Whether ecclesiastical or lay, the Carolingian 'intellectual' was no 'ivory-towered' philosopher lost in abstract thought, secluded from and uninterested in the turmoil of the world. To the contrary, he (or she) was a public person who actively engaged in the political and religious disputes of the day. Lay intellectuals, as Scott Ashley astutely observes, 'were more than merely "learned" people, they actively participated in shaping the values and ideologies of their societies and of mediating them to its members, at all levels of the social hierarchy'.[9] Possessed of the skills of literacy, well versed in the writings of Christian and classical authorities, often of aristocratic or royal descent, Carolingian lay intellectuals used their learning to promote and legitimise the established authorities, whether royal, ecclesiastical or familial. But they did not do so uncritically. Their engagement in political conflicts and doctrinal disputes, as well as their recognition of the gulf between ideal and reality, often necessitated that they critique its practical exercise.

The agenda of the aristocratic ideology they shared and helped shape was to implement in practice the central tenets of the Carolingian *renovatio*. In this ethos of 'secular sanctity' (as Thomas Noble characterises it), secular authority was conceived of as a *ministerium*, a responsibility and an opportunity to perform Christian service for the betterment of the soul, and the lay nobility was seen as corporately forming a *schola humani servitii*.[10] God's City as it existed imperfectly in this world was maintained through a chain of ministerial duty and a hierarchy of mutually reinforcing loyalties to God, king and family. The ideal noble in this schema was a *vir sanctus* whose sanctity manifested itself not in his withdrawal from the world but through the proper use of the secular authority entrusted to him. Doing God's work meant using his public and private authority wisely, to advance the spiritual welfare of those entrusted to him, promote justice and public utility, and fulfil his responsibilities to *familia* and kin. Alfred and

[9] S. Ashley, in this volume, above, p. 222. See also T. Noble, above, pp. 40–5.
[10] See Noble, above, pp. 39–40; Kershaw, pp. 22–3, 241–2; Nelson, p. 290.

other lay intellectuals believed that a judge could not fulfil his duties adequately if he lacked *sapientia*, and that this wisdom was instilled, at least in part, through literacy and learning. And, as Alfred and his contemporaries also knew, if the lay nobleman was to be a true *miles in Christo* he needed to arm himself as well with courage, prudence and practical know-how (*scientia*), to fight effectively sin, disorder and injustice.

Each of the authors examined in this book – Alfred, Einhard, Nithard, Dhuoda and Æthelweard – wrote within the general discourse of the ethos of 'secular sanctity'. In the *Vita Karoli* Einhard represented Charlemagne as a lay intellectual and a Christian hero, a ruler both *sapiens et fortis*. Einhard follows the Suetonian model in reporting Charlemagne's many successful wars and describing his domestic life. But he also emphasises Charlemagne's intellectual interests and endeavours, self-consciously shaping the image of the king and his court to conform to a Ciceronian notion of civilisation. Asser, who had a copy of Einhard's work before him, portrayed Alfred in a similar light, although his hero went well beyond his Charlemagne in terms of his personal intellectual accomplishments. In the hands of Einhard and Asser, Charlemagne and Alfred became the living embodiments of the reform programmes they sponsored. Charlemagne played a similar role in Nithard's increasingly wintry *Histories*, although the author's purpose in writing changed as he became increasingly disillusioned by the failure of his contemporaries to live up to the ideals they espoused.[11] By the end of his work, Nithard almost seems to be writing a mocking counterpoint to the moral advice Dhuoda offered her son William in her *Liber manualis*, as he depicts kings and nobles competing with one another for worldly advantage without regard either for the good of their souls or the common weal. Nithard's original purpose, to justify the claims of his lord and cousin Charles the Bald during a period of political crisis, comes close to the aims of the late tenth-century English ealdorman Æthelweard in composing his free Latin translation of the Anglo-Saxon Chronicle. In Æthelweard's hands the Chronicle was transformed into a 'work of family piety and remembrance' justifying the claims of the Alfredian dynasty. Whereas Nithard detailed the treacheries and conflicts of his day in creating what ultimately became a negative 'mirror of princes', Æthelweard, himself the descendent of an *ætheling* who died contesting the royal succession of his cousin Edward the Elder, consciously manipulated his sources to eliminate all indications of political tensions

---

[11] S. Airlie, above, pp. 165–9, 176–7.

and conflict, so that the history of tenth-century England became one in which royal authority passed peacefully from ruler to heir within a single charismatic agnatic lineage, the dynasty of Alfred.[12]

King Alfred's intellectual credentials are well established by his literary endeavours. Although his understanding of Boethius, Augustine, Gregory the Great, the Psalms and the Book of Exodus was undoubtedly shaped in spirited discussions with his clerical entourage of scholars, Alfred left his own mark on these works, not only through his choice of words, but through the unique insights that he brought to them based upon his experience as both king and *ætheling* in the courts of his father and brothers. As an author, Alfred may not have been unique among early medieval rulers, but he was certainly a rarity. Learned kings and nobles more often participated in this intellectual world through the patronage they extended to writers and artists. The evidence of the learning of the Emperor Charles the Bald or of King Æthelstan or of great Frankish noblemen such as Eberhard, margrave of Friuli, comes not from any book or poem that they wrote but indirectly from the complexities of symbol and allusion in artistic and literary works they commissioned or were given as gifts. Celia Chazelle demonstrates how the ivory crucifixion scene now on the cover of the early eleventh-century Pericopes of Henry II can serve as a window to the learning of its intended audience, Charles the Bald. Similarly, Paul Kershaw and Michael Wood examine, respectively, the patronage given and book collections owned by Eberhard of Friuli and of Alfred's grandson King Æthelstan as reflections of their learning, or at least of the opinion of their learning by ecclesiastical contemporaries. Whether in the form of an ivory *Fürstenspiegel* designed according to the thought of Hincmar of Rheims or of a praise poem by Sedulius Scottus, the lay patron was expected to comprehend and appreciate sophisticated visual and literary allusions to biblical exegesis, liturgy and patristic and classical literature. Although court scholars undoubtedly helped their lay patrons to unpack the layers of allusion and symbol buried in a work, that these patrons were thought capable of engaging in such a level of learned discourse marked them as intellectuals.

The term 'lay' is nearly as problematic. Although the Carolingian world drew a formal distinction between clergy and laity based upon the former's acceptance of holy orders, these two categories were not nearly as clear as the capitulary-formula *laicus et clericus* might suggest. Einhard and

---

[12] S. Ashley, above, pp. 232–6.

Nithard, for instance, were not only laymen but abbots, and, as we have seen, the aristocratic ethos embraced by the Carolingian laity was one infused with Christian values and beliefs. Ninth- and tenth-century Frankish and English bishops were important royal agents with worldly authority, while Carolingian counts and nobles and English ealdormen and thegns were conceived of as possessing Christian *ministeria*. The boundaries between the orders at times grew blurry. But there were recognised differences. The lay noble may have been idealised as a *miles in Christo* but what he was above all else was a warrior. Although the ethos of secular sanctity was promoted by lay and clerical intellectuals alike, it had to be accommodated within an aristocratic culture that mandated young nobles to demonstrate their manhood through fighting, hunting, drinking, feasting and engaging in sexual activities. A noble layman was expected to master the arts of war and the court, and, eventually, to marry and have sons to continue his lineage.

To be complete, then, a lay intellectual needed not only the divine wisdom (*sapientia*) revealed in books but practical know-how (*scientia*) and skills obtained through experience and practice.[13] Both Alfred and Hrabanus Maurus acknowledged that, for laymen, the time to master one's letters was in early youth, before (in Asser's words) 'they had the requisite strength for manly skills (hunting, that is, and other skills appropriate to noblemen)'.[14] Alfred took pride in his knowledge of the fine points of the hunt.[15] By far the most important *scientia* for noblemen, however, was the art of warfare. Although the skills needed for the battlefield, like those of the hunt, were most likely acquired largely through training under the guidance of older men experienced in war, book learning was thought to have a role in mastering the arts of war. Thus both Eberhard of Friuli and Charles the Bald received copies of Vegetius's *Epitoma rei militaris* as gifts from bishops. Whatever its practical utility for ninth-century warfare, lay intellectuals of the era apparently valued the *Epitoma*, at least for the veneer of classical learning it gave to their bellicose activities.[16] The same may have

---

[13] Isidore of Seviille, *Liber secundus de differentiis rerum*, ch. 37: 'scientia ad agnitionem pertinet, sapientia ad contemplationem. Scientia temporalibus bene utitur ... sapientia autem tantummodo aeterna contemplatur'.

[14] *VA* c. 75, Stevenson, p. 58; trans. KL, p. 90. Cf. *King Alfred's Pastoral Care*, ed. Sweet, pp. 6–7. See discussion by Kershaw, above.

[15] *VA* c. 76, p. 59.

[16] The applicability of Vegetius' *Epitoma* to Carolingian armies and warfare, *pace* Bernard S. Bachrach, is questionable. As Guy Halsall warns, '[W]e cannot be sure that the popularity of Vegetius was not mainly a matter of antiquarianism and the desire to acquire classical learning ... [E]arly medieval people were quite prepared to accord great authority to classical works, even while recognising that they

been true of the law-books in Eberhard's collection; like much of the education received today in elite law schools, Lupus' *Liber legum* may have been more valuable for teaching the theory and philosophy of law than for guidance in its actual practice.

Thomas Noble emphasises that the aristocratic ethos of secular sanctity was exclusively a masculine affair, designed by males for the guidance of 'powerful, public men' in the exercise of their public offices.[17] Ironically, the work that most clearly lays out the moral attributes, personal traits and skills required by this code, Dhuoda's *Liber manualis*, was a handbook of instruction for a young nobleman written by his mother. Dhuoda's authorship raises the question of how a learned ninth-century Frankish laywoman, who, by definition, belonged to the domestic sphere, could influence actions in the political and public realm of men. Nonetheless, Dhuoda has as good a claim to the title of 'lay intellectual' as any of her male contemporaries. Not only does her handbook reveal an impressive array of biblical, patristic and classical citations and allusions reflecting her deep learning, Dhuoda intended it for a public audience. She wrote not simply as a mother to a son – although her claim to authority rested in part upon maternity – but also as a noblewoman whose extensive book learning was complemented by her life experiences in the royal court at Aachen. Through the agency of her son William, moreover, she hoped that her book would reach a wider audience at court, so that the wisdom she offered might teach others how to be 'useful in the *saeculum* and please God'.[18]

Dhuoda's foray into the public and political world reserved for males was legitimised by her maternal authority. Like other mothers, she was concerned for the welfare of her son and wrote ostensibly that he might continue to benefit from her spiritual encouragement and advice even *in absentia*. In this guise she was able to transcend the limitations placed upon women by a culture that discouraged them from teaching in public.[19]

---

had nothing to do with the world in which they lived. There is no evidence at all that Vegetius' detailed tactical and organisational recommendations were ever put into practice, and it seems unlikely that his advice on campaigning was followed closely either.' G. Halsall, *Warfare and Society in the Barbarian West, 450–900* (London and New York, 2003), p. 145 and p. 268, n. 35. See also R. P. Abels and S. Morillo, 'A Lying Legacy? A Preliminary Discussion of Images of Antiquity and Altered Reality in Medieval Military History', *Journal of Medieval Military History* 3 (2005), pp. 1–13. But cf. Bernard S. Bachrach's careful delineation of the differences between Hrabanus Maurus' *De Procinctu romanae miliciae* and his source, Vegetius, and how, from that, he infers ninth-century military practices. Bachrach, *Early Carolingian Warfare: Prelude to Empire* (Philadelphia, PA, 2001), pp. 84–131.

[17] Noble, above, p. 72. [18] J. L. Nelson, above, pp. 112–13.
[19] Theodulf of Orléans, *Opus Caroli Contra Synodum*, ed. A. Freeman, *MGH Conc.* II, Supplementum 1, p. 389, cited by V. Garver, above, p. 135, and n. 68.

Perhaps more typical of aristocratic laywomen was Dhuoda's contemporary, Liutberga. Liutberga's activities, at least until she became a recluse, were confined to the domestic sphere, the family and estates of her mentor and patron, the Lady Gisla and her son. Although the *Vita Liutbirgae Virginis* is a portrayal of the life of a woman as mediated by a male, it nonetheless provides valuable insights into the sort of learning and expertise deemed appropriate for noblewomen in the ninth century. Whereas young male nobles learned to ride and handle weapons, noble girls mastered the skills of embroidery and weaving, which formed a key part of the household knowledge that they were expected to possess as wives and mothers. While her husband (or son) engaged in political and military affairs, the noblewoman managed the domestic affairs of her husband's household. This included transmitting basic religious knowledge to her sons and daughters, modelling and encouraging right behaviour within the family, and managing her husband's estates and resources. Liutberga and the other noblewomen in her *Vita* possessed, as Valerie Garver writes, 'a social competence that included making rational decisions, shrewdly managing daily tasks, using often limited resources skillfully, and looking after the material and spiritual needs of those around them'.[20] The example of Liutberga underscores how exceptional Dhuoda was in her claim to be a female intellectual and raises interesting questions about the gendering of learning in the early middle ages.

Finally, the presence of two Anglo-Saxon kings, Alfred and his grandson Æthelstan, and an ealdorman, Æthelweard, in a volume of essays on 'lay intellectuals in the Carolingian world' is a useful reminder that England in the ninth and tenth centuries formed part of a wider intellectual and cultural world. Perhaps it is misleading to term this wider culture 'Carolingian'. The debt that Charlemagne's *renovatio* owed to the Insular learning of Alcuin and others ought not to be forgotten. Nor should Alfred's own originality in fostering an educational system that promoted learning in both the vernacular as well as in Latin. But if Charlemagne looked towards the learning of the Church of York for inspiration, a century later Alfred would return the compliment by seeking the services of continental scholars such as Grimbald and John the Old Saxon. Even more so, his grandson Æthelstan imported Frankish learning and artistic and architectural fashions, perhaps not surprising given Æthelstan's desire to reshape English kingship along the lines of Carolingian *imperium*. The

[20] Garver, above, p. 137.

career of one of Æthelstan's court scholars, Israel of Trier, which took him variously to Rome, Francia, the Rhineland and England, is indicative of the wide expanse of this shared intellectual world.[21] In short, from at least the reign of Alfred, the intellectual culture of Anglo-Saxon England might best be thought of as 'European'. And given how disproportionately richer the artistic and literary remains of Francia are in comparison to those of ninth- and tenth-century England, it would not be inappropriate to label this European culture as 'Carolingian'.

Read as a whole, the essays in this volume, then, present a coherent portrait of a lay intellectual culture that flourished in Francia and England in the ninth and tenth centuries. But the gulf between ideal and reality, as Nithard bitterly chronicled, could be very wide. 'The ability to excel in learning and on the battlefield was a powerful ideal in Frankish panegyric', Paul Kershaw argues, 'in large part precisely because it ran counter to reality.'[22] This ideal probably did not appeal to all noblemen. The Carolingian ethos of secular sanctity promoted by ecclesiastical and lay intellectual alike attempted to reconcile the contrary demands made on nobles by Christian clerics and the traditional values of a military aristocracy. The attempt to negotiate among them could well produce anxieties and tensions, and perhaps even illness, as the cases of Alfred and Gerald of Aurillac suggest. Asser's portrayal of Alfred as a devotee of the hunt and an ever-victorious warrior who impetuously rushed into battle at Ashdown may perhaps be seen as a defence of the hero's masculinity against those who otherwise might have questioned it. How widespread the appeal of learning, of pursuing holy wisdom, actually was among the lay elites of Carolingian Francia and Anglo-Saxon England must remain an open question.

---

[21] Wood, above, pp. 205–6. [22] Kershaw, above, p. 89.

Index

Adalbert, count of Metz 53, 69–71
Adalhard, abbot of Corbie 45–6, 75, 118
  see also Hincmar, *De ordine palatii*
Adalhard 'the seneschal' 57–9, 69, 74
Addula, abbess of Pfalzel 126, 134, 135
Ælfgifu, wife of Eadwig 224, 225, 226, 227, 228–43
Ælfheah, ealdorman of Central Wessex 226, 227
Ælfhere, ealdorman of Mercia 226, 227, 228, 229, 237
Ælfric 99, 163, 198, 239, 240, 241, 242
Ælfthryth, wife of Edgar 228, 229
Æthelgifu, mother of Ælfgifu and Æthelweard 225, 227
Æthelmaer, son of Æthelweard 239–41
Æthelred I, king of the West Saxons 220, 223–34
Æthelred II, king of the English 224, 228, 229–30
Æthelstan, king of the English
  biography of, *see* William of Malmesbury, 'old book' of
  books of 192, 194–5, 206–8, 208–9, 214
  childhood of 194–6
  court of 192, 193, 200, 203–6, 212
  education of 193–4, 197–9
  empire of 200, 201–2, 203, 216
  as intellectual 192, 193, 199, 203, 215
  learning of 192–3, 197, 208, 209–10
  legal activity of 192, 202–3
  patronage of 209–11, 212–13
    translations 211, 213–15
  piety of 196, 199, 202, 208, 212
  poems connected to 192, 193–4, 195–6, 197–9, 200, 204, 212–13, 213–14
  Psalter of (BL Cotton Galba A. xviii) 206–8, 211
  as reformer 192, 200, 216
  succession of 197, 199
  titles of 200, 201

Æthelstan Half-King, ealdorman of East Anglia 226, 227, 228, 237
Æthelweard, ealdorman of the Western Shires 54
  Chronicon 201, 220, 242, 249–50
  aims of 219–20, 222, 224, 230–1, 232–3
  and *Anglo-Saxon Chronicle* 219, 220, 226–7, 230, 232–3, 237
  ethnic terminology of 231–2, 236, 245
  genealogy in 232–3, 236, 237, 243
  manuscript of 218
  omissions of 220, 224, 226–7, 230, 233, 234, 237
  on pagans 223–34, 231–2, 243
  structure of 224, 231, 245
  style of 218–19, 241
  education of 225
  family of 220, 224–5, 225–6, 227, 228–9, 236–7, 238, 239–41
  as intellectual 218–19, 242, 244
  as layman 222, 234–5, 239, 242
  learning of 220, 244
  patronage of 220, 239–40
  piety of 239–41, 242
  political role of 220, 222, 225, 227–9, 230
  as royal 223, 232, 234, 237–8, 242
Æthelwine, ealdorman of East Anglia 228, 229
Æthelwold, son of Æthelred I 224
Æthelwold, bishop of Winchester, 195, 198, 208, 210, 211, 212, 216
  Benedictional of (BL Add. 49598) 208
Æthelwulf, king of the West Saxons 44, 223, 232–4, 231–3, 238, 243
Agobard, bishop of Lyons 9, 14, 15, 25
Aistulf, Lombard wife-killer 17
Alcuin 9, 18, 19, 24, 42, 46, 51, 108, 116, 132
  De virtutibus et vitiis 5, 9, 15–16, 27, 28, 86, 100, 112, 115, 134
  letters of 6, 209, 210
Aldhelm, bishop of Sherborne 11, 195, 201, 209, 211–12
  De virginitate 194, 195

Alfred the Great 92, 105, 223
  agency of 166, 167–8, 169, 172–3, 176
  as author 163–4, 170, 172–3, 173–4, 174–5, 178–9, 183, 191, 250
    see also Alfredian corpus
  coinage of: see coinage
  court of 168, 169, 171, 173–4, 179, 184, 190, 194
  education of 171–2, 175–6
  as educator 174, 190
  as exemplar 171–2, 175
  illness of 165, 174, 179
  as intellectual 162
  investiture of 196
  on kingship 195, 233
    see also Alfredian corpus, kingship in
  law-code of 166, 169, 179
  learning of 174, 175–7
  as reformer 170–1, 246–7
  self-presentation of 164, 165, 170, 171–2, 173–5, 178, 179–80, 185, 189, 190–1
  as translator 163, 171, 173, 174, 175
  will of 166
  see also courts
Alfredian corpus 164, 166–8, 172–3, 189–90, 215
  audience of 171, 173–4, 182, 185, 189, 209
  compositional methods of 177–8, 185
  dialect of 166, 167, 168–9
  influences on 168–9
  kingship in 179, 183–4
  lordship in 179, 180, 181, 184–5, 186, 187–8, 188–9, 190
  style of 166–7, 177, 179
  use of *personae* in 165, 173, 178–9, 179–80
  see also Alfred, law-code of; Augustine, *Soliloquia*; Boethius; Gregory the Great, *Regula pastoralis*; Psalms, OE translation of
Amalarius, bishop of Metz 209, 210
Ambrose, bishop of Milan 46, 99–100, 152–3
Ambrosius Autpertus 9, 11, 117
Angelbert, poet 59
Angilbert, abbot of St Riquier 64
Anglo-Saxon Chronicle 166–7, 168, 172, 229, 233, 235
  see also Æthelweard
Anskar, Archbishop of Hamburg 34, 131
arms and armour 17–18, 45, 72, 84, 90, 105, 196
Arnulf, bishop of Metz 61, 64, 235
Arnulf I, count of Flanders 234–5, 236
asceticism 12, 17, 44–5, 99
  see also ethos, noble
Ashburnham Pentateuch (Paris BN Nouv. acq. lat. 2334) 207
assemblies 25, 26, 199, 200, 202–3
  see also Hincmar, *De ordine palatii*

Asser, bishop of Sherborne 168
  as biographer 56, 165, 174
  Life of King Alfred 10–13, 171–2, 174, 187–8, 196, 233, 247
  education in 171–2, 174, 175–6, 198–9
Astronomer 8, 20, 37, 61, 65, 72, 196
  as biographer 47, 56, 73, 74
audiences: see Alfredian corpus, audience of; courts as audiences; Dhuoda, *Liber manualis*; literacy; Nithard, *Histories*; translation, audience for
Augustine, bishop of Hippo 41, 46, 95, 99, 101, 113, 116, 240
  City of God 48, 113, 157–8, 159–60
  De videndo Deo 185, 186
  Enchiridion 91–2, 92–3, 100
  Old English translation of *Soliloquia* 166, 169, 172, 177–8, 184–5, 246
  'Augustinus' 179, 184
  '*Gesceadwisnes*/Reason' 180–3, 184, 186, 187, 189
  personae of 173, 180
  testimony and authority in 186–7
Augustine Gospels (Cambridge, Corpus Christi College 286) 207
authorship
  anonymity and 163, 172–3
  meaning of 163–4, 172, 173–4
  post-structuralism and 163, 164, 166, 170, 172
  royal 61–2, 162–3, 164, 165
  see also Æthelweard; Alfred; Nithard
  see also laypeople as authors

Bale, John 213–14
Basil, bishop of Caesarea 101
Bateley, Janet 166–8, 177–8
Bede 40, 41, 46, 97, 194, 209, 231, 240, 243
  Historia Ecclesiastica 215–16
  OE translation of *Historia Ecclesiastica* 166, 167, 168, 177
Benedict of Aniane 34
Benedict the Irishman 204
Bernard, king of Italy 64
Bernard of Septimania 59, 65, 69, 73, 118, 119
  see also Dhuoda
Bernard, son of Gisla 124, 125–7, 129, 130
biography 45–9, 56–7, 72
  see also Asser, *Life of King Alfred*; Astronomer; Einhard, *Vita Karoli*; Thegan, *Gesta Hludowici imperatoris*
Boethius 49
  OE translation of *Consolatio philosophiae* 166, 169, 177–8, 190
  'Boethius' 178, 180–1
  '*Mod*/Mind' 181–2

personae of 172, 180
'*Wisdom*' 180, 181–2
Boniface, archbishop of Mainz 42, 126–7, 128

capitularies 9, 14, 26, 29, 85, 162
  of Charlemagne 19, 85, 86, 115, 132
  of Louis the Pious 19, 85
Carolingian dynasty 48, 61–2, 63–7, 74, 221, 223, 235
  conflicts within 73
    see also Charles the Bald, family relations of; Lothar I, family relations of; Louis the Pious, family relations of
'Carolingian Renaissance'
  influence on England 3, 168, 169, 193, 209–10, 211, 215, 221, 253–4
  see also reform
Cathedra Petri, *see* Charles the Bald, throne of
Cerdic, king of the West Saxons 232, 236
chaplains 97, 240
Charlemagne 21, 25, 75
  court of 25, 48, 89, 210
  as intellectual 48, 89, 139
  learning of 27
  Nithard's attitude to 62–3, 67, 73
  patronage of 46–7
  piety of 47
  as reformer 13, 18, 19, 36, 43, 86, 171
  see also Einhard, *Vita Karoli*
Charles the Bald, king of the West Franks 75, 88
  books of 80, 140, 195
  court of 52, 140
  education of 139
  as emperor 156–7, 159–60
  family relations of 52–3, 56, 65–6, 73, 235
  images of 140, 142, 155, 156–7, 158
  and Ivory of the Pericopes 142–3
  learning of 89, 139–40, 144–5, 161
  as lord 60
  marriage of 73–5
  Nithard's attitude to 63, 64, 71–4, 75
  Prayerbook of 140, 142, 159
  throne of 140–2, 145, 155, 156, 159
charters 28, 29, 38, 59–60, 123, 166, 199, 200–1, 204, 208, 212, 216, 228
Christianisation 2, 35–6, 242–3
  of warfare 32, 54, 92–3
  see also miles Christi,
  see also ethos, noble; paganism; reform
Cicero 46, 48, 49
Clement the Irishman 20, 22, 108
Codex Aureus of St. Emmeram (Munich, Bayerische Staatsbibliothek clm. 14000) 143, 154
coinage 166, 201

confraternity books 21, 39, 42
conversatio see ethos, noble
counts 14, 24–6, 28, 86
  see also ealdormen
courts 50, 54–5, 68, 90–1, 108, 115, 118–20
  as audiences 75, 119–20, 174
  as intellectual centres 25, 28, 48, 89
  moral role of 26, 58, 116, 118, 171
  see also Æthelstan; Alfred; Charlemagne; Charles the Bald; Louis the Pious
crises 12–13, 50, 57–61, 71, 108, 224, 235
  see also Carolingian dynasty, conflicts within; Vikings; West Saxon royal dynasty, conflicts within
Cross, devotion to: 39, 44, 90–1, 140
  see also Hrabanus Maurus, *De laudibus sancti crucis*
crucifixion 149–53
  see also Ivory of the Pericopes
Cynewulf 163, 165
Cysoing 78, 79, 81, 90, 97

demons 39, 70, 127
Desiderius, bishop of Cahors 41
Dhuoda 27, 30–1, 88, 106–20, 223, 252
  books of 28–9
  claims to authority of 109–11
  as courtier 118–19
  family of 22
  as intellectual 117–20
  learning of 101, 113–14, 116–17, 132
  Liber manualis 10, 57, 69, 101, 109, 122
    audience of 119–20
    manuscripts 119
    structure of 112–15, 116
  as mother 109–11, 134
  piety of 11, 15, 31, 53, 113–15, 132
  on social duties, 15, 58, 68, 112–13, 115–16
  as spiritual mother 113–14, 120
  as wife 109–11, 130
  see also Bernard of Septimania
Drogo, bishop of Metz 63–4
Drogo Gospelbook (Paris BN lat. 9383) 147–8, 154
Drogo Sacramentary (Paris BN lat. 9428) 143, 146, 148, 149–50
Dunstan, archbishop of Canterbury 195, 202–3, 225, 226

Eadwig, king of the English 224, 225–7, 238
ealdormen 228, 244
  see also counts
Eberhard, margrave of Friuli 77–105
  autograph of 82
  books of 28–9, 80–2, 92, 97–105

Eberhard, margrave of Friuli (cont.)
  education of 87–9
  family of 78, 83, 86–7
    see also Gisela; Unruoch
  as Frank 103–4
  and Gottschalk 91–7
  learning of 82–90, 94–6, 98, 105
  military role of 77–8, 79, 80–1, 83–4, 90–1, 92, 105
  patronage of 85, 89, 91, 97
  piety of 90–1, 91–2, 94–6, 97, 98–100, 102, 105
  will of Eberhard and Gisela 81–2, 90, 97–105
Ebo, archbishop of Rheims 19–20, 21–2, 25, 53
Eccard, count of Mâcon 28–9
Ecgberht, king of the West Saxons 231
Edgar, king of the English 210, 224, 226, 239
Edmund the Martyr, king of East Anglia 202
Edward the Elder, king of the Anglo-Saxons 197, 198, 224, 237
Edward the Martyr, king of England 224, 228, 229–30
Einhard 37–50, 108, 109, 223
  as abbot 37–8, 42
  as biographer 45, 46–50, 56, 73, 74
  as layman 37, 38
  letters of 38–9, 44, 50, 94–6
  piety of 42–4
  sense of sinfulness of 38–9, 41, 43–4
  Translatio et Miracula SS. Marcellini et Petri 38–9, 44, 50
  Vita Karoli 8, 54, 58, 62, 68, 72, 87, 171, 249
    as mirror for princes 195
Ephrem the Syrian 101
epic 47, 233, 237, 241
Eric, margrave of Friuli 11, 12, 27, 84
  see also Paulinus, *Liber exhortationis*
Ermengard, wife of Lothar I 57, 58, 59
Ermentrude, wife of Charles the Bald 66, 74
Ermoldus Nigellus 9, 81, 82, 88
estate management 129–30, 132–3
ethos, noble 8–36, 48, 52, 58–9, 75, 100–2, 170–1, 182, 185, 240–1, 248
  failure to live up to 34, 67–70, 71, 74, 229–30, 254
  and gender 34, 112, 252
  honour 57–8, 71
  lay response to 26–7, 30–1, 44–5, 86, 87, 102, 104–5, 242
  lay role in creation of 24, 111–12, 115–16, 179, 183, 191, 234–5, 248–9
    see also Æthelweard; Alfred; Alfredian corpus; Dhuoda; Nithard
  noblemen as exemplars 5, 12–14, 33, 35, 49, 73, 115, 116

  see also Alfred; Gerald of Aurillac
  noblewomen as exemplars 5, 110–14, 115, 134, 135–6
    see also Liutberga
  official duties 10, 13, 19, 23–4, 31, 36, 86, 87, 113, 248–9
    see also counts; ealdormen; *ministerium*
  personal morality 10–13
    see also asceticism; good works
  sources for 8–10, 24–30 see also arms and armour; laypeople; mirrors for laity; nobility, military role of; reform; virtues and vices
Eucharist 32, 151–3, 160–1
  see also ivory of the Pericopes

families 15–16, 109–11, 122, 227, 236–8
  see also marriage; Carolingian dynasty; Dhuoda; marriage; mothers; West Saxon royal dynasty
florilegia 133, 177
Fontenoy, battle of 52, 56, 59, 69, 77, 101
Fortune 49
Foucault, Michel: see authorship, post-structuralism and
Frankishness 48, 103–4, 157, 242
Friuli 79, 84–5, 104
Fulda 70, 90, 91, 123, 126–7, 211

genealogies 232–5, 236
  see also Æthelweard, *Chronicon*
Gerald, count of Aurillac 10, 12, 15–16, 28, 29, 32, 33, 44, 51
Germanus, bishop of Paris 41
Gisela, wife of Eberhard of Friuli 78, 82, 83, 91, 98, 132, 135
  see also Eberhard
Gisla 129, 134, 137
  family of 124
  patronage of 121, 125–6
Godden, Malcolm 164–5, 173, 178–9, 183, 184, 186, 188
godparenthood 24, 35, 73, 119
good works 10, 12, 44, 94–5, 116, 134
Gospels, OE translation of 213–15
Gottschalk of Orbais 91–7, 102
Greek, knowledge of 201, 205, 206–7, 208, 244
Gregory, bishop of Utrecht 126–7
Gregory the Great, pope 11, 41, 96, 97
  OE translation of *Dialogues* 166, 167, 172, 177, 187
  OE translation of *Regula pastoralis* 166, 168, 171, 174, 179, 194
  Regula pastoralis 179–80
Guy see Wido

hagiography 32–4, 45, 103, 126–7, 128, 202
  see also Gerald of Aurillac; sanctity; *Vita
    Liutbirgae virginis*
Halitgar, bishop of Cambrai 25
Hartgar, bishop of Liège 80, 97, 98
Heiric of Friuli *see* Eric of Friuli
heresy 91–2, 94–6
Hibernicus Exul 18, 198, 200–3
hierarchy, ideas of 16–21, 31, 41, 234
Hildegard, daughter of Louis the Pious 65–6
Hildegard, wife of Charlemagne 20, 65
Hincmar, archbishop of Rheims 15, 25, 94, 108,
    120, 135, 143, 151
  Annales Bertiniani 94, 160
  De cavendis vitiis 9, 27, 29, 160
  De ordine palatii 25, 118
  on kingship 141, 145–6, 154, 157, 159–61, 188
  letters of 28, 97
history, writing of 55–7, 71, 103, 222, 223, 230,
    244–5
honour *see* ethos, noble
Hrabanus Maurus, archbishop of Mainz 9, 15,
    24–5, 37, 52, 135, 148, 209
  adaptation of Vegetius 88, 92
  De laudibus sancti crucis 89–90, 97, 102
  and Gottschalk 91, 94, 102
  letters of 9, 16, 24–5, 91, 92, 101
  sermons of 9

intellectuals 5–6, 106–9, 116, 117, 220, 230
  laypeople as intellectuals 6, 45, 49–50, 94,
    95–6, 222–3, 234, 248
    see also Æthelstan; Æthelweard; Alfred;
      Charlemagne; Nithard
  types of 223, 243–4
  women as intellectuals 109, 117–20, 137,
    252–3
    see also Dhuoda; public life
Isidore, bishop of Seville 11, 97, 101, 104, 251
  Etymologiae 39, 46–7, 110, 148
Israel of Trier 205–6, 244
ivories 140, 142, 156
  see also Paris Psalter
ivory of the Pericopes, the 140
  connection to Charles the Bald 142–3
  doctrines expressed by 149–53
    crucifixion 149–53
    Eucharist 151–3
  iconography of 140–2, 146–7, 150, 153, 158
    angels 146, 147, 150, 151–2, 158
    crucified Christ 146, 150, 152–3
    Ecclesia 146, 150, 152–3, 153–4, 158
    Longinus 146, 147, 150, 151, 152–3
    Oceanus 143, 147, 149, 150, 151, 158–9
    parallels to 142–3, 145–6, 154–7, 159

  snakes 146–7, 148, 150, 151
  Stephaton 146, 150, 152, 153
  Tellus 146, 154–8, 159
  Temple 147–8, 149, 150, 151, 152
  Terra 143, 147, 148–9, 150, 151
  originality of 143–4

Jerome 49, 152–3, 198
John Scottus Eriugena 145, 205
John the Old Saxon 168, 194–5
Jonas, bishop of Orléans 13, 27, 188
  De institutione laicali 9, 12, 16, 25, 32, 132,
    134–5
Judith, wife of Louis the Pious 15, 20, 55, 74, 118
justice 3, 14, 57, 188
  see also law

Khludov Psalter (Moscow Historical Museum,
    cod. 129) 152
kingship 56, 59–60, 65, 67, 140–2, 153, 159,
    192–3, 235, 236
  iconography of 155–6
  see also Alfredian corpus; Charles the Bald;
    Hincmar; lordship; mirrors for princes;
    Tellus
knighthood *see* arms and armour; *miles Christi*;
    nobility, military role of

Laon 65–6
law 2, 3–4, 93
  see also Æthelstan, legal activity of; justice
law-codes 85, 102–3
  of Æthelstan *see* Æthelstan, legal activity of
  of Alfred *see* Alfred
laypeople
  as abbots 37–8, 52, 54, 58
  attitudes to clerics 14, 52–3
    see also chaplains
  as authors 26, 38–9, 45, 50, 51–5, 57–9
  book ownership of 27, 28–9
    see also Æthelstan; Charles the Bald;
      Dhuoda; Eberhard
  clerical attitudes to 4–5, 12, 13, 20, 51, 83, 94,
    95–6, 134–5, 137, 240–1
  education of laymen 48, 72, 87–9, 126–7, 221
  education of laywomen 48, 124–5, 126–7, 136,
    137–8, 198
  lay/clerical distinctions 37, 44–5, 48, 51–2,
    54–5, 91, 93, 115, 222, 238–9, 241, 250–1
    see also Æthelweard; Einhard; Nithard
  literacy of *see* literacy
  patronage of 250
    see also Æthelstan; Æthelweard;
      Charlemagne; Eberhard; Gisla
    see also ethos, noble; intellectuals; piety, lay

Leo III, pope 20, 21
Leo IV, pope 93, 196
life-cycles
  of kings 72–3, 195–6
  of noblemen 87–8
  see also youth
Lindau Gospels (New York, Pierpont Morgan Library, M.1) 142
literacy 2
  of laymen 27–30, 83, 89, 97, 114, 170, 187–8, 193–4
  of laywomen 114, 132–3
  meaning of 176
  and orality 30, 60, 177–8
  see also vernacular
liturgy 31, 32, 97, 157, 204, 210
  see also Eucharist; prayer
Liudger, bishop of Münster 126
Liutberga
  authority of 129, 130
  childhood of 121, 126
  as educator 129, 130–1
  education of 127
  as exemplar 124, 130, 134, 135–6
  as recluse 124, 128, 130–1, 136
  skills of 128
  social status of 125–6
  work of 124, 129–30, 134
Liutward, bishop of Vercelli 22
lordship 15, 179, 230
  see also Alfredian corpus; Charles the Bald; Lothar I
Lothar I, emperor of the Franks 59
  family relations of 53, 54
  as lord 57–8, 59–60, 77
  Nithard's attitude to 67, 73
Louis the German, king of the East Franks 52, 60, 69–70, 91, 215
Louis the Pious, emperor of the Franks, 47, 196
  court of 25, 118–19
  family relations of 54–5, 64, 67
  see also Judith
  as *miles Christi* 89–90
  Nithard's attitude to 63–4, 74
  as reformer 13, 19, 36
Louis II 13, 85, 157
loyalty 15–16, 52, 57–8, 59, 184
  see also lordship
Lupus of Ferrières 9, 22, 24, 28, 42, 85, 94, 108

MacDurnan Gospels (London, Lambeth 1370) 214
Malmesbury 212, 213

manuscripts
  Boulogne
    Bibliothèque municipale, 82 211
  Cambridge
    Corpus Christi College 183 204, 208, 211
    Corpus Christi College 448 211
    Trinity College B.16. 3 211
    Trinity College R 15.14 pt. 1 213
    see also Augustine Gospels
  Chicago
    Newberry Library, MSS Fragments no. 15 210
  Florence *see* Rabbula Gospels
  London
    BL, Add. 40618 214
    BL, Cotton Claudius B.v 209
    BL, Cotton Cleopatra A.iii 212
    BL, Cotton Otho B.ix 204, 209
    BL, Cotton Tiberius A.ii 204
    BL, Cotton Titus D.xviii 206
    BL, Cotton Titus D.xxvii 207
    BL, Cotton Vespasian B.vi 194
    BL, Harley 647 209
    BL, Royal 1. A. xviii 214
    BL, Royal 1. E. vi 214
    BL, Royal 7. D. xxiv 211
    BL, Royal 17.A 213
    Lambeth 208 210
    see also Æthelstan, Psalter of; Æthelwold, Benedictional of
  MacDurnan Gospels 214
  Moscow *see* Khludov Psalter
  Munich *see* Codex Aureus of St Emmeram; Ivory of the Pericopes; Charles the Bald, Prayerbook of
  New York *see* Lindau Gospels
  Oxford
    Bodleian Library, Junius 27 211
    Bodleian Library, Rawlinson B. 484 207
    Bodleian Library, Rawlinson C. 697 194–5, 196
    Corpus Christi College 221 205, 206
  Paris
    BN lat.12949 206
    see also Ashburnham Pentateuch; Drogo Gospelbook; Drogo Sacramentary; Paris Psalter; Paris Sacramentary
  Rome *see* San Paolo Bible
  St Petersburg
    Russian National Library, cod. lat. Oct. v. I.5 151
  Utrecht *see* Utrecht Psalter
  Vatican City
    Biblioteca Apostolica, reg. lat. 11 82
  Worcester
    Cathedral Library, Q.5 205

Index

marriage 16, 32, 83, 115–16
  royal 55, 72, 73–5
  see also families
Martin, archbishop of Braga 100–1
masculinity 72, 105, 254
  see also ethos, noble; life-cycle
Matfrid, count of Orléans 14, 25, 27
Matilda, abbess of Essen 219, 221, 235, 237
Michelstadt 37, 38
miles Christi 11, 83–4, 90–1, 99–100, 105, 113
  see also Louis the Pious as *miles Christi*
ministerium 9, 13, 16, 19, 36, 170
mirrors
  for laity 9, 13, 24–9, 71, 100–2, 118
    see also Alcuin, *De virtutibus et vitiis*;
      Dhuoda, *Liber manualis*; Jonas of
      Orléans, *De institutione laicali*;
      Paulinus of Aquileia, *Liber
      exhortationis*
  for princes 9, 71, 100–1, 111, 159, 160, 210
    see also Hincmar on kingship
mothers
  authority of 109–11, 129, 130
  as educators 110–14, 131–2, 133–5
  spiritual 113–14
  see also Dhuoda

Nithard 51–76, 82, 108, 223
  as abbot 52, 54
  attitude to Charlemagne 62–3, 67, 73
  attitude to Charles the Bald 63, 64, 71–4, 75
  attitude to Lothar 67, 73
  attitude to Louis the Pious 63–4, 74
  bias of 58, 69–71
  family of 61, 64–5, 110
  Histories 51–4, 55–7, 56–7, 60–74, 249
  audience of 75
  as intellectual 75–6
  as layman 52–4, 55, 89
  pessimism of 51, 57, 63, 66, 68, 73–5
  as social critic 51, 56, 61, 66–76
nobility
  definitions of 17, 21–4, 125
  ethos of *see* ethos, noble
  military role of 21, 88–9, 92–3, 251
    see also miles Christi
  political role of 60, 68–71
    see also Æthelweard; counts; ealdormen
  social mobility of 19–20, 21–2
  structure of 21–4, 235
    see also families; hierarchy, ideas of;
      laypeople; sanctity, noble; women,
      role in noble society
Noting, bishop of Verona 92, 97

Notker the Stammerer 20, 22, 55, 74, 108
nutritor 46, 58, 73, 126–7

Oda, archbishop of Canterbury 226, 244
Odo of Cluny *see* Gerald of Aurillac
Orosius 104, 167
  OE translation of *Historiae adversus paganos*
    166–7, 168, 177
Otgar, archbishop of Mainz 53
Ottonian dynasty 205, 221, 244–5
Ovid 113–14

paganism 47, 141, 145, 159, 201, 241, 242
  see also Æthelweard, *Chronicon*;
    Christianisation; Tellus; Vikings
Paris Psalter (Paris BN lat.1152) 140, 142, 156, 159
Paris Sacramentary (Paris BN lat.1141) 143
Paschasius Radbertus 11, 45–6, 151, 153
Paschal I, pope 20–1
Patrick, Saint 40
patronage *see* Æthelstan; Æthelweard;
  Charlemagne; Eberhard; Gisla; laypeople,
  patronage of; *nutritor*; women, patronage of
Paul the Deacon 46, 103
Paulinus, patriarch of Aquileia 9, 17, 18
  Liber exhortationis 11, 12, 15–16, 27, 35, 84–7,
    101, 134
Paulinus, bishop of Nola 41
penance 12–13, 17, 40, 59
Pericopes of Henry II (Munich Bayerische
  Staatsbibliothek, clm. 4452)
  see ivory of the Pericopes
Petrus, chaplain of Æthelstan 200, 204
physiognomy 103
piety
  lay 10, 12, 31–2, 98–100
  see also Æthelstan; Æthelweard;
    Charlemagne; Dhuoda; Eberhard;
    Einhard; ethos, noble; prayer;
    salvation; sanctity; sinfulness
Pippin, son of Bernard of Italy 64, 67
poetry
  Old English 233, 240, 241, 242
  Latin 80–1, 85, 89–90, 103
  see also Æthelstan, poems connected to
post-structuralism *see* authorship,
  post-structuralism and
prayer 5, 40, 41–4, 112, 133
  prayer books 28–9, 99, 114–15, 176
  see also Charles the Bald, Prayerbook of;
  see also psalms; psalters
predestination 43, 91–5
Prosper of Aquitaine 95, 209
prudentia see wisdom
Prudentius 11, 117, 194, 240

psalms 116, 117, 128, 131, 136
  OE translation of 166, 169, 173, 179, 211
  reciting of 5, 131, 132, 176
psalters 29, 82, 99, 131–2
  see also Æthelstan, Psalter of; Khludov Psalter; Paris Psalter; Utrecht Psalter
public life, ideas of 12, 16, 38, 68–9, 74–6, 107–9, 114, 120

queens *see* women, royal
Quinity 207

Rabbula Gospels (Florence, Biblioteca Medicea-Laurenziana Cod. Pluteus I, 56) 150, 207
Rather, bishop of Verona 9, 16, 22, 40
reform 50, 170–1, 183, 215–16, 242–3, 248
  Benedictine 195, 208, 212, 239–41
  Carolingian 3, 16, 31–2, 35–6, 86–7, 102
  see also Æthelstan; Alfred; Charlemagne; ethos, noble; Louis the Pious
Regino of Prüm 49
Reichenau 21, 70
relics 38, 103, 202
  see also Cross; Einhard, *Translatio et Miracula SS. Marcellini et Petri*
Rigrannus, Frankish noble 37

St Bavo, Ghent 37, 38
St-Bertin 78, 87, 234
St Cuthbert, Chester-le-Street 204, 211
St Peter, Salzburg 21
St Riquier 53–4
St Servatius, Maastricht 37, 39
salvation 10–13, 30–1, 86–93, 94, 95, 102, 105, 114, 153
  see also predestination; sinfulness
sanctity
  noble 32–3
  secular 8, 33–4
  see also ethos, noble; Gerald of Aurillac
San Paolo Bible 140, 142, 156, 159
San Salvatore, Brescia 22, 102
sapientia see wisdom
Sceaf, ancestor of Æthelwulf 233, 234, 238
scientia see wisdom
Sedulius 147, 152
Sedulius Scottus 80, 81, 85, 87–8, 90, 102
Seligenstadt 37, 38, 42
sermons 26–7, 99–100, 133
sinfulness 38–41, 43–4, 50
Smaragdus 9, 13–14, 117
Strasbourg oaths 60

Suetonius 46, 48, 49
Sulpicius Severus 45, 103, 175

Tellus, 'Great Mother' goddess 146, 157–8
  see also ivory of the Pericopes
Thegan 87
  as biographer 47, 55, 56, 72, 73
  on Ebo 19–20, 21–2, 53
  Gesta Hludowici imperatoris 8, 65, 72, 74
Theodore of Tarsus, archbishop of Canterbury 206–8, 216
Theodulf, bishop of Orléans 14, 18, 25, 43, 135, 139
Translatio Sancti Calixti 79, 81
translation 163, 165, 167, 172–3, 177–8, 185, 188
  audience for 171
  see also Æthelweard, *Chronicon*; Alfred; Alfredian corpus; Gospels, OE translation of

Unruoch, father of Eberhard of Friuli 78, 86–7, 101
Unruoch, son of Eberhard of Friuli 22, 81, 83, 88, 90, 98, 99–100, 101
Utrecht Psalter (Utrecht, University Library, MS 32) 143, 144, 154–5, 207

Varro 157
Vegetius 80–1, 88, 92, 103, 195, 251
Venantius Fortunatus 195, 198
vernacular 30, 49, 52, 60, 170, 176
  see also Alfredian corpus; Strasbourg oaths; translation
Vikings 40, 44, 180, 201, 220, 224, 238
Virgil 84–5, 197, 209
virtues and vices 10–11, 25, 27, 100–1
  see also Alcuin, *De virtutibus et vitiis*
visions 44, 202
Vita Liutbirgae virginis
  author of 121
  reliability of 123–4

Wærferth, bishop of Worcester 168, 172
  see also Gregory the Great, OE translation of *Dialogues*
Waltharius 17–18, 32
warfare *see* Christianisation of warfare; *miles Christi*; nobility, military role of; Vegetius
West Saxon royal dynasty 230, 232–3, 235–8
  conflicts within 199, 224, 225–7, 227–8, 229, 230
Wido, count of Breton march 24, 27, 115

Widukind of Corvey 222, 244–5
Willehad, bishop of Bremen 34
William, count of Gellone 22
　see also Dhuoda
William of Malmesbury, 176, 192, 195–8,
　　213–14, 218, 239, 240
　'old book' of 197–9, 203, 210, 214
Williams, Raymond 107
wills
　of Alfred 166
　of Charlemagne 49–50
　of Eberhard and Gisela 81–2, 90, 97–105
wisdom 108, 170, 171, 180–3, 189, 190, 246,
　　249
　prudentia 85, 101, 123, 135
　sapientia 123, 249, 251
　scientia 118, 123, 251
　see also Boethius, OE translation of *Consolatio philosophiae*
Witger, author of *Genealogia Arnulfi Comitis*
　　234–5, 238
women 59, 68
　education of: *see* laypeople, education of laywomen
　as educators 121–2, 122–3, 129, 133–5, 136–8
　　see also Liutberga; mothers as educators
　estate management by 129–30, 132–3
　as exemplars *see* ethos, noble; Liutberga
　group activities of 111, 118, 127–8
　as intellectuals *see* intellectuals
　learning of 81
　　see also Dhuoda
　literacy of *see* literacy
　patronage of 219, 239–40
　　see also Gisla
　religious 127–8, 136–7, 138
　　see also Liutberga; Matilda
　role in noble society 123, 137
　royal 49, 54, 65–6, 78, 89, 132–3
　　see also Ælfgifu; Ælfthryth; Ermengard; Ermentrude; Hildegard; Judith
　singing of 128, 131
　textile work by 127–9
　see also mothers
Wormald, Patrick 1–7
Wulfad, bishop of Bourges 41
Wulfstan, archbishop of York 163, 230
Wulfstan Cantor 195, 197

youth 72, 87, 88, 171
　see also life-cycles; Æthelstan, childhood of; Liutberga, childhood of

Zachary, pope 21

Lightning Source UK Ltd.
Milton Keynes UK
UKHW012209291219
356094UK00001B/19/P